SMALL-COMPANY
ENVIRONMENT

AGILITY
FOCUS
INNOVATION

BIG-COMPANY
IMPACT

STABILITY
OPPORTUNITIES
GLOBAL REACH

EMPOWERED
LEADERSHIP

Johnson & Johnson
Family of Companies

small-company environment
big-company impact.

As an MBA degree candidate you've demonstrated a passion for acquiring knowledge and advancing your career. You understand the advantages of working within a small company, where you can be closer to the business and where your contributions will be recognized. At the same time, you value the breadth of career opportunities and international perspective that a global organization can provide.

Who says you have to choose?

Within the Johnson & Johnson Family of Companies you can experience an entrepreneurial atmosphere that encourages teamwork and innovation— in fast-paced environments that have the feel of a small company— where people are empowered to grow as leaders and to drive their own careers. But you'll also find the impact of the world's most comprehensive and broadly based manufacturer of health care products.

Discover the many small-company environments behind the big-company impact of the Johnson & Johnson companies.

MEDICAL DEVICES &
DIAGNOSTICS   CONSUMER   PHARMACEUTICAL

find more
www.jnj.com/careers

ASIA-PACIFIC
EUROPE/MIDDLE EAST/AFRICA
LATIN AMERICA
NORTH AMERICA

The media's watching Vault!
Here's a sampling of our coverage.

"For those hoping to climb the ladder of success, [Vault's] insights are priceless."
– *Money magazine*

"The best place on the web to prepare for a job search."
– *Fortune*

"[Vault guides] make for excellent starting points for job hunters and should be purchased by academic libraries for their career sections [and] university career centers."
– *Library Journal*

"The granddaddy of worker sites."
– *US News and World Report*

"A killer app."
– *New York Times*

One of Forbes' 33 "Favorite Sites"
– *Forbes*

"To get the unvarnished scoop, check out Vault."
– *Smart Money Magazine*

"Vault has a wealth of information about major employers and job-searching strategies as well as comments from workers about their experiences at specific companies."
– *The Washington Post*

"Vault has become the go-to source for career preparation."
– *Crain's New York*

"Vault [provides] the skinny on working conditions at all kinds of companies from current and former employees."
– *USA Today*

THE VAULT
MBA CAREER BIBLE

THE VAULT
MBA CAREER BIBLE

VAULT EDITORS

Acknowledgments

We are also extremely grateful to Vault's entire staff for all their help in the editorial, production and marketing processes. Vault also would like to acknowledge the support of our investors, clients, employees, family, and friends. Thank you!

Visit Vault at **www.vault.com** for insider company profiles, expert advice, career message boards, expert resume reviews, the Vault Job Board and more.

VAULT CAREER LIBRARY   vii

Does it matter who you are?

Or does it matter what you can do?

At Deloitte, our firm's success is measured by the quality of our team's insights and solutions. So, the more diverse our people's backgrounds and expertise, the better. With more than 120,000 professionals worldwide, sharing their unique perspectives across our functions, service lines and offices, we are uniquely positioned in the global marketplace to understand our clients' complex needs and exceed their expectations. Are you ready to be yourself and make a difference in everything you do?

Deloitte.

Audit.Tax.Consulting.Financial Advisory.

www.deloitte.com/us

About Deloitte

Deloitte, one of the nation's leading professional services firms, provides audit, tax, consulting, and financial advisory services through nearly 30,000 people in more than 80 U.S. cities. Known as an employer of choice for innovative human resources programs, the firm is dedicated to helping its clients and its people excel. "Deloitte" refers to the associated partnerships of Deloitte & Touche USA LLP (Deloitte & Touche LLP and Deloitte Consulting LLP) and subsidiaries. Deloitte is the U.S. member firm of Deloitte Touche Tohmatsu. For more information, please visit Deloitte's Web site at www.deloitte.com/us.

Deloitte Touche Tohmatsu is an organization of member firms devoted to excellence in providing professional services and advice. We are focused on client service through a global strategy executed locally in nearly 150 countries. With access to the deep intellectual capital of 120,000 people worldwide, our member firms, including their affiliates, deliver services in four professional areas: audit, tax, consulting, and financial advisory services. Our member firms serve more than one-half of the world's largest companies, as well as large national enterprises, public institutions, locally important clients, and successful, fast-growing global growth companies.

Deloitte Touche Tohmatsu is a Swiss Verein (association), and, as such, neither Deloitte Touche Tohmatsu nor any of its member firms has any liability for each other's acts or omissions. Each of the member firms is a separate and independent legal entity operating under the names "Deloitte," "Deloitte & Touche," "Deloitte Touche Tohmatsu," or other, related names. The services described herein are provided by the member firms and not by the Deloitte Touche Tohmatsu Verein. For regulatory and other reasons, certain member firms do not provide services in all four professional areas listed above.

Member of Deloitte Touche Tohmatsu
Copyright © 2004 Deloitte Development LLC. All rights reserved.

Table of Contents

Visit Vault at **www.vault.com** for insider company profiles, expert advice, career message boards, expert resume reviews, the Vault Job Board and more.

VAULT CAREER LIBRARY   ix

Visit Vault at **www.vault.com** for insider company profiles, expert advice,
career message boards, expert resume reviews, the Vault Job Board and more.

VAULT CAREER LIBRARY

xi

Visit Vault at **www.vault.com** for insider company profiles, expert advice,
career message boards, expert resume reviews, the Vault Job Board and more.

VAULT CAREER LIBRARY   xiii

Visit Vault at **www.vault.com** for insider company profiles, expert advice,
career message boards, expert resume reviews, the Vault Job Board and more.

VAULT CAREER LIBRARY

xv

Introduction

The MBA degree opens up worlds of opportunity for its bearers. Many business positions require an MBA for advancement. For example, investment banking and management consulting firms hire large classes of newly minted MBAs each year at six-figure salaries into the "associate" level – those without MBAs generally don't advance past the "analyst" level. At major consumer products companies like Procter & Gamble, Kraft and Colgate-Palmolive, MBAs are hired as "assistant brand managers" into the brand management department – those without MBAs are generally not eligible for the department. And it is from this function that these companies' senior executives are generally drawn.

In other industries such as media and entertainment and the federal government, while the MBA isn't necessary for advancement, it is increasingly becoming a major asset.

In this new career guide, Vault provides an overview of career topics most relevant to the MBA job search, including a look at some of the most prominent career paths for MBAs. Sectors covered in this guide include:

- Aerospace and Defense
- Agriculture
- Biotech and Pharmaceuticals
- Brand Management/Consumer Products
- Energy/Oil and Gas
- Fashion
- Financial Services and Insurance
- Government and Politics
- Health Care
- Hedge Funds
- High Tech
- Investment Banking
- Investment Management
- Management Consulting
- Manufacturing
- Media and Entertainment
- Real Estate
- Sales and Trading
- Technology Consulting
- Telecommunications
- Transportation and Airlines
- Venture Capital

Visit Vault at **www.vault.com** for insider company profiles, expert advice, career message boards, expert resume reviews, the Vault Job Board and more.

VAULT CAREER LIBRARY

1

THE MBA
JOB SEARCH

Use the Internet's
MOST TARGETED
job search tools.

Vault Job Board

Target your search by industry, function, and experience level, and find the job openings that you want.

VaultMatch Resume Database

Vault takes match-making to the next level: post your resume and customize your search by industry, function, experience and more. We'll match job listings with your interests and criteria and e-mail them directly to your in-box.

VAULT
> the most trusted name in career information™

Recruiting and Internships

Hiring Overview

MBA hiring continues to strengthen

MBA hiring continued to strengthen in 2004 and 2005, according to surveys focused on the hiring landscape for new business school graduates.

• In its annual Corporate Recruiters Survey, published in spring 2005, the Graduate Management Admission Council (GMAC), found that companies planned to do more MBA hiring in 2005 than in 2004, as measured by planned on-campus recruiting, percentage of new hires expected to be new MBAs and other metrics.

• In a survey published in February 2005, the National Association of Colleges and Employers (NACE) found that employers planned on hiring 24.9 percent more new MBA graduates in 2004-2005.

• And in a survey released in May 2005, the MBA Career Services Council (MBA CSC) found that recruiting activity increased in the fall 2004/winter 2005 at 84 percent of schools surveyed.

MBA CSC president Mindy Storrie, who is director of Career Services at the University of North Carolina at Chapel Hill's Kenan-Flagler Business School said "Companies have stepped up recruiting at business schools and MBAs are getting more job offers."

The 2005 GMAC survey, released in the spring of 2005, was based on the responses of 1,691 recruiters representing 1,019 companies. The companies reported, on average, that they expected about 22 percent of their new hires to be new MBA graduates – an increase from 19 percent in 2004. (The companies reported in 2005 that they expected 25% of their new hires to be new undergraduates, 14% to be graduates of non-MBA graduate programs, and 39% to be direct-from-industry hires.)

The improving recruiting picture drawn by the surveys is reflected in the recruiters' assessments of the economy. According to the GMAC survey, the percentage of corporate recruiters who said the economy was constraining recruiting plans dropped from 69 percent in 2001-2002 to 57 percent in 2002-2003 to 50 percent in 2003-2004 and finally down to 30 percent in 2004-2005.

What they make

The surveys reported average starting salaries in the $70,000 to $80,000. The MBA CSC survey found that 2004 graduates received an average base salary of $71,096. The NACE survey reported that recruiters expected to offer an average base salary of $72,930. The GMAC survey reported an expected average salary of $78,040. However, all surveys showed a wide range of potential salaries. For example, the GMAC survey had estimated salaries that ranged from $25,000 to $150,000.

On-Campus recruiting and internships

For many full-time business school students, on-campus recruiting and summer internships following the first year of business school are the most important methods of finding employers. According to the GMAC survey, 31 percent of MBA graduates hired in 2004 had served as interns at their companies.

On-campus recruiting is expected to increase in 2005. Of the more than 1,000 MBA employers surveyed in the GMAC survey, 82 percent said they planned to visit school campuses to recruit new MBAs (up from 78 percent in 2004). The GMAC survey also discovered that companies plan to visit more campuses (an average of 9.3 in 2005, up from 8.5 in 2004).

Visit Vault at **www.vault.com** for insider company profiles, expert advice, career message boards, expert resume reviews, the Vault Job Board and more.

VAULT CAREER LIBRARY

5

While companies will make presentations and send representatives to business schools throughout the year, actual on-campus interviewing and recruiting tends to be structured on a predictable schedule. Investment banking and consulting firms, which hire large classes of both summer interns full-time hires from business schools, tend to interview second-year students for full-time positions in October and November, and first-year students for summer internships in January and February. On-campus interviewing for Fortune 1000 companies usually happens later, with interviews in March and April for both full-time and internship hiring.

Choosing Between Summer Internships – Why Not Split 'Em?

Getting summer internships, especially in business school, is incredibly competitive, and the MBA who has two or more tempting internships to choose between is lucky indeed. Most students feel they must choose one over the other, but there is another option. Vault estimates that about one in 10 MBAs split their summer internships – that is, intern at more than one company. In the vast majority of cases, internships are split between companies in different industries, say, consulting and investment banking.

While split summers are still relatively uncommon, the question has arisen often enough for many top firms to establish policies designed to stamp out internship excess, whether these policies be informal or formal. But in many cases, with enough effort, it is still possible to spend your summer doing two separate internships. You won't get any time off during the summer, however – most firms will ask for a minimum of eight or nine weeks, and many will require you spend at least 10 or 12 weeks at the company. Since many business schools have summers lasting only 16-18 weeks, splitting your summer may even require you to take a couple of weeks off from school, either during finals week, the first week or two of your second year, or both. In general, smaller firms and firms in less formal industries, like high tech, will be more open to fitting you in at a time convenient for you, while at most investment banks and consulting firms, the time limitations are likely to be more stringent and the internship programs themselves less flexible.

The pros and cons of splitting

Let's weigh the pros and cons: On the one hand, splitting your summer will allow you an inside look at two different companies or industries, and you'll have two valuable names on your resume. However, remember that internships are, in part, designed to reflect your deep and abiding interest in a particular firm or industry when you go looking for a full-time offer. Splitting your summer may suggest that you lack commitment – not a good sign to hold up to companies who want to make sure that you'll stay with them. You'll also have to show up late to at least one of your internships which "never looks good, and then you'll have to explain to everyone where you were the first half of the summer," one MBA tells Vault. In addition "you run the risk of pissing off the companies who've offered you the internship," says one MBA student. "So, if you think you might definitely want to work for one of the companies, you should take that into account."

A quantitatively-inclined MBA student who split his summer advises: "You shouldn't split your summer if you are only 5 or 10 percent curious about what it might be like in another industry. Your minimum curiosity level should be around 25 percent." In general, says one MBA grad, "it makes more sense to split your summer if you're interested in the two industries involved, but perhaps not the firms in particular. Remember that summer internships are normally much more difficult to get than permanent employment, so you may be able to trade up to better firms during full-time job interviews. In other words, if you split a summer interning at two places you're not interested for permanent employment, you don't have to worry about what the firms think."

Structuring a split summer

According to insiders who've done it, here are some useful strategies for structuring a split summer internship. First of all, never let on that you intend to split your summer during your interviews. Express full enthusiasm for corporate finance, or strategy consulting, or whatever you're interviewing for – you can bring up a split summer if you get a job offer. Secondly, decide which internship is your priority internship, and put that one at the beginning of your summer. That way, you'll enter with the rest of the intern class, and your leaving early will attract less notice.

Questions to Ask During Your Summer Internship Interviews

Not all internships are created equal. Some involve dedicated training, exposure to managers, and significant responsibility. Others involve grunt work and sitting around with nothing to do.

How do you make sure you're getting a good deal when you sign on for an internship? Take the time during your interview to make sure you understand what's involved in the internship by asking these questions.

- Can you give me an example of my summer responsibilities? Try to make sure the answer you receive is as specific as possible. Particularly if you're new to the industry, you want to ensure that you will perform work that is representative of a full-time associate.

- How many people are typically given permanent job offers? And ask for percentages too. This shows you're interested in opportunities after graduation at the firm, and allows you to plan your strategic options. Some firms, like Goldman Sachs, are known for giving offers to a small proportion of the summer class. You may want to try better odds at another firm.

- Will I be able to rotate between departments? Again, the more you know about the company, the better you will be able to determine which department interests you most, or whether you want to work at the firm at all. If there's a specific department you want to work in, you should make this known.

- Do you provide any assistance with relocation? Many firms will help locate, and even subsidize, summer housing. If this makes a difference in whether you take the position, ask.

Visit Vault at **www.vault.com** for insider company profiles, expert advice, career message boards, expert resume reviews, the Vault Job Board and more.

V/\ULT CAREER LIBRARY   7

Resumes

Ten Seconds

Studies show that regardless of how long you labor over your resume, most employers will spend 10 seconds looking at it. That's it.

Because of the masses of job searchers, most managers and human resource employees receive an enormous number of resumes. Faced with a pile of paper to wade through every morning, employers look for any deficiency possible to reduce the applicant pool to a manageable number. Thus, your resume must present your information quickly, clearly, and in a way that makes your experience relevant to the position in question. That means condensing your information down to its most powerful form.

So distill, distill, distill. Long, dense paragraphs make information hard to find and require too much effort from the overworked reader. If that reader can't figure out how your experience applies to the available position, your resume is not doing its job.

Solve this problem by creating bulleted, indented, focused statements. Short, powerful lines show the reader, in a glance, exactly why they should keep reading.

Think about how to write up your experience in targeted, clear, bulleted, detail-rich prose. Here are some examples.

Before

Primary Duties: Computer repair and assembly, software troubleshooter, Internet installation and troubleshooting, games.

After

Primary Duties:

- Assembled and repaired Dell, Compaq, Gateway, and other PC computers

- Analyzed and fixed software malfunctions for Windows applications

- Installed and debugged Internet systems for businesses such as Rydell's Sports, Apple Foods, and Eric Cinemas

---

Before

Responsibilities included assisting with artist press releases, compiling tracking sheets based on information from reservationists and box office attendants, handling photo and press release mailings to media, assisting in radio copywriting, and performing various other duties as assigned.

After

Experience includes:

- Wrote artist press releases that contributed to an increase in sales by 23%

- Compiled and maintained mailing list of 10,000 – Cambridge Theater's largest-ever list

- Handled press release mailings to *Anchorage Daily News*, and Fox Four Television

- Contributed to copywriting of promotion radio commercials for selected events

---

Visit Vault at **www.vault.com** for insider company profiles, expert advice, career message boards, expert resume reviews, the Vault Job Board and more.

VAULT CAREER LIBRARY

9

It's What You Did, Not What Your Name Tag Said

Resumes should scream ability, not claim responsibility. Employers should be visualizing you in the new position, not remembering you as "that account assistant from Chase." While some former employers can promote your resume by their mere presence, you don't want to be thought of as a cog from another machine. Instead, your resume should present you as an essential component of a company's success.

Think Broadly

Applicants applying for specific job openings must customize the resume for each position. Many job-hunters, particularly those beginning their careers, apply to many different jobs.

A person interested in a career in publishing, for example, might apply for jobs as a writer, proofreader, editor, copywriter, grant proposal writer, fact-checker, or research assistant. The applicant may or may not have the experience necessary to apply for any of these jobs. But you may have more skills than you think.

When considering the skills that make you a valuable prospect, think broadly. Anyone who has worked a single day can point to several different skills, because even the most isolated, repetitive jobs offer a range of experience. Highway toll collection, for instance, is a repetitive job with limited variation, but even that career requires multiple job skills. Helping lost highway drivers read a map means "Offering customer service in a prompt, detail-oriented environment." Making change for riders translates as "Financial transactions in a high-pressure, fast-paced setting." But unless these toll-booth workers emphasize these skills to prospective employers, it'll be the highway life for them.

Selected History

A lot of things happen in everyone's day, but when someone asks, "How was your day?" you don't start with your first cough and your lost slippers. You edit. Resumes require that same type of disciplined, succinct editing. The better you are at controlling the information you create, the stronger the resume will be.

When editing your history to fit the resume format, ask yourself, "How does this particular information contribute towards my overall attractiveness to this employer?" If something doesn't help, drop it. Make more space to elaborate on the experiences most relevant to the job for which you are applying.

Similarly, if information lurks in your past that would harm your chances of getting the job, omit it. In resume writing, omitting is not lying. If some jobs make you overqualified for a position, eliminate those positions from your resume. If you're overeducated, don't mention the degree that makes you so. If you're significantly undereducated, there's no need to mention education at all. If the 10 jobs you've had in the last five years make you look like a real life Walter Mitty, reduce your resume's references to the most relevant positions while making sure there are no gaps in the years of your employment.

Sample MBA Resume

EUGENE H. HUANG
5050 S. Lake Shore Dr., Apt. 1407
Chicago, IL 60615
(773) 555-1234
ehuang@uchicago.edu

EDUCATION

MIDWAY SCHOOL OF BUSINESS Chicago, IL
Master of Business Administration – Finance and Strategic Management June 2004

- Dean's Honor List
- Active member of Management Consulting, Corporate Management and Strategy, and High Tech Clubs.

ANDERSEN COLLEGE Boston, MA
Bachelor of Arts in Physics (Cum Laude) June 1999
- Andersen College Scholarship for academic distinction; Dean's List all semesters
- Violinist in Andersen College Symphony
- Physics tutor for Bureau of Study Counsel; active participant in Habitat for Humanity
- Completed dissertation in the field of condensed matter theory

EXPERIENCE

SMART BROTHERS New York, NY
Technology Project Manager – Investment Banking June 2000 – July 2002

- Managed project teams to develop profit and loss systems for Proprietary Trading group
- Promoted to project leadership role in two years, well ahead of department average of four
- Developed an original mathematical algorithm for trading processing module, improving performance by 1200%
- Led team of six analysts in firmwide project to reengineer loan syndicate trading flows in firm's largest technology project of 1999. Recommendations established new firmwide standard for real-time trade processing
- Appointed lead developer of interest accrual team after just three months in department. Initiated and designed project to create customized, improved interest accrual and P&L applications for fixed income controllers
- Selected to work on high-profile project to reengineer corporate bond trading P&L system. Reduced overnight processing time from six hours to 20 minutes and improved desktop application speed by 350%
- Devoted 20-25 hours a month to instructing junior members of the team in interest accrual and trading

FINANCIAL TECHNOLOGY GROUP New York, NY
Analyst June 1999 – May 2000

- Developed cutting-edge analytic software for use by Wall Street traders
- Worked on a daily basis with clients to create and implement customized strategic software solution for equity traders. Helped create and deliver extensive training program for clients
- Initiated, created, and documented new firmwide standard for software module development

OTHER

- Winner of Mastermaster.com stock trading competition in November 2000. Won first place out of over 1,600 entrants worldwide with one-month return of 43.3%
- Other interests include violin, soccer, and the harmonica
- Recent travel to Yemen, Egypt, and Venezuela

Visit Vault at **www.vault.com** for insider company profiles, expert advice, career message boards, expert resume reviews, the Vault Job Board and more.

VAULT CAREER LIBRARY 11

Cover Letters

The Cover Letter Template

Your Name
Your Street Address, Apartment #
Your City, State Zip
Your Email Address
Your Home Phone Number
Your Fax Number

WONDERING WHAT GOES ON A COVER LETTER? HERE'S A STEP-BY-STEP GUIDE

Contact's Name
Contact's Title
Contact's Department
Contact's Name
Contact's Street Address, Suite #
Company City, State Zip
Company Phone Number
Company Fax Number

Date

Dear Ms./Mr. CONTACT,

The first paragraph tells why you're contacting the person, then either mentions your connection with that person or tells where you read about the job. It also quickly states who you are. Next it wows them with your sincere, researched knowledge of their company. The goal: demonstrating that you are a worthy applicant, and enticing them to read further.

The second and optional third paragraph tell more about yourself, particularly why you're an ideal match for the job by summarizing why you're what they're looking for. You may also clarify anything unclear on your resume.

The last paragraph is your goodbye: you thank the reader for his or her time. Include that you look forward to their reply or give them a time when you'll be getting in contact by phone.

Sincerely,

Sign Here

Visit Vault at **www.vault.com** for insider company profiles, expert advice, career message boards, expert resume reviews, the Vault Job Board and more.

VAULT CAREER LIBRARY   13

Date

Placement of the date, whether left justified, centered or aligned to the right, is up to your discretion, but take the time to write out the entry. If you choose to list the day, list it first, followed by the month, date, and year, as follows: Tuesday, July 9, 2004. (Europeans commonly list the day before month, so writing a date only in numbers can be confusing. Does a letter written on 4/7/04 date from April 7, or July 4?)

Name and address

Your name and address on the cover letter should be the same as the one on your resume. Uniformity in this case applies not only to the address given, but the way the information is written. If you listed your street as Ave. instead of Avenue on your resume, do so on your cover letter too.

Your header can be displayed centrally, just like the resume header – including your name in a larger and/or bolded font. But in most cases, the heading is either left justified or left justified and indented to the far right hand side of the page.

If you choose to list your phone number, make sure that you don't list it somewhere else on the page.

Next comes the address of the person you are writing. In many circumstances, you'll have the complete information on the person you're trying to contact, in which case you should list it in this order:

• Name of contact

• Title of contact

• Company name

• Company address

• Phone number

• Fax number

However, in many cases, you have less than complete information to go on. This is particularly true when responding to an advertisement. If you have an address or phone or fax number but no company name, try a reverse directory, such as Superpages (www.superpages.com), which lets you trace a business by either its address or phone number.

When you're trying to get a name of a contact person, calling the company and asking the receptionist for the name of the recipient (normally, though not always, head of HR) may work. But usually, companies don't list this information because they don't want you calling at all. So if you call, be polite, be persistent, ask for a contact name, say thank you and hang up. Don't identify yourself. If you have questions, wait until the interview.

If you don't get all of the info, don't worry. There are several salutations to use to finesse the fact that you've got no idea who you're addressing. Some solutions are:

To whom it may concern: A bit frosty, but effective.

Dear Sir or Madam: Formal and fusty, but it works.

Sirs: Since the workforce is full of women, avoid this outdated greeting.

Omitting the salutation altogether: Effective, but may look too informal.

Good morning: A sensible approach that is gaining popularity.

Format

Unlike the resume, the cover letter offers the writer significant room for flexibility. Successful cover letters have come in various different forms, and sometimes cover letters that break rules achieve success by attracting attention. But most don't. Here are some basic guidelines on what information the body of a cover letter should deliver.

First paragraph

To be successful, this first paragraph should contain:

• A first line that tells the reader why you're contacting them, and how you came to know about the position. This statement should be quick, simple and catchy. Ultimately, what you're trying to create is a descriptive line by which people can categorize you. This means no transcendental speeches about "the real you" or long-winded treatises on your career and philosophy of life.

• Text indicating your respect for the firm's accomplishments, history, status, products, or leaders.

• A last line that gives a very brief synopsis of who you are and why you want the position. The best way to do this, if you don't already have a more personal connection with the person you're contacting, is to lay it out like this:

I am a (your identifying characteristic)

+

I am a (your profession)

+

I have (your years of experience or education)

+

I have worked in (your area of expertise)

+

I am interested in (what position you're looking for)

And thus a killer first paragraph is born.

Middle paragraph(s)

The middle paragraph allows you to move beyond your initial declarative sentences, and into more expansive and revealing statements about who you are and what skills you bring to the job. This is another opportunity to explicitly summarize key facts of your job history. The middle paragraph also offers you the opportunity to mention any connection or prior experience that you may have with the company.

Tell the employer in this paragraph how, based on concrete references to your previous performances, you will perform in your desired position. This does not mean making general, unqualified statements about your greatness such as "I'm going to be the best you've ever had" or my "My energetic multi-tasking will be the ultimate asset to your company."

Comments should be backed up by specific references. Try something along the lines of "My post-graduate degree in marketing, combined with my four years of retail bicycle sales would make me a strong addition to Gwinn Cycles' marketing team."

Or: "Meeting the demands of a full-time undergraduate education, a position as student government accountant, and a 20-hour-a-week internship with Davidson Management provided me with the multi-tasking experience needed to excel as a financial analyst at Whittier Finance."

Visit Vault at **www.vault.com** for insider company profiles, expert advice, career message boards, expert resume reviews, the Vault Job Board and more.

VAULT CAREER LIBRARY   15

Many advertisements ask you to name your salary requirements. Some avoid the problem altogether by ignoring this requirement, and this may be the safest route – any number you give might price you out of a job (before you have the chance to negotiate face-to-face at an interview). Alternatively, you might be pegged at a lower salary than you might otherwise have been offered. If you must give a salary requirement, be as general as possible The safest bet is to offer as general a range as possible ("in the $30,000s"). Put the salary requirement at the end of the paragraph, not in your first sentence.

Some cover letter writers use another paragraph to describe their accomplishments. This makes sense if, for example, your experience lies in two distinct areas, or you need to explain something that is not evident on your resume, such as "I decided to leave law school to pursue an exciting venture capital opportunity" or "I plan to relocate to Wisconsin shortly." Do not get overly personal – "I dropped out of business school to care for my sick mother" is touching, but will not necessarily impress employers.

Final paragraph

The final paragraph is your fond farewell, your summation, a testament to your elegance and social grace. This should be the shortest paragraph of the letter. Here, tell your readers you're pleased they got so far down the page. Tell them you look forward to hearing from them. Tell them how you can be reached. Here's some sample sentences for your conclusion.

Thank you sentences:

Thank you for your time.

Thank you for reviewing my qualifications.

Thank you for your consideration.

Thank you for your review of my qualifications.

Way too much:

It would be more than an honor to meet with you.

A note of confidence in a callback:

I look forward to your reply.

I look forward to hearing from you.

I look forward to your response.

I look forward to your call.

Over the top:

Call me tomorrow, please.

MBA Summer Internship Cover Letter

February 1, 2005

Kimberly Sharpe, Recruiting Manager
Hexagonal Consulting
666 Avenue of the Americas
13th Floor
New York, NY

Dear Ms. Sharpe,

I am a first-year MBA student at State Business School. I was extremely impressed with Hexagonal Consulting's approach to management consulting after attending the presentation given by your firm earlier this year. I also learned more about your firm by talking with William Field and several other summer interns. My discussions with them confirmed my interest in Hexagonal Consulting, and I am now writing to request an invitation to interview for a summer associate consulting position.

After graduating from Northern College with a degree in accounting, I worked as an associate in the Finance department of AutoCo, a well-known automotive manufacturer. I gained solid analytical and problem solving skills there. I was responsible for identifying and resolving financial reporting issues, as well as generating innovative methods to improve our processes. I also fine-tuned my communication and consensus building skills, as I often needed to present and market my work to middle and upper management. Finally, during my last year of employment, I took on a team leadership role, managing the daily work of five junior members of our team and taking an active role in our training for new hires.

I am excited by the strong potential fit I see with Hexagonal Consulting. I feel that the analytical, leadership and teamwork abilities gained through my employment and academic experience have provided me with the tools and skills necessary to perform well in a consulting career, and will allow me to make a significant contribution at your firm. I am particularly intrigued by the shareholder value focus of Hexagonal Consulting's methodology, since it fits well with my experience in finance.

I have enclosed my resume for your review. I welcome the opportunity to meet with you when you recruit at SBS for summer internships later this month, and I would greatly appreciate being included on your invitational list.

Thank you for your time and consideration. I look forward to hearing from you.

Sincerely,

Laura Haley
314 Broadway, Apt. 15
New York, NY 10007
lbethhaley@hotmail.com

Visit Vault at **www.vault.com** for insider company profiles, expert advice, career message boards, expert resume reviews, the Vault Job Board and more.

V\ULT CAREER LIBRARY   17

MBA Full-Time Cover Letter

Ms. Margaret Jones, Recruiting Manager
Mainstream Consulting Group
123 21st Street
Boston, Massachusetts 02145

November 19, 2004

Dear Ms. Jones:

It was a pleasure to meet you in person last week at the Mainstream Consulting invitational lunch on the Boston Business School campus. Having spoken with your colleagues at the event, I believe that Mainstream would be an exciting and challenging firm in which to build my career.

My background fits well with a position in strategy consulting. As a Midway University physics undergraduate, I developed an analytic, creative mind geared towards solving complex problems. I applied and enhanced my problem solving skills as a technology project leader at Smart Brothers Investment Bank, where I focused on making business processes faster, more effective, and more efficient. Creating these results for traders, financial analysts, and senior management taught me how to effectively partner with clients throughout the various phases of business transformation. In addition, I gained valuable team leadership experience at Smart Brothers, guiding many project teams through the successful design and implementation of cutting-edge technology strategies.

As a telecommunications strategy intern at Global Consulting Associates this summer, I confirmed that strategy consulting is indeed the right career for me. Our project team helped a major telecommunications provider formulate a wireless data services strategy. I led the industry analysis and market opportunity assessment. This experience showed me that I am an effective contributor in a consulting environment, where industry knowledge, creative problem solving skills, fact-based analysis, and client focus are rewarded.

Mainstream appeals to me over other firms because of its focus on pure strategy projects, small firm atmosphere, and accelerated career growth opportunities. Please consider me for your invitational campus interviews this fall. I am particularly interested in positions in the San Francisco and Chicago offices, and I have enclosed my resume for your review.

Thank you for your time, and I look forward to hearing from you soon.

Sincerely,

Michael A. Thomas
100 Wellany Way
Boston, MA 02111
michaelt3@bostonu.edu

MBA Interviews

MBA Interviews

Interviewing during on-campus MBA recruiting can be a harrowing process for several reasons. First, there is the sheer volume of interviewing: some students interview with a dozen or more companies within a few week period, all while maintaining a busy class schedule.

At each interview, students work to convince interviewers that they represent a good "fit" with the company. Part of being a good fit, of course, means that students have specific interest and knowledge of the companies they are interviewing with. This crucial element of interview performance requires students to research the employers as thoroughly as possible in order to convincingly make their cases to many companies, a feat made more difficult by the large number of companies many students interview with. To help students prepare for their interviews with specific companies, Vault publishes 50-page employer profiles of major MBA employers, as well as "snapshots" of thousands of other major employers online at www.vault.com.

Interviewers use a variety of techniques to test students. According to the Graduate Management Admission Council's (GMAC) Corporate Recruiters Survey survey of more than 1,000 MBA employers, behavior-based interviews (during which candidates describe specific examples of skills such as leading a team or managing a difficult employee) are used by 79 percent of recruiters, and are the most common technique used by MBA recruiters. More than half of the recruiters surveyed (53 percent) use "case" or situational interviews in which the interviewers describe a hypothetical or real business situation and ask the job seeker to work through a course of action out loud. And more than one-third (36 percent) use question that measure position-specific knowledge (such as the ability to price a bond for a fixed income finance position).

Case interviews and technical finance interviews can be particularly stress-inducing, as students cannot as easily predict questions and prepare answers for these types of interviews as they can for behavior-based interviews. (In fact, some interviewers, most notoriously in the investment banking industry, choose to deliberately make interviews stressful in order to assess how business school students respond to stressful situations.) To help students prepare for these types of interviews, we discuss case and finance interviews in detail in the next two sections.

Case Interviews

What is a case interview?

Simply put, a case interview is the analysis of a business question. Unlike most other interview questions, it is an interactive process. Your interviewer will present you with a business problem and ask you for your opinion. Your job is to ask the interviewer logical questions that will permit you to make a detailed recommendation. The majority of case interviewers don't have a specific answer that you, the candidate, are expected to give. What the interviewer is looking for is a thought process that is both analytical and creative (what consultants love to call "out-of-the-box" thinking). Specific knowledge of the industry covered by the case question is a bonus but not necessary. Business school students and candidates with significant business world experience receive case questions that require a deeper understanding of business models and processes.

The interview with a consulting company normally lasts about half an hour. Of this time, about five to 10 minutes is taken up with preliminary chat and behavioral questions and five minutes of you asking questions about the company. This leaves five to 15 minutes for your case interview question or questions. Make them count!

Visit Vault at **www.vault.com** for insider company profiles, expert advice, career message boards, expert resume reviews, the Vault Job Board and more.

VAULT CAREER LIBRARY　　19

Why the case?

Your impressive resume may get you an interview with a consulting firm, but it won't get you the job. Consultants know that a resume, at its very best, is only a two-dimensional representation of a multi-faceted, dynamic person.

And because consulting firms depend on employing those multi-faceted, dynamic people, the firms rely heavily on the case interview to screen candidates. The interview process is especially pertinent in the consulting industry, since consulting professionals spend the lion's share of their business day interacting with clients and colleagues and must themselves constantly interview client employees and executives.

Consultants must have a select set of personality and leadership traits in order to be successful. The consultant's work environment is extremely turbulent. There are nonstop co-worker changes, hostile client environments, countless political machinations, and near-perpetual travel. These factors mandate that an individual be cool under pressure, be influential without being condescending, be highly analytical, have the ability to understand the smallest aspects of a problem (while simultaneously seeing the big picture), and have the ability to maintain a balance between the personal and professional.

Consultants are often staffed in small groups in far-flung areas. As a result, the individual must be able to function, and function well, without many of the traditional workplace standards: a permanent working space, the ability to return home each night, easily accessed services such as administrative assistance, faxing, and photocopying, and the camaraderie that develops among co-workers assigned to the same business unit.

All these factors necessitate a unique interview structure focused on assessing a candidate's ability to manage these particular circumstances with professionalism and excellence. The case interview has evolved as a method for evaluating these characteristics.

Types of case interviews

What case interviews are not designed to do is to explore educational, professional, or experiential qualifications. If you've reached the case interview stage, take a deep breath – the consulting firm has already weighed your background, GPA, and experience and found you worthy of a deeper skill assessment. This means that the case interview is yours to lose. Triumph over your case interviews and chances are that a slot at the firm will open for you.

Case interviews vary widely, but in general they fall into three groups: business cases, guesstimates, and brainteasers.

Case interviews

Case interviews vary somewhat in their format. The classic and most common type of case interview is the business case, in which you're presented with a business scenario and asked to analyze it and make recommendations. Most cases are presented in oral form, though some involve handouts or slides, and a few (like Monitor Company's) are entirely written. (In a written case, the interviewer will not contribute any other information besides what's on the handout.) Another variation on the case interview is the group case interview, where three to six candidates are grouped together and told to solve a case cooperatively. Consultants from the firm watch as silent observers. Though you should certainly be prepared for these variations on case interviews, you are most likely to come across the traditional, mano-a-mano case interview.

Guesstimates

Whether free-standing or as part of a case, learning how to make "back-of-the-envelope" calculations (rough, yet basically accurate) is an essential part of the case interview. As part of a guesstimate, you might be asked to estimate how many watermelons are sold in the United States each year, or what the market size for a new computer program that organizes your wardrobe might be. (For example, you might need to figure out the market size for the wardrobe software as a first step in determining how to enter the European market.) You will not be expected to get the exact number, but you should come close

– hence the guesstimate. Non-business school students and others who appear to be weak quantitatively may get stand-alone guesstimates – guesstimates given independently of a case.

Brainteasers

Brainteasers are normally logic puzzles or riddles. They may be timed. Often, brainteasers are meant to test both analytic and "out-of-the-box" thinking, as well as grace under pressure.

Skills assessed in the case interview

Following your case interview, your consulting interviewer will complete a written evaluation form. The evaluation forms often include a list of qualities, traits, and abilities and ask the interviewer to assess the candidate against the list. Following is a list of these special traits that, according to consulting insiders, interviewers will be keeping an eye out for as you work through the case interview:

Leadership skills

You'll hear this from every consulting firm out there – they want leaders. Why, you might ask, would a consulting firm need a leader? After all, many beginning consultants are consigned to independent number-crunching and research. The fact is, however, that consultants are often called upon to work independently, shape projects with very little direction, and direct others. You should demonstrate your leadership skills by taking charge of the case interview. Ask your questions confidently. Inquire whether the case interview relates to the interviewer's own experience. While your resume and previous leadership experience will probably most strongly convey your leadership ability, your demeanor in the case interview can help.

Analytical skills

The core competency of consulting is analysis – breaking down data, formulating it into a pattern that makes sense, and deriving a sensible conclusion or recommendation. You should display this skill through your efficient, on-target, and accurate questions while wrestling your case to a solution.

Presentation skills

Presenting your analysis is an essential part of consulting. Once consultants have analyzed their case engagement and decided on the proper course of action, they must present their findings and recommendations to their case team and to their clients. Interviewers will be watching you closely to see if you stumble over words, use inadvisable fillers like "um" or "like" frequently, or appear jittery under close questioning. Remember: When you're speaking, slow down and smile. If asked a question that temporarily stumps you, take a deep breath and pause. It's always better to pause than babble. Ask the interviewer to restate information if necessary.

Energy

Even the most qualified and analytical hire won't be much good if she quits at 5 p.m. during a long and arduous engagement. Interviewers look for zest and energy – firm handshake, sincere and warm smile, bright eyes. Remember that consulting firms expect you to take a long flight and show up at work the next day alert, perky, and ready to go. If you must, drink lots of coffee and use eyedrops – just be energized.

Attention to detail/organization

Consultants must be as painstaking as scientists in their attention to detail. And consultants who juggle two or more flights a week and engagements all over the world must be extremely organized. You can display this skill through a disciplined, logical approach to your case solution, and by showing up for your interview prepared. You'll want to take notes, so bring a pad of paper and a pen. Interviewers notice when candidates must ask for these materials. You must arrive on time.

Visit Vault at **www.vault.com** for insider company profiles, expert advice, career message boards, expert resume reviews, the Vault Job Board and more.

V∧ULT CAREER LIBRARY 21

Quantitative skills

Those spreadsheets you'll be working with as a management consultant need numbers to fill them. Consulting interviews will inevitably test your grasp of numbers and your ability to manipulate them. Many interviewers will assess your quantitative skills by giving you a "guesstimate," either within the case question or separately.

Flexibility

Consultants may have to arrive at the office one day and be packed off to Winnipeg for six months the next. This kind of flexibility of schedule is mirrored in tests for mental flexibility. To test your grasp of a case interview, the interviewer may suddenly introduce a new piece of information ("Okay, let's say the factories must be opened either in Canada or China") or flip the terms of the case interview ("What if this labor contract is not guaranteed, as I said earlier?") and then watch how quickly you're able to alter your thinking.

Maturity

Consultants must often work with executives and company officials decades older than they are. (This is why consultants are taught the right way to answer the question, "How old are you?") Eliminate giggling, fidgeting, and references to awesome fraternity events you may have attended, even if the interviewer seems receptive.

Intelligence, a.k.a. "mental horsepower"

Rather straightforward – consulting interviewers are looking for quickness of analysis and depth of insight. Don't be afraid to ask questions for fear of looking stupid – smart people learn by asking questions and assimilating new information. At the same time, asking your interviewer to repeat an elementary (or irrelevant) concept 20 times will not do you any favors.

What kind of case will I get?

While there's no way to tell for sure what case question you'll get, there are some things that can tip you off to the kind of case you'll receive.

If you're an undergraduate or other non-MBA student, you can probably be safely assured of getting a creative or "open-ended" question. "We don't expect our undergraduate candidates to know that much about business," confides one interviewer. "What we do expect is the ability to break down and articulate complex concepts." Undergraduates are also much more likely to get guesstimates and brainteasers than MBAs.

Are you a business school student or graduate? Then your case question will probably be less open-ended and drive toward an actual solution. Your interviewer may posit something from her own experience – knowing what course of action the consultancy actually ended up recommending. This doesn't mean you have to make the same recommendation – but you'd better be able to back up your reasoning! Alternatively, one thing case interviewers love to do is look at your resume and give you a case question that relates to your past experience. "For example," says one consultant, "if you were on the advertising staff for the school newspaper, you might be given a question about investing in advertising agencies." For this reason, advise consultants, "it makes sense to follow up on your field in The Wall Street Journal because you may be asked about recent developments in it. If you know what's going on you'll be that much more impressive." Some guesstimates, like figuring out the total worldwide revenues of Tarzan, are broad enough so that most people can make a reasonable assumption of numbers.

Sample Case

You are advising a credit card company that wants to market a prepaid phone card to its customers. Is this a good idea?

Whoa! Better find out more about this prepaid phone card first before you even begin to think about recommending it.

You: What is the role of our company? Do we simply market the card or must we create them ourselves? Are we expected to provide the telephone services?

Interviewer: This card will be co-marketed with an outside phone company. We do not need to perform telecommunications functions.

You: What are our expenses connected with the card?

Interviewer: We must pay 15 cents for every minute we sell. We also have to pay $1.00 as a start-up cost for the card and card systems.

You: What are our marketing expenses?

Interviewer: We normally use slips of paper that are attached to the backs of our credit card payment envelopes. We sometimes also send customers a direct mailing – in a separate envelope. Or we can have telemarketers call selected customers.

You: What's the cost of each of these marketing techniques, and what is their response rate?

Interviewer: Telemarketers have a 2 percent response rate and cost $1.00 per call. Direct mailings cost us 40 cents per mailing and have a 0.50 percent rate of response. Our payment attachments have a 0.25 percent rate of response, but only cost us 5 cents each.

You: I'm going to assume we will sell one-hour phone cards. That will cost us $9.00 for the minutes and a dollar per card – so each card costs us $10.

Interviewer: Okay, that sounds reasonable.

You: And what is our expected revenue on a one-hour phone card? What is the current market rate for a 60-minute phone card?

Interviewer: Assume it's 50 cents a minute.

You: So if we sell the cards for $30, we have a $20 profit, minus our expenditures on marketing.

Interviewer: What's our cost structure look like?

You: Okay, let's figure this out. To sell 1,000 cards through telemarketing, we would need to contact 50,000 people. That would cost us $50,000. To use direct mail, we would have to contact 200,000 thousand people, which, at 40 cents per mailing, costs us $80,000. Since the envelope inserts aren't very reliable, we will need to contact 800,000 people using that method. But at 5 cents each, it costs only $20,000 to sell 1,000 cards.

We make $20 profit on each card. But even using the cheapest promotional vehicle, at $20 profit, we would only break even, because our profits on 1,000 cards would be $20,000. We shouldn't market this card, unless we can further cut our marketing costs or increase the price of the card. If we could slice the cost of the envelope attachments a penny or so, or sell the card for $35, or convince our co-marketer to reduce our costs, it might be worth selling.

Interviewer: What are some other issues you might want to consider? (Notice how the interviewer is nudging you to add to your analysis.)

Visit Vault at **www.vault.com** for insider company profiles, expert advice, career message boards, expert resume reviews, the Vault Job Board and more.

V∧ULT CAREER LIBRARY   23

You: We should also consider the competitive landscape for this business. Is the per-minute rate for calling card minutes expected to fall? If so, and our costs are held constant, we may lose money. Of course, we can learn more from marketing these cards. It could be that the people likely to buy these cards might be frequent travelers and could be targeted for other promotions

Sample Guesstimate

How many square feet of pizza are eaten in the United States each month?

Take your figure of 300 million people in America. How many people eat pizza? Let's say 200 million. Now let's say the average pizza-eating person eats pizza twice a month, and eats two slices at a time. That's four slices a month. If the average slice of pizza is perhaps six inches at the base and 10 inches long, then the slice is 30 square inches of pizza. So four pizza slices would be 120 square inches. Therefore, there are a billion square feet of pizza eaten every month. To summarize:

- There are 300 million people in America.
- Perhaps 200 million eat pizza.
- The average slice of pizza is six inches at the base and 10 inches long = 30 square inches (height x half the base).
- The average American eats four slices of pizza a month.
- Four pieces x 30 square inches = 120 square inches (one square foot is 144 inches), so let's assume one square foot per person.
- Your total: 200 million square feet a month.

Finance Interviews

An overview of finance interviews

Investment banking positions and other finance positions are some of the more stressful and demanding positions on the planet, and this is reflected in the interview. In fact, insiders say that occasionally, an interviewer will yell at an applicant to see how he or she will react. Interviews normally go three or four rounds (sometimes as many as six or more rounds), and these rounds can have up to six interviews each, especially in the later rounds. Investment banking and finance interviews are also known for being deliberately stressful (as opposed to the attendant nervousness that goes with any interview). Some firms may ask you specific and detailed questions about your grades in college or business school, even if your school policy prohibits such questions. At other firms, interview rounds may be interspersed with seemingly casual and friendly dinners. Don't let down your guard! While these dinners are a good opportunity to meet your prospective co-workers, your seemingly genial hosts are scrutinizing you as well. (Hint: Don't drink too much.)

There are generally two parts to the finance hiring process: the fit part and the technical part. In asking technical questions, the interviewer wants to judge your analytical and technical skills. If you don't know the basic concepts of finance and accounting, your interviewers will believe (rightly) that you are 1) either not interested in the position 2) not competent enough to handle the job. An important part of the interviews is what is called "fit." As you go through recruiting in finance interviews, understand that you compete with yourself. Most firms are flexible enough to hire people that are a good fit.

The fit interview

They call it the O'Hare airport test, the Atlanta airport test, or the whatever-city-you-happen-to-be-applying-in airport test. They also call it the fit interview or the behavioral interview. It means: "Could you stand to be stranded in an airport for eight hours with this person?" Although bankers may have reputations for being aggressive individuals, don't act that way in your interview.

And while your performance in the fit interview partly depends – as the airport test suggests – on how well you gel with your interviewer, it also depends on your ability to portray yourself as a good fit as an investment banker, asset manager, etc. In other words, interviewers will try to figure out what your attitude towards work is like, how interested you are in a career in the industry, and how interested you are in the job for which you are applying.

I'm a hard worker

As a general rule, you should emphasize how hard you have worked in the past, giving evidence of your ability to take on a lot of work and pain. You don't have to make things up or pretend that there's nothing you'd want more than to work 100-hour weeks. In fact, interviewers are sure to see through such blatant lying. Says one I-banking interviewer, "If somebody acted too enthusiastic about the hours, that'd be weird." If you ask investment bankers and others in finance what they dislike most about their jobs, they will most likely talk about the long hours. Be honest about this unpleasant part of the job, and convince your interviewer that you can handle it well. For example, if you were in crew and had to wake up at 5:00 a.m. every morning in the freezing cold, by all means, talk about it. And if you put yourself through school by working two jobs, mention that, too.

Got safe hands?

As with all job interviews, those for finance positions will largely be about figuring out whether you can handle the responsibility required of the position. (In many cases with finance positions, that responsibility will mean making decisions with millions or billions of dollars at stake.)

An interviewer will try and figure out if you've got safe hands and won't be dropping the ball. "This is a critical I-banking concept," says one banker about safe hands. "The idea is: 'Can I give this person this analysis to do and feel comfortable that they will execute it promptly and correctly?' The people with safe hands are the ones who advance in the company. They are not necessarily the hardest workers but they are the most competent." Make sure you bring up examples of taking responsibility.

A mind to pick things apart

The world of finance is largely about number crunching and analytical ability. While this doesn't mean you have to be a world-class mathematician, it does mean that you have to have an analytic mind if you are to succeed. Explains one insider at a numbers-heavy Wall Street firm, "You can't be any old English major. You've got to have a really logical, mathematical head." Make sure you have examples of your problem-solving and analytic strengths.

T-E-A-M! Go team!

Teamwork is the buzzword of these days not just for the investment banking industry, but for every employer. Every finance position (except, perhaps, for research) requires that an employee work closely with others – whether this be in the form of investment banking deal teams, or finance officials working with marketers at a corporation. Interviewers will ask questions to make sure that you have experience, and have excelled, in team situations. Yeah, you can break out those glory days stories about the winning touchdown pass, but lots of other situations can also help describe your teamwork ability – previous work experience, volunteer activities, etc.

Preparing for finance interviews

When you review career options, don't discount the amount of time it takes to prepare for finance interviews. First of all, you should evaluate whether you actually want to be in investment banking, commercial banking, venture capital, etc. In

Visit Vault at **www.vault.com** for insider company profiles, expert advice, career message boards, expert resume reviews, the Vault Job Board and more.

V/\ULT CAREER LIBRARY   **25**

short, you should know what you're getting into. Not only should you know this for your own sake (this is your future, after all), but your interviewers want to know that you understand the position and industry.

You should use the opportunity of non-evaluative settings (i.e., not an interview) to get answers to these questions. These are questions to which we strongly suggest you have answers to before interviewing. Make a point to attend recruiting presentations by firms. Your informational interviews with alumni and (for those in business school) second-years are also good ways to get answers to some of your questions.

As for written materials, you can start with general business publications like *The Wall Street Journal*, *The Economist*, *BusinessWeek*, and the *Financial Times*. From there, you can move on to trade publications that will give more industry-specific news and analysis. *American Banker*, *Institutional Investor*, *Investment Dealers' Digest* and *The Daily Deal* are some examples.

Your interaction with alumni can have direct results. The results can be good if you prepare properly before contacting them. You can also assure yourself a ding if you don't handle a meeting or phone conversation correctly.

Here are some questions about finance positions you should ask before you have your first interview:

• What is a typical day like?
• What are the hours in the industry really like? Are they 100 hours every week or every other week? Is it the same for every firm?
• How do people cope with the lifestyle issues in the industry?
• What kind of money do people make in the industry?
• What are the things I-bankers (or commercial bankers, venture capitalists, etc.) like about their jobs? What would they like to change?
• What is the future of the industry for the next few years? How will the industry change? How will the margins change? The return on equity?
• What is the career track in the industry? What skills are required at what stage?
• What is so exciting about this job?
• What is the culture of an I-banking firm as compared to a Fortune 500 company? Compared to a startup?
• What are the exit opportunities after 10 years in the industry? After two years?

Research individual firms

Once you've answered questions about the industry, you should begin to narrow your research to specific firms – both to know which firms to target, and to be knowledgeable for your interviews. Good sources for research are easily accessible publications like *The Wall Street Journal*, *BusinessWeek* and *Fortune*. If you have the resources (perhaps at a school library), you can also read through recent issues of trade publications like *Investment Dealers' Digest*.

Insiders at business school who have gone through the recruiting process suggest that you form research and interview practice teams. There is a lot of material to cover, and it is not possible to do it all by yourself. Form teams for researching industries and firms. Later, you can use the same teams to practice interviews. If you are in business school, your school will undoubtedly have such a club, or you may want to team up with other students who are looking into finance careers. Teams of four to six work quite well for this research process.

Practice your interviews

You should prepare answers to common questions given at finance interviews – whether they be fit questions, technical questions, or brainteasers. While this may be easiest for technical questions and brainteasers (after all, we can help you to nail those questions with the right answers), it is also important to prepare for fit questions even if there are no right or wrong answers. We can steer you onto the right path with these questions, but you'll need to fill in the blanks. What's the hardest thing you've ever had to do? Can you give me an example of a time when you came up with a creative solution? You don't want to be cursing yourself after an interview, thinking about what you should have said, or examples you could have brought up.

One of the best ways to prepare answers to these questions is to use mock/practice interviews. You can practice by role-playing with your friends and classmates, or by taking advantage of interview training offered by your school. Many MBA career centers offer students the opportunity to perform mock interviews, which are normally videotaped. These practice sessions are conducted either by professional career counselors or by second-year students. The mock interviewees are given the videotape of their critique to watch at home (again and again). Students may choose what kind of interview they'd like to receive: finance, consulting, etc.

What mistakes are commonly unearthed by the videotaped interview? One business school career counselor says that he finds that "most MBAs don't have their story down. They can't elaborate why they came to business school, and why they want to work in the industry." The best candidates are able to describe their background and career history, and make a pitch about why they are interested in a firm, all in a minute or less, career counselors say. Another problem is that many students apparently "can't elaborate their strengths. They have them, but can't sell them. They are too modest." While there's no use demurring when explicating your good points, career center professionals warn that "there is also a danger of tooting your horn too much" – so make sure you're not making any claims for competency you can't back up with relevant experience.

To take full advantage of their mock interviews, career counselors say, students should take them as seriously as possible. Dress professionally "to get into the interviewing mindset." Afterwards, the interviewer will go over the session, assessing the candidate's strengths and weaknesses. It's a good idea to take notes on this feedback.

Mock interviewers also coach students on appropriate answers. "For example," explains one mock interviewer, "many candidates are asked to name their top three weaknesses. Answering with your actual weaknesses is not a good idea. So when I identify a student's weaker point – maybe they are weak on real teamwork experience – we strategize on an appropriate answer. It's better to say something like 'I wouldn't call them weaknesses, but there are three areas in which I still have room to grow,' and then choose three areas that are not deal-breakers."

Do interviewers thus end up hearing the same canned answers over and over again? "I do hear from some interviewers at certain schools – not mine! – that they do hear identical answers to certain questions," says one insider. "My advice to students is to always put answers into their own words."

Prepare questions

Finally, don't forget that finance interviewers often ask candidates whether they have any questions. Don't get caught looking like a job applicant who hasn't done research and is not curious about the opportunities. Read about the firms, read about the industries, and prepare some intelligent questions.

Sample Finance Interview Questions

What happens to each of the three primary financial statements when you change a) gross margin b) capital expenditures c) etc.

This problem tests your understanding of the interconnection between all three statements.

a) If gross margin were to say, decrease, then your income statement would first be affected. You would pay lower taxes, but if nothing else changed, you would have lower net income. This would translate to the cash flow statement on the top line. If everything else remained the same, you would have less cash. Going to the balance sheet, you would not only have less cash, but to balance that effect, you would have lower shareholder's equity.

Visit Vault at **www.vault.com** for insider company profiles, expert advice, career message boards, expert resume reviews, the Vault Job Board and more.

V\ULT CAREER LIBRARY   **27**

b) If capital expenditure were to say, decrease, then first, the level of capital expenditures would decrease on the Statement of Cash Flows. This would increase the level of cash on the balance sheet, but decrease the level of property, plant and equipment, so total assets stay the same. On the income statement, the depreciation expense would be lower in subsequent years, so net income would be higher, which would increase cash and shareholder's equity in the future.

c) Just be sure you understand the interplay between the three sheets. Remember that changing one sheet has ramifications on all the other statements both today and in the future.

How do you calculate the terminal value of a company?

The value of the terminal year cash flows (usually calculated for 10 years in the future) is calculated by calculating the present value of cash flows from the terminal year (in our case, Year 10) continuing forever with the following formula:

$$\text{TY FCF} = \frac{FCF_{10}\,(1 + g)}{(r_{d} - g)}$$

Here "g" is an assumed growth rate and rd is the discount rate. (Remember that you could also calculate the terminal value of a company by taking a multiple of terminal year cash flows, and discounting that back to the present to arrive at an answer. This alternative method might be used in some instances because it is less dependent on the assumed growth rate (g).

If you add a risky stock into a portfolio that is already risky, how is the overall portfolio risk affected?

a. It becomes riskier

b. It becomes less risky

c. Overall risk is unaffected

d. It depends on the stock

Answer: D. It depends on the stock. In modern portfolio theory, if you add a risky stock into a portfolio that is already risky, the resulting portfolio may be more or less risky than before.

A portfolio's overall risk is determined not just by the riskiness of its individual positions, but also by how those positions are correlated with each other. For example, a portfolio with two high-tech stocks might at first glance be considered risky, but if those two stocks tends to move in opposite directions, then the riskiness of the portfolio overall could be significantly lower. So the risk effect of adding a new stock to an existing portfolio depends on how that stock correlates with the other stocks in the portfolio.

When should a company issue stock rather than debt to fund its operations?

There are several reasons for a company to issue stock rather than debt. If the company believes its stock price is inflated it can raise money (on very good terms) by issuing stock. The second is when the projects for which the money is being raised may not generate predictable cash flows in the immediate future. A simple example of this is a startup company. The owners of startups generally will issue stock rather than take on debt because their ventures will probably not generate predictable cash flows, which is needed to make regular debt payments, and also so that the risk of the venture is diffused among the company's shareholders. A third reason for a company to raise money by selling equity is if it wants to change its debt-to-equity ratio. This ratio in part determines a company's bond rating. If a company's bond rating is poor because it is struggling with large debts, they may decide to issue equity to pay down the debt.

If inflation rates in the U.S. falls relative to the inflation rate in Russia, what will happen to the exchange rate between the dollar and the ruble?

The dollar will strengthen relative to the ruble.

Visit Vault at **www.vault.com** for insider company profiles, expert advice, career message boards, expert resume reviews, the Vault Job Board and more.

V\ULT CAREER LIBRARY   **29**

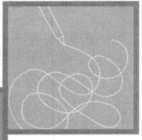

Connect.

At Mattel, we connect with our customers and our consumers. But most of all, we connect with each other. We welcome every race, gender, religion... to work with us as one.

With worldwide headquarters in El Segundo, Calif., Mattel employs more than 25,000 people in 36 countries and sells products in more than 150 nations throughout the world. The Mattel vision is to be the world's premiere toy brands—today and tomorrow. Mattel, Inc. (NYSE: MAT, www.mattel.com) is the worldwide leader in the design, manufacture and marketing of toys and family products, including Barbie® the most popular fashion doll ever introduced.

MBA
DIVERSITY

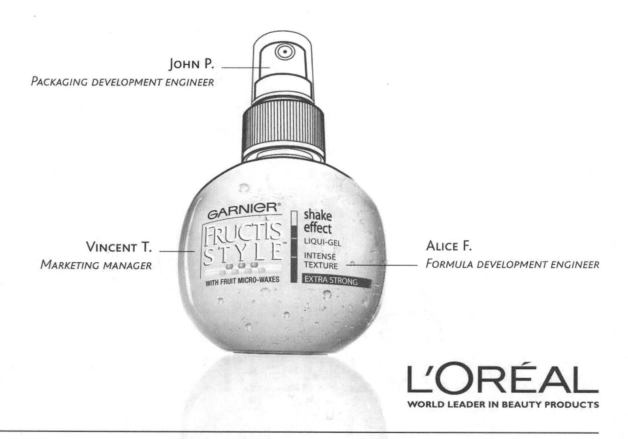

TO BUILD BEAUTY, WE NEED TALENT.

"A DIVERSE WORKFORCE ENHANCES OUR CREATIVITY AND OUR UNDERSTANDING OF CONSUMERS AND ALLOWS US TO DEVELOP AND MARKET HIGHLY RELEVANT PRODUCTS."
JEAN-PAUL AGON, PRESIDENT AND CEO L'ORÉAL USA

JOHN P.
PACKAGING DEVELOPMENT ENGINEER

VINCENT T.
MARKETING MANAGER

ALICE F.
FORMULA DEVELOPMENT ENGINEER

L'ORÉAL
WORLD LEADER IN BEAUTY PRODUCTS

JOIN US. STAYING ON TOP OF A DYNAMIC INDUSTRY MEANS WE NEED AMBITIOUS, FLEXIBLE AND HIGH-PERFORMING PEOPLE. L'ORÉAL USA: IT'S FAST-PACED. IT'S STIMULATING. IT'S REWARDING. AND MOST OF ALL, IT'S WHAT YOU MAKE IT.

L'ORÉAL USA MANAGEMENT DEVELOPMENT PROGRAM
MARKETING ▪ SALES ▪ FINANCE ▪ INFORMATION SYSTEMS ▪ LOGISTICS ▪ MANUFACTURING ▪ RESEARCH & DEVELOPMENT

IF YOU ARE AN IMAGINATIVE AND RESULTS-FOCUSED GRADUATING SENIOR WITH AN ENTREPRENEURIAL SPIRIT AND COMMITMENT TO EXCELLENCE, THEN L'ORÉAL USA MAY HAVE THE OPPORTUNITY FOR YOU. UPON ENTERING OUR ROTATIONAL TRAINING PROGRAM, YOU WILL BECOME AN INTEGRAL PART OF OUR TEAM, WITH CONCRETE RESPONSIBILITY FROM DAY ONE. YOU WILL WORK ALONGSIDE TOP PROFESSIONALS WHO SHAPE THE INDUSTRY, CONTRIBUTING TO THE CREATION OF IDEAS AND THE PROCESSES THAT TURN THOSE IDEAS INTO REALITIES. IN ADDITION TO PROFESSIONAL DEVELOPMENT TRAINING HELD AT OUR MANAGEMENT DEVELOPMENT CENTER, WE OFFER COMPETITIVE COMPENSATION AND BENEFITS. LEARN MORE ABOUT THIS EXCITING FULL-TIME OPPORTUNITY AND APPLY AT **WWW.LOREALUSA.COM.** EQUAL OPPORTUNITY EMPLOYER.

The Importance of Mentors

What makes the difference between a career that thrives and one that stalls? For many women and minorities, the narrow gap between failure and success is bridged by mentorships. Mentors are people who share their general business knowledge, as well as their knowledge of a specific company, with lucky mentees (someone who is mentored). Here is some advice on how to make these valuable relationships work for you.

Mentors can keep you with an employer

After several years at the prestigious consulting firm Booz Allen Hamilton, Cathy Mhatre had her first child. Mhatre credits her mentors at Booz Allen with keeping her at the firm. "I've now been at Booz Allen for six years, which is unusual for any consultant. One of the main reasons I am still here is because there were people who wanted to keep me here." Mhatre estimates that she has "four to six" mentors at the firm, and advises, "Because women mentors are scarce in general, find enlightened men."

Have many mentors for many reasons

Do you need help on balancing your family life and career without sacrificing your career viability? You could probably use some help from a mentor who's done just that at your company. Your work-life balance mentor, however, may not be the same person who can help you polish your presentation skills and confidence. If you seek someone who will be your advocate at performance and promotion reviews, look for someone at least two levels above you (or with four or more years of experience at the company).

Find out if your employer assigns you a mentor - then keep looking

Increasingly, employers assign mentors to incoming associates – a practice that has been common at law firms for some time and is spreading rapidly to other industries as well. Some consulting firms have entire mentor family trees – with a "founder" mentor, his or her mentees, their mentees, and so on. Make sure to take advantage of these mentors, who have specifically volunteered to serve as resources.

At the same time, the most valuable mentors are normally the ones that evolve from everyday working relationships. If someone appears willing to share their experience and skills with you and takes an interest in your career, it is likely that they would like to mentor you in some way.

Don't expect your mentor to share your background.

While it's terrific to have mentors that share your ethnicity or gender, it's no sure thing. Some of the MBAs we spoke to indicate that the old "succeed and close the door behind you" ethos is still in existence. "When I was working," says Lanchi Venator, a NYU Stern MBA graduate, "it seemed that most successful women were not open to helping other women out. It was almost as if they were saying, 'I made it when it was tough on me. Why should I soften for you?'"

Be careful of having only one mentor.

One-on-one mentorship has its pitfalls. Corporate historians may recall the case of Mary Cunningham and William Agee at Bendix Corp. After rising rapidly through the ranks of Bendix, Cunningham, a 1979 graduate of Harvard Business School, was accused of sleeping with her mentor. Cunningham eventually left the firm. Even when the shadow of romance doesn't

Visit Vault at **www.vault.com** for insider company profiles, expert advice, career message boards, expert resume reviews, the Vault Job Board and more.

VAULT CAREER LIBRARY   33

enter a close mentorship, mentees with only one advisor run the risk of being seen as an appendage or sidekick, not a full professional. Whenever possible, seek mentorship from a wide variety of people.

Tips for mentees

It's not enough to find a good mentor – it's just as important to use them correctly. Here are a few tips to make the most of your mentor relationship.

- **Find mentors at all levels of the company.** The classic mentor is someone a few levels above you in an organization – close enough to your experience to guide you upwards in the ranks, experienced enough to have some pull. But you can also gain experience from mentors at your level and at other companies as well. Your business school professors are another invaluable set of potential mentors.

- **Don't approach someone and formally ask them to be your mentor.** This kind of artificiality is akin to handing your business card to someone and asking them to be your contact – it's too artificial to take root. If someone wants to be your mentor, they will indicate that fact through the interest they take in you.

- **Keep in touch with your mentors.** Mentorship is a relationship, and relationships are built from frequent, informal contact. This is important even when your mentor is assigned to you by your company. If you move on from a company, stay in touch with your mentor there.

- **Establish trust.** Everything you discuss with your mentor is between the two of you.

- **Have realistic expectations.** Your mentor is an advisor and advocate – not someone to do your career networking for you, or someone to cover your errors.

- **Find your own mentees.** Mentorship is a two-way street. As soon as possible, start finding people who are willing to learn from you. You never know when the mentee will become the mentor!

- **Don't pass up the opportunity to have a mentor.** Having a mentor can make a major difference in your career path and your self-confidence.

Vault Diversity Q&A: Pipasu Soni, Financial Analyst, Honeywell

Pipasu Soni is a 2003 graduate of the Johnson School of Management at Cornell University. A former engineer of Indian descent, he previously worked at Ingersoll-Rand before getting an MBA. He currently works in Minneapolis as a financial analyst with Honeywell's Automation and Control Solutions (ACS) division, an $8 billion division encompassing seven different strategic business units including environmental controls, fire solutions, security systems and more. He took time out to talk to Vault a bit about being a minority MBA and working at Honeywell.

Vault: How did you end up in your current position? Did you go to business school knowing you wanted to do finance?

Soni: Actually, I was initially interested in going into marketing, but after the very first semester, my focus shifted to finance. Previously I worked in new product development for Ingersoll-Rand. There's always some tension between the engineering and marketing side during new product introduction, and I was interested in exploring the marketing/product management aspect, to get more of a general management perspective.

But as an engineer, I enjoyed the technical side of finance and the role it played within an organization. When it came to recruiting, I really liked the Finance Pathways Program and the fact that the finance group at Honeywell is one of the keys to implementing the strategic vision of the organization.

Vault: Did you intern at Honeywell?

Soni: No actually, I interned with a consulting firm. I wanted to find out more about the consulting field, and decided it wasn't for me. I enjoyed being part of the day-to-day operations of an organization where I could influence the performance and visibly see the product. I knew Honeywell would be a great place to leverage my past experience with Ingersoll-Rand.

Vault: What sort of program were you hired into?

Soni: I was hired into Honeywell's Finance Pathways Program. It's one of their career development programs for MBA graduates. The program consists of two 18-month assignments across different Honeywell businesses. I'm in my first rotation, which ends this December. My current assignment consists of working in the corporate finance group supporting the annual operating plan, strategic plan, corporate initiatives, and other functional areas – Six Sigma and Technology. At the end of the assignment I'll move into an operational finance role at a business unit level.

Vault: Is there a formal mentorship program with the Pathways program?

Soni: No, not "formal." Mentoring takes several forms at Honeywell. All employees are encouraged to seek out mentors as well as offer to mentor others. My particular businesses assisted me in identifying a formal mentor at the beginning of my assignment. The main focus of my mentor is to provide a contact that can give me insight and advice as I move throughout my career.

In addition, you receive mentoring through working with managers on assignments. Also, your supervisor gives you regular feedback on performance and instructs you on training you should pursue.

Vault: Are there diversity organizations for you at Honeywell?

Soni: Yes, there's an Indian and Asian Association that meets on a regular basis. These groups usually meet once a month for a networking hour or a guest speaker presentation. Honeywell also has several other minority employee groups throughout the company. like the Hispanic Network and the Black Employees Network.

Vault: Did you get the feeling during recruiting that Honeywell targets minorities and women for diversity hiring purposes?

Soni: No, I don't think Honeywell specifically targets minorities, but focuses on recruiting individuals that are the right fit with the company. Honeywell defines diversity more as individual uniqueness. I don't think it's just gender, race, and ethnic background but also things such as educational and cultural background and work experience.

With that said, Honeywell's incoming Pathways class is a diverse group similar to what you would find in a typical MBA class.

Vault: What attracted you to Honeywell?

Soni: The things that attracted me the most were the people and the job assignments. For me, having a first assignment in financial planning and analysis at the corporate level allowed me to understand the strategic vision of the organization before moving into a business unit role.

Other things unique to Honeywell included the ability to work across several functions, mandatory green-belt training and certification for all incoming MBAs, and ability to switch roles – from finance to marketing if desired. I spoke with several Cornell alumni and other Pathway program members before joining and it seems that our perspective of Honeywell is very similar.

Vault: What aspects of your MBA education do you think have proved most helpful in your experience so far at Honeywell?

Soni: In my current assignment, finance, accounting, and leadership classes have been the most helpful. The classes in accounting and finance have been invaluable in reviewing business unit results. The classes in leading, communicating and team building have been also valuable in day-to-day communication getting people to meet deadlines and goals.

Visit Vault at **www.vault.com** for insider company profiles, expert advice, career message boards, expert resume reviews, the Vault Job Board and more.

VAULT CAREER LIBRARY   **35**

Job Fair ■ Seminars ■ Networking Reception

5th Annual
ASIAN DIVERSITY
CAREER EXPO

The Largest Career Event For Asian Americans in the United States.

May 5, 2006
New York City
Madison Square Garden

EVENT HIGHLIGHTS:

- Speak with recruiters from prestigious companies, attend an onsite interview, FIND A JOB!
- Corporate cultural training session by Cross Cultural Connections
- Get FREE resume critiquing and attend FREE workshops on "Targeting the Job You Want", "Leadership Development in Today's Competitive Corporate Climate" and "Turning Your Interviews Into Offers/Acing Your Meetings" by the Five O' Clock Club
- Attend FREE seminars on "Jobs in Asia" and "Asian Americans in the Workplace" hosted by the Asian Pacific Islander American Corporate Leadership Network (ACLN)
- Utilize DELL's FREE CYBERCAFE!

Confirmed Exhibitors

Memorial Sloan Kettering Cancer Center	Oxford Health Plans A United Healthcare Co.	Bank of America
Dell	The New York State Education Department	Milton Hershey School
Healthfirst	DaimlerChrysler Services	The Intelligence Community
Primerica Financial Services	New York Life	Enterprise Rent-A-Car
Bear Stearns & Co., Inc.	Internal Revenue Service	Federal Bureau of Prisons
Pepsi Co.	HSBC Bank USA, NA	BP America
AT&T	Department of Defense – Recruitment Assistance Division	Intel Corporation
United States Secret Service	The Procter & Gamble Company	Starbucks Coffe Company
Kiss Products, Inc	Johnson & Johnson Family Of Companies	Merck & Co.
Mercedes-Benz USA, LLC	Central Intelligence Agency	New York City Police
USAREC MOPS Army-Starcom Worldwide	MasterCard International	Metro Recruiting Station
National Instruments	U.S. Postal Service	LG Electronics
Time Warner Cable	U.S. Department of Labor	
Federal Bureau of Prisons-Metropolitan Correctional Center	The Hershey Company	
National Geospatial-Intelligence Agency	The U.S. Department of Commerce	
New Jersey Judiciary Administrative Office of The Courts	School District of Philadelphia	
U.S. Federal Bureau Of Investigation	Department of Energy	
U.S. Department of Justice Drug Enforcement Administration	Colgate Palmolive Co	
Sandia National Laboratories	MetLife Auto & Home	
State Farm Insurance	Daimler Chrysler Corporation	
US Dept of State/Diplomatic Security Recruitment	ARAMARK	
Choice Hotels International, Inc.	International Broadcasting Bureau/Voice of America	
National Credit Union Administration	New York State Police	
Talbots	American International Group (AIG)	
Social Security Administration	Stryker Orthopaedics	

REGISTER NOW by visiting www.asiandiversity.com/event

- Online Pre Registration **Free**
- On Site Registration **$10**

Presented By: 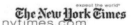 The New York Times
nytimes.com

Platinum sponsor: DELL

Silver Sponsor: AT&T   Mercedes-Benz   LG

Media Sponsor: The Korea Daily 世界新聞網 WorldJournal.com News India

You learn about metrics in business school and using metrics to drive performance, but you don't realize the significance until you actually use it. It's been a great experience, and I feel like I'm going to the next level in my ability to lead teams and drive results.

Vault Diversity Q&A: Ann Silverman, M&T Bank

A 2004 graduate of the Wharton School at the University of Pennsylvania, Ann Silverman was a project manager and exhibition developer at the Smithsonian Institution in New York prior to business school. She decided to get an MBA in order to have a greater impact on the community in which she lives and ended up choosing to join the Executive Associate program at M&T Bank in the Washington, DC metro area after graduation. She took time out to talk with Vault about her choice of regional banking and about being a woman professional in finance.

Vault: Going into business school, did you know that you wanted to go into finance and commercial banking?

Silverman: I knew that I wanted to go into finance, but I suppose coming from such a different background, I didn't know what individual buckets [in finance] there were. Once I got into business school and understood more, I knew that commercial banking in particular was what I wanted, and that I wanted a regional bank.

Vault: What in particular about regional banks and commercial banking appeals to you?

Silverman: At the Smithsonian, one of the things I loved most was the community impact of the job, but I felt that I wasn't going to have a real impact until I had a profession that hits people's wallets. When I looked at the landscape out there I thought "Wow, commercial banking is really a wonderful area that contributes to the businesses in the community and the community at large."

Vault: Why did you choose M&T?

Silverman: Looking at all of the mergers and acquisitions activity that have gone on in the banking industry, I really wanted to find a place where I would have opportunities for business development and client interaction earlier rather than later and a smaller, regional bank seemed the best place to get this experience and the chance to contribute in meaningful ways. And M&T's mission emphasizes being really involved in the community, and I take that very seriously.

Vault: Can you describe the program that you were hired into? Is it a rotational program?

Silverman: M&T has what's called the Executive Associate program. It's not really a formal rotation program; you're hired into a functional position. I was hired into commercial lending as knew I wanted to be a lender. In my case, my title is Relationship Manager. "Executive Associate" is more of a hiring title.

Vault: How long are you in the Executive Associate program?

Silverman: The first year is the more defined part of the program, though the bank does track us as Executive Associates throughout our career.

The first year has really been a mix of both project work, which gives you exposure to people throughout the bank, and learning the skills to being a lender, everything from the financial and industry analysis and the business development skills to integrating yourself into the community.

Vault: Are there training sessions for Executive Associates outside of on-the-job-training?

Silverman: In the first year, we have seminars. Almost once a month, all the MBAs are brought together at the Bank's headquarters in Buffalo. Each time, there's a lunch with one of the members of the executive committee, and bookending that in the morning and afternoon are presentations from departments throughout the Bank. This way, you get a chance to meet the other EAs that you've been hired with and the managers and staff that work across the Bank.

Visit Vault at **www.vault.com** for insider company profiles, expert advice, career message boards, expert resume reviews, the Vault Job Board and more.

V\ULT CAREER LIBRARY   37

Vault: How many Executive Associates were there in your class?

Silverman: I believe there were 21 that were hired in my class.

Vault: Did you have any concerns about going into finance, which is notoriously male-dominated? And do you find, in comparing notes with your business school classmates, that commercial banking is any better than other areas of finance, such as investment banking or investment management?

Silverman: I would agree that finance is an area where women are underrepresented. I knew that that would be part of the world that I would enter regardless of where I went into finance. I don't feel that there's a difference between investment banking and commercial banking.

With the issue of representation of women in finance, it's only going to change as more of us come into the field. There are a lot of women who have certainly gone before me, and we need to keep that momentum. Taking my peer group at Wharton as an example, many of the women that I was friends with are going into finance, so there's continued progress.

Vault: How many women are there in your Executive Associate class at M&T?

Silverman: There were three of us. I know them quite well – we speak frequently and try to foster close relationships with each other.

One thing that was important to me about M&T is that it has a Diversity Council. It's a bank-wide initiative that's headed up by a gentleman on the senior committee of the bank. Particularly as the bank has grown in the last three years, it has made an effort to takes issues of diversity seriously, as evidenced by the formation of this group. The idea that you've really got to grow and nurture that, it doesn't happen overnight.

Vault: What types of companies and organizations are you working with as a lender?

Silverman: We service middle market companies, which are companies that have revenues above $10 million. The economy in DC is incredibly diverse. There are lots of life sciences and biotechnology companies, there are government related contractors, high technology companies. Just everything under the sun.

Vault: And how do you go about developing business with these organizations?

Silverman: One of the ways that we get a lot of business is through referrals. And one of the ways to do that is to make sure you're really well networked with accountants and lawyers in the region and others that work with businesses. People in the bank are very generous about making sure you get the external introductions you need. There are many business organizations in the county that have breakfasts, lunches, dinners, etc. Let's just say that my evenings are quite full.

Vault: Do you work with professional groups for women with respect to business development initiatives?

Silverman: Oh, yes. In the DC region, there's a group called Women in Bio, there's one called Women in Information Technology – there are a lot of those groups, and those are definitely resources I tap into.

Diversity Employer Directory

Bristol-Myers Squibb Co.

345 Park Avenue
New York, NY 10154-0037
Phone: 212-546-4000
www.bms.com/career/data/workdive.html

 Bristol-Myers Squibb
Hope, Triumph and the Miracle of Medicine™

Different perspectives make it possible. At Bristol-Myers Squibb, we're a diverse team of talented and creative people -- each with a different perspective. We value each person's unique contributions and inspire each other to develop the innovative solutions that extend and enhance the lives of our patients around the world.

Opportunities make your growth possible. Ask yourself - how far do you want to go? At Bristol-Myers Squibb, we're determined to be the company where our employees can achieve their career goals. We offer a range of opportunities to help you get there. It's simple. Your growth helps us to better extend and enhance the lives of patients around the world.

Business Schools Bristol-Myers Squibb Co. Recruits from

BMS offers opportunities for MBA students and graduates to join Summer and Full-Time Associate Programs in the following areas: Marketing, Finance, Information Management, Human Resources and Technical Operations.

Campbell Soup Company

1 Campbell Place, Box 35D
Camden, NJ 08103
Phone: 856-342-4800
Diversity Recruiting E-mail: Csc_Diversity@Campbellsoup.com

At Campbell, we define diversity as the vast array of human differences and similarities, inclusive of everyone. In order to compete and succeed in a changing marketplace we must cultivate and embrace a diverse employee population that fuels our growth and enriches our global culture.

As part of our Campbell's Vision, "Together We Will Do Extraordinary Things in the Workplace and Marketplace," our commitment to building and strengthening teams has the greatest focus of our leadership. We must have diverse perspectives, talents and teams to meet this business challenge. You won't find a better place for your talent, ideas and experience than at Campbell Soup Company.

Business schools Campbell's recruits from

Wharton (Penn); Cornell; University of North Carolina (Kenan Flagler); University of Michigan (Ross); Darden (UVA); Carnegie Melon (Tepper); University of Maryland (Smith)

Credit Suisse First Boston

11 Madison Avenue
New York, New York 10010
www.csfb.com

Tanji Dewberry – Head of Diversity Recruiting
Phone: 212-538-2594
E-mail: Diversity.recruiting@csfb.com

 **CREDIT SUISSE | FIRST BOSTON**

CSFB MBA Explorer Program – First Year MBA Students

The MBA Explorer Program is a two-day educational outreach program that brings together women and students of color who are entering business school in the fall. This unique program offers students who may not have an investment banking background a chance to learn first-hand about Wall Street and specifically CSFB. Participants learn about the firm's core businesses and culture and get to meet with school teams and recruiters months in advance of the Summer Associate recruiting season.

The CSFB MBA Fellowship Program – First Year MBA Students

The MBA Fellowship Program is designed to increase the level of interest in, and awareness of careers in the investment banking industry among students of color attending business school. Credit Suisse First Boston (CSFB) will offer a one-year, full-tuition fellowship to top MBA students of Black and/or Hispanic heritage at the following business schools: Chicago Graduate School of Business • Columbia Business School • Cornell Johnson School of Management • Harvard

Business School • IT Sloan School of Management • tern School of Business • Stanford Graduate School of Business • The Wharton School •

Eligible candidates must be admitted as entering first-year MBA students and be interested in pursuing a career in the investment banking industry including sales, trading, research, investment banking, and alternative capital.

Once selected the fellowship recipients will be assigned junior and senior mentors at the beginning of the academic year. Finally, the CSFB Fellowship requires that recipients participate in and complete the CSFB summer internship interview process.

Business schools CSFB recruits from

Columbia Business Schools; Cornell Johnson School of Management; Harvard Business School; Stanford Graduate School of Business; Wharton School of Business; Sloan School of Management; Stern School of Business; University of Chicago Graduate School of Business

Visit Vault at **www.vault.com** for insider company profiles, expert advice, career message boards, expert resume reviews, the Vault Job Board and more.

V∆ULT CAREER LIBRARY 39

Cox Communications, Inc.

1400 Lake Hearn Drive
Atlanta, Georgia 30319
Phone: (404) 843-5000
www.cox.com

Your Friend in the Digital Age™

Cox Communications is a multi-service broadband communications company serving approximately 6.3 million customers nationwide. Cox Communications, Inc. and its subsidiaries are Equal Opportunity Employers with a tradition of encouraging a wide diversity of talents through a broad range of hiring practices. Cox Communications, Inc. is the 2004 recipient of the Forerunner Accolade for the Best Operator for Women in Cable. On September 22, Cox Media of Northern Virginia was recognized with the American Advertising Federation's (AAF) prestigious Mosaic Award for increasing its partnership with minority employees. For a partial list of Cox-Supported Organizations visit: www.cox.com/about/Diversity/Community/organizations.asp

Fitch Ratings

One State Street Plaza
New York, NY 10004
Phone: 212-908-0500

FitchRatings

Fitch Ratings is a leading global rating agency committed to providing the world's credit markets with accurate, timely and prospective credit opinions. Fitch Ratings is dual-headquartered in New York and London, operating offices and joint ventures in more than 40 locations and covering entities in more than 75 countries. Fitch Ratings complies with federal, state, and local laws governing employment, and provides equal opportunity to all applicants and employees. All applications will be considered without regard to race, color, religion, gender, national origin, age, disability, marital or veteran status, sexual orientation, and other status protected by applicable laws.

Business schools Fitch Ratings recruits from
NYU; Cornell; Brown; Columbia

Honeywell

101 Columbia Road
Morristown, New Jersey 07962
Phone: (973) 455-2000
www.honeywell.com\careers

Honeywell

Honeywell International is a $23 billion diversified technology and manufacturing leader, serving customers worldwide with aerospace products and services; control technologies for buildings, homes and industry; automotive products; turbochargers; specialty chemicals; fibers; and electronic and advanced materials. Based in Morris Township, N.J., Honeywell's shares are traded on the New York, London, Chicago and Pacific Stock Exchanges. It is one of the 30 stocks that make up the Dow Jones Industrial Average and is also a component of the Standard & Poor's 500 Index.

Business Schools Honeywell recruits from
University of Arizona; Arizona State University; Brigham Young University; Carnegie Mellon University; Columbia; Cornell; Emory; Georgia Tech; University of Illinois; University of Maryland; University of Michigan; Michigan State; University of Minnesota; Massachusetts Institute of Technology; Northwestern; Notre Dame; Ohio State; Penn State; Purdue University; University of Tennessee; Thunderbird; UCLA; USC; Vanderbilt; University of Virginia

Pitney Bowes Inc.

1 Elmcroft Road
Stamford, CT 06926-0700
Phone: 203-356-5000
www.pb.com/careers

Engineering the flow of communication™

Pitney Bowes is the world's leading provider of integrated mail and document management systems, services and solutions. The $5.0 billion company helps organizations of all sizes efficiently and effectively manage their mission-critical mail and document flow in physical, digital and hybrid formats. Its solutions range from addressing software and metering systems to print stream management, electronic bill presentment and presort mail services.

Pitney Bowes values, actively pursues, and leverages diversity in our employees, and through our relationships with customers, business partners and communities, because it is essential to innovation and growth. Pitney Bowes' commitment to diversity is also consistent with and further supports the company's values and practices.

Business schools Pitney Bowes recruits from
Open to all competitive MBA programs

Visit Vault at **www.vault.com** for insider company profiles, expert advice, career message boards, expert resume reviews, the Vault Job Board and more.

V∧ULT CAREER LIBRARY   41

Johnson & Johnson

One Johnson & Johnson Plaza
New Brunswick, NJ 08933
Phone: 732-524-0400
www.jnj.com/careers

Johnson & Johnson
Family of Companies

Johnson & Johnson has $47.3 billion in sales and is the world's most comprehensive and broadly based manufacturer of health care products, as well as a provider of related services, for the consumer, pharmaceutical, and medical devices and diagnostics markets. Johnson & Johnson has 109,900 employees and over 200 operating companies in 57 countries around the world, selling products throughout the world.

We keep our leadership positions fresh and vital through constant innovation. Our commitment to a superior rate of innovation has been accompanied by a superior rate of profitability, enabling the development of unique new products and new leadership positions – thereby spurring added breadth and enhancing consistency. This successful cycle in the pursuit of leadership has given us the wherewithal to deliver consistently outstanding performance since the Company was founded in 1886.

M & T Bank

One M&T Plaza, 11th Floor
Buffalo, N.Y. 14203
Phone: (716) 842 – 5157
E-mail: college@mandtbank.com
www.mandtbank.com

 M&T Bank

At M&T, employees are our most important asset. In fact, our success is attributable to the talent and dedication of our employees. Therefore, M&T demonstrates its return commitment by supporting both diversity and the unique talents of our employees throughout the organization. To foster an inclusive environment, M&T continually drives initiatives such as diversity awareness training, diversity recruitment, supplier diversity and community involvement. In addition the bank has a dedicated diversity council focused on important employee issues. Through these efforts, M&T strives to deliver on our commitment to become one of the best companies to work for in the nation.

Business schools M&T Bank recruits from:
American University (Kogod); Carnegie Mellon (Tepper); Univ. of Chicago; Columbia; Cornell (Johnson); Dartmouth (Tuck); Duke (Fuqua); Georgetown University (McDonough); Harvard Business School; University of Maryland (Robert H. Smith); University of Michigan; New York University (Stern); Northwestern (Kellogg); Penn State (Smeal); University of North Carolina (Kenan-Flagler); University of Rochester (Simon); University of Virginia (Darden); University of Buffalo; University of Pennsylvania (Wharton)

Mattel, Inc.

333 Continental Blvd.
El Segundo, CA 90245
Phone: 310-252-3777
www.mattel.com

Recruiting E-mail
MBAIntern@Mattel.com
UndergradIntern@Mattel.com

Mattel, Inc., (NYSE: MAT, www.mattel.com) is the worldwide leader in the design, manufacture and marketing of toys and family products, including Barbie®, the most popular fashion doll ever created. The Mattel family is comprised of such best-selling brands as Hot Wheels®, Matchbox®, American Girl® and Tyco® R/C, as well as Fisher-Price® brands (www.fisher-price.com), including Little People®, Rescue Heroes®, Power Wheels® and a wide array of entertainment-inspired toy lines. With worldwide headquarters in El Segundo, Calif., Mattel employs more than 25,000 people in 42 countries and sells products in more than 150 nations throughout the world. Mattel's vision is: the world's premier toy brands – today and tomorrow.

Osram Sylvania

100 Endicott St.
Danvers, MA 01923
Phone: (978) 750-2761 or (978) 750-2078
REcruiting E-mail: Leah.Weinberg@sylvania.com
www.sylvania.com/AboutUs/Careers/Diversity

 OSRAM SYLVANIA

OSRAM SYLVANIA is committed to building an increasingly diverse workforce. We are developing strategic partnerships with colleges, universities, and professional organizations that have significant female and minority populations. We are establishing a corporate commitment to programs that serve minority student populations, such as INROADS. Programming and strategies driving diversity inclusion and retention are Affinity Groups, Mentoring, as well as increasing commitment to succession planning and employee development. With the powerful commitment of our management team, OSRAM SYLVANIA is expanding its reputation as the type of environment where every talented individual will be proud to work.

Business schools Osram Sylvania recruits from
Dartmouth (Tuck); University of Illinois

Roche

9115 Hague Road
Indianapolis, Indiana 462520
Recruiting Website: careers.ind.roche.com
www.roche.com

Roche Diagnostics is the world's leading provider of diagnostic systems and decision-oriented health information. Roche Diagnostics is a diverse, inclusive company that seeks, celebrates and leverages diversity to maximize the competitive advantage of people. We are always looking for people who want to become part of our winning team, whose daily work involves finding solutions that help people live better lives. We offer a variety of opportunities at our U.S. diagnostics marketing and sales headquarters in Indiana and at our global molecular business area headquarters in California.

Business schools Roche Diagnostics recruits from

University of Chicago; Northwestern (Kellogg); Indiana University (Kelley); Harvard Business School, Duke University (Fuqua); U.C.L.A.; University of Michigan; Purdue University; MIT (Sloan); University of Pennsylvania (Wharton); Yale University, Stanford University; UC Berkeley (Haas); Washington University (Olin)

Sodexho

200 Continental Drive,
Suite 400
Newark, DE 19713
Phone: 302 738-9500 ext 5209
E-mail: John.lee@sodexhousa.com
www.sodexhousa.com

Sodexho is the leading provider of food and facilities management in the U.S. and Canada, with $4.9 billion in annual sales. Sodexho offers innovative outsourcing solutions in food service, housekeeping, grounds keeping, plant operations and maintenance, asset and materials management and laundry services to corporations, health care and long term care facilities, retirements centers, schools, college campuses, military and remote sites. Headquarters in Gaithersburg, MD, the company has more than 100,000 employees in 50 states and Canada.

The Hartford Financial Services Group, Inc.

690 Asylum Street
Hartford Plaza
Hartford, Connecticut 06115
Phone: (860) 547-5000
www.thehartford.com

Founded in 1810, The Hartford Financial Services Group, Inc. (NYSE: HIG) is one of the largest investment and insurance companies in the United States. The Hartford is recognized for its financial strength and stability, operational excellence and superior customer service. Our Stag logo is a trusted symbol of dependability.

Diversity and Inclusion are among our core values at The Hartford. We understand that sustainable competitive advantage comes from leveraging the diversity of ideas and people to achieve our business goals. Building a more inclusive work environment means actively seeking out, welcoming and utilizing different voices, skills, work experiences, and perspectives as distinct capabilities. Respect and integrity are cornerstones of The Hartford's reputation.

We're very proud of our company and are always searching for talented and motivated individuals who represent the broadest possible diversity. Please visit us at www.thehartford.com/career to explore career opportunities and register with The Hartford's job matching system.

Visit Vault at **www.vault.com** for insider company profiles, expert advice, career message boards, expert resume reviews, the Vault Job Board and more.

VAULT CAREER LIBRARY   **43**

Use the Internet's
MOST TARGETED
job search tools.

Vault Job Board

Target your search by industry, function, and experience level, and find the job openings that you want.

VaultMatch Resume Database

Vault takes match-making to the next level: post your resume and customize your search by industry, function, experience and more. We'll match job listings with your interests and criteria and e-mail them directly to your in-box.

MBA
ROTATIONAL
PROGRAMS

Diversity

is a source of strength for our people and our businesses.

At Citigroup, we have worked hard to create a workplace with an emphasis on inclusion, innovation and merit, rooted in our shared values and respect for our colleagues and the millions of people we serve. We aspire to be a company where the best people

MBA Rotations

The internship after the first year of business school is a great opportunity for MBA students to experiment a bit and get a taste of a specific job or company. What if you're now in your second year and looking for your first position after business school, but still would like to try your hand at a variety of positions?

Some major employers provide rotational MBA hiring programs for new business school graduates that provide just this opportunity. MBAs who join rotational programs are hired into a specific function such as finance or marketing, but then can rotate through different specialties within the broader function (for example, treasury vs. risk management in finance). Rotations also allow for new MBA hires to gain experience with different business units at a large organization.

The following Vault Q&As will help give you a sense of how some of these rotational programs work.

Vault Q&A: Federico Sercovich, Citigroup

Upon graduating from the University of Maryland's Robert H. Smith School of Business in 2003, Federico Sercovich, joined Citigroup's rotational MBA Management Associate program with the company's North American credit card division. The program consists of two one-year rotations. Now finishing up his second rotation, he spoke with Vault about why he chose a rotational program and his experience with it.

Vault: Tell me a little bit about your pre-business school background.

Sercovich: I'm originally from Argentina. I spent four years doing marketing in Chile, in a variety of industries and functions within marketing. First I worked with the country's largest global advertising firm, BBDO, then at L'Oreal in brand management, then with B2B marketing for a smaller regional telecom.

Vault: Did you want to do a career change from marketing when you went to get your MBA?

Sercovich: Overall the idea of doing the MBA was the opportunity to expand my skill set and move on to a more general management-oriented career path.

The Management Associate program at Citigroup allowed me – in a rather "safe environment" – to gain more experience in different business functions. While marketing is still my passion, I've expanded my skill base to achieve my long-term aspirations.

Vault: What do you mean by a "safe environment?"

Sercovich: You know it's a 1-year term job, and so you get to learn a lot and to add value at the same time. However it's not something you will be doing for more than 12 months, it has a defined term, which allows you to go beyond your professional comfort zone

For example, during my current rotation which I'm finishing up this week, I'm in a CFO role supporting a new product -function clearly outside my comfort zone. I was encouraged to take the risk and I've seen other people doing it and succeeding at it. The program gives you the opportunity to go ahead and do these kinds of things.

Vault: So tell me a little bit about the program and the rotations that you've done.

Sercovich: It's a two-year program, with two one-year rotations in different areas. My first rotation was in a marketing/strategy role in our merchant acquiring business. With that group – the customer is not the cardholder unlike the rest of the North America Cards, it's merchants who want to take credit cards as payment instruments. During said rotation, I had the opportunity to leverage my B2B skills, and it provided me with a broad view of the payment landscape and the consumer's behavior at the point of sale.

Visit Vault at **www.vault.com** for insider company profiles, expert advice, career message boards, expert resume reviews, the Vault Job Board and more.

VAULT CAREER LIBRARY   47

Vault: Did you know that you were going to that type of position when you joined the Management Associates program?

Sercovich: I was actually first a summer associate during the summer between my first and second years of business school. I was in the E-business department, working with the strategic alliances team with various partners on different cross-sell initiatives.

At the end of the summer, at the end of my performance evaluation I was offered a position in the MA Program, which I happily accepted. The way it works – you know you have a job, but you initially don't know in which business you're going to be working. When it's closer to the point of joining, you start an interview process. You meet with different managers and network. I think it's pretty cool because you are completely in charge of your career choices – you get to decide for which opportunities you want to interview.

Vault: So what about your second rotation, your current role.

Sercovich: It's a CFO role in an area called cross-sell. Iprovide Financial Planning & Analysis support for a new set of products under the umbrella of the alternate lending franchise. The products are unsecured personal loans.

These are new products, and this is a function I haven't been exposed to in my past. In this role, I do financial forecasting and profitability analyses, I have been solely in charge of the development of the 2006 financial plan for these products.

Vault: As a role outside of your "comfort zone" how have you found this experience?

Sercovich: Well, it's definitely stressful, but very exciting. The numbers I report roll up all the way to the CEO of Citi Cards and that's a big responsibility. The value I contribute to the business is clear and tangible.

Vault: So what are you drawing on to do your job, given that your background is in marketing?

Sercovich: It's part business school theory, part on-the-job training, and a lot of common sense. It's not rocket science – the math is fairly straightforward – but it was definitely a good challenge. I was able to put together from scratch the forecasting models for the business, which are now used every month.

Vault: Is there a formal mentorship program component to the program?

Sercovich: Last year, we joined the overall Citi Cards mentorship program, through which the MAs are paired up with a mentor who has been in the company for a while. But I think there is a huge component that is totally informal. As an MA, many doors are open, many times you can just call up a senior member of the organization and ask them for some time in their calendar. They are open to help you, and they give you wise career advice. It's sort of weird sometimes to be talking with these senior leaders who are dedicating part of their valuable time to giving career advice to a Management Associate.

Vault: So what will you be doing once you finish this rotation?

Sercovich: I have accepted a role in Citigroup International Cards, I will be working on strategic initiatives with different regions – global competitor analysis, different practices and products, taking a look at what's been successful in North America which could be rolled out elsewhere.

Vault Q&A: Rebecca Preston, Chevron

After graduating in 2001 with her MBA from the University of Michigan Business School, Rebecca Preston joined Chevron's Finance MBA Development Program, one of several MBA hiring programs maintained by the company. After stints in London and Houston in a variety of roles, Preston returned to the company's corporate headquarters in California to oversee the program. She talked to us about the program, which has been around for close to 60 years.

Vault: How many MBAs does Chevron hire a year?

Preston: For the finance program, we just increased the target this year. Historically it's been six to eight and it's now eight to 10. The HR program does about four, the marketing program hires about four, supply and trading out of Houston hires about three, global gas is considering starting and MBA program, and procurement hires in the neighborhood of four. Every group has MBA summer interns. Finance has also increased its intern target, from six to eight; the other programs do between two and four.

Vault: How long has the finance MBA program been running?

Preston: The program started in 1946. We'll be 60 years old next year. The other programs are more recent.

Vault: I'd imagine that would mean that a lot of the company's leaders have come through the program.

Preston: Yes. The former chairman came through the program. The current vice chairman is off the program, our head of international upstream (exploration and production), vice president of government and public affairs, and our CFO are all program alumni. The finance heads for major strategic business units are off the program; the comptroller, the Treasurer, they're all from the program.

Vault: Is there any crossover between the various MBA programs in terms of rotations?

Preston: Not in terms of rotations. Functionally the programs are quite different. However, we do some joint events. Typically these would be around general industry or company knowledge. For example, we bring in external instructors – last week we had a geophysics professor, Dr. Hines from University of Tulsa, lecture about topics from how the earth was formed and how oil was created through to drilling and production of resources. It's a very complex industry, so getting fluency outside of your discipline is important.

Vault: In what types of roles and locations are incoming MBA hires for the Finance program placed?

Preston: I've got eight people coming in this year. Six are starting here in California, two are overseas…

Vault: You're already sending them overseas for their first positions?

Preston: These two are returning interns. If they've had an internship at HQ and so grounding with us, we're comfortable in sending them overseas right off the bat. One's in Aberdeen [Scotland] in the North Sea, and another's in Singapore with our Treasury function. The international component is increasingly important.

Vault: How long is the program and how many rotations do employees do?

Preston: It's a two-year program. They do three or four rotations. Domestic rotations are typically six months long. Sometimes the international assignments will be longer, and someone may elect to do three rotations with a longer, more in-depth experience overseas. This is particularly true of people who have interned here. Other people might feel strongly they need to see four different areas while on the program.

We always try to maximize the diversity of experience with different business units, and different finance functions. I get contacted from Chevron businesses all over the world looking for the talent. Every month I send out an update that shows where everyone in the program is in the company, and what opportunities have come in.

Visit Vault at **www.vault.com** for insider company profiles, expert advice,
career message boards, expert resume reviews, the Vault Job Board and more.

V/\ULT CAREER LIBRARY

49

We encourage people to do a rotation outside of the finance discipline, too, and we have had many people cross over in past years.

Vault: What sort of rotations would they do outside of finance?

Preston: Typically people cross over into two areas: planning and business development. The planning roles are corporate strategy roles within the business units – developing the business plan, the strategic plan for the organization, within overall corporate strategy. The business development roles might be supporting commercial teams looking for new opportunities. For example, you might be supporting a team that's negotiating for new opportunities in Russia.

Vault: With the program having been in place for so long, there must be a lot of alumni from the program.

Preston: Yes. There are about 150 alumni and we've got a very active alumni network for the program. As the program manager I maintain all that information. We have two to three events a year that pull in all the alumni. We do a "family picnic" every year. We have a summer cocktail, where people meet the interns and the new hires. This year, the CFO was there, the head of investor relations was there, and other senior people. And every year we do the holiday luncheon and that pulls in all the alumni as well. These are typically in the Bay Area.

About a quarter of the alumni are international now. There are alumni in Moscow, Kuwait, London, Singapore, Scotland, Barbados, Beijing, Bogotá, Angola, Venezuela…

Vault: Is there any resentment among other finance professionals toward what might be thought of as an elite group?

Preston: There's definitely the risk of it becoming sort of an elitist group, and if that were to happen, the program would lose much of its effectiveness. But that hasn't happened because we're highly selective in who we bring in. Our industry is enormously comples, so you have to be humble and learn from the experienced people around you. You also have to be very capable so that you can take these learnings and produce superior results in a short period of time (6 months or less for the rotations). Fit is very important – we have a highly collaborative and cooperative culture at Chevron.

Bringing in people with strong teamwork orientation, combined with demonstrated performance, means that rather than resentment, there's a lot of respect for the program and its members. They're able to perform at a high level quickly so people are clamoring for program members to work on their teams.

There's brisk, brisk demand for program graduates once their 24 months on the program is over. A big part of my job is matching the right opportunity with a program member's individual interests and development goals. It's quite common to move every 18 months to three years after you're off the program, because you're building up a broad base of experience.

Vault: Do most of the people who join the program have energy industry experience?

Preston: Not necessarily. I'd say it's less than a quarter that have direct industry experience, although a lot of them have technical backgrounds, such as engineering or geosciences. A lot of people have finance backgrounds or economics backgrounds.

Vault: But when interviewing, you're trying to make sure they are interested in the industry.

Preston: That's very important. In the first round for full-time hires, I spend almost all of the time trying to understand fit and motivation – is energy something they're passionate about? Will they thrive in our culture or clash with it? I then use the second round to push on the technical skills. Can they do the job? We're looking for every hire to be a career hire. We have 90% retention over 10 years. Fit and motivation is what's going to sustain you over the long run.

Vault: Is there a formal mentoring program?

Preston: We do not do a formal mentor matching in the Finance Program, but some of the other programs do. Intead, our alumni are very receptive to program members. I facilitate connections and our members find diverse and successful mentoring relationships that way. For interns we do match them with a "buddy," someone who's currently on the program and can help them evaluate us as a full-time employer.

Employer Directory

Citigroup

1 Court Square, 9th Floor, Zone 11
Long Island City, NY 11120
www.citigroup.com/citigroup/oncampus/
Recruiting E-mail: citigrouprecruiting@citigroup.com

Citigroup's Management Associate Programs provide candidates with ample opportunity to experience multiple aspects of the business while gaining valuable insights and experiences. Citigroup offers the following Management Associate Programs for graduate students:

- Global Consumer Group Management Associate Program
- Commercial Business Group Management Associate Program
- Citi Cards Management Associate Program
- Citi Cards Operations & Technology Management Associate Program
- Consumer Finance North America Management Associate Program
- CitiMortgage Management Associate Program
- Financial Management Associate Program
- Human Resources Management Associate Program
- Risk Management Associate Program
- Citigroup International Country Programs

For more information please visit: For more information please visit:
www.citigroup.com/citigroup/oncampus/

Graduate Schools Citigroup Recruits from:

Michigan/Ross; Columbia GSB; Wharton; Rochester/Simon; Cornell/Johnson; Georgetown GSB; NYU/Stern; Texas/Austin; Carnegie Mellon; Harvard Business School; Maryland GSB; Cornell/ILR; Duke/Fuqua; Howard GR; Northwestern/Kellogg

Visit Vault at **www.vault.com** for insider company profiles, expert advice, career message boards, expert resume reviews, the Vault Job Board and more.

VAULT CAREER LIBRARY   51

INDUSTRY
OVERVIEWS

V/AULT
THE MOST TRUSTED NAME IN CAREER INFORMATION

Vault guides and employer profiles have been published since 1997 and are the premier source of insider information on careers.

Each year, Vault surveys and interviews thousands of employees to give readers the inside scoop on industries and specific employers to help them get the jobs they want.

V/AULT

Aerospace and Defense

Industry Overview

The aerospace and defense industry immediately felt the impact of the attacks of September 11 and the war on terrorism that followed. The severe economic blow to the commercial airlines led to a sharp decline in orders for new planes after 2001. And in 2002, the top ten commercial airlines – which place the orders for these aircraft when business is good – lost more than $12 billion, with key players like United Airlines' parent company UAL and US Airways filing for bankruptcy. All of this has resulted in an anticipated 18 percent decrease in overall employment for aerospace products and parts manufacturing between 2002 and 2012 (compared to a projected 16 percent growth for all industries combined), according to the Bureau of Labor Statistics (BLS). There are signs, though, that business is at least stabilizing. By the end of 2004, aerospace sales, orders, exports, and employment all increased significantly, according to data from AIA's Aerospace Research Center, with growth expected to continue into 2005. Overall sales in aerospace in 2004 rose from $12 billion to a whopping $161 billion, the highest level of current-dollar sales in industry history. Not surprisingly, the biggest gains came from defense contracts.

Drumming up defense

At the same time, since 2001, military action in Afghanistan and Iraq, as well as an increased need for U.S. defense, has led to stepped-up demand for military aircraft, missiles and defense contractors. In fiscal year 2004, for example, the Pentagon boosted its budget for procurement and research and development by 8 percent. While this trend is predicted to slow in coming years, defense budgets overall should continue to grow between 4 percent and 6 percent through the end of the decade, according to an analysis from *BusinessWeek Online*. As military equipment continues to age, manufacturers are calling for increased attention to R&D and procurement. For the fiscal year 2006, the newly created Department of Homeland Security boasts a budget of $39 billion, while the Department of Defense requested $419.3 billion.

Bidding for planes

Traditionally, the federal government has been the aerospace industry's largest customer. There were about 2,800 establishments in the aerospace industry as of 2002, according to BLS. Of these firms, a handful fly above the crowd, reaping contracts from the Department of Defense after submitting to a competitive bidding process. The amount of time elapsing from the DOD's initial call for military aircraft or missile systems – through the bidding system and on into production of a prototype, approval, production of the equipment and delivery – can be several years. This time span has been trimmed in recent years, however, owing to new computer-aided design (CAD) technologies that bring the design of equipment into the virtual realm.

The bulk of the industry is taken up by firms producing civil (non-military) aircraft, including planes for commercial airlines and cargo transportation, as well as those for general aviation, like leisure planes and corporate jets. In 2004, the number of U.S. commercial jetliners delivered increased for the first time in two years, following the post-9/11 industry downturn, while revenue in the civil aircraft sector increased to $35 billion. The sector also includes the production of military aircraft and helicopters, along with guided missiles and missile propulsion units. But not all of this equipment is used to serve defense purposes – it also covers space vehicles and the rockets that launch them. This industry also spans the seas, with shipbuilding added to the mix – in fact, analysts anticipate strong growth in this area as ships with average life spans of 30 years are phased out and replaced.

The commercial sector

In the private sector, commercial airlines and private businesses specify their requirements and then invite manufacturers to submit bids. Usually, a new aircraft won't go into production until a large contract is secured. For example, in April 2004, Boeing finally got the OK to start cranking out its new 7E7 Dreamliner commercial planes after sealing a deal worth approx-

Visit Vault at **www.vault.com** for insider company profiles, expert advice, career message boards, expert resume reviews, the Vault Job Board and more.

VAULT CAREER LIBRARY 55

imately $6 billion with Japanese carrier Al Nippon Airways, which placed an order for 50 of the fuel-efficient flyers – the largest launch order ever for a new Boeing jet. Reportedly, the Dreamliner fleet could enter service by 2008. The efficiency of the Dreamliner – said to offer 20 percent more fuel efficiency over Boeing's 767 jet – could draw new airlines like JetBlue to the table to increase their competitiveness in the cutthroat low-cost carrier arena, observers say. In addition, French and Japanese aerospace industry groups agreed to work together in June 2005 on researching technologies to build a commercially viable supersonic jet in the same vein as the Concorde, minus the high fuel consumption and loud engine noise.

High flyers

Traditionally, Boeing has run neck-and-neck with rival Airbus for dominance of the aircraft manufacturing sector. Both giants have stumbled since 2001, with Boeing's aircraft orders plummeting by 45 percent and Airbus' by 28 percent during that year alone. The shaky situation led Boeing to slash 30,000 jobs, or about 30 percent of its commercial aircraft workforce, in 2002 as Airbus slipped into the No. 1 spot in the industry worldwide. Both are bouncing back, albeit slowly – Airbus, based in Europe, is in the development process for the world's biggest jetliner, the 555-seat A380, while Boeing is hard at work on its Dreamliner. The A380 shares the Dreamliner's fuel efficiency and boasts an impressive 262-foot wingspan. A historic market shift for the two industry giants began in 2003, when Airbus for the first time delivered more airplanes than Boeing for the year – 300, compared to 280 from Boeing, according to *BusinessWeek*.

The tides may be turning back to Boeing's favor, though. In June 2005, Airbus revealed that the first of its A380 deliveries would be delayed up to six months due to unspecified production difficulties. Then, Emirates airlines, expected to make a big order for the A350, announced instead that it was not ready to make a decision. Boeing, meanwhile, has racked up 255 orders on the year so far (as of June 2005), while Airbus claimed only 196. Boeing's new 787 has also garnered the attention of major airlines, who have placed 266 orders for the jets, while Airbus has yet to announce a deal for its comparable A350. Plus, delivery delays will no create multimillion-dollar penalties for Airbus to contend with if it cannot get orders out on time. Boeing has spent its time recently expanding its market abroad, discussing potential business deals with Kuwait while increasing its market presence in Latin America – all the while weathering potentially damaging headlines regarding former CEO Harry Stonecipher's acknowledgement of an affair with a female executive in March 2005.

Still, Boeing, with its wealth of (sometimes controversial) defense contracts in addition to its commercial airplane business, dominates the aerospace and defense industry as a whole, followed, in order of sales, by European Aeronautic Defence and Space Company, Lockheed Martin Corporation, Airbus, and Northrop Grumman Corporation. Other major players in the sector include Raytheon Corporation and the National Aeronautics and Space Corporation (more familiar as NASA).

In the industry's regional aircraft market (defined as planes with less than 100 seats), Bombardier, Gulfstream, and Textron's Cessna unit dominate. GE Aircraft Engines, Pratt & Whitney, and Rolls Royce are tops among manufacturers of jet engines.

Dominating defense

In the area of defense contractors specifically, Lockheed Martin and Northrop Grumman lead the pack, followed by Boeing, Raytheon, and BAE Systems. European companies are not far behind, though. European Aeronautic Defense and Space, the EU's biggest defense and aerospace company, announced in June 2005 plans to build an assembly site stateside should the Pentagon award the company a contract to produce an aerial-refueling plane. With U.S. companies increasing spending and reeling in contracts, transatlantic rivals have no choice but to step up efforts to compete, and are slowly building up U.S. market share. Major players on the international end include British Aerospace and Marconi Electric Systems (BAES), which picked up U.S.-based United Defense Industries for $4.1 billion in March 2005, and Italy's Finmeccanica. EADS has also established several partnerships recently with Northrop Grumman and Lockheed Martin.

Lockheed maintains a healthy dominance in the sector thanks in part to its score of one of the richest defense deals in history, when in 2001 it beat out Boeing for a fighter jet contract worth $200 billion. More than 80 percent of Lockheed's overall revenue comes from government orders, working with a variety of Washington agencies, including the U.S. Census Bureau, Social Security Administration, Federal Aviation Administration, and even the U.S. Postal Service. More recently, though, Boeing was the winner over Lockheed for a contract to build a new submarine-hunting airplane for the Navy in a June 2004 contract estimated at up to $15 billion over 10 years. Boeing will subcontract with fellow defense heavies Northrop Grumman and Raytheon on the project. Controversy dogged Boeing in 2003 following an Air Force tanker deal that drew intense Congressional scrutiny after Darleen Druyun, a former Air Force executive in charge of acquisitions, admitted to under-the-table deals with Boeing to first gain employment for her daughter and son-in-law, and then drum up sales for the billion-dollar business at the expense of the Air Force budget. Lockheed and Boeing made headlines together with their May 2005 announcement of an alliance to combine their missile development and manufacturing capabilities. Meanwhile, Northrop execs forecast a big year for 2005, expecting sales to climb 7.1 percent, with at least 10 percent growth on the year and earnings of $30 billion.

The defense portion of the industry has been affected not only by the call to arms following the U.S. terror attacks, but also mega mergers and a shift in the way warfare is practiced. In 2002, the aerospace and defense industry spent about $30 billion on M&A. Northrop Grumman has been one of the most aggressive players, according to Hoover's, acquiring both Litton Industries and Newport News Shipbuilding in 2001 and TRW in 2002. However, the competition is catching up: 2004 brought a string of buyouts in the industry. Raytheon picked up privately held Photon Research Associates (provider of physics modeling for government agencies and private companies); Lockheed bought Stasys Ltd. (a technology and consulting firm) and Soflinx Corp. (a wireless sensor affair firm); and BAE purchased STI Government Systems (high-tech defense contractor), Alphatech (inventor of electronic image processing systems), and DigitalNet Holdings (a network security software seller).

Since the Cold War, priorities among Pentagon types have shifted, from a philosophy of overwhelming force to a focus on equipment that's smarter, leaner, and more mobile. For instance, the firm General Atomics saw success in Afghanistan with the use of its unmanned Predator drones. Unmanned jets and other computer-guided equipment are seen as preferable to the traditional manned craft, being less costly to operate and posing less risk to military personnel in combat. Other buzz on the war front of the industry concerns "network-centric warfare," an area the top defense contractors have shifted resources toward in recent years. In this approach, computers, satellites, and sensors are all integrated so that soldiers and their planes, tanks and other equipment get a constant stream of precise, real-time information about what's happening on the front lines. One example is General Dynamics Corp., traditionally known as a manufacturer of ships and tanks, which told BusinessWeek its IT systems and technology operations alone would make up a third of total revenues in 2004.

A new world for defense

Another major shift in the defense industry since 2001 is the growth of companies focusing on homeland security. This sector includes everything from audio and video surveillance equipment, to disease and bioterror identification, to secure communications equipment. In addition, the Pentagon is increasingly – and controversially – relying on manpower from private military contractors (PMCs) to bolster its missions in Iraq, Afghanistan, and elsewhere. These projects might include rebuilding power and sanitation systems and other logistical support, or (more notoriously) conducting interrogations and security operations. While the military outsourced just one percent of its work, mainly for airfield maintenance, during the first Gulf War in the 1990s, contractors are handling as much as 30 percent of the military's services, including reconstruction, during the ongoing activities in Iraq today, according to Brookings Institution fellow P.W. Singer. These contractors include well-known giants like Kellogg Brown & Root (Halliburton), with a $3.97 billion contract for oil field reconstruction and maintenance in Iraq, and smaller PMCs.

These latter companies are catching the eye of traditional aerospace and defense giants like Northrop Grumman, which recently acquired smaller PMC Vinnell. But all PMCs are catching the eye of Congress, the media and the public, who question the oversight of these companies and wonder if the military should be outsourcing so much of its operations to people

Visit Vault at **www.vault.com** for insider company profiles, expert advice, career message boards, expert resume reviews, the Vault Job Board and more.

VAULT CAREER LIBRARY   **57**

who, in some cases, are seen as "mercenaries." An April 2004 report in *The Washington Post* noted that private security firms working on-site in Iraq banded together, creating their own private armies – nearly 20,000 strong, a number unprecedented in U.S. history – after falling under attack by insurgents. The situation as such these days - PMCs in the fray, somewhere between getting their jobs done and defending themselves from attack – has led to a "shoot and scoot attitude" and "blue-on-blue incidents" in which U.S. military and PMCs engage in accidental combat, according to Peter Singer of The Brookings Institute, and author of a recent book on PMCs. "They're in roles that you wouldn't want private soldiers in, roles that affect how we win hearts and minds there, and so sometimes it really backfires on us," said Singer in a June 2005 interview. "Unfortunately, it's not been dealt with at the senior leadership level."

The final frontier

In the space sector, made up of manufacturers of satellites and rocket manufacturing and launch services, familiar names lead the pack, including Boeing, Northrop Grumman, and Lockheed Martin, which picked up a hefty NASA contract in June 2005 capped at $700 million to develop a satellite designed to collect scientific data on Jupiter and the solar system as a whole. According to Hoover's, major aerospace and defense companies continue to build space activities into their long-term investment plans – even though shooting for the stars isn't very profitable in the near-term. Other, more specialized leaders include Alcatel Space, Astrium, Orbital Sciences, and Arianespace. As the NASA budget continues to grow, though, the organization has seen research capital reduced drastically for aeronautics research and development in favor of other outer-worldly pursuits, such as President Bush's Moon, Mars, and Beyond directive. By 2010, R&D funding is expected to have dropped by more than $800 million since 1995 levels, which has AIA President and CEO John Douglass in a tizzy. In a March 2005 article in Space News, Douglass declared such losses will have "dire consequences" for the aviation industry, including development of conventional turbine engines and rotorcraft.

These star players are keeping an eye on a pack of upstarts in the space race, private companies that rely on individual investors rather than federal dollars. If successful, these private liftoff firms promise to radically alter the space exploration game by stripping it of the costs, bureaucracy, and other padding that often accrue to federally funded projects. June 2004 saw the historic liftoff of SpaceShipOne, the first privately funded rocket. Later in 2004, an unmanned rocket built by a small California company was set to carry an experimental satellite into orbit for the Defense Department in a project involving no federal dollars. The Bush Administration has come out in favor of increased involvement by such private companies in missions to send people to the moon and, one day, to Mars. In addition to these types of missions, many space visionaries – some of whom formerly headed the dot-com pack back in the Internet boom days – see all sorts of opportunities up beyond the clouds, ranging from tourism to mining for precious metals.

The employment outlook

Professionals who work in the aerospace product and parts manufacturing sector, the BLS reports, enjoy earnings that are substantially higher, on average, than those of their counterparts in other manufacturing sectors. Most jobs in the sector are in the areas of skilled production and management. The BLS reports that in 2002, 64 percent of jobs in aerospace manufacturing were in large establishments employing 1,000 or more workers. In addition, aerospace employment stopped a five-year skid in 2004, as the industry added 18,900 new jobs. Women are still scarce in the industry, making up only 11.3 percent of U.S. aerospace engineers in 2004, according to data by the BLS, despite the fact that women earning doctoral degrees in aerospace increased by 150 percent between 1994 and 2001.

Employer Directory

Honeywell

101 Columbia Road
Morristown, New Jersey 07962
Phone: (973) 455-2000
www.honeywell.com\careers

Honeywell International is a $23 billion diversified technology and manufacturing leader, serving customers worldwide with aerospace products and services; control technologies for buildings, homes and industry; automotive products; turbochargers; specialty chemicals; fibers; and electronic and advanced materials. Based in Morris Township, N.J., Honeywell's shares are traded on the New York, London, Chicago and Pacific Stock Exchanges. It is one of the 30 stocks that make up the Dow Jones Industrial Average and is also a component of the Standard & Poor's 500 Index.

Business schools Heneywell recruits from

University of Arizona; Arizona State University; Brigham Young University; Carnegie Mellon University; Columbia; Cornell; Emory; Georgia Tech; University of Illinois; University of Maryland; University of Michigan; Michigan State; University of Minnesota; Massachusetts Institute of Technology; Northwestern; Notre Dame; Ohio State; Penn State; Purdue University; University of Tennessee; Thunderbird; UCLA; USC; Vanderbilt; University of Virginia;

BAE Systems

Warwick House, PO Box 87, Farnborough Aerospace Center
Farnborough
Hampshire GU14 6YU, United Kingdom
Phone: +44-1252 373232
Fax: +44-1252 383000
www.baesystems.com

General Dynamics Corporation

3190 Fairview Park Dr.
Falls Church, VA 22042-4523
Phone: (703) 876-3000
Fax: (703) 876-3125
www.gendyn.com

General Electric Company

3135 Easton Tpke.
Fairfield, CT 06828-0001
Phone: (203) 373-2211
Fax: (203) 373 3131
www.ge.com

L-3 Communications Holdings

600 3rd Ave.
New York, NY 10016
Phone: (212) 697-1111
Fax: (212) 867-5249
www.L-3Com.com

Lockheed Martin

6801 Rockledge Dr.
Bethesda, MD 20817-1877
Phone: (301) 897-6000
Fax: (301) 897-6704
www.lockheedmartin.com

Northrop Grumman Corporation

1840 Century Park East
Los Angeles, CA 90067-2199
Phone: (310) 553-6262
Fax: (310) 553-2076
www.northgrum.com

Parker Hannifin Corporation

6035 Parkland Blvd.
Cleveland, OH 44124-4141
Phone: (216) 896-3000
Fax: (216) 896-4000
www.parker.com

Raytheon Company

870 Winter St.
Waltham, MA 02451-1449
Phone: (781) 522-3000
Fax: (781) 522-3001
www.raytheon.com

Textron Inc.

40 Westminster St.
Providence, RI 02903-2596
Phone: (401) 421-2800
Fax: (401) 421-2878
www.textron.com

United Technologies Corporation

One Financial Plaza
Hartford, CT 06103
Phone: (860) 728-7000
Fax: (860) 728-7979
www.utc.com

Visit Vault at **www.vault.com** for insider company profiles, expert advice, career message boards, expert resume reviews, the Vault Job Board and more.

VAULT CAREER LIBRARY

59

Agriculture

Industry Overview

Feed me

No nation can do without food, so no prosperous nation lacks a well-developed agricultural system. The industry's scope includes farmers and ranchers, but also scientists who splice the genes of disparate plants and animals to create new and better food sources and the businesspeople who keep it all running. The various disciplines within the agricultural industry seek ways to more efficiently feed Earth's ever-growing population while improving profit margins for food-related businesses.

This industry cannot live on bread alone

Agriculture includes everything grown or raised for consumption, not just food. Cotton and wool are agricultural products, as are animal byproducts, ornamental plants, tobacco, lumber and the various fruits and grains used to produce alcohol. Agriculture, not surprisingly, is a huge industry, accounting for 2 percent of the U.S. GDP. That might not seem like a lot, but it speaks of the efficiency with which industrialized nations can produce their produce.

Cotton struggles

Cotton has become a hot topic in the agribusiness world. As the global trading arena develops and changes, industry experts predict the U.S. textile mill sector will average only five million to seven million bales of yearly U.S. cotton consumption, while the U.S. cotton export market is expected to hit 13 billion bales, roughly two-thirds of the overall cotton market. W. G. Winburne, president of the American Cotton Shippers Association, acknowledged when he took office in 2004 the industry's challenge to maintain its competitiveness in a global economy that has seen the rise of Chinese cotton production and increased rivalry from third-world and developing countries. Neal Gillen, general counsel to the ACSA, lamented the loss of U.S. manufacturing capacity overseas, creating a situation in which consumption exceeded production. Meanwhile, leaders of the Cotton Belt in the southeast U.S., fearful that farm law will be compromised in the future as the nation struggles with a budget deficit, continue to challenge current farm legislation to protect their cotton interests, and to secure disaster assistance from Congress for producers who suffered losses during the 2001 and 2002 production years.

Bread and circuses

Agriculture rides a fine line of profitability, despite its iconic representation as the Horn of Plenty. The more volume it produces beyond a certain point, the less money it makes; yet too little production is just as much of a problem. The tricky relationship of productivity and profit has plagued agribusiness for decades. Efforts to lessen the burden on farmers have included federal bailout money ($8.7 billion in 1999, the largest ever) and subsidies for farmers who reduce their output.

Some plagues are less figurative; natural disasters, droughts, disease and adverse weather patterns are just some of the uncontrollable circumstances that can have wide-reaching effects on the industry. Easily recognizable examples include the extended drought in several African nations; the excessive rainfall and flooding in America's heartland in 1997 and 1998; hurricanes in Honduras and Nicaragua that destroyed those nations' export capabilities in 1998; 2004's harsh hurricane season along the Florida panhandle; and the tsunamis that devastated Southeastern Asia in the closing days of 2004.

Visit Vault at **www.vault.com** for insider company profiles, expert advice, career message boards, expert resume reviews, the Vault Job Board and more.

VAULT CAREER LIBRARY 61

Mad Cow mania

In addition, many cattle ranchers have been hit hard by back-to-back appearances of bovine spongiform encephalopathy, a fatal brain-wasting disease more commonly referred to as "Mad Cow," in cows on U.S. soil. The disease was discovered in Europe in 2000, and first reared its ugly head stateside in December 2003, after a Canadian bovine afflicted with Mad Cow was transported to Washington State. The discovery sent shock waves through the industry, as dozens of countries banned U.S. beef imports. Beef exports plummeted from $3.1 billion on 2003 to a mere $550 million in 2004. Then, in June 2005, the first homegrown case of Mad Cow was discovered in Texas. Ranchers publicly admonished the USDA for its alleged "don't look, don't find" policy with regards to Mad Cow. Industry insiders predict another subsequent downturn in the market, but do not anticipate as drastic a slip as reported after the first case in 2003.

Begun, this clone war has

Biotechnology and cloning have recently become major issues in the agriculture industry. Steroids and antibiotics are routinely fed to meat and dairy animals. Scientists have begun breeding modified crops with higher yield, greater disease resistance and other desirable qualities. These days, nearly all soy and half the corn crop in the country is genetically engineered, while 75 percent of the cotton crop is also genetically engineered.

Scientists are also beginning to explore these methods for use on farm animals, increasing egg and milk production, changing fat content and speeding maturity, among other changes. However, this genetic tinkering has spawned a number of advocacy groups who fear potential unseen drawbacks. They argue that direct genetic manipulation might produce harmful side effects that simple hybridization and crossbreeding wouldn't. Nigeria, Zambia and Zimbabwe have refused or plan to refuse shipments of genetically modified corn, fearing that it is unsafe. Another concern is that rising demand for genetically modified crops will depress the prices of more traditional crops such as wheat, corn and soybeans.

Organic farming was the subject of a June 2005 federal court ruling demanding stricter standards for organic food that many fear will slow industry growth. While consumer advocates were pleased with the ruling (which banned synthetic ingredients in products labeled organic and required dairy farmers to feed cows 100 percent organic feed), the organic dairy industry says the regulations will make it more expensive to convert to organic from conventional feed, and will potentially discourage farmers from becoming organic. Consumer groups reject the argument of the U.S. House Organic Caucus that the new rules could "decimate every sector of the organic industry," and claim the ruling will increase the integrity of the organic label and create a steady increase in the strength of standards.

The business of food

Producers formed a number of agricultural cooperatives at the grassroots level in the 1990s to divide the burdens of low commodity prices. Co-ops (as opposed to coops, where chickens are raised) allow farmers to share costs, market their goods in greater bulk and speak with a louder voice, in much the same way that labor unions benefit workers through collective bargaining. This approach is reminiscent of the grange societies of the early 19th century. Larger agribusinesses also merge: In December 2000, Cargill acquired Agribrands International for $580 million. The next year it acquired 56 percent of European grain conglomerate Cerestar. In September 2002, ConAgra, the world's No. 2 producer of packaged foods, sold its fresh beef and pork business to a group of investors led by Hicks, Muse, Tate & Furst Inc. and Booth Creek Management for $1.4 billion.

The big guns

In the agricultural industry, the biggest names include Cargill, Archer Daniels Midland, Tyson, Perdue, Bunge, and Pilgrim's Pride. ConAgra, a once major player in the industry, is currently divesting its agricultural business to focus on branded and value-added packaged foods. In addition, Bayer, Dow, and DuPont all have a stake in biotechnology, each with its own crop science division. Monsanto is also a leader in the genetic engineering field.

Jobs from farmhand to finance

The agriculture industry is exceptionally diverse when you consider the number of different segments it encompasses. Operations include fish hatcheries, apple orchards, flower nurseries and slaughterhouses. Farm workers (who comprise 90 percent of industry employees) require minimal training, but inspectors must have a relevant college degree or valid experience. Managers include farm and ranch owners, as well as those who operate ripening facilities or cold storage. These professionals generally require both an agriculture degree and a background in the field – literally. Agronomists (researchers in the many disciplines involving agriculture) start at the bachelor degree level, and many have masters or doctorates to perform "pure" research. Commodities brokers, who manage business deals and trade in futures, have their own specialty within the agriculture industry.

Vault Q&A: Bernard Swanson, Archer Daniels Midland

After getting his undergraduate degree from Millikin University in Illinois in 2000, Bernard Swanson began his working life as a purchasing agent at Illinois Power. He eventually changed companies to work in purchasing Archer-Daniels Midland. While working at ADM, he received his MBA through an 18-month night program, also from Millikin. Currently a global sourcing specialist at ADM, Swanson talked to Vault about getting an MBA while working full-time and the opportunities he sees ahead of him at ADM.

Vault: Why did you switch companies from Illinois Power to ADM?

Swanson: I decided to switch to ADM based on ADM's size and stability as a corporation. At the time, the energy/utility industry was a little unstable. But more importantly, ADM presented a wealth of opportunities that no other corporation in the Midwest could offer.

Vault: What do you mean when you talk about opportunities?

Swanson: Just the size of ADM offers many upward mobility opportunities. ADM offers many vertical and horizontal opportunities. There's also the experience I could gain from working in the Sourcing department at such a large organization.

The culture of ADM is very professional; they present you with your required duties and expect you to complete them within a timely manner. You're not micro-managed.

Vault: What sort of products are you responsible for purchasing?

Swanson: The Sourcing department currently writes contracts for chemicals that are used for the production plants, such as antioxidants, resin, acids. We also write contracts for manufacturing MRO equipment, such as fasteners and small tools.

Vault: How many sourcing specialists are there in your department?

Swanson: There are seven in North America, one in South America, and one in Europe.

Vault: How do you know what you need to purchase?

Swanson: The requests are given to us by the vice president of the operations divisions for each division. At the beginning of the year, they tell us what they want to source for that year. ADM has approximately 450 plants located all across North America. They are organized into multiple divisions, such as corn, Grain Group, cocoa, specialty food ingredients, and specialty feed ingredients.

Visit Vault at **www.vault.com** for insider company profiles, expert advice, career message boards, expert resume reviews, the Vault Job Board and more.

V\ULT CAREER LIBRARY   63

Vault: Are you responsible for the logistics of actually getting the products to the plant?

Swanson: When we source a contract, we try to include the logistics (transportation) into the price of the agreement. In addition, we do handle some of the issues that may arise with transportation logistics.

Vault: Have you found the skills you learned at your MBA program helpful in your position?

Swanson: Absolutely. I believe that the organizational skills, in addition to the analytical skills, and accounting and financial skills, have played a large part in my success here at ADM. I'm talking about skills such as creating P&L statements, analyzing ROI [return on investment] and cost-analysis – they've played a large part in being able to analyze viable suppliers for ADM.

Also, we negotiate contracts on a continuous basis, so excellent negotiating skills are mandatory for this position to ensure that the plants are getting the best price and service. [At Millikin] we studied negotiation as an art and I acquired additional skills through the training. Small group communication skills were also discussed and beneficial. All of these skills together are necessary for facilitating the teams for each of these contracts – that is, to ensure a success full working environment. had negotiating skills training. The training we had in small group communication skills has been helpful too as this is necessary for facilitating the teams for each of these contracts – that is, working with the plant locations.

Vault: Do you foresee yourself staying in purchasing with your MBA?

ADM offers so many opportunities that you really can't limit yourself. ADM has sales positions, logistics positions, IT positions, HR positions. There's no need to limit myself. I believe as the opportunities present themselves, I'll be available.

Employer Directory

Archer Daniels Midland Company (ADM)

4666 Faries Parkway
P.O. Box 1470
Decatur, Illinois 62525
Phone: 217-451-4906
Recruiting web site: www.admworld.com/naen/careers/
Recruiting e-mail: michaelmarty@admworld.com

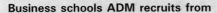

Archer Daniels Midland Company (ADM) is a world leader in agricultural processing. ADM is one of the world's largest processors of soybeans, corn, wheat and cocoa. ADM is also a leader in the production of soy meal and oil, ethanol, corn sweeteners and flour. In addition, ADM produces value-added food and feed ingredients. Headquartered in Decatur, Illinois, ADM has over 25,000 employees, more than 250 processing plants and net sales for the fiscal year ended June 30, 2005 of $35.9 billion. Additional information can be found on ADM's Web site at http://www.adm-world.com.

Business schools ADM recruits from

Thunderbird; University of Illinois; University of Chicago; University of Michigan; Indiana University

---

Archer Daniels Midland Company (ADM)
4666 Faries Pkwy.
Decatur, IL 62525
Phone: (217) 424-5200
Fax: (217) 424-6196
Toll Free: (800) 637-5843
www.admworld.com

Associated British Foods plc
Weston Centre, 10 Grosvenor St.
London
W1K 4QY, United Kingdom
Phone: +44-20-7399-6500
Fax: +44-20-7399-6580
www.abf.co.uk

Bunge Limited
50 Main Street
White Plains, NY 10606, United States
Phone: (914) 684-3300
www.bunge.com

Cargill
15407 McGinty Rd. West
Wayzata, MN 55391
Phone: (952) 742-7575
Fax: (952) 742-7393
www.cargill.com

ConAgra Foods, Inc.
1 ConAgra Dr.
Omaha, NE 68102-5001
Phone: (402) 595-4000
Fax: (402) 595-4707
www.conagra.com

Corn Products International, Inc.
5 Westbrook Corporate Center
Westchester, IL 60154
Phone: (708) 551-2600
Fax: (708) 551-2570
Toll Free: (800) 443-2746
www.cornproducts.com

Perdue Farms Incorporated
31149 Old Ocean City Rd.
Salisbury, MD 21804
Phone: (410) 543-3000
Fax: (410) 543-3292
www.perdue.com

Pilgrim's Pride Corporation
4845 US Hwy. 271 North
Pittsburg, TX 75686-0093
Phone: (903) 855-1000
Fax: (903) 856-7505
www.pilgrimspride.com

Smithfield Foods, Inc.
200 Commerce St.
Smithfield, VA 23430
Phone: (757) 365-3000
Fax: (757) 365-3017
www.smithfieldfoods.com

Tate & Lyle PLC
Sugar Quay, Lower Thames St.
London
EC3R 6DQ, United Kingdom
Phone: +44-20-7626-6525
Fax: +44-20-7623-5213
www.tate-lyle.co.uk

Tyson Foods, Inc.
2210 W. Oaklawn Dr.
Springdale, AR 72762-6999
Phone: (479) 290-4000
Fax: (479) 290-4061
www.tysonfoodsinc.com

Visit Vault at **www.vault.com** for insider company profiles, expert advice, career message boards, expert resume reviews, the Vault Job Board and more.

VAULT CAREER LIBRARY   65

Discover the satisfaction of working for an organization that improves the quality of life for people everywhere by joining our talented team. Roche Diagnostics is the number one *in vitro* diagnostics company in the world! With our North American headquarters based in Indianapolis, we have some of the most talented and dedicated individuals in the industry. Our work is exciting, challenging and highly rewarding. Our success comes from having a clear focus on the needs of our customers.

Roche is one of the world's leading research-oriented healthcare groups in the fields of pharmaceuticals and diagnostics. Our innovative products and services address needs for the prevention, diagnosis and treatment of disease, thus enhancing people's well-being and quality of life.

We are always looking for people who want to become part of our winning team, whose daily work involves finding solutions that help people live better lives. Roche values our employees and recognizes their achievements through advancement opportunities and personal rewards.

We offer an excellent compensation and benefit program including 401(k). For information on our current openings, please visit our career site: **http://careers.ind.roche.com**. Roche is committed to providing equal opportunity to a diverse workforce.

We're People Helping People Enjoy Life

Biotech and Pharmaceuticals

What's in a Name: Big Pharma, Big Biotech and Biopharma?

Strictly speaking, the term "pharmaceuticals" refers to medicines composed of small, synthetically produced molecules, which are sold by large, fully integrated drug manufacturers. The largest of these players - companies like Pfizer, GlaxoSmithKline and Merck - as well as a handful of others are referred to as "Big Pharma" because they are huge research, development, and manufacturing concerns with subsidiaries all over the globe. Indeed, Big Pharma is where over 50% of the industry's sales are generated. Big Pharma is responsible for all those television commercials urging us to contact our doctors if we suspect we suffer from everything ranging from acid reflux disease to social anxiety disorder. Yet despite life-saving, cancer-fighting drugs and significant corporate philanthropy, Big Pharma's recent product recalls and safety testing troubles (Vioxx and Celebrex) have made it the industry we've come to love to hate.

Most biotechs are small, research-oriented companies dedicated to applying genetics to curing a multitude of heartbreaking diseases, ranging from Alzheimer's to multiple sclerosis. A handful of companies - such as Amgen, Genentech and Chiron - have broken through the rest of the pack to become "fully integrated" like their Big Pharma cousins. The term "fully integrated" means that they manufacture as well as sell their own products. These "products" are proteins, which need to be injected since they are very large molecules compared to the synthetic molecules Big Pharma sells. The largest biotechs are actually mid-size pharmaceutical companies in the way they function and are sometimes called "Big Biotech."

As for the largest Big Pharma players, most are either gobbling up small biotechs through outright acquisitions or, alternatively, are entering licensing agreements. This has been happening over the last decade, and is likely to continue throughout the rest of this decade, since it is increasingly difficult to find innovative new drugs through traditional science. In fact, innovation is the industry's biggest current challenge. Companies are using acquisitions and alliances to round out their product pipelines and meet investor expectations. Big drug manufacturers can now claim to research, manufacture and sell both synthetics and biologics. What this means to you is that you should include the largest biotechs as well as the largest traditional pharmaceuticals when planning a marketing career. That's good news since it increases the number of players and potential employers.

What you should keep in mind, however, is that the marketing models around which traditional pharmaceuticals and biotechs are developed are complementary. Pharmaceutical companies are generally organized around the "blockbuster" model, i.e., they derive most of their sales and profits from a handful of broadly acting drugs, which are mass-marketed to a broad patient population by a network of sales representatives, or "detail" people. This is the same model that brought Vioxx to the market and it is increasingly under attack. By industry consensus, a "blockbuster" is a drug whose annual revenues reach or exceed $1 billion. The biotech firms, on the other hand, tend to be organized around smaller franchises, i.e., their products are targeted to small patient populations with rare genetic diseases. Their biologics are sold by specialty sales representatives, who often have a relatively high degree of scientific knowledge. Because of this focus, biotech products are often referred to as specialty pharmaceuticals. To complicate matters, some biologics reach blockbuster status with respect to their revenues, since they are usually much more expensive than therapeutics. Considering that some biologics cost $10,000 per patient per year, you would need a mere 100,000 patients to reach $1 billion in revenues. Compare this to the millions of patients who ingest small molecule drugs like Prozac or Viagra.

Because this transition is ongoing, the dividing line between the two industries will continue to blur. That leaves us with the problem of how to refer to the emerging industry. Some people use the term "Biopharma" to include both types of products.

The Global Biopharmaceutical Industry

The global industry is dominated by three major market segments: North America is the largest and comprises 49% of the total market, Europe is second with some 28%, and Japan third at 11% in 2003 sales. Although these combined markets

Visit Vault at **www.vault.com** for insider company profiles, expert advice, career message boards, expert resume reviews, the Vault Job Board and more.

VAULT CAREER LIBRARY 67

account for 78% of global sales, the remaining emerging market segments - Other Asian, Africa, and Australia and Latin America - are growing rapidly.

Although the industry is dominated by a handful of super-large companies, the global industry is actually highly fragmented. Over 2,000 pharmaceutical and biotech companies exist worldwide. In the top tier are the large, multinational companies that dominate the market or Big Pharma. In the middle tier are the specialty companies. Many large companies have tended to absorb second-tier companies before they can grow enough to pose a competitive threat. That trend has a contracting effect on the number of firms. The opposite happens on the third and lowest tier, which is composed of an ever increasing group of start-ups mostly focused on discovery research.

According to IMS Health, Inc., a healthcare research and information company, as recently as 1998, the global pharmaceutical market was valued at $280 billion. By 2003, total global sales had grown 9% over 2002 levels to $492 billion or nearly half a trillion dollars! This figure was derived retail sales in major global markets. This astonishing growth over five-year period reflects the increasing role pharmaceuticals is taking as a first-line treatment option in many disease conditions in the developed world.

Economic activity is concentrated in both products and therapeutic areas. As we noted, most of the industry's revenues are based on mega-sales of blockbuster products, i.e., those that generate at least $1 billion in sales. In 2000, the highest selling 20 drugs generated sales revenues of $100 billion or roughly 50% of total sales of the top 500 drugs. In 2002, 58 products each generated sales over $1 billion. Reflecting the stress-ridden, developed world's disease vulnerabilities, the most profitable products treated heart disease, gastric distress, mood and mental disorders, and inflammatory conditions.

The U.S. pharmaceutical industry

The U.S. pharmaceutical industry is comprised of approximately 100 companies, according to the Pharmaceutical Research and Manufacturers of America (PhRMA), a leading industry trade and lobbying organization. This does not include biotech companies, which number approximately 325 publicly traded companies, with hundreds more private, discovery research oriented firms. The U.S. drug market is concentrated - the top ten largest companies accounted for 60% of total retail sales in 2003, according to IMS Health, Inc.

The U.S. has not only the largest pharmaceutical market in the world but also the only one without government controls. That characteristic has major consequences on drug pricing, innovation, and R&D investment. Standard & Poor's expects the U.S. to continue to be the largest of the top 10 pharmaceutical markets for the foreseeable future as well as the fastest growing.

Although pharmaceutical companies are scattered throughout the continental United States, the industry is geographically concentrated in the Mid-Atlantic States (New York, New Jersey, and Pennsylvania) and on the West Coast in California. A handful of companies can also be found in Massachusetts, Illinois, and North Carolina. New Jersey is the heart of the industry and has by far the largest number of companies within a single state. (Note the geographic distribution of the biotech industry in the Guide to Biotech.)

MBA Level Sales and Marketing Jobs

Most companies consider sales and marketing to be one function, but with two basic areas of activity. Within the Sales function, you can typically find three career tracks: Field Sales, Sales Management, and Managed Markets. A fourth track, Sales Training is closely associated with Sales and is distinct from the broader Training and Development function, which is usually associated with Human Resource Departments. Sales Training groups bridge the sales and marketing function: in some companies, they are considered part of marketing support, and hence part of the marketing function. The main point, however, is that all companies that have Field sales forces have rigorous sales training departments.

Within the marketing function are two main areas of activity: marketing management and marketing support. The latter is actually composed of several distinct groups, some of which are quite large, but all of which serve essentially the same purpose: to provide support services for marketing managers. Depending on the size of the company, the distinction between the two areas may be either blurred on non-existent. Typical groups include training and development, advertising and promotion, market analysis, customer call center, e-business, and commercialization and strategic planning.

Fully integrated Big Biotech companies have their own sales and marketing infrastructure and essentially the same job classifications. The main difference from their Big Pharma cousins is that biotech sales reps are specialty reps, who market products to specific and highly defined patients groups. On an experiential level, the big difference is that that very focus prevents the overreaching to the mass market that is now plaguing the marketers of broadly acting agents.

The good thing about the sales and marketing function in the biopharmaceutical industry is that, once you get hired in a particular work area, it is possible, and even encouraged, to gain experience in other areas.

Sales management

Managing a sales force can be one of the most lucrative tracks in the pharmaceutical industry. District sales manager is the first rung on the management ladder, followed by regional sales manager, area sales director, and vice president of sales. Each level has increasing responsibility for the sales of a broader geographic area. This is not an entry-level job and usually requires several years of direct sales experience plus evidence of leadership potential. In particular, the first level, district sales manager, is a position people from several areas of activity can move in and out of to get perspective on sales activity.

Like field reps, the responsibilities of a sales manager fall into three distinct categories. Management responsibilities require a sales manager to lead assigned sales district in meeting upper management goals; recruit, hire and train sales reps; ensure efficient coverage of their assigned geographic area; plan and lead meetings to review sales achievements; and manage Reps' activities when coordinating educational events (e.g., symposia, speakers bureaus, seminars, etc.). Administrative responsibilities require sales managers to develop business plans and plans of action (POA's), implement market strategies, monitor progress of ongoing sales activity, stay current on industry and company issues that impact the sales force, ensure optimal distribution and consistent stocking of product samples, monitor the district's budget, and control it's expenses. Professional Development responsibilities require the sales manager to maintain a work environment that maximizes motivation, act as a coach and mentor to the sales reps, and create individualized development plans for each direct report.

Marketing management

Marketing management is the core work of the marketing function and is where strategy is formulated and implemented. Many companies organize marketing management according to therapeutic areas (i.e., oncology drugs, cardiovascular drugs, anti-hypertensives, etc.). Until recent years, marketing had a single upward path to senior positions. With large companies merging into mega-companies (e.g., Pfizer acquired both Warner-Lambert and Pharmacia to become the largest company in the industry), some companies have opted to organize therapeutic areas and their associated products into separate business units, so that marketing management decisions get made with fewer layers of oversight and with closer contact with customer physicians and targeted patient groups.

The main job title in marketing management is product manager and is consistent throughout the industry. From there, titles like product director, group product manager, and vice president of marketing represent higher level marketing management jobs. None of these are entry-level positions at the BS level, although MBAs with previous marketing experience can work in product management groups, as assistant or associate product managers.

Visit Vault at **www.vault.com** for insider company profiles, expert advice, career message boards, expert resume reviews, the Vault Job Board and more.

V\ULT CAREER LIBRARY   **69**

A product manager's responsibilities fall into two main categories. Product management responsibilities require the product manager to develop and manage the short term product strategy and marketing plans for assigned products, oversee development of business plans, specify the positioning of a product among its competitors, monitor those competitor products, acquire both a quantitative and intuitive feel for customer needs, and act as an in-house champion for a product or brand. From an administrative perspective, a product manager must develop budgets, maintain records of expenses, and manage and develop entry-level support staff.

In companies organized as business units, product managers effectively become mini-CEOs and are involved in virtually every aspect of getting a product to market. Most product managers also have substantial communication and negotiation skills, as they are required to interact with professionals from every part of the organization.

Marketing support: Market analysis

Market analysis groups are responsible for gathering and analyzing business information in specific geographic areas to understand the economic profile of specific disease conditions in which the company specializes, the associated targeted patient populations - including demographic trends and shifts and progression of disease conditions - and the competitive landscape for the products under development. Jobs have titles like market analyst or regional analyst. Although these jobs are usually not entry-level with only a Bachelor's degree, many MBAs target market analyst jobs after graduation and can land them if they have basic science education and can demonstrate evidence of some understanding of the industry's marketing issues.

A market analyst has primarily analytical responsibilities, which are consistent throughout the industry. Typical tasks are to perform local healthcare marketplace assessments, provide analysis and consulting support to sales and marketing management, develop and implement tools and processes for standard sales performance measurement, identify opportunities and assess threats for the company's products, measure financial ratios (e.g., return on investment or ROI, market share, etc.), and analyze tactical plans based on historic performance.

Business Development in Biotech

Business development

On the business development side, research analysts provide the extensive research and analysis needed to determine how and with whom a biotech company should partner with. Analysts generate the assessments that help business development management determine how to meet its goals. Analysts answer such questions as, "Should we expand organically or acquire other companies to grow?" and "Who should we partner with to become more competitive?" Research analysts work with attorneys to assess intellectual property and licensing issues, help develop and enforce agreements, and secure licenses for ongoing operations. Many companies have senior analyst positions with the same responsibilities, but operating more autonomously. Analysts can bring home salaries ranging from $90,000 to $110,000.

It's a significant step up to manager of corporate planning, a job that generally appears at the larger companies. They prepare long-range and strategic plans (usually several years out) and short-range/tactical plans (up to a year out). Other activities include designing and executing financial planning processes, setting targets, and planning guidelines. The manager of corporate planning works closely with the CFO to develop the company's financial plans for senior management, industry analysts, and investors. They complete competitive analysis and continually assess the prospects for the company. This senior position usually has salaries ranging from $110,000 to $120,000.

At the head of the group is the vice president of business development, a very important position in most biotech companies. The VP of biz dev oversees all efforts to identify, evaluate, and pursue potential strategic partners, joint ventures, and alliances. This person also directs the assessment of the licensing potential of targets, leads and drug candidates as well as the managing of all collaborations. They maintain partnership agreements and address the inevitable issues that arise in any relationship. Most companies ask for impressive credentials to reach this level: an MBA, a science degree and nearly a decade of experience that includes knowledge of due diligence, asset valuation, alliance integration, and portfolio management. As an executive, the VP can expect to earn a salary ranging from $160,000 to $190,000 and also receive additional incentive compensation.

A Day in the Life: Business Development Manager

A business development manager at a mid-sized company (about 300 employees) gives Vault the inside scoop on job responsibilities as a biotech MBA. He holds a BS in Microbiology and an MBA.

There is no routine to my days. My days are divided between proactive and reactive work. Although you have much more control on the proactive side, I'm often on the reactive side of things. This makes my days much less predictable. You have to be able to plan both sides to be productive.

Proactive work: My typical proactive tasks include:

- Getting back to any potential customers
- Scheduling meetings with prospects
- Sending draft proposals to potential clients to go through the details in preparation for negotiating contract terms
- Conducting project review board meetings to screen potential projects at a high level (e.g., senior executives, subject matter experts or SMEs) to make a go/no go decision. This involves collecting information, drafting, or editing proposals
- Conducting commercial review meetings with existing clients to review current projects and determine whether we are meeting our agreed-upon terms (usually either monthly or biweekly meetings)
- Coordinating and scheduling conferences and trade shows
- Regularly and routinely contacting key industry players who we may not have business with (i.e., maintaining relationships)

Reactive Work: My reactive work typically involves:

- Responding to potential client inquiries (phone, e-mail, referral) to set up meetings, collect information, draft proposals, review them with clients, respond to their questions, and set up the terms of the contract
- Setting up negotiations with internal clients (e.g., senior executives) as well as external clients

It's important to react in a structured way, but the points of reaction are not that predictable. The challenge is always scheduling, since multiple people with multiple schedules can make coordination unpredictable.

Visit Vault at **www.vault.com** for insider company profiles, expert advice, career message boards, expert resume reviews, the Vault Job Board and more.

V∧ULT CAREER LIBRARY

71

Business Development Manager Uppers and Downers

Uppers

• Travel can be either a pro or a con, depending on whether you are single or have a family.

• I am often in conversations with leading researchers, who are on the cutting-edge of science, discussing how products are going to be commercialized – that's exciting.

• Bringing products to market that are helping to save people's lives is also very satisfying.

• I like having the flexibility and freedom that comes from having a job with limited structure and a measure of unpredictability.

Downers

• I am quite often the giver of bad news and the receiver of client reactions to that news. For example, when their schedule changes, and they don't make promised deliveries, that impacts everything we do, and often delays our ability to manufacture the product.

• You also have to have a thick enough skin to not react to their disappointment and anger.

Employer Directory

Bristol-Myers Squibb Co

Bristol-Myers Squibb
345 Park Avenue
New York, NY 10154-0037
Phone: 212-546-4000
www.bms.com/career

BMS offers opportunities for MBA students and graduates to join Summer and Full-Time Associate Programs in the following areas: Marketing, Finance, Information Management, Human Resources and Technical Operations.

Johnson & Johnson

One Johnson & Johnson Plaza
New Brunswick, NJ 08933
Phone: 732-524-0400
www.jnj.com/careers

Johnson & Johnson has $47.3 billion in sales and is the world's most comprehensive and broadly based manufacturer of health care products, as well as a provider of related services, for the consumer, pharmaceutical, and medical devices and diagnostics markets. Johnson & Johnson has 109,900 employees and over 200 operating companies in 57 countries around the world, selling products throughout the world.

We keep our leadership positions fresh and vital through constant innovation. Our commitment to a superior rate of innovation has been accompanied by a superior rate of profitability, enabling the development of unique new products and new leadership positions – thereby spurring added breadth and enhancing consistency. This successful cycle in the pursuit of leadership has given us the wherewithal to deliver consistently outstanding performance since the Company was founded in 1886.

Roche Diagnostics

9115 Hague Road
Indianapolis, Indiana 462520
careers.ind.roche.com
www.roche.com

Roche Diagnostics is the world's leading provider of diagnostic systems and decision-oriented health information. We are dedicated to the discovery, development, manufacturing, marketing and servicing of products and solutions for medical laboratories, physicians and patients, as well as for research and industry. Roche Diagnostics is a diverse, inclusive company that seeks, celebrates and leverages diversity to maximize the competitive advantage of people. We offer a variety of opportunities at our U.S. diagnostics marketing and sales headquarters in Indiana and at our global molecular business area headquarters in California.

Business schools Roche Diagnostics recruits from

University of Chicago; Northwestern (Kellogg); Indiana University (Kelley); Harvard Business School, Duke University (Fuqua); U.C.L.A.; University of Michigan; Purdue University; MIT (Sloan); University of Pennsylvania (Wharton); Yale University, Stanford University; UC Berkeley (Haas); Washington University (Olin)

Visit Vault at **www.vault.com** for insider company profiles, expert advice, career message boards, expert resume reviews, the Vault Job Board and more.

VAULT CAREER LIBRARY

73

Life.
Enhanced.

New Breakthroughs, New Opportunities.

If you're looking for an exciting place to work with a future full of opportunities, consider Bristol-Myers Squibb. We recently launched four major medicines in just over two years. And we have a robust pipeline of investigational products to treat serious diseases with unmet needs, including diabetes, rheumatoid arthritis and related medical disorders. Help us fulfill our mission *to extend and enhance human life*. You'll not only enrich the lives of others, but also have the opportunity for a rewarding career with personal and professional advancement in a high-caliber, team-oriented environment.

Find out more at
www.bms.com/career/

BMS offers opportunities for MBA students and graduates to join Summer and Full-Time Associate Programs in the following areas: Marketing, Finance, Information Management, Human Resources and Technical Operations.

Undergraduate-level students and other advanced-degree graduates may also pursue internship, co-op and permanent job opportunities in many business divisions and functions across BMS and its family of companies.

 Bristol-Myers Squibb

Hope, Triumph and the Miracle of Medicine™

Bristol-Myers Squibb Company
P.O. Box 5335 Princeton, NJ 08543-5335

Abbott Laboratories
100 Abbott Park Rd.
Abbott Park, IL 60064-6400
Phone: (847) 937-6100
Fax: (847) 937-1511
www.abbott.com

Amgen Inc.
1 Amgen Center Dr.
Thousand Oaks, CA 91320-1799
Phone: 805-447-1000
Fax: 805-447-1010
www.amgen.com

AstraZeneca
15 Stanhope Gate
London W1Y 1LN
United Kingdom
Phone: +44-20-7304-5000
Fax: +44-20-7304-5183

AstraZeneca: U.S. headquarters
1800 Concord Pike
Wilmington, DE 19850-5438
Phone: (302) 886-3000
Fax: (302) 886-2972
www.astrazeneca.com

Aventis (Sanofi-Aventis Group)
Espace Européen de l'Entreprise,
16, Avenue de l'Europe
67917 Strasbourg, France
Phone: +33-3-88-99-11-00
Fax: +33-3-88-99-11-01

U.S. headquarters:
200, 400 Crossing Blvd.
Bridgewater, NJ 08807
Phone: (908) 304-7000
www.aventis.com

Bausch & Lomb
1 Bausch & Lomb Place
Rochester, NY 14604-2701
Phone: (585) 338-6000
Fax: (585) 338-6007
Toll Free: (800) 344-8815
www.bausch.com

Baxter International, Inc.
1 Baxter Pkwy.
Deerfield, IL 60015
Phone: (847) 948-2000
Fax: (847) 948-3642
Toll Free: (800) 422-9837
www.baxter.com

Bayer Corporation
100 Bayer Rd.
Pittsburgh, PA 15205-9741
Phone: (412) 777-2000
Fax: (412) 777-2034
www.bayerus.com

BD
Human Resources
1 Becton Drive
Franklin Lakes, NJ 07417-1880
Phone: (201) 847-6800
www.bd.com

Bristol-Myers Squibb
345 Park Avenue
New York, NY 10154-0037
Phone: (212) 546-4000
Fax: (212) 546-4020
www.bms.com

Chiron
4560 Horton Street
Emeryville, CA 94608-2916
Phone: (510) 655-8730
Fax: (510) 655-9910
www.chiron.com

Eli Lilly & Co.
Lilly Corporate Center
Indianapolis, IN 46285
Phone: (317) 276-2000
Fax: (317) 277-6579
www.lilly.com

Genentech
1 DNA Way
South San Francisco, CA 94080-4990
Phone: (650) 225-1000
Fax: (650) 225-6000
www.gene.com

Genzyme Corporation
500 Kendall Street
Cambridge, MA 02142
Phone: (617) 252-7500
Fax: (617) 252-7600
www.genzyme.com

GlaxoSmithKline
980 Great West Road
Brentford, London
TW8 9GS, United Kingdom
Phone: +44-20-8047-5000
Fax: +44-20-8047-7807
www.gsk.com

Johnson & Johnson
One Johnson & Johnson Plaza
New Brunswick, NJ 08933
Phone: (732) 524-0400
Fax: (732) 524-3300
www.jnj.com

McKesson Corporation
1 Post Street
San Francisco, CA 94104
Phone: (415) 983-8300
Fax: (415) 983-7160
www.mckesson.com

Merck & Co., Inc.
1 Merck Drive
Whitehouse Station, NJ 08889-0100
Phone: (908) 423-1000
Fax: (908) 735-1253
www.merck.com

Novartis AG
Lichtstrasse 35
CH-4056 Basel
Switzerland
Phone: +41-61-324-1111
Fax: +41-61-324-8001
www.novartis.com

Pfizer Inc.
235 E. 42nd St.
New York, NY 10017-5755
Phone: (212) 573-2323
Fax: (212) 573-7851
www.pfizer.com

Visit Vault at **www.vault.com** for insider company profiles, expert advice,
career message boards, expert resume reviews, the Vault Job Board and more.

VAULT CAREER LIBRARY

75

Pharmacia Corporation
100 Rte. 206 North
Peapack, NJ 07977
Phone: (908) 901-8000
Fax: (908) 901-8379
www.pnu.com

Roche Group
Grenzacherstrasse 124
CH-4070 Basel, Switzerland
Phone: +41-61-688-1111
Fax: +41-61-691-9391
www.roche.com

Schering-Plough Corporation
2000 Galloping Hill Rd.
Kenilworth, NJ 07033-0530
Phone: (908) 298-4000
Fax: (908) 298-7653
www.schering-plough.com

Wyeth
5 Giralda Farms
Madison, NJ 07940-0874
Phone: (973) 660-5000
Fax: (973) 660-7026
www.wyeth.com

Brand Management/Consumer Products

Functional Overview

What is a marketer? The allure of brand management

Marketing encompasses a wide variety of meanings and activities. Some marketing positions are very close to sales, while others set overarching marketing strategy. What marketing positions have in common is the sense of ownership over the product or service, as well as the need to understand customer needs and desires and translate those needs into some kind of marketing communication, advertising campaign or sales effort. The manager of product or service marketing is called the brand manager – he or she is the ruler of that marketing universe.

Careers within the marketing/branding arena are high-profile. The business world is now realizing that strong brands and solid marketing programs drive shareholder value, and that companies can no longer make fundamental strategy decisions without truly understanding how to market a product. Today's business challenges – the quest for company growth, industry consolidation and deregulation, economic webs, and the emergency of new channels and technologies – make marketers even more valuable.

The titles of brand manager, product manager, and to a lesser extent, marketing manager are often used to describe the same function – some companies use one title, others use another. Marketing manager tends to be used in industries other than consumer packaged goods; product manager is often used in tech industries. "Brand management" implies more complete supervision of a product. The typical brand management framework gives a brand "group" or "team" – generally comprised of several assistant brand or assistant marketing managers and one supervising brand manager – responsibility for all matters relevant to their product or products. Whether this responsibility is in fact complete depends somewhat on the size of the company relative to the number of brands it has, the location of the brand group, and most importantly, on the company's attitude toward marketing.

How important is the individual brand manager?

Consider the company to determine the level of brand manager responsibility. The first factor: the size of the company relative to its number of brands. For a company with hundreds of different brands – Nabisco, for example – brand managers, or even assistant brand managers, may have a great deal of power over a specific brand. At companies with a few core products, brand managers will focus on narrower aspects of a brand. As one assistant brand manager at Coca-Cola comments: "They're not going to take an MBA and say, 'Okay, you're in charge of Sprite.'" Brand managers at such companies will instead be focused on marketing to a particular demographic or geographic group, or perhaps handling one aspect of the product's consumption (plastic bottles, cases of aluminum cans, and so forth).

International brand managers have historically held more sway than managers in the company's home market, but keep in mind that the daily tasks of international brand managers often lean more toward questions of operations, rather than questions of strategy or marketing. ('How much should we produce?' or 'How is our distribution network affecting sales?' rather than 'What do we want our brand identity to be?') International brand management is sometimes split into two positions. Global brand managers are more strategic, concentrating on issues such as protecting brand equity and developing product offerings that can be rolled out into subsidiaries. Local brand managers are more tactical. Local managers focus on executing global plans that are delivered to them, and tweak them for local consumers. Also know that with the increasing trend toward globalization and the truly global presence of certain brands, companies have sought to impose more centralization and tighter controls on the marketing of those brands from country to country. In the past, individual country managers have

Visit Vault at www.vault.com for insider company profiles, expert advice,
career message boards, expert resume reviews, the Vault Job Board and more.

VAULT CAREER LIBRARY

77

had more discretion and leeway to make decisions about a brand's packaging, advertising, etc. Now, companies have established tighter guidelines on what can be done with regard to a brand around the world, with the goal of protecting and enhancing the value of the brand and ensuring a consistent product and message worldwide.

Finally, consumer products companies place varying levels of importance on their brand or marketing departments. Some companies, such as the Ford Motor Company, are driven as much by financial analyses of production costs or operations considerations as by marketing. The level of emphasis on finance or operations matters at a firm will influence not only the independence and authority of marketing managers, but also potential marketing career paths. At some companies, marketing is the training ground for general management. At General Mills, marketing is considered so important that employees in other functions who show promise are plucked from their positions and put into the department.

Careers in Marketing

Taking charge of a brand involves tackling many diverse job functions – and different subspecialties. Decide where you'd like your main concentration to lie.

Brand management

In a typical brand management organizational structure, positions are developed around responsibility for a particular product rather than a specific functional expertise (i.e. you're an assistant brand manager for Cheerios). This structure enables you to be the "master of all trades," acquiring an expertise in areas such as manufacturing, sales, research and development, and communications. In brand management, the marketing function is responsible for key general management decisions such as long-term business strategy, pricing, product development direction and, in some cases, profit and loss responsibility. Brand management offers a terrific way to learn intensively about a particular product category (you could be a recognized expert on tampons!) and to manage the responsibility of running a business and influencing its performance.

The core of brand work is brand strategy. Brand managers must decide how to increase market share, which markets and demographic groups to target, and what types of advertising and special promotions to use. And at the very heart of brand strategy is identifying a product's "brand identity." Brand groups then figure out how to exploit brand strategy, or, in some cases, how to change it. PepsiCo's Mountain Dew has built the drink's popularity among youth as a high-caffeine beverage into a "brand identity" of cutting-edge bravado that has boosted market share, while the Banana Republic chain underwent a transformation from an outdoor adventure store that sold actual Army-Navy surplus to an upscale, chic clothing store. In both cases, the brands have benefited from a shift in brand identity, and consequently, a shift in their market. Brand identity is normally created and confirmed through traditional print, radio, and TV advertising. Advertising is usually produced by outside agencies, although brand insiders determine the emphasis and target of the advertising.

Some liken a brand manager to a hub at the center of a hub and spoke system, with the spokes going out to departments like finance, sales, manufacturing, R&D, etc. It is the job of the brand manager to influence the performance of those groups – over whom he or she has no direct authority – in order to optimize the performance of his or her brand or product line.

Direct marketing

Ever wonder who is responsible for making those coupons you receive in the mail? Or the Saab videotape you've received every two years since you bought your car in 1993? You can thank direct marketers. Direct marketers are masters in one-to-one marketing. Direct marketers assemble databases of individual consumers who fit within their target market, go after them with a personal approach, and manage the production process from strategy inception to out-the-door distribution.

Direct marketers have two main objectives: to stay in touch with their current consumer base and to try and generate more business by finding individuals who fit a target set of criteria but are not currently using their particular product. For instance, if you've ever checked out of the supermarket and got a coupon for Advil after buying a bottle of Tylenol, chances are a direct marketer is trying to convince you to switch brands by offering you a monetary incentive.

It's important to note that direct marketing isn't just through snail mail. It operates in multiple media such as the Web, tele-marketing, and in-store promotions. Direct marketers have a powerful new tool in their arsenal – the Internet. Marketers are able to track the online habits and behavior of customers. They can then serve up customized banner advertisements that are much more likely to be relevant to them. Many consumers have agreed to receive promotional offers on certain subjects – marketers can then send them targeted e-mail messages that allow for much easier access to purchase or action (a click on a link, for example) than a conventional mail direct marketing programs.

Affiliate/property marketing

If you're working with a major brand company like Nike, Disney, Pepsi, or L'Oreal, chances are you'll do a lot of cross-promotion, or "affiliate marketing." For instance, Nike has marketing relationships with the NBA, NFL, and a variety of individual athletes and athletic teams. Disney has a strong relationship with McDonalds; cute toys from the entertainment company's latest flick are often packaged with McDonalds Happy Meals upon the release of each new movie. L'Oreal works with celebrities like Heather Locklear and sponsors events such as the annual Academy Awards.

Marketers must manage the relationship between any two entities. If Disney wants to promote the cartoon du jour with McDonalds, or Pepsi wants to make sure that all Six Flags theme parks have a Pepsi Ride, then marketers ensure both parties are getting what they need out of the deal and staying true to their own brand image.

Price marketing/sales forecasting

Pricing is largely driven by market pressure. Most people, for example, won't pay more than $2.00 for a hamburger in a fast food restaurant. On the other hand, brand managers always have some pricing leeway that can greatly affect market share and profitability. An increase of a nickel in the price of a product sold by the millions can make huge differences in revenue – assuming the price rise doesn't cause equivalent millions less of the products to be sold. Brand managers need to figure out the optimal pricing strategy for their product, though it's not always a case of making the most money. Sometimes it makes more sense to win market share while taking lower profits. How do brand managers justify their prices? Through extensive research. Paper towels, for example, may be much more price-sensitive than a luxury item like engagement rings or foie gras.

Brand and marketing managers don't always have free reign over pricing. At some companies, such as those that sell largely through mail order, or those with complex pricing systems, pricing and promotional offers may be limited to what the operational sales system can handle. Explains one marketing manager at a long-distance phone company (an industry with notoriously tangled pricing plans): "It's very easy to offer something to the customer. It's very difficult to implement that in the computer system."

Another large part of the general management duties of brand managers is forecasting product sales. This means not only keeping track of sales trends of one's product, but anticipating responses to marketing campaigns and product launches or changes. The forecasts are used to determine production levels. Once a year, brand groups draw up budgets for their production, advertising and promotion costs, try to convince the finance folks that they absolutely need that amount, get less than they ask for, and then rework their budgets to fit the given budget. As one international brand manager at one of the world's biggest consumer goods companies puts it: "You don't determine the production and then get that budget; you get the budget, and then determine the production."

Visit Vault at **www.vault.com** for insider company profiles, expert advice, career message boards, expert resume reviews, the Vault Job Board and more.

VAULT CAREER LIBRARY   79

High-tech marketing

Not everyone markets applesauce for a living. Many people choose to enter the world of high-tech marketing because they want to work with products and technologies that reshape and improve the word around us. These marketers feel that they would rather change the way a person interacts with the world in a sophisticated way, rather than spend time understanding what hair color teenagers find most appealing. High tech marketers spend much of their time understanding research and development issues and working on new product launches.

Technology companies like Intel, Dell, and Microsoft have recognized the power of branding and are utilizing traditional marketing tactics more and more. Amazon's extensive marketing campaign in 1998 helped brand that company in the mind of consumers still new to e-commerce as the company to purchase books (and other products) online. Intel became perhaps the first semiconductor company readily identifiable to the public through its heavily branded "bunny people." Marketing in the high tech world will continue to grow in importance over the next decade, as technology companies become more consumer-oriented (see Microsoft's X-Box). Marketing a service or software product versus a more tangible product is a bit different. It may be a bit more challenging to understand how consumers relate to the product. Inventory and distribution issues may be tracked differently.

Market research

If you are an analytical person who enjoys numbers and analysis, and enjoys tracking consumer behavior, then market research may be the field for you. A product is much more effective when a company understands the consumer it is targeting. That's where market researchers come in. Market researchers employ a variety of different qualitative and quantitative research techniques to understand consumers. Surveys, tracking systems, focus groups, satisfaction monitors, psychographic and demographic models, and trial/repurchase estimations are all methods researchers use to understand how consumers relate to their products. Researchers who find that consumers associate lemon scents with cleanliness, for example, may suggest that cleansers could drive up sales by adding a lemon aroma.

Marketing consulting

Although most well-known consulting firms are known for their expertise in general strategy, many consulting firms now hire industry or functional experts that focus on marketing issues. These firms need people with expertise in the areas of branding, market research, continuous relationship marketing, pricing strategy, and business-to-business marketing – they tend to hire people with previous marketing experience and value consultants who have been successful marketing managers and have lived through the full range of business issues from the inside. McKinsey and Monitor are two general strategy firms that have begun to hire marketing specialists. Other boutique marketing consulting firms, such as Kurt Salmon, focus on certain product categories like beverages, healthcare, and retail. Major ad agencies are also attempting to reinvent themselves as marketing partners focused on marketing strategy beyond simple advertising.

A Day in the Life: Assistant Brand Manager

You can often spot the assistant brand manager because they are the ones running around like a chicken with its head cut off. You must learn how to balance your time and prioritize. Here's a look at how your time might be spent:

Responsibilities	% of time per day
Meetings	30%
Analysis/data tracking	30%
Writing memos	30%
Answering management queries	30%
Interfacing with other departments	30%
Actually marketing	Optional

Although this is a humorous take on the day of an ABM (talk about giving 150%), there is some truth to it. Days and weeks will go by where you feel like you've just been pushing paper and trying to stay afloat. It is very easy to get comfortable maintaining the businesses rather than creating new opportunities. Although the role of an ABM is mostly one of maintenance, if you want to be a "star," you must shape your brand, not just maintain it.

A more realistic look at a day in the life of a brand manager

8:30 a.m. Get into work. Listen to voice mails. Check e-mails. Print out calendar of today's events. Skim the Markets section of The Wall Street Journal to find out what's happening "on the street." Go to the cafeteria and grab breakfast. (Of course, you're only eating products that your company produces or has some relationship with!)

9:00 a.m. Meet with market research department to discuss specifics of your latest round of quantitative research. You are trying to understand why people are not repurchasing your product, but you don't feel that the data presented actually answers your questions. You decide that you'll need to design another round of research – but where's the money going to come from?

10:00 a.m. Budget meeting to determine how you will be spending 2nd quarter funds. Given the decision to spend more money on research, you might need to cancel an instant redeemable coupon or a local promotion in a poorly performing market.

10:30 a.m. You head to the long-awaited product development meeting. Your team has recently discussed reformulating your product to take advantage of new technology. This new technology may raise your product's performance levels, but it will cost more to manufacture and will take some advertising effort (and more money) to explain the changes to the consumer. The group must decide whether these changes are strategically and financially justified. As always, very few people agree. You decide to summarize all the costs and benefits to the project and present the issues to your brand manager at the status meeting you have scheduled for the end of the day.

12:00 pm. A fancy lunch with a *People* magazine salesperson. For months the magazine has tried to convince you that your product should be advertised in *People*. During lunch the represenative explains to you how the publication can effectively reach x percent of your target audience and how it can provide you with the extended reach you need to communicate with potential new users. You leave lunch with a fancy *People* backpack and a headache. Where can I find the money to add *People* to my media plan? Let's ask the media department (Note: While lunch with ad reps happens occasionally, the days of most brand managers are packed, without the time to spend schmoozing with ad reps. More often, brand managers, who are very focused on their jobs, grab lunch at a corporate cafeteria and take it back to their desks.)

1:30 p.m. Media planning meeting. Because sales of your product have come in slightly under budget, you have been forced to give up 10 percent of your media budget. You now must meet with the media department to determine how to cut media

Visit Vault at **www.vault.com** for insider company profiles, expert advice, career message boards, expert resume reviews, the Vault Job Board and more.

VAULT CAREER LIBRARY   **81**

funds without sacrificing your goals (to reach 20 percent of your target group, and to have a continuous presence on TV). Maybe you can cut out two weeks of TV advertising in July when not many people are home anyway. But isn't that your product's peak purchase cycle? Decisions, decisions.

2:30 p.m. Time to review changes to the latest advertising campaign. Your ad agency presented a new concept about three weeks ago that needed work. You and your brand manager made comments to the storyboard (a drawing that explains a commercial) and now you are anxious to see what the agency has produced. You review the changes with the agency via conference call and promise to present the new work to your brand manager at your status meeting later in the day.

3:15 p.m. Keep the ad agency on the phone and bring in the in-house promotions department. This ad campaign will be introduced into a promotional campaign in the top 20 performing markets in the country. You want to make sure that before you get the promotions people working on a concept, they agree with the agency on the strategy going forward. The following 45 minutes is a creative brainstorming session that offers wonderful possibilities. You promise to type all ideas up and distribute them to the group later in the week.

4:00 p.m. Strategy development with sales manager. Your category manager is insisting that all brands work to gain a better presence in supermarkets. You meet with the regional sales manager to understand what types of strategies might work to get better shelf space and more consistent in-store promotions. Once you hear his ideas, you start to price options and see if this is possible within your (reduced) current budget.

5:00 p.m. Status meeting with brand manager. You present your proposal for increased research expending as well as the implications of the new product development issue. You also review the latest advertising changes and the changes to the media plan. You aggressively present your data and your opinion and discuss these with your boss. The two of you decide on next steps.

6:00 p.m. End of the day. You spend an hour checking the 23 e-mail/voice mail messages you received during the day but failed to return. You go through your "in box" to read any documents relevant to your product. You start to attack all of the work you have to do and promise that tomorrow you'll block out some time to make some progress.

Vault Q&A: Nir Liberbolm, L'Oreal

After interning at NY-based L'Oreal Paris as an MBA summer intern in 2003, Nir Liberboim joined the beauty company full-time as an Assistant Brand Manager upon graduating from business school in 2004. A graduate of Harvard Business School, Liberboim took time out from his hectic schedule to speak with us about L'Oreal's MBA hiring program - and starting his career at L'Oreal by making sure that the shelves at Wal-Mart were stocked properly.

Vault: What was your background prior to L'Oreal?

Liberbolm: I spent two years in investment banking at Goldman Sachs, followed by two years in venture capital in Boston. I really wanted a switch for two reasons: I wanted a combination of business and creativity, as well as operational experience.

Vault: Have you found that you're getting that experience?

Liberbolm: Definitely. You really focus on all the different functions – marketing, sales, advertising, product development. It's a tremendous opportunity from that perspective.

Vault: Tell me about the L'Oreal MBA program. Is there a rotational aspect to it?

Liberbolm: When I came in, it wasn't so much a rotational program. It's a brand management role and you're constantly working with other functional areas on a daily basis, but it wasn't rotational when I came in. Having said that, the new class that's coming in will spend six months to a year rotating across different brands before they get placed in one. I believe the new class might also have a three-month stint in sales when they come in, too.

Vault: What brand are you working on?

Liberbolm: I'm working on Feria, which is a hair color brand. Feria is considered a more edgy, young trendy brand, and I think they were looking for someone more interested in trend or fashion. It is very advertising- and media-focused -some brands are heavily advertised, others less so. Because Feria is about vibrant and shimmering color, we try to promote it through a lot of advertising. So it was a great fit.

Vault: You mentioned working with different functions. In what way do you work with different functions?

Liberbolm: We're constantly working closely with Sales and Consumer Promotions on developing the trade and promotions grid – these are all the promotions inside a store or that a consumer receives. For example if we're working with Wal-Mart, maybe we want to have displays, whereas at CVS we might want to have something on the shelf, say a dangler that says "new shades."

My direct contact in Sales is a Manager in Sales Planning. I'm always asking her, "Hey, what's happening in CVS? What's happening in Wal-Mart? Are you hearing anything from accounts about new competitive launches?" We're constantly talking; I'd say daily.

We work very closely with Product Development as well. When we are launching a new product, the Product Development team would help us cost out new cartons, components or tools. We would also work with them on creating a timeline for when different milestones must be met in order to phase-in our new product by a certain date.

We work very closely with advertising agencies on new print and TV campaigns. We're constantly going back and forth with them. It is a very creative and fascinating process.

We also work very closely with Finance. For example, Feria has a media budget, Feria has both a media and a consumer promotions budget – they are managed in total as a P&L, and we kind of come up with a plan. If we're getting x million dollars for media, we decide how that's spent. A lot of it is working with Finance to understand the budget.

Vault: Was there an orientation or training period to start?

Liberbolm: Yes. We actually began in the field, where we spent about three to four weeks resetting the shelves.

Vault: You're saying you were actually in stores rearranging shelves?

Liberbolm: Yes. They split us into teams of two or three, and we drove around New York City and New Jersey. We did it in Wal-Mart, Target, Duane Reade. We were putting in new product, taking off the defective product off the shelves, making sure the pricing was right.

It seems strange, but it really gives you a sense of how the products look on the shelves, how they end up there, and what people see. Then you can better understand where things get defective, and therefore you understand that you need to use new material or package the product differently. Actually, L'Oreal's one of the few companies that internally handles its store displays. We have our own department who is responsible for this and they do a fantastic job.

Vault: What happened after you finished that period?

Liberbolm: Then we had training for about a month. We met with all the different function groups, and there were people who came in to explain how the products actually work, why they affect the skin the way they do, for example.

We did one week in New Jersey staying in a hotel, where we toured the plants. Then we were back in New York talking with the different functional areas. It was great exposure to the company at large.

Visit Vault at **www.vault.com** for insider company profiles, expert advice, career message boards, expert resume reviews, the Vault Job Board and more.

V\ULT CAREER LIBRARY

83

Vault: What is your understanding of the career path from here?

Liberbolm: The next move is to Brand Manager. Many times you do work with a specific brand for a year or two and then you move to another brand or category. Usually they move you to a new brand where you can hone a new skill set. You keep honing the different skills that are necessary to run a company.

Also, there's international mobility – they are definitely big on providing you with international experience if you want it after several years. I think that's something that's really compelling.

One of the things that I feel is really unique about L'Oreal Paris is the constant exposure with senior management – the President, the SVP of Marketing, etc. You get to see how they make significant decisions, which is really unique within a large organization. Just recently I had a presentation to the President of L'Oreal Paris about what our plans for 2006 will be for Feria. It is a terrific experience to hear feedback and learn from an accomplished person.

Employer Directory

Campbell Soup Company

1 Campbell Place
Box 35D
Camden, NJ 08103
Recruiting Contact Phone: 856-342-4800
careers.campbellsoupcompany.com

At Campbell we have an unwavering commitment to Our Mission, "Together We Will Build The World's Most Extraordinary Food Company" and Our Vision, "Nourishing People's Lives, Everywhere, Every Day." Our Mission and Our Vision are supported by an integrated framework that clearly defines how we pursue quality growth in the workplace and the marketplace.

We empower our people to do their best. We're committed to building and strengthening teams, providing the right resources, celebrating successes, rewarding excellence and creating a thriving work environment. We believe extraordinary things are achieved by people who are determined to leave a legacy that is second-to-none.

Business schools Campbell recruits from

Wharton (Penn); Cornell; University of North Carolina (Kenan Flagler); University of Michigan (Ross); Darden (UVA); Carnegie Mellon (Tepper); University of Maryland (Smith)

Honeywell International

101 Columbia Road
Morristown, New Jersey 07962
Phone: (973) 455-2000
www.honeywell.com\careers

Honeywell International is a $23 billion diversified technology and manufacturing leader, serving customers worldwide with aerospace products and services; control technologies for buildings, homes and industry; automotive products; turbochargers; specialty chemicals; fibers; and electronic and advanced materials. Based in Morris Township, N.J., Honeywell's shares are traded on the New York, London, Chicago and Pacific Stock Exchanges. It is one of the 30 stocks that make up the Dow Jones Industrial Average and is also a component of the Standard & Poor's 500 Index.

Business schools Honeywell recruits from

University of Arizona; Arizona State University; Brigham Young University; Carnegie Mellon University; Columbia; Cornell; Emory; Georgia Tech; University of Illinois; University of Maryland; University of Michigan; Michigan State; University of Minnesota; Massachusetts Institute of Technology; Northwestern; Notre Dame; Ohio State; Penn State; Purdue University; University of Tennessee; Thunderbird; UCLA; USC; Vanderbilt; University of Virginia;

Visit Vault at **www.vault.com** for insider company profiles, expert advice, career message boards, expert resume reviews, the Vault Job Board and more.

 VAULT CAREER LIBRARY   **85**

L'Oréal USA

575 Fifth Avenue
New York, New York 10017
Phone: 212-818-1500
lorealusa.com

The L'Oréal USA Management Development Program is designed for graduating MBA's who want to pursue a career in Marketing. This rotational program is designed to give you the opportunity to gain exposure and hone your skills through hands-on assignments. It puts a strong emphasis on professional development through formal training held at our Management Development Center and individual check-points with members of the HR community.

L'Oréal USA offers a formal internship program consisting of three main elements (1) The day to day functional job assignment (2) A business related project to be completed and presented to management (3) Educational and Professional Development sessions.

Business schools L'Oreal recruits from:

University of California Berkeley (Haas); Clark Atlanta; Cornell (Johnson); Harvard Business School; Northwestern (Kellogg); NYU (Stern); Columbia Business School; Georgetown; Stanford (Thunderbird (Garvin); University of Michigan; University of Pennsylvania (Wharton).

We do, however, consider students from all MBA programs and students from schools where we don't have a presence should apply on-line. Go to lorealusa.com/careers

Miller Brewing Company

3939 W. Highland Blvd.
P.O. Box 482
Milwaukee, WI 53201
www.millerbrewing.com

Founded in 1855 in Milwaukee, Wisconsin, Miller Brewing Company has over 150 years of history in producing fine, high quality - award winning - beer. With six major breweries and a portfolio of beer brands, Miller is one of America's major brewers. Miller Brewing Company is a subsidiary of SABMiller plc, one of the world's largest brewers, with brewing presence in over 40 countries.

People are a competitive advantage. While many companies say it, we mean it! If you want to make great beer your business, take your career to the next level, be rewarded for your results...join the Miller Team.

Business schools Miller recruits from

Duke (Fuqua); Indiana University (Kelley); University of Michigan (Ross); University of Texas-Austin (McCombs); Northwestern (Kellogg); University of Wisconsin-Madison; University of Pennsylvania (Wharton)

Procter & Gamble

PO Box 599
Cincinnati, OH 45201
Phone: 1-888-486-7691
E-mail: careers.im@pg.com
www.usjobs.pg.com

Two billion times a day, P&G brands touch the lives of people around the world. We have one of the largest and strongest portfolios of trusted, quality brands, including Pampers, Tide, Ariel, Always, Whisper, Pantene, Bounty, Pringles, Folgers, Charmin, Downy, Lenor, Iams, Crest, Clairol Nice'n Easy, Actonel, Dawn and Olay. Nearly 98,000 P&G people working in almost 80 countries worldwide make sure P&G brands live up to their promise to make everyday life just a little better.

Business schools Procter & Gamble recruits from

Because we do web-based recruiting, students from any MBA program can apply for U.S. jobs at Procter & Gamble. See our website for a listing of schools where we have "in person" campus presence.

Roche Diagnostics

9115 Hague Road
Indianapolis, Indiana 462520
careers.ind.roche.com
www.roche.com

Roche Diagnostics is the world's leading provider of diagnostic systems and decision-oriented health information. We are dedicated to the discovery, development, manufacturing, marketing and servicing of products and solutions for medical laboratories, physicians and patients, as well as for research and industry. Roche Diagnostics is a diverse, inclusive company that seeks, celebrates and leverages diversity to maximize the competitive advantage of people. We offer a variety of opportunities at our U.S. diagnostics marketing and sales headquarters in Indiana and at our global molecular business area headquarters in California.

Business schools Roche Diagnostics recruits from

University of Chicago; Northwestern (Kellogg); Indiana University (Kelley); Harvard Business School, Duke University (Fuqua); U.C.L.A.; University of Michigan; Purdue University; MIT (Sloan); University of Pennsylvania (Wharton); Yale University, Stanford University; UC Berkeley (Haas); Washington University (Olin)

Sodexho

200 Continental Drive,
Suite 400
Newark, DE 19713
Phone: 302 738-9500 ext 5209
John.lee@sodexhousa.com
www.sodexhousa.com

Sodexho is the leading provider of food and facilities management in the U.S. and Canada, with $4.9 billion in annual sales. Sodexho offers innovative outsourcing solutions in food service, housekeeping, grounds keeping, plant operations and maintenance, asset and materials management and laundry services to corporations, health care and long term care facilities, retirements centers, schools, college campuses, military and remote sites. Headquartered in Gaithersburg, MD, the company has more than 100,000 employees in 50 states and Canada.

Visit Vault at **www.vault.com** for insider company profiles, expert advice,
career message boards, expert resume reviews, the Vault Job Board and more.

VAULT CAREER LIBRARY

87

3M Company
3M Center
St. Paul, MN 55144
Phone: 651-733-1110
Fax: 651-736-2133
www.mmm.com

Alberto-Culver Company
2525 Armitage Ave.
Melrose Park, IL 60160
Phone: (708) 450-3000
Fax: (708) 450-3354
www.alberto.com

Altria Group Inc.
120 Park Avenue
New York, NY 10017
Phone: (917) 663-5000
Fax: (917) 663-2167
www.altria.com

Anheuser-Busch Companies, Inc.
1 Busch Place
St. Louis, MO 63118
Phone: (314) 577-2000
Fax: (314) 577-2900
www.anheuser-busch.com

Avon Products, Inc.
1345 Avenue of the Americas
New York, NY 10105-0196
Phone: (212) 282-5000
Fax: (212) 282-6049
www.avoncompany.com

Black & Decker
701 E. Joppa Road
Towson, MD 21286
Phone: (410) 716-3900
Fax: (410) 716-2933
www.bdk.com

Bose Corp.
The Mountain
Framingham, MA 01701
Phone: (508) 879-7330
Fax: (508) 766-7543
www.bose.com

Campbell Soup Company
1 Campbell Place
Camden, NJ 08103-1799
Phone: (856) 342-4800
Fax: (856) 342-3878
www.campbellsoup.com

Canon U.S.A., Inc.
1 Canon Plaza
Lake Success, NY 11042
Phone: (516) 328-5000
Fax: (516) 328-5069
www.usa.canon.com

Clorox Company
1221 Broadway
Oakland, CA 94612-1888
Phone: (510) 271-7000
Fax: (510) 832-1463
www.clorox.com

Coca-Cola Company, The
1 Coca-Cola Plaza
Atlanta, GA 30313-2499
Phone: (404) 676-2121
Fax: (404) 676-6792
www.cocacola.com

Colgate-Palmolive
300 Park Avenue
New York, NY 10022
Phone: (212) 310-2000
Fax: (212) 310-2475
www.colgate.com

ConAgra Foods Inc.
1 ConAgra Drive
Omaha, Nebraska 68102
Phone: (402) 595-4000
Fax: (402) 595-4707
www.conagra.com

Dial Corporation
15501 N. Dial Blvd.
Scottsdale, AZ 85260-1619
Phone: (480) 754-3425
Fax: (480) 754-1098
www.dialcorp.com

Dole Food Company, Inc.
1 Dole Drive
Westlake Village, CA 91362
Phone: (818) 879-6600
Fax: (818) 879-6615
www.dole.com

Eastman Kodak Company
343 State Street
Rochester, NY 14650
Phone: (585) 724-4000
www.kodak.com

The Estée Lauder Companies
767 Fifth Avenue
New York, NY 10153
Phone: (212) 572-4200
Fax: (212) 572-6633
www.elcompanies.com

General Mills
1 General Mills Blvd.
Minneapolis, MN 55426
Phone: (763) 764-7600
Fax: (763) 764-7384
www.generalmills.com

The Gillette Company
Prudential Tower Building
Boston, MA 02199
Phone: (617) 421-7000
Fax: (617) 421-7123
www.gillette.com

The Goodyear Tire & Rubber Company
1144 E. Market Street
Akron, OH 44316-0001
Phone: (330) 796-2121
Fax: (330) 796-2222
www.goodyear.com

Hallmark Cards, Inc.
2501 McGee Street
Kansas City, MO 64108
Phone: (816) 274-5111
Fax: (816) 274-5061
www.hallmark.com

Hasbro, Inc.
1027 Newport Avenue
Pawtucket, RI 02862
Phone: (401) 431-8697
Fax: (401) 431-8535
www.hasbro.com

Hershey Foods, Inc.
100 Crystal A Drive
Hershey, PA 17033
Phone: (717) 534-6799
Fax: (717) 534-6760
www.hersheys.com

HJ Heinz
600 Grant St.
Pittsburgh, PA 15219
Phone: (412) 456-5700
Fax: (412) 456-6128
www.heinz.com

Hormel Foods
One Hormel Place
Austin, MN 55912-3680
Phone: (507) 437-5611
Fax: (507) 437-5129
www.hormel.com

Johnson & Johnson
1 Johnson & Johnson Plaza
New Brunswick, NJ 08933
Phone: (732) 524-0400
Fax: (732) 524-3300
www.jnj.com

Kimberly-Clark Corporation
351 Phelps Drive
Irving, TX 75038
Phone: (972) 281-1200
Fax: (972) 281-1490
www.kimberly-clark.com

Kraft Foods Inc.
Three Lakes Drive
Northfield, IL 60093
Phone: (847) 646-2000
Fax: (847) 646-6005
www.kraft.com

Land O'Lakes
4001 Lexington Avenue North
Arden Hills, MN 55126
Phone: (651) 481-2222
Fax: (651) 481-2000
www.landolakesinc.com

Liz Claiborne, Inc.
1441 Broadway
New York, NY 10018
Phone: (212) 354-4900
Fax: (212) 626-3416
www.lizclaiborne.com

L'Oréal SA
41, rue Martre
92117 Clichy, France
Phone: +33-1-47-56-70-00
Fax: +33-1-47-56-80-02
www.loreal.com

LVMH Moët Hennessy Louis Vuitton SA
22 avenue Montaigne
75008 Paris, France
Phone: +33-1-44-13-22-22
Fax: +33-1-44-13-21-19
www.lvmh.com

Mary Kay, Inc.
16251 Dallas Parkway
Addison, TX 75001
Phone: (972) 687-6300
Fax: (972) 687-1611
www.marykay.com

Mattel, Inc.
333 Continental Blvd.
El Segundo, CA 90245-5012
Phone: (310) 252-2000
Fax: (310) 252-2180
www.mattel.com

Molson Coors Brewing Company
311 10th Street
Golden, CO 80401-0030
Phone: (303) 279-6565
Fax: (303) 277-6246
www.molsoncoors.com

Nestlé USA
800 N. Brand Blvd.
Glendale, CA 91203
Phone: (818) 549-6000
Fax: (818) 549-6952
www.nestleusa.com

Newell Rubbermaid Inc.
10 B Glenlake Pkwy., Suite 600
Atlanta, GA 30328
Phone: (770) 407-3800
Fax: (770) 407-3970
www.newellrubbermaid.com

NIKE, Inc.
1 Bowerman Drive
Beaverton, OR 97005-6453
Phone: (503) 671-6453
Fax: (503) 671-6300
www.nike.com

PepsiCo, Inc.
700 Anderson Hill Rd
Purchase, NY 10577-1444
Phone: (914) 253-2000
Fax: (914) 253-2070
www.pepsico.com

Procter & Gamble
1 Procter & Gamble Plaza
Cincinnati, OH 45202
Phone: (513) 983-1100
Fax: (513) 983-9369
www.pg.com

Revlon, Inc.
237 Park Avenue
New York, NY 10017
Phone: (212) 527-4000
Fax: (212) 527-4995
www.revloninc.com

Sara Lee Corporation
3 First National Plaza
Chicago, IL 60602-4260
Phone: (312) 726-2600
Fax: (312) 726-3712
www.saralee.com

Visit Vault at **www.vault.com** for insider company profiles, expert advice,
career message boards, expert resume reviews, the Vault Job Board and more.

V/AULT CAREER LIBRARY   89

S.C. Johnson & Son, Inc.
1525 Howe Street
Racine, WI 53403-5011
Phone: (262) 260-2000
Fax: (262) 260-6004
www.scjohnson.com

Smithfield Foods
200 Commerce Street
Smithfield, VA 23430
Phone: (757) 365-3000
Fax: (757) 365-3017
www.smithfieldfoods.com/home.asp

Sony Corporation
7-35, Kitashinagawa, 6-chome,
Shinagawa-ku
Tokyo, 141-0001, Japan
Phone: +81-3-5448-2111
Fax: +81-3-5448-2244
www.sony.net

Stanley Works
1000 Stanley Dr.
New Britain, CT 06053
Phone: (860) 225-5111
Fax: (860) 827-3987
www.stanleyworks.com

Unilever
Unilever House
Blackfriars
London, UK EC4P 4BQ
United Kingdom
Phone: +44-20-7822-5252
Fax: +44-20-7822-6191
www.unilever.com

Whirlpool Corporation
2000 N. M-63
Benton Harbor, MI 49022-2692
Phone: (269) 923-5000
Fax: (269) 923-5443
www.whirlpoolcorp.com

Energy/Oil and Gas

What is the Energy Sector?

The energy sector produces, converts and distributes fuels to produce heat, light and propulsion. Oil, natural gas, and coal are burned to make heat and electricity. Wind, flowing water, and sunlight are converted into electricity. Oil is refined to propel cars, planes, and industrial machines. And to achieve these things, the companies who are producing, transporting, converting and distributing these energy sources are supported by a variety of service firms, investors, equipment providers, and government regulators.

There is a great divide in the energy sector between the oil and gas "side" and the electricity "side," each of which accounts for about half of the business jobs across the sector. "Oil and gas" refers to the exploration for and extraction and processing of oil and natural gas. In contrast, the electric power business revolves around converting fuel to electricity in power plants and distributing that electricity to consumers. The economics of the two fields, and the regulations that govern them, are quite distinct. Generally, people make their energy careers in one camp or the other, without too much crossover. Natural gas is one arena that bridges the oil & gas versus electricity divide – it is extracted from the earth together with oil, and is also a primary fuel for generating electricity.

When people refer to the "energy sector," they can actually mean any of the following: electric power, oil & gas, or both together. This guide takes a broad view of the industry, covering upstream (exploration), midstream (refining) and downstream (distribution and sales) oil and gas activities, electric power generation and transmission, equipment manufacturing, regulatory oversight, and lending to, investing in, and advising companies involved in the sector.

Just how big is the industry that comprises all those diverse activities? Companies in the energy sector take in nearly $1 trillion in revenue annually, out of the $17 trillion earned by all U.S. businesses. Energy-related businesses employ about 2.5 million people, or 2% of the U.S. workforce – far more than banking, high tech or telecommunications. Energy companies as a whole employ a high percentage of production workers (the people who drive local utility repair trucks, laborers on oil rigs, and gas station attendants), compared to other industries; of the 2.5 million energy jobs in the U.S., about 90% of them are blue-collar jobs or technical positions. The subject of this guidebook is the one-quarter-million energy-related business jobs out there: the business analysts, finance associates, marketing managers, economic modelers, and operations consultants, to name a few roles.

Energy sector positions capture about 2% of new MBA graduates, an amount roughly proportional to the industry's size. In contrast, the investment banking and investment management sectors together capture 40% of graduates, and consulting absorbs another 20%. Even the significantly smaller high tech industry takes on 3 times the number of new MBAs as does the energy sector. What this means for you as a job seeker is that the energy sector is not as dominated by people with graduate business degrees as some other popular arenas. There is plenty of opportunity for smart, well-trained college graduates to rise through the ranks without going back to school.

Sector	US employees in managerial, business or financial positions
Pharmaceuticals and biotechnology	50,000
Telecommunications	140,000
High technology	200,000
Banking and investment management	250,000
Energy	*250,000*
Consulting	500,000
Entire economy	11,500,000

Visit Vault at **www.vault.com** for insider company profiles, expert advice, career message boards, expert resume reviews, the Vault Job Board and more.

VAULT CAREER LIBRARY

91

Which Job Function?

In order to pursue a job in the energy sector, your first decision is what type of position you want – in other words, what functional role you want to play. Your function has a lot more impact on the nature of your job than does the type of company in which you work.

You can have a wide variety of business jobs in the energy sector:

- Asset development
- Corporate finance
- Quantitative analytics, risk management
- Trading, energy marketing
- Investment analysis
- Consulting
- Business development
- Banking
- Strategy and planning
- Economics and policy analysis

Different companies can have widely varying names by which they refer to these roles. For example, "marketing" in one company involves advertising and product promotion, whereas "marketing" in another can mean commodities trading. Similarly, "business development" can be more akin to sales in one company, or synonymous with strategic planning in another.

What Type of Company?

Job functions and company types intersect in numerous ways – for example, you can do corporate finance in a large oil company or with a small fuel cell manufacturer, or choose between asset development and trading within a given utility. Below, we have summarized the characteristics of each of the major energy sector employer types:

Oil companies

Oil companies engage in exploration and production of oil ("upstream" activities), oil transportation and refining ("midstream"), and petroleum product wholesale and retail distribution ("downstream"). The largest companies, known as the "majors," are vertically integrated, with business operations along the entire spectrum from exploration to gas stations. Smaller oil companies, known as "independents," are often exclusively involved in exploration and production. Upstream is considered the glamorous place to be, where all the big decisions are made. Upstream jobs also involve heavy international work, with many employees sent off to new postings around the world every 3 years or so. We should also note that E&P businesses are fairly similar in nature among oil companies and companies mining other natural resources like uranium or coal – moving among these types of firms during a career can be a logical path.

The majors are known for excellent rotational training programs, and a fair number of people take advantage of those programs and then jump over to independents for good salaries. Oil companies pay well in general, but jobs are not necessarily as stable as one might think. When oil prices drop, company operating profits are dramatically impacted, and layoffs are fairly common. American oil jobs are overwhelmingly concentrated in Houston. International hot spots include London, Calgary, and the Middle East.

Some oil companies focus exclusively on midstream and downstream activities. They operate refineries to distill crude oil into its many commercially useful petroleum derivatives, like gasoline, jet fuel, solvents, and asphalt. Refineries are, in theory, built to last 40 years, but some have been around for as long as 80 years. That means that new refineries are rarely built, and the refinery business is mostly about managing the razor-thin margins between purchased crude oil inputs and revenues from refined product outputs.

Oil services companies

Oil services companies provide a very wide range of outsourced operational support to oil companies, such as owning and renting out oil rigs, conducting seismic testing, and transporting equipment. The fortunes of these companies follow the price of oil: when oil is expensive, oil companies drill a lot and make a lot of money, so business volume and revenue increase for their oil services contractors. Working for an oil services company probably means working in Texas or internationally, and can feel very much like working for an oil company, given the similarity in issues and activities.

Pipeline operators

Pipeline operators own and manage tens of thousands of miles of petroleum products and natural gas pipelines. Many of them also operate oil intake terminals, engage in commodities trading and energy marketing, and own natural gas storage facilities or petroleum refineries as well. Unlike the major oil companies, pipeline operation companies are not household names – nonetheless, the largest ones take in several billion in annual revenue, comparable to the scale of a medium-sized oil company.

Utilities

Utilities are, by definition, located all over the country..everyone has to get their electricity and gas from somewhere, of course. However, as a result of massive consolidation among utility holding companies, the corporate offices for your local utility may not necessarily be that local. There are presently about 50 investor-owned utilities in the country, but industry insiders predict that in a few years mergers may leave us with as few as 10. The "graying" of the utility industry is a well-documented trend; 60% of current utility employees are expected to retire by 2015 – meaning there's lots of opportunity today for young job seekers.

"Utility" is actually a loose term that we use to succinctly refer to gas utilities and all types of power generation companies: investor-owned utilities, government-owned utilities, municipal power companies, rural electric co-ops, and independent power producers (IPPs) or non-utility generators (NUGs). Utilities differ greatly in terms of their lines of business: some have sold off most of their generation assets and are primarily distribution companies with power lines as their primary assets; others may own large amounts of regulated power plants, and may also own non-utility generators or individual independent power plants. As the electricity market fell apart starting in 2001, most IPPs sold off their assets piecemeal to large utility holding companies or financial institutions.

Transmission grid operators

Transmission grid operators, known as Independent System Operators (ISO) or Regional Transmission Operators (RTO), provide a power generation dispatch function to a regional electricity market. They don't own the transmission lines, but coordinate how much power is generated when and where, such that supply and demand are equal at every moment. This is an extremely complex process, and necessitates the analytical skills of electrical engineers and other generally quantitative and analytical operations staff.

Visit Vault at **www.vault.com** for insider company profiles, expert advice, career message boards, expert resume reviews, the Vault Job Board and more.

V/\ULT CAREER LIBRARY   93

Equipment manufacturers

Equipment manufacturers make turbines, boilers, compressors, pollution control devices, well drilling and pipeline construction equipment, software control systems, pumps, and industrial batteries. Many of them also provide engineering services and construction/installation of their equipment. The major gas turbine manufacturers, for example, also offer engineering, procurement and construction of entire power plants. Oil-related equipment makers are often characterized as "oil services" firms (above). The equipment manufacturers in the energy industry are not particularly concentrated in one geographic area, though of course many of the oil business-oriented ones have major offices in Texas.

Investment funds

Investment funds are a diverse bunch: mutual funds, private equity funds, and hedge funds. As a whole, the investment fund world is fairly concentrated in Boston, New York and San Francisco, but there are small funds dotted all over the country as well.

Mutual funds hire stock analysts primarily out of MBA programs to track, value, and recommend stocks in a particular sector (e.g. energy, natural resources, consumer products) to the fund managers. However, there are a lot of other finance-related positions inside these massive firms where undergrads are sought after as well.

The number of hedge funds in the U.S. has been growing at a phenomenal rate in the past few years, but they are still notoriously difficult places to get jobs. Hedge funds often hire people out of investment banking analyst programs. They tend to not hire people out of the mutual fund world, given that their valuation approach is so different, their investing horizon is so much shorter, and their orientation many times is towards short-selling as well as buying stocks. While some hedge funds may focus exclusively on energy, most are generalist and opportunistic with respect to their target sectors.

Private equity funds invest money in private (i.e. not publicly traded) companies, often also obtaining operating influence through a seat on the portfolio company's board of directors. As a result, an analyst's work at a private equity fund is vastly different from that at a mutual fund or hedge fund. You are not following the stock market or incorporating market perception issues into your valuations and recommendations; instead, you are taking a hard look at specific operating issues, identifying concrete areas where the portfolio company can lower costs or enhance revenue. A few private equity firms specialize in energy investing, and many more do occasional deals in the energy space as part of a broader technology or manufacturing focus. Private equity firms hire just a few people straight out of college or MBA programs, and many others from the ranks of investment banking alumni.

Banks

Banks are primarily involved in lending money to companies, but they also have their own trading operations, private wealth management, and investment analysis groups. Commercial and investment banks arrange for loans to energy companies, as well as syndicate loans (i.e. find other people to lend the money) for them. Investment banks manage IPOs and mergers and acquisitions (M&A) activities as well. The banking world is overwhelmingly centered in New York (and London), with some smaller branches in Chicago and San Francisco.

Consulting firms

Consulting firms offer rich opportunities for those interested in the energy industry. Consulting on business issues (rather than information technology or technical, scientific issues) is done at three types of firms: management consultancies, risk consulting groups, and economic consulting shops. Consulting firms are often interested in hiring people with good functional skills rather than requiring specific industry expertise, and provide a broad exposure to energy sector business issues.

as well as good training. Business consulting firm offices are located in most major cities, but much of the energy sector staff may be located in Houston, Washington D.C., and New York.

Nonprofit groups

Nonprofit groups are tax-exempt corporations (pursuant to IRS code 501(c)3) engaged in issue advocacy or public interest research. Advocacy groups may focus on developing grassroots support for public policy changes, publicizing public interest issues or problems through direct actions, or working to influence politicians to enact or change legislation. Most of the energy-related advocacy groups focus on environmental topics, though some also cover corporate financial responsibility and investor protection issues. Think tanks are public policy research institutes, staffed mainly by PhDs who generate research and opinion papers to inform the public, policy-makers and media on current issues. Interestingly, the think tank is primarily a U.S. phenomenon, although the concept is slowly catching on in other countries. Some think tanks are independent and nonpartisan, whereas some take on an explicit advocacy role. Nonprofits are funded by individual donations and grants from foundations, and accordingly a substantial portion of their staffs are dedicated to fundraising. Most energy nonprofits are based in Washington, D.C., where they have access to the federal political process, but many of them have small regional offices or grassroots workers spread out across the country.

Government agencies

Government agencies at the federal and state levels regulate the energy markets and define public energy and environmental policy. Federal agencies are mostly located in Washington D.C., and each state has staff in the state capital. Jobs can include policy analysis, research project management, or management of subcontractors. The energy agencies tend to hire people with environmental or engineering backgrounds, and are lately following a policy of hiring people with general business and management education and experience.

Energy services firms

Energy services firms help companies (in any sector) reduce their energy costs. Working for an energy services firm is similar in many respects to consulting-except that you go much further down the path of implementation. Typically, an energy services firm first conducts an energy audit to understand where a company spends money on energy: electricity, heat, and industrial processes. Then, the firm actually implements energy-saving measures "inside the fence" of the client company. This can involve investments and activities such as putting lightbulbs on motion sensors, upgrading the HVAC (heating, ventilation, air conditioning) system, negotiating better rates with the utility suppliers, or developing a cogeneration power plant adjacent to the factory. Often, the energy services firm receives payment for these services in the form of a share in the net energy cost savings to the client. These firms are located across the country, with a few of the largest clustered in Boston.

Visit Vault at **www.vault.com** for insider company profiles, expert advice, career message boards, expert resume reviews, the Vault Job Board and more.

VAULT CAREER LIBRARY   95

Job Function	Possible Employer Types
Asset Development	Utility; Oil Company; Pipeline Operator; Energy Services Firm
Corporate Finance	Utility; Pipeline Operator; Oil Company; Equipment Manufacturer
Quantitative Analytics, Risk Management	Utility; Oil Company; Transmission Grid Operator; Pipeline Operator; Investment Fund; Bank
Trading, Energy Marketing	Utility; Oil Company; Pipeline Operator; Investment Fund; Bank
Investment Analysis	Investment Fund; Bank
Consulting	Consulting Firm; Oil Services Company
Business Development	Equipment Manufacturer; Utility; Oil Services Company; Pipeline Operator; Energy Services Firm
Banking	Bank
Strategy and Planning	Utility; Oil Company; Pipeline Operator; Oil Services Company; Equipment Manufacturer
Economic and Policy Analysis	Government Agency; Nonprofit Group; Consulting Firm

Who Gets Hired?

As in other technology-intensive sectors, the energy sector is populated by a disproportionate number of people with technical degrees, i.e. BS, MS, or PhD in engineering, hard sciences, and math. Whether it's true or not, traditional energy company employers often feel that success in a job correlates to having a certain degree. This pickiness about your undergraduate major or master's degree field gets even stronger during economic downturns, when companies act more conservatively and have more bargaining power in terms of new hires.

In many energy jobs, the prevalence of people with technical pedigrees is somewhat a function of self-selection: individuals interested enough in the energy sector to make it their career were usually also interested enough in related topics to focus on them academically. On top of that, the prevalence of technical people is also self-reinforcing; in other words, engineers like to hire other engineers. There is also arguably an element of reality underpinning the preference for people with certain academic backgrounds – engineers communicate best with other engineers, and have proven in school that they can learn the ins and outs of a complex subject area.

This tendency is most characteristic of hiring preferences among oil companies, oil services firms, refineries, pipelines, grid operators, equipment manufacturers, energy services companies, and utilities. These firms want to hire people who have their heads around how their technologies work – people who can master the jargon quickly, and who can fit into their culture. Even for their MBA hires, these companies often look for technical undergraduate degrees or pre-MBA work in energy or another technical field.

However, there are certainly many people with liberal arts backgrounds doing great work at these types of companies. A non-technical degree does not in any way shut you out of any energy sector career path; it simply makes you slightly more unusual in the eyes of some interviewers. If you can craft a compelling story about why you are passionate about and deeply understand the energy world, your degree becomes far less relevant. In addition, if you are applying for a finance, economics or accounting job with a degree in those fields, you are also less subject to scrutiny about your knowledge of geology, electrical engineering, or chemistry. Once you have a couple years of experience in the industry, that serves as a degree equivalent and you will have established your credibility.

Many of the service jobs in energy are interested in simply hiring smart people who demonstrate an ability to learn a new industry quickly. Energy consulting, banking, and investing jobs often screen for nothing different than their counterparts in other industries. Similarly, the newer, alternative energy companies are often heavily filled with people who studied liberal arts, economics, and government in college. These companies are progressive in terms of their business strategies, and usually this comes across in their approach to hiring as well. In addition, nonprofits typically first look for passion and commitment to advocacy work before they look for technical background.

Apart from academic background, traditional energy employers are also keenly interested in people who have a strong connection to the geographic region in which the company is located. These companies like to hire for the long term, so will often grill out-of-state candidates about why they would want to move to, for example, Houston or Atlanta. This can mean that, for a Houston oil company position, an MBA from Rice is a more attractive candidate than one from Wharton.

In fact, the energy sector offers particularly rich opportunities for students from second-tier undergraduate and graduate schools. Energy companies know that their industry is not typically considered as hot and glamorous as some other industries, and they can therefore often be skeptical about recruiting from name-brand undergraduate and graduate schools. The bottom line is that energy, as an industry, is simply less hung up on name-brand schools than some other industries, i.e. consulting, law and banking.

Moreover, during the past few years of our sluggish economy, many traditional energy companies tightened their recruiting budgets and reduced focus on first-tier schools – at the same time as service companies like consulting and banking firms reacted to a slow economy by canceling recruiting at second-tier schools and concentrating on only a limited set of top schools. Of course, those in the know are well aware that the energy sector is one of the most intellectually challenging, influential arenas in which to work! If you want to work in the sector, you can certainly seek out the energy employers, regardless of whether they visit your campus or target people from your alma mater.

In general, the best time to jump into the energy sector is right out of undergraduate or graduate (MA/MS, MBA or PhD) school. Like most employers, energy companies expect less in the way of industry experience from people who have just graduated, so it's a good time to get your foot in the door of a new field. Lateral hires of people a few years out of college or post-MBA are relatively rare, unless you have some specific industry background or functional experience a company needs. For example, a pipeline company might realistically hire someone with a couple years of general banking experience into a corporate finance role, but would be very unlikely to hire someone with a couple years of, say, real estate experience into that same role – so if you had just graduated and never spent those couple of years in real estate, you'd have a better shot at the job.

This reluctance to hire laterally from other industries is far less common in the services sector (consulting, banking, investing, nonprofits). These employers are more interested in functional knowledge and pure brainpower, rather than a track record in one particular industry or another (though they have their own intransigence about hiring people laterally from other functional areas, i.e. it's awfully hard to get into consulting or banking if you don't do so your first year out of school). As a result, these jobs are an excellent way to get into the energy sector, and offer lots of options down the road – in other words, for example, it's relatively easy to go from an energy consulting role into a corporate job at other energy firms.

One caveat for those who move from one firm to another to position themselves for a future job: traditional energy employers like stability. If you have a lot of different jobs on your resume, you should make sure to have a good story to explain the necessity of your job-hopping, and why you are long-term play for the company (whether you truly are or not). This is true when interviewing with any firm, but large, traditional energy firms are certainly more sensitive to the issue.

Visit Vault at www.vault.com for insider company profiles, expert advice, career message boards, expert resume reviews, the Vault Job Board and more.

VAULT CAREER LIBRARY   97

Employer Directory

Chevron Corporation

6001 Bollinger Canyon Rd
San Ramon, CA 94583
Phone: (925) 842-1000
Finance MBA Development Program: fmbadp@chevron.com
Marketing MBA Development Program: OrgCapab@chevron.com
HR Development Program: HRDEVPROG@Chevron.com
www.chevron.com

Chevron is the second largest US energy company and one of the largest in the world. We operate in more than 180 countries and develop vital energy resources worldwide. Integral to everything we do is our commitment to valuing the talent of each individual, harnessing the strengths of a diverse work force, and respecting and learning from the communities in which we operate. The people of Chevron are committed to partnership as a key building block of the company's overall performance. Our success demands the highest standards of social, economic and environmental responsibility across our operations worldwide. We take pride in producing safe, reliable and affordable energy, knowing that it is critical for economic development, and helping to improve the standard of living around the world.

Business schools Chevron recruits from

Finance: University of Michigan (Ross); University of Chicago (GSB); Northwestern (Kellogg); University of Texas (McCombs); Penn (Wharton); Cornell University (Johnson); University of California (Haas); University of California (Andersen); University of Southern California (Marshall); University of Rochester (Simon); and others

Marketing: University of North Carolina (Duke); University of Texas (McCombs); University of California (Haas); University of California (Andersen); University of Southern California (Marshall); Dartmouth (Tuck); and others

HR: Michigan State, University of Minnesota; and others

Alliant Energy Corporation
4902 North Biltmore Lane
Madison, WI 53718
Phone: (800) 255-4268
www.alliantenergy.com

Amerada Hess Corporation
1185 Avenue of the Americas
New York, NY 10036
Phone: (212) 997-8500
Fax: (212) 536-8593
www.hess.com

American Electric Power Company, Inc.
1 Riverside Plaza
Columbus, OH 43215-2372
Phone: (614) 716-1000
Fax: (614) 716-1823
www.aep.com

Anadarko Petroleum Corporation
1201 Lake Robbins Dr.
The Woodlands, TX 77380-1046
Phone: (832) 636-1000
Fax: (832) 636-8220
www.anadarko.com

Baker Hughes Incorporated
3900 Essex Ln., Ste. 1200
Houston, TX 77027-5177
Phone: (713) 439-8600
Fax: (713) 439-8699
Toll Free: (888) 408-4244
www.bakerhughes.com

BP p.l.c.
1 St James's Square
London SW1Y 4PD
United Kingdom
Phone: +44 (0)20 7496 4000
Fax: +44 (0)20 7496 4630
www.bp.com

ChevronTexaco Corp.
6001 Bollinger Canyon Road
San Ramon, CA 94583
Phone: (925) 842-1000
Fax: (925) 842-3530
www.chevrontexaco.com

ConocoPhillips Company
600 N. Dairy Ashford
Houston, TX 77079
Phone: (281) 293-1000
Fax: (281) 293-1440
www.conocophillips.com

Consolidated Edison, Inc.
4 Irving Place
New York, NY 10003
Phone: (212) 460-4600
Fax: (212) 982-7816
www.conedison.com

Duke Energy Corporation
526 S. Church St
Charlotte, NC 28202
Phone: (704) 594-6200
Fax: (704) 382-3814
www.duke-energy.com

Eaton Corporation
Eaton Center
1111 Superior Ave.
Cleveland, OH 44114-2584
Phone: (216) 523-5000
Fax: (216) 523-4787
www.eaton.com

Edison International
2244 Walnut Grove Ave.
Rosemead, CA 91770
Phone: (626) 302-1212
Fax: (626) 302-2517
www.edison.com

Exelon Corporation
10 S. Dearborn St., 37th Floor
Chicago, IL 60680-5379
Phone: (312) 394-7398
Fax: (312) 394-7945
www.exeloncorp.com

Exxon Mobil Corporation
5959 Las Colinas Blvd.
Irving, TX 75039-2298
Phone: (972) 444-1000
Fax: (972) 444-1350
www.exxonmobil.com

FirstEnergy Corp.
76 S. Main St.
Akron, OH 44308
Phone: (800) 646-0400
Fax: (330) 84-3866
www.firstenergycorp.com

GE Energy
4200 Wildwood Parkway
Atlanta, GA 30339
Phone: (678) 844-6000
Fax: (678) 844-6690
www.gepower.com

Halliburton
5 Houston Center
1401 McKinney, Ste. 2400
Houston, TX 77020
Phone: (713) 759-2600
Fax: (713) 759-2635
www.halliburton.com

Marathon Oil Corporation
5555 San Felipe Rd.
Houston, TX 77056
Phone: (713) 629-6600
Fax: (713) 296-2952
www.marathon.com

Occidental Petroleum Corporation
10889 Wilshire Blvd.
Los Angeles, CA 90024
Phone: (310) 208-8800
Fax: (310) 443-6690
www.oxy.com

Pacific Gas and Electric Company
77 Beale Street
San Francisco, CA 94177
Phone: (415) 973 7000
Fax: (415) 267 7268
www.pge.com

Schlumberger Limited
153 E. 53rd St.
57th Floor
New York, NY 10172
Phone: (212) 350-9400
Fax: (212) 350-9457
www.slb.com

Shell Oil Company
One Shell Plaza
Houston, TX 77002
Phone: (713) 241-6161
Fax: (713) 241-4044
www.shellus.com

Sunoco, Inc.
10 Penn Center
1801 Market St.
Philadelphia, PA 19103
Phone: (215) 977-3000
Fax: (215) 977-3409
Toll Free: (800) 786-6261
www.sunocoinc.com

TXU Corp.
Energy Plaza, 1601 Bryan St.
Dallas, TX 75201-3411
Phone: (214) 812-4600
Fax: (214) 812-7077
www.txucorp.com

Unocal Corporation
2141 Rosencrans Avenue
Suite 4000
El Segundo, CA 90245
Phone: (310) 726-7600
Fax: (310) 726-7817
www.unocal.com

Valero Energy Corporation
One Valero Place
San Antonio, TX 78212-3186
Phone: (210) 370-2000
Fax: (210) 370-2646
www.valero.com

Williams Companies Inc., The
One Williams Center
Tulsa, OK 74172
Phone: (918) 573 2000
Fax: (918) 573 6714
www.williams.com

Visit Vault at **www.vault.com** for insider company profiles, expert advice,
career message boards, expert resume reviews, the Vault Job Board and more.

V\ULT CAREER LIBRARY   99

This section was excerpted from the *Vault Career Guide to the Energy Industry*. Get the inside scoop on energy industry careers with Vault:

- **Vault Guides:** *Vault Career Guide to the Energy Industry*, *Vault Guide to the Top Energy and Oil/Gas Employers*

- **Vault Employee Surveys:** Vault's exclusive employee surveys for ExxonMobil, BP, Halliburton and other top energy industry employers

- **Employer Research:** Company snapshots providing business descriptions and the latest news on top energy employers

- **Career Services:** Vault Resume and Cover Letter Reviews, rated the "Top Choice" by *The Wall Street Journal* for resume makeovers

Go to www.vault.com/energy

or ask your bookstore or librarian for other Vault titles.

Fashion

Fashion and the MBA

Like the entertainment industry, the fashion industry considers education to be less important than experience. So, if you want to go into the industry but don't have the previous experience, get a part-time job in sales or merchandising for an introduction to the industry. Unfortunately, most companies won't care much about your MBA unless it's a large corporation, such as Gap, Levi Strauss, Eddie Bauer, Limited or Nike. These companies tend to hire for finance, supply chain issues or CRM. Typically, you need a consulting, finance or marketing background to get a post-MBA job in the industry. Very few apparel companies have established programs to specifically hire MBAs. A few companies that do hire MBAs for the more creative positions include Cartier, LVMH, Federated and the Gap.

Hillary Shor recruits for the Strategy & Business Development and Consulting and Assurance Services groups of Gap, Inc. These groups are relatively small (about 20 to 30 people per group). Almost all candidates have an MBA, although many are not hired directly as MBA graduates. Hillary says, "We actually look at what a candidate did prior to business school. The Strategy and Consulting groups look for candidates with consulting or industry experience (such as consumer products, goods or retail). Some of our candidates come from consulting firms such as A.T. Kearney and McKinsey."

The Strategy & Business Development group at Gap identifies, develops and drives longer-term strategies and initiatives that will result in profitable growth (usually with a focus on new opportunities). "Strategy involves brand management, research, as well as planning," says Hillary. Consulting and Assurance Services involves financial/operational analysis, process analysis and design and project management. Basically, this group acts as an internal consulting group for Gap. They may work with outside consultants and vendors.

Getting Hired

Build your resume correctly and you can get the interviews you need. In apparel, most of the job functions are very specific, such as design, merchandising, marketing, production and so on. Because many of the companies are small, there aren't very many traditional MBA "management" positions. Many of the people who work at these companies may have gone to trade schools or been in the industry for a long time. For example, the president of Gucci used to work as vice president at Richard Tyler. He was young when he left Richard Tyler for Gucci, but he had started working there when he was 18.

The Gap, Limited, and Eddie Bauer all have internal consulting groups that traditionally hire MBAs. If you are interviewing for an internal consulting position, more than likely it will resemble a traditional consulting interview. You may be given a case study as part of the interview. (See the Vault Guide to the Case Interview for more information on this type of business interview.) Other jobs at fashion companies for MBA graduates may include planning, finance, or strategy.

Pay and Perks

MBA jobs in the fashion industry will not pay well in comparison with other MBA graduate options. Salaries may hover around the $50,000 mark. There are several options here – you work to get the experience or to learn enough to start your own business. If you are thinking of the latter, gain experience that will help you manage your own business. For example, if you want to open your own jewelry store, get a job merchandising or selling jewelry. The best way to learn all sides of the business is to experience it yourself. The pay in the fashion industry is more negotiable than other industries. Most companies will not release this information and, because these jobs are not necessarily geared toward MBAs, the salaries are not standard.

Visit Vault at **www.vault.com** for insider company profiles, expert advice, career message boards, expert resume reviews, the Vault Job Board and more.

VAULT CAREER LIBRARY 101

Vault Profile: Judy Chang, Fashion MBA

Judy Chang graduated from the Anderson School at UCLA with a MBA in 2002. Her previous education included a BS and Master's in industrial and operations engineering from the University of Michigan. After college, she worked as a Program Manager for DaimlerChrysler to coordinate the launch of a particular program in the automotive plants. Judy says, "I would work on program launches for each car model year and style (for specific windshield specifications). I came to Anderson knowing that I wanted to do something totally different." Judy also says, "If you really want to change careers, getting an MBA is essential. Without my MBA, I don't think I would have been able to switch careers successfully. Fashion companies would have looked at my resume and questioned my interest."

At the Anderson School, her emphasis was marketing, and it was the first time she began to seriously consider a fashion career. She had worked at Armani Exchange during college and enjoyed it – but didn't think that fashion would be a practical career choice. At Anderson, she joined the Fashion and Retail Association and began to do her research so that she could merge her interests and career goals. On campus, Macy's and Neutrogena came for interviews. Through the database, she found alumni and contacted them to speak about their experiences. Judy landed a summer internship in Planning at Macy's West. She worked there for three months in the summer and is now there full-time.

At Macy's West, Judy did two projects over the summer. (The department store Macy's is split into two regions and run completely separately. Macy's East is headquartered in NYC, while Macy's West is based in San Francisco.) To her surprise, Judy's operations experience was extremely relevant during the internship. Her first project was about handbag assortments. Her goal was to figure the optimum assortment level. Judy analyzed the number of styles bought for each cluster of stores, available table space for the handbags and discounted handbag sales versus regular stock. She used Macy's sales data as well as active visits to the Macy's floor to make her recommendations. Her second project was to standardize colors across a group of buyers. Each buyer used an individual color coding system. Macy's had no way of tracking sales by color or across categories. For example, although each buyer bought "red," each red item could be a completely different shade. Judy created a color tracking system that allowed the planners to analyze the sales by color and buyer. Macy's could now see which color sold during any a one-week period.

During her internship, Judy was excited to go to work everyday (especially compared to her previous position). She found everyone to be supportive and very friendly. Macy's was a very different experience for her. Judy says, "At Macy's, it seemed like the workforce was 90 percent women and only 10 percent men. At DaimlerChrysler, I used to work with 90 percent men and 10 percent women. If there is something you really think will make you happy, you should do it – even in this difficult economy."

Employer Directory

Abercrombie & Fitch Co.
6301 Fitch Path
New Albany, OH 43054
Phone: (614) 283-6500
Fax: (614) 283-6710
www.abercrombie.com

Ann Taylor Stores Corporation
100 Ann Taylor Drive
P.O. Box 571650
Taylorsville, UT 84157-1650
Phone: (212) 541-3300
Fax: (212) 541-3379
www.anntaylor.com

The Body Shop International PLC
Watersmead
Littlehampton
West Sussex BN17 6LS, United Kingdom
Phone: +44-1-903-731-500
www.the-body-shop.com

Chanel S.A.
135, Avenue Charles de Gaulle
92521 Neuilly-sur-Seine Cedex, France
Phone: +33-1-46-43-40-00
www.chanel.com

Dolce & Gabbana SPA
Via Santa Cecilia, 7
20122 Milan, Italy
Phone: +39-02-77-42-71
www.dolcegabbana.it

Donna Karan International Inc.
550 Seventh Avenue
New York, NY 10018
Phone: (212) 789-1500
Fax: (212) 921-3526
www.donnakaran.com

Eddie Bauer, Inc.
15010 NE 36th St.
Redmond, WA 98052
Phone: (425) 755-6100
Fax: (425) 755-7696
www.eddiebauer.com

Estee Lauder Companies Inc.
767 Fifth Ave.
New York, NY 10153-0023
Phone: (212) 572-4200
Fax: (212) 572-6633
www.elcompanies.com

Federated Department Stores
7 West Seventh Street
Cincinnati, OH 45202
Phone: (513) 579-7000
Fax: (513) 579-7555
www.federated-fds.com

Gap Inc.
One Harrison Street
San Francisco, CA 94105
Phone: (415) 427-2000
Fax: (650) 874-7828
www.gapinc.com

Guess?, Inc.
1444 S. Alameda St.
Los Angeles, CA 90021
Phone: (213) 765-3100
Phone: (213) 744-7838
www.guess.com

J. Crew Group Inc.
770 Broadway
New York, NY 10003
Phone: (212) 209-2500
Fax: (212) 209-2666
www.jcrew.com

Tommy Hilfiger
25 West 39th St., 14th Floor
New York, NY 10018
www.tommy.com

Kenneth Cole Productions, Inc.
603 West 50th St.
New York, NY 10019
Phone: (212) 265-1500
Fax: (212) 830-7422
www.kennethcole.com

L'Oreal USA
575 5th Ave.
New York, NY 10017
Phone: (212) 818-1500
Fax: (212) 984-4999
www.lorealusa.com

Levi Strauss & Co.
1155 Battery St.
San Francisco, CA 94111
Phone: (415) 501-6000
Fax: (415) 501-7112
www.levistrauss.com

Limited Brands
3 Limited Parkway
Columbus, OH 43216
Phone: (614) 415-7000
Fax: (614) 415-7440
www.limited.com

Nike, Inc.
One Bowerman Drive
Beaverton, OR 97005-6453
Phone: (503) 671-6453
Fax: (503) 671-6300
www.nikebiz.com

Nordstrom, Inc.
1617 Sixth Ave.
Seattle, WA 98101-1742
Phone: (206) 628-2111
Fax: (206) 628-1795
www.nordstrom.com

Pacific Sunwear of California, Inc.
3450 E. Miraloma Ave.
Anaheim, CA 92806-2101
Phone: (714) 414-4000
Fax: (714) 414-4251
www.pacsun.com

OshKosh b'Gosh, Inc.
112 Otter Ave.
Oshkosh, WI 54901 (Map)
Phone: (920) 231-8800
Fax: (920) 231-8621
www.oshkoshbgosh.com

Polo Ralph Lauren Corporation
650 Madison Avenue
New York, NY 10022
Phone: (212) 318-7000
Fax: (212) 888-5780
www.polo.com

Reebok International Ltd.
1895 J. W. Foster Blvd.
Canton, MA 02021
Phone: (781) 401-5000
Fax: (781) 401-7402
www.reebok.com

Revlon, Inc.
237 Park Ave.
New York, NY 10017
Phone: (212) 527-4000
Fax: (212) 527-4995
www.revloninc.com

Visit Vault at **www.vault.com** for insider company profiles, expert advice, career message boards, expert resume reviews, the Vault Job Board and more.

V∧ULT CAREER LIBRARY   **103**

FitchRatings

Fitch Ratings Corporate Description

Fitch Ratings is a leading global rating agency committed to providing the world's credit markets with accurate, timely and prospective credit opinions. Built on a foundation of organic growth and strategic acquisitions, Fitch Ratings has grown rapidly during the past decade gaining market presence throughout the world and across all fixed income markets.

Fitch Ratings is dual-headquartered in New York and London, operating offices and joint ventures in more than 49 locations and covering entities in more than 80 countries. Fitch Ratings is a wholly owned subsidiary of Fimalac, S.A., an international business support services group headquartered in Paris, France.

ANALYTICAL POSITIONS

Entry level analysts are key contributors to all analytical departments: Structured Finance, Corporate Finance, Public Finance, Credit Products, Credit Policy, and Fitch Risk Management. If you join Fitch, you will:

- Provide support to lead analyst on new issue ratings.
- Gather and analyze financial statements, as well as the latest industry, regulatory, and economic information.
- Develop an understanding of legal and accounting issues affecting a security.
- Run computer models and spreadsheet-based applications to evaluate credit risk and cash flow coverage. Present analysis at rating committee meetings.
- Develop an ability to differentiate among rating categories.
- Write research reports and press releases.
- Adopt Fitch style: high level of service to our clients and a team-oriented approach to ratings analysis.

CANDIDATES MUST POSSESS

- BA/BS or MBA degree.
- Ability to apply advanced mathematical concepts.
- Excellent verbal and written communication skills.
- Proficiency in Microsoft Word/Excel.

For more information about career opportunities as a Financial Analyst in New York or Chicago, please log on to www.fitchratings.com and visit the "Careers at Fitch" section of our website.

Summer Internships available
Equal Opportunity Employer M/F/D/V

www.fitchratings.com

| opportunity for advancement | dental insurance | life insurance | medical insurance | 401(k) | annual salary increases | tuition reimbursement |

Financial Services and Insurance

Brokerage Services

Sales is a core area of most securities firms, comprising the vast majority of people and relationships and accounting for a substantial portion of revenues. Securities salespeople can take the form of a classic retail broker, an institutional salesperson, or a private client service representative. Retail, brokers develop relationships with individual investors and sell securities and advice to the average Joe. Institutional salespeople sell securities to and develop business relationships with large institutional investors – those that manage large groups of assets such as pension funds or mutual funds. Lying somewhere in between retail brokers and institutional salespeople are private client services (PCS) representative, who provide brokerage and money management services for extremely wealthy individuals. A firm's PCS unit is often referred to as its Wealth Management department. All salespeople, no matter who they're selling to, make money through commissions on trades made through their firms.

This guide focuses on firms with retail brokers or private client service representatives; these types of salespeople are usually separate from a financial firm's banking operations. The *Vault Career Guide to Sales & Trading* is where you'll find more information on institutional salespeople, who typically fall under a firm's banking operations.

Retail brokers

Some firms call them account executives, others call them financial advisors, and still others give them the financial consultant moniker. Regardless of the official designator, firms are still referring to your classic retail broker. The broker's job involves managing the account portfolios for individual investors – usually called retail investors. Brokers charge a commission on any stock trade and also give advice to their clients regarding stocks to buy or sell and when to buy or sell them. To get into the business, retail brokers must have an undergraduate degree and demonstrated sales skills. The Series 7 and Series 63 examinations are also required before selling commences. Having connections to people with money offers a tremendous advantage for a starting broker.

Private client cervices

As a private client services (PCS) representative, your job is to bring in individual accounts with at least $2 million in assets. The PCS job can be exhilarating, exhausting and frustrating – all at once. It involves pounding the pavement to find clients, and then advising them on how to manage their wealth. PCS is a highly entrepreneurial environment. Building a roster of clients is all that matters, and managers typically don't care how PCS reps spend their time – whether it be on the road, in the office or at parties – as long as they're bringing in cash. Culture-wise, therefore, one typically finds a spirited entrepreneurial group of people in PCS, working their own hours and talking on the phone for the better part of the day.

Recent Trends

Typically, where the equities markets go, the brokerage industry follows. Which means the brokerage industry is alive and kicking, after enjoying two straight years of solid gains. All of the major stock indices have posted positive results as of late. After rising 25 percent in 2003, the Dow Jones Industrial Average increased another 3.15 percent in 2004. The S&P 500 also enjoyed two good years, following up a 26 percent gain in 2003 with a 9 percent rise in 2004. And the Nasdaq Composite Index, which had a killer 2003, growing 50 percent, rose 8.6 percent in 2004. As far as 2005 is concerned, more good news is expected. In its 2004 year-end report on the market, *The Wall Street Journal* reported that "the consensus view is that 2005 will be a good, although not a spectacular year for stocks."

Visit Vault at **www.vault.com** for insider company profiles, expert advice, career message boards, expert resume reviews, the Vault Job Board and more.

VAULT CAREER LIBRARY   105

As a result of the gains in the equity markets, some of the top retail brokerage firms have been cashing in. Merrill Lynch's Global Private Client unit boosted net revenues by 11 percent to $9.8 billion in 2004, and increased pre-tax earnings by 23 percent to $1.9 billion. Additionally, financial advisor headcount increased by 420 during the year to approximately 14,100, and GPC's assets ended the year at $1.4 trillion on net inflows of $24 billion. Another giant in the industry, Morgan Stanley also recently reported healthy increases in 2004. Net revenues in its Individual Investor group were $4.6 billion in fiscal 2004, a 9 percent increase over a year earlier. And total client assets increased to $602 billion, up 7 percent from fiscal 2003. The number of global financial advisors, though, slightly decreased by 124 to 10,962 versus fiscal year end 2003.

Credit Card Services

Issuing credit cards is one of the most common ways in which financial services firms provide credit to individuals. Via the credit card, firms provide individuals with the funds required to purchase goods and services, and in return, individuals repay the full balance at a later date, or make payments on an installment basis. While you're most likely familiar with a how a credit card works, you might not be familiar with just how large the credit card industry is today. According to the Nilson Report, more than 1.9 trillion credit or debit cards were circulating worldwide at the beginning of 2004, representing $4.7 billion in total volume. In the U.S., more than 847 million cards were in circulation, representing $2.1 trillion in total volume. The largest issuers of U.S. credit and debit cards were Citigroup and MBNA, with Visa the top brand of choice (429 million cards) followed by MasterCard (326 million). According to the Tower Group, the average U.S. household has 7.8 cards and approximately $10,000 in credit card debt.

History

Heavy metal

The credit card traces its roots back to 1914 when Western Union began doling out metal cards, called "metal money," which gave preferred customers interest-free, deferred-payment privileges. Ten years later, General Petroleum Corporation issued the first metal money for gasoline and automotive services, and by the late 1930s, department stores, communication companies, travel and delivery companies had all began to introduce such cards. Then, companies issued the cards, processed the transactions and collected the debts from the customer. The popularity of these cards grew until the beginning of World War II, when "Regulation W" restricted the use of cards, and as a result, stalled their growth.

After the war, though, cards were back on track. Modes of travel were more advanced and more accessible, and more people were beginning to buy expensive modern conveniences such as kitchen appliances and washing machines. As a result, the credit card boomed in popularity, as consumers could pay for these things on credit that otherwise they couldn't afford to buy with cash.

Charge-it

In 1951, New York's Franklin National Bank created a credit system called Charge-It, which was very similar to the modern credit card. Charge-It allowed consumers to make purchases at local retail establishments, with the retailer obtaining authorization from the bank and then closing the sale. At a later date, the bank would reimburse the retailer and then collect the debt from the consumer. Acting upon the success of Franklin's Charge-It, other banks soon began introducing similar cards. Banks found that cardholders liked the convenience and credit line that cards offered, and retailers discovered that credit card customers usually spent more than if they had to pay with cash. Additionally, retailers found that handling bank-issued cards was less costly than maintaining its own credit card program.

Also in the 1950s, the Diner's Club charge card was created. This card, which gave users 60 days to make repayment, was the first to allow consumers to pay for goods and services from a variety of retailers. Another 1950s credit card milestone was the BankAmericard, created by California's Bank of America. The BankAmericard was the first "revolving credit" card

– it gave cardholders the option to pay their debts in whole, or in monthly minimum payments while the issuers charged interest on the remaining balances.

The association and the Master

Bank of America continued its credit card innovations in the 1960s with the introduction of the bank card association. In 1965, Bank of America began issuing licensing agreements that allowed other banks to issue BankAmericards. To compete with the BankAmericard, four banks from California formed the Western States Bankcard Association and introduced the MasterCharge. By 1969, most credit cards had been converted to either the MasterCharge (which changed its name to MasterCard in 1979) or the BankAmericard (which was renamed Visa in 1977).

Cutting the cost of transaction processing and decreasing credit card fraud were the next innovations introduced to the industry. Electronic authorizations, begun in the early 1970s, allowed merchants to approve transactions 24 hours a day. By the end of the decade, magnetic strips on the back of credit cards allowed retailers to swipe the customer's credit card through a dial up terminal, which accessed the issuing bank card holder's information. This process gave authorizations and processed settlement agreements in a mater of minutes. In the 1980s, the ATM (Automatic Teller Machine) began to surface, giving cardholders 24-hour access to cash.

The debut of the debit, the climb of the cobrand

The 1990s saw the debit card rise in popularity. The debit card grew from accounting for 274 million transactions in 1990 to 8.15 billion transactions in 2002. The 1990s also witnessed the surge of cobranded and affinity cards, which match up a credit card company with a retailer to offer discounts for using the card (think Citibank's AAdvantage cards and American Express' Mileage Rewards program). Although cobranded cards took a dip in the late 1990s – according to some industry experts, this was because issuers had exhausted the most lucrative partners – they've recently returned in full force. Consider that in 2003 alone, MBNA, which BusinessWeek has called "King of the Plastic Frontier," struck some 400 new deals with various companies such as Merrill Lynch, Royal Caribbean and Air Canada. Additionally, it renewed deals with another 1,400 organizations, including the National Football League and the University of Michigan. And in 2004, MBNA signed agreements with numerous other companies and organizations such as A.G. Edwards & Sons, the Massachusetts Institute of Technology, Arsenal Football Club (U.K.), Starwood Hotels and Resorts, and Charles Schwab.

And then there were four

In September 2003, a federal court upheld a lower court ruling that cost credit card powerhouses Visa and MasterCard a combined $3 billion. The court found Visa and MasterCard rules preventing the companies' member banks from also issuing American Express and Morgan Stanley's Discover cards to be illegal and harmful to competition. MasterCard was forced to pay $2 billion in damages and Visa paid $1 billion.

In October 2004, the U.S. Supreme Court decided not to hear Visa and MasterCard's appeal in the government's antitrust suit against them, effectively ending the two companies' rules that have prevented banks from issuing cards on rival networks. As a result, Amex and Discover became free to partner with the thousands of banks that issue Visa and MasterCard, which should allow Amex and Discover to gain ground on the two credit powerhouses that, together, control about 79 percent of the U.S. credit card market (as of August 2004).

Upon the initial ruling in September 2003, Amex CEO Kenneth I. Chenault said, "We plan to add more partnerships with other issuers on a selective basis, ensuring they are a strategic fit for our brand and can drive more high-spending customers to the merchants on our network." In 2004, David W. Nelms, chairman and CEO of Morgan Stanley's Discover Financial Services unit, told BusinessWeek that the ruling "will create competition in our industry for the first time."

That competition is expected to be intense, say insiders. According to *BusinessWeek*, U.S. consumers use cash or checks to pay for about 59 percent of their $8.2 trillion in transactions each year. That leaves $4.8 trillion in cash outlays for credit card companies to capture. The Nilson Report estimates that debit- and credit-card spending will grow 13 percent a year from

Visit Vault at **www.vault.com** for insider company profiles, expert advice, career message boards, expert resume reviews, the Vault Job Board and more.

VAULT CAREER LIBRARY **107**

At M&T Bank, we understand that you want more than just a job.

M&T Bank can help you make the most of your ambition and abilities. As one of the best performing banks in the country, we've fostered a diverse, challenging and professional environment where you'll find exceptional growth opportunities and a team-oriented culture.

M&T's **Executive Associate** positions are career tracks for MBA students that offer immediate responsibility and a significant amount of latitude in decision making. You can expect a rigorous and challenging environment in which you'll quickly become involved in extensive, high profile projects and have frequent interaction with the bank's senior management. Unlike similar graduate level positions, you'll be given a high degree of autonomy and flexibility in determining your career path.

Find out what it's like to work for one of the strongest and most highly regarded regional banks in the country. For more information about the Executive Associate career track at M&T Bank, visit our website at www.mandtbank.com/campus. An equal opportunity employer M/F/D/V.

M&T Bank

Understanding what's important®

2005 to 2008. "You're talking about the most profitable retail banking product in the world," Nilson publisher David Robertson told *BusinessWeek* in August 2004. "The competition among the titans is going to be fierce." He added, "They are already clobbering each other."

Insurance

Risky business

The insurance industry combines to form a multi-trillion-dollar market dealing in risk. In exchange for a premium, insurers promise to compensate, monetarily or otherwise, individuals and businesses for future losses, thus taking on the risk of personal injury, death, damage to property, unexpected financial disaster, and just about any other misfortune you can name.

The industry often is divided into categories such as life/health and property/casualty. Life insurance dominates the mix, making up about 60 percent of all premiums. The bigger categories can be subdivided into smaller groups; property insurance, for instance, may cover homeowner's, renter's, auto, and boat policies, while health insurance is made up of subsets including disability and long-term care.

But these days, you can find insurance for just about anything – even policies for pets (a market that grew 342 percent from 1998 to 2002, with sales of up to $88 million, according to research firm Packaged Facts), weddings and bar mitzvahs, and the chance of weather ruining a vacation. Even insurance companies themselves can be insured against extraordinary losses – by companies specializing in reinsurance. Celebrity policies always get a lot of press – while rumors that Jennifer Lopez had insured her famous asset (sorry) for $1 billion proved to be unfounded, other such policies do indeed exist. In fact, the phrase "million dollar legs" comes from Betty Grable's policy for that amount (a similar policy is held by TV's Mary Hart); other notable contemporary policies include Bruce Springsteen's voice, reportedly covered at around $6 million.

The world's top five

Though the U.S. is, on average, ahead of the rest of the world in terms of insurance coverage, insurance is a truly global industry. Ranked by 2003 revenue data from the Insurance Information Institute, the top five insurance companies are Germany's Allianz, France's AXA, the Netherlands' ING, New York-based American International Group, Inc. (AIG), and Italy's Assicurazioni Generali. Other leading U.S. insurers include State Farm, MetLife, Allstate, Prudential, Aetna and Travelers.

Consolidation is the name of the game – Hoovers reports that the top ten property/casualty insurers account for nearly half of all premiums written. Perhaps the most notable example of the mergers and acquisitions mania in the industry was the $82 billion merger in 1998 between Citicorp and the Travelers Group, which created Citigroup. Some insurance companies have also begun to reconfigure themselves from mutual insurers, or those owned by policyholders (e.g., State Farm), to stock insurers, or those held by shareholders (e.g., Allstate). This process, known as "demutualization," promises to raise even more capital for insurance companies to indulge in more acquisitions.

Insurance investigations

These days, life at the top for a number of insurance heavyweights has been less than perfect. An investigation by federal and state prosecutors into AIG's accounting practices revealed accounting problems that forced the company to reduce reported profits by nearly $4 billion over five years, largely the fault of former CEO Maurice Greenberg and former CFO Howard Smith. Greenberg, personally picked by AIG founder Cornelius Vander Starr to steer the company, stepped down from his perch in March 2005 after nearly four decades on the job. That May, New York State Attorney General Eliot Spitzer filed a

Visit Vault at **www.vault.com** for insider company profiles, expert advice, career message boards, expert resume reviews, the Vault Job Board and more.

VAULT CAREER LIBRARY   **109**

complaint against AIG, Greenberg, and Smith, over accusations of securities fraud, common law fraud, and a number of violations of insurance and securities laws.

Investigations into insurance industry practices are not uncommon these days. The federal government has taken a keen interest in what is known as "finite" or "financial reinsurance," a specific type of insurance that, at its most basic level, typically involves "a premium laid down by a corporation large enough to cover all the expected losses into an account held with the insurer," according to CFO.com. The carrier is allowed "to return the difference to the insured if the cost of losses is less than the premium; if the losses turn out to be greater, the insured pays an additional premium."

Additional investigations are popping up. In May 2005, the Chubb Corp received a subpoena from federal prosecutors investigating its use of nontraditional insurance that could artificially boost financial results. The announcement came on the heels of a November 2004 statement that Spitzer's team, in an investigation into bid-rigging practices between insurance brokers and insurers, requested information from Chubb, along with a number of other companies. At that point, executives at AIG and Ace had already pleaded guilty to such practices. And, in June 2005, Allstate Insurance agreed to pay $34 million in restitution and fine to settle claims from California insurance regulators, accusing the company of overcharging on 250,000 policies over a five-year period. Also, as of July 2005, Marsh & McLennan stands accused of manipulating bids and receiving kickbacks for funneling business.

Though the headlines have mostly come from major corporations, the ripple effects of such negative press have leaked across the entire industry. To this end, the FBI launched a nationwide review of insurance practices at more than 7,000 companies in May 2005, looking for problems in accounting patterns similar to those at AIG. According to a report in The New York Times the same month, many industry officials were surprised at the FBI review, while some declared it was "premature" for the FBI to associate AIG's faulty accounting with the entire industry.

Branching out

The last 25 years have seen a shift in the industry away from life insurance toward annuity products, focusing on managing investment risk rather than the (inevitable) risk of mortality. With increasing deregulation in the U.S. and Japan, these insurers are moving ever closer to competition with financial services firms. Indeed, the business of the insurance industry doesn't end with insurance. The world's top insurance companies have broadened their array of financial services to include investment management, annuities, securities, mutual funds, health care management, employee benefits and administration, real estate brokerage, and even consumer banking. The move towards financial services follows the 1999 repeal of the Glass-Steagall Act, which barred insurance companies, banks and brokerages from entering each other's industries, and the Gramm Leach-Bliley Act of 1999, which further defined permissible acts for financial holding companies. Now insurance companies are free to partner with commercial banks, securities firms, and other financial entities.

At the speed of the Internet

Like many other industries, the insurance market has been transformed in recent years by the Internet. Traditionally, insurance products have been distributed by independent agents (businesspeople paid on commission) or by exclusive agents (paid employees). But insurers who sell over the Web reap the benefits of lower sales costs and customer service expenses, along with a more expedient way of getting information to consumers. is transforming those traditional methods by cutting costs and increasing the amount of information available to consumers. By 2005, Celent Communications estimates that the online insurance market will top $200 billion, or 37 percent of personal insurance premiums, up from 19 percent in 2003. Of course, an automated approach to doing business means fewer salespeople are needed – Celent reports that insurance giant Cigna, for instance, eliminated 2,000 jobs in 2002 because of increased efficiencies.

With more IT comes a greater need for IT security – Celent estimated that U.S. insurers would spend roughly $770 million by 2006 on security alone. Aside from the threat of viruses, hackers, and the like, regulations have made security a top priority – the Health Information Portability and Accountability Act (HIPAA), for instance, which went into effect in 2003, sets strict standards for the privacy and security of the patient information transferred between health insurers and providers.

Response to 9/11

The September 11 terrorist attacks sent shockwaves through the industry, not only costing insurers roughly $23.5 billion in property-related losses and $40 billion in other associated claims, but also causing insurers and re-insurers to take a hard look at how they would handle the risks associated with possible future terrorist acts. The Terrorism Risk Insurance Act, signed into law by President Bush in November 2002, aimed to deal with the nearly incalculable risk posed by this threat. Among other things, the law defines a terrorism-related event as one with a minimum of $5 million in damages. It provides for the sharing of risk between private insurers and the federal government over a three-year period, with each participating company responsible for paying a deductible before federal assistance is available. If losses are incurred above the insurer's deductible, the government is obliged to pay 90 percent. While the measure met with a considerable amount of grumbling from all parties involved, for the most part the industry acknowledged that the plan at least allows for the potential risk to insurers from terrorism-related disasters to be quantified.

With TRIA set to expire at the end of 2005, lawmakers are currently considering legislation to renew the Act. Those in favor of the law might have an uphill battle ahead of them: a June 2005 statement from Treasury Secretary John W. Snow, speaking on behalf of the Bush administration, said the law should not be extended in its current form since it had "achieved temporary objectives" of stabilizing the private insurance sector during the period of economic uncertainty following the attacks. Though Secretary Snow admitted removing the law would likely result in "less terrorism insurance written by insurers, higher prices, and lower policyholder take-up," in the wake of the ongoing economic revival, the administration would not support the act unless the insurance industry agreed to shoulder more costs. Industry insiders worry removing the "government backstop" would increase insurance premiums for owners of office space in high-risk cities, and claim they cannot afford to cover terrorism without some government assistance.

Meanwhile, analysts with the Consumer Federation of America agree with Secretary Snow that the existing program was too generous and has created a situation in which taxpayers could potentially be liable for "taking on huge amounts of risk that insurance companies can afford to take on for themselves." The Property Casualty Insurers Association set up a task force in February 2005 to evaluate how terrorism affects workers' compensation insurance and commercial coverage. Christopher Zwygart, a task force member and assistant vice president for finance at West Bend Mutual Insurance Co., calls terrorism "a very troubling risk to insurance companies" because of its unpredictable nature.

When disaster strikes...

Despite the catastrophic disaster level of 9/11, the nation's most costly insurance incidents come straight from the hands of Mother Nature. 2004's hurricane season, during which a succession of four hurricanes battered the Southeast corner of the country, racked up insured property losses estimated at $22.9 billion, exceeding the property damage incurred during the 9/11 attacks, which registered at $18.8 billion. Florida lawmakers passed a bill that December, eliminating multiple hurricane deductibles as of May 2005. Currently, consumers can choose either a 2 or 5 percent deductible; most choose 2 percent. The 2004 hurricane season also brought on more than two million insurance claims, a number far greater than the 750,000 filed following 1992's Hurricane Andrew – to date the industry's single most costly natural disaster. For the full year 2004, insured catastrophe losses (including tornadoes, hurricanes, terrorism, winter storms, earthquakes, wind/hail/flood, and fire) were estimated at a record $27.5 billion.

Visit Vault at **www.vault.com** for insider company profiles, expert advice, career message boards, expert resume reviews, the Vault Job Board and more.

V/\ULT CAREER LIBRARY   **111**

Fraud: The $100 billion challenge

Another trend in the industry is the problem of fraud, which costs an estimated $85 billion to $120 billion per year, according to the Insurance Information Institute. III data shows property/casualty insurance fraud cost the industry $29 billion in 2003, while auto insurance fraud racked up $14 billion in false claims in 2004. Topping the cake is health care fraud – costing the nation a whopping $95 billion on an annual basis, according to some estimates. Fraud comes in two flavors, "hard" and "soft," with hard fraud being a deliberate invention or staging of an accident, fire, or other type of insured loss to reap the coverage. Soft fraud covers policyholders' and claimants' exaggeration of legitimate claims, such as when victims of burglaries overstate the value and amount of lost property, or when car accident claimants pad damage claims to cover their deductibles.

Unhealthy healthcare

Medical malpractice is another hot topic. Health insurers generally get a bad rap from the public, with a 2003 Harris Poll indicating that just 40 percent of health insurance companies do a good job of taking care of their customers (in fact, only the tobacco industry ranked lower in the poll). The media and politicians give plenty of air time to horror stories about managed care companies slighting critically ill patients, and insurers refusing to cover necessary treatments or technologies. Is this reputation deserved? Depends on who you ask, but the industry has its own battles in health care – for example, it sees medical malpractice claims, which have skyrocketed in recent years, as a true crisis. Indeed, according to the Insurance Information Institute, some insurers have quit writing malpractice policies entirely rather than shoulder the risk (the median malpractice award in 2001, the latest year for which this figure is available, was $1 million). Insurance company Farmers, which racked up more than $100 million in malpractice-related losses in 2003, announced it would get out of malpractice overage in September of that year.

Interestingly, a July 2005 study by the Center for Justice and Democracy found that malpractice rates had increased 120 percent between 2000 and 2004, while the amount of money paid in claims increased by a paltry 5.7 percent in comparison, and the surpluses collected by insurers increased by 33 percent. Researchers culled data from annual statements filed with state insurance departments from the nation's 15 biggest medical malpractice insurers. Insurers blasted the study's methodology, and claimed it failed to take into account additional costs insurers face, such as underwriting. The Physician Insurers Association of America reports an average wait time of four and a half years between the time an accident occurs and the claim is paid, a lapse which forces companies to collect premiums "based on future cost expectations."

Lawrence Smarr, president of the PIAA, called the study a "meaningless comparison no respectable actuary would consider." Connecticut Attorney General Richard Blumenthal asked the National Association of Insurance Commissioners to review the study, indicating that such disparate numbers warranted "the need for more much tougher and aggressive oversight to prevent and punish profiteering." Jay Angoff, a former state insurance commissioner of Missouri, agreed, "In recent years, medical malpractice hasn't been unprofitable, but it's been phenomenally profitable." In the meantime, the Bush administration is working on litigation to cap some malpractice damages in an effort to drive down health care costs.

The whole(sale) story

In a curious twist, Costco Wholesale Corp., the largest wholesale club operator in the U.S., announced the start of a pilot program in July 2005 designed to offer individual health insurance policies to California shoppers maintaining "executive membership" status. The company says the program is geared toward people who cannot get group insurance, such as the jobless or owners of family businesses. For now, Costco insurance is only available in the Golden State – representatives for the company say spreading insurance to its 18 million members nation wide is most likely unfeasible, as some states have larger membership bases than others. Though most analysts say the plan will likely have little effect on the 45 million uninsured Americans from coast to coast, some have suggested that discounters like Costco may spur growth in locally based, low-premium niche plans. Meanwhile, insurance brokers are quietly wondering if Costco's wholesale plan could have ramifications of Wal-Mart proportions on brokerage firms. Glenn Melnick, director of the USC Center for Health Financing, Policy and Management, claims low-priced health products have the potential to "really shake up the market" and force insurers to develop more low-cost products.

Working in insurance

According to the U.S. Bureau of Labor Statistics, the industry employed 2.2 million people in 2002. Of these jobs, three out of five were with insurance carriers, while the remainder were with insurance agencies, brokerages, and providers of other insurance-related services 2 out of 5 jobs. Another 141,000 workers in the industry were self-employed in 2002, mostly as insurance sales agents. Most insurance agents specialize in life and health insurance, or property and casualty insurance. But a growing number of "multi-line" agents sell all lines of insurance. An increasing number of agents also work for banking institutions, non-depository institutions, or security and commodity brokers. Medical, financial, and health insurance are among the fastest growing industry sectors.

Common jobs in the industry include claims adjusters, appraisers, examiners, and investigators; marketing and sales managers; customer service representatives; insurance sales agents; underwriters; lawyers; computer systems analysts; computer programmers; and computer support specialists. Data provided by the BLS suggests that though corporate downsizing and changes in business practices will limit growth in the industry in the next few years, "numerous" job openings are expected as older workers leave or retire.

Visit Vault at **www.vault.com** for insider company profiles, expert advice, career message boards, expert resume reviews, the Vault Job Board and more.

VAULT CAREER LIBRARY

113

Employer Directory

Citigroup

1 Court Square, 9th Floor, Zone 11

Long Island City, NY 11120

Recruiting E-mail: citigrouprecruiting@citigroup.com

www.citigroup.com/citigroup/oncampus/

The largest bank in the U.S. and the No.5 company on the Fortune 500, Citigroup offers seemingly every financial service under the sun to consumer and corporate customers, catering to some 200 million customer accounts and doing business in more than 100 countries. The company is organized into FOUR broad divisions: the Global Consumer Group, Corporate and Investment Banking, Global Wealth Management, and Alternative Investments. The Global Consumer Group typically accounts for over half of Citigroup's profits and includes the firm's Citibank cards, consumer finance and retail banking units. The cards unit provides MasterCard, VISA, Diner's Club and private label credit and charge cards. The firm's investment banking arm is one of the most respected in the industry, consistently at or near the top of every conceivable league table.

Business schools Citigroup recruits from

Michigan/Ross; Columbia GSB; Wharton; Rochester/Simon; Cornell/Johnson; Georgetown GSB; NYU/Stern; Texas/Austin; Carnegie Mellon; Harvard Business School; Maryland GSB; Cornell/ILR; Duke/Fuqua; Howard GR; Northwestern/Kellogg

Deloitte

1633 Broadway

New York, NY 10013-6754

www.deloitte.com/careers

Deloitte, one of the nation's leading professional services firms, provides audit, tax, consulting, and financial advisory services through nearly 30,000 people in more than 80 U.S. cities. Known as an employer of choice for innovative human resources programs, the firm is dedicated to helping its clients and its people excel. "Deloitte" refers to the associated partnerships of Deloitte & Touche USA LLP (Deloitte & Touche LLP and Deloitte Consulting LLP) and subsidiaries. Deloitte is the U.S. member firm of Deloitte Touche Tohmatsu.

Business schools Deloitte recruits from

There are too many to list. All candidate are to submit to opportunities via our career website located at www.deloitte.com

Fitch Ratings

One State Street Plaza

New York, NY 10004

Phone: 212-908-0500

Fitch Ratings is a leading global rating agency committed to providing the world's credit markets with accurate, timely and prospective credit opinions. Fitch Ratings is dual-headquartered in New York and London, operating offices and joint ventures in more than 40 locations and covering entities in more than 75 countries. Fitch Ratings complies with federal, state, and local laws governing employment, and provides equal opportunity to all applicants and employees. All applications will be considered without regard to race, color, religion, gender, national origin, age, disability, marital or veteran status, sexual orientation, and other status protected by applicable laws.

Schools Fitch Ratings recruits from

NYU; Cornell; Brown; Columbia

M&T Bank Corporation

One M&T Plaza, 11th Floor

Buffalo, N.Y. 14203

(716) 842-5157

college@mandtbank.com

www.mandtbank.com

M&T Bank Corporation is the 18th largest bank-holding company in the nation, with $50 billion in assets as of March 31, 2004.

As one of the most respected regional banks in the country, M&T Bank is recognized for financial strength and stability built on our belief that we succeed when our employees, customers and communities do. We are proud of our record of civic and charitable support and our employees' leadership and volunteerism.

We work hard to understand what's important to our customers and to create a supportive, inclusive culture and work environment where employees can succeed personally and professionally.

Business schools M&T Bank recruits from

American University (Kogod); Carnegie Mellon (Tepper); Univ. of Chicago; Columbia; Cornell (Johnson); Dartmouth (Tuck); Duke (Fuqua); Georgetown University (McDonough); Harvard Business School; University of Maryland (Robert H.Smith); University of Michigan; New York University (Stern); Northwestern (Kellogg); Penn State (Smeal); University of North Carolina (Kenan-Flagler); University of Rochester (Simon); University of Virginia (Darden); University of Buffalo; University of Pennsylvania (Wharton)

Nationwide

One Nationwide Plaza

Columbus, OH 43215

www.nationwide.com/jobs/colrecruiting/grad.htm

If you're seeking an organization that would value the unique skills and abilities you bring to the workplace, consider Nationwide. Nationwide is one of the largest insurance and financial services companies in the world, with more than $148 billion in assets. We are an industry leader in property and casualty insurance, life insurance and retirement savings, and asset management. Our leadership and continued growth provides a variety of employment opportunities for qualified individuals to begin or advance their careers. We do business in all 50 states, the District of Columbia, and the Virgin Islands, Asia, Europe, and Latin America.

A.G. Edwards & Sons

One North Jefferson Ave.

St. Louis, MO 63103

(314) 955-3000

Fax: (314) 955-5402

www.agedwards.com

Aetna Inc.

151 Farmington Ave.

Hartford, CT 06156

Phone: (860) 273-0123

Fax: (860) 273-3971

Toll Free: (800) 872-3862

www.aetna.com

Aflac Incorporated

1932 Wynnton Road

Columbus, GA 31999

Phone: (706) 323-3431

Fax: (706) 324-6330

Toll Free: (800) 992-3522

www.aflac.com

The Allstate Corporation

2775 Sanders Rd.

Northbrook, IL 60062

Phone: (847) 402-5000

Fax: (847) 836-3998

Toll Free: (800) 574-3553

www.allstate.com

Allianz Group

Königinstrasse 28

D-80802 Munich, Germany

Phone: +49-89-3800-0

Fax: +49-89-3800-3425

www.allianz.com

Allianz Global Investors of America L.P.

888 San Clemente Dr.

Suite 100

Newport Beach, CA 92660

Phone: (949) 219-2200

Fax: (949) 219-3949

www.adam-us.com

Visit Vault at **www.vault.com** for insider company profiles, expert advice, career message boards, expert resume reviews, the Vault Job Board and more.

VAULT CAREER LIBRARY **115**

American Express
World Financial Center
200 Vesey St.
New York, NY 10285
Phone: (212) 640-2000
www.americanexpress.com

American International Group
70 Pine St.
New York, NY 10270
Phone: (212) 770-7000
Fax: (212) 509-9705
www.aig.com

AON Corporation
Aon Center, 200 E. Randolph St.
Chicago, IL 60601
Phone: (312) 381-1000
Fax: (312) 381-6032
www.aon.com

Bank of America Corporation
100 North Tryon Street
Charlotte, NC 28255
Phone: (800) 432-5000
Fax: (704) 386-6699
www.bankofamerica.com

Berkshire Hathaway Inc.
1440 Kiewit Plaza
Omaha, NE 68131
Phone: (402) 346-1400
Fax: (402) 346-3375
www.berkshirehathaway.com

Blackstone Group, The
345 Park Ave.
New York, NY 10154
Phone: (212) 583-5000
Fax: (212) 583-5712
www.blackstone.com

Blue Cross and Blue Shield Association
225 N. Michigan Avenue
Chicago, IL 60601-7680
Phone: (312) 297-6000
Fax: (312) 297-6609
www.bcbs.com

Capital One Financial
1680 Capital One Dr.
McLean, VA 22012
Phone: (703) 720-1000; (800) 801-1164
www.capitalone.com

Charles Schwab
101 Montgomery Street
San Francisco, CA 94104
Phone: (415) 627-7000
Fax: (415) 636-5970
www.schwab.com

Chubb Corporation, The
15 Mountain View Road
Warren, NJ 07061-1615
Phone: (908) 903-2000
Fax: (908) 903-3402
www.chubb.com

CIGNA
1 Liberty Place
Philadelphia, PA 19192-1550
Phone: (215) 761-1000
Fax: (215) 761-5515
www.cigna.com

Citigroup
399 Park Avenue
New York, NY 10043
Phone: (212) 559-1000
Fax: (212) 793-3946
www.citigroup.com

Conseco
11825 N. Pennsylvania Street
Carmel, IN 46032
Phone: (317) 817-6100
Fax: (317) 817-2847
www.conseco.com

Countrywide Financial
4500 Park Granada
Calabasas, CA 91302
Phone: (818) 225-3000
www.countrywide.com

Edward Jones
12555 Manchester Road
Des Peres, MO 63131
Phone: (314) 515-2000
Fax: (314) 515-2622
www.edwardjones.com

Equitable Life Assurance Society
Walton Street
Aylesbury
Buckinghamshire HP21 7QW, United Kingdom
Phone: +44-870-901-0052
www.equitable.co.uk

Erie Indemnity Company
100 Erie Insurance Place
Erie, PA 16530
Phone: (814) 870-2000
Fax: (814) 870-3126
Toll Free: (800) 458-0811
www.erie-insurance.com

Fannie Mae
3900 Wisconsin Ave., NW
Washington, DC 20016-2892
Phone: (202) 752-7000
Fax: (202) 752-3868
www.fanniemae.com

Fitch Ratings
1 State Street Plaza
New York, NY 10004
Phone: (212) 908-0500; (800) 753-4824
Fax: (212) 480-4435
www.fitchratings.com

Freddie Mac
8200 Jones Branch Drive
Mclean, VA 22102-3100
Phone: (703) 903-2000; (800) 424-5401
www.freddiemac.com

GE (financial services businesses)
260 Long Ridge Road
Stamford, CT 06927
Phone: (203) 357-4000
Fax: (203) 357-6489
www.ge.com/en/financial

Golden West Financial

1901 Harrison Street

Oakland, CA 94612

Phone: (510) 446-4000

Fax: (510) 446-4259

www.gdw.com

Guardian Life Insurance

7 Hanover Sq.

New York, NY 10004-2616

Phone: (212) 598-8000

Fax: (212) 919-2170

Toll Free: (866) 425-4542

www.guardianlife.com

Hartford Financial Services Group

Hartford Plaza, 690 Asylum Ave.

Hartford, CT 06115-1900

Phone: (860) 547-5000

Fax: (860) 547-2680

www.thehartford.com

Hilb Rogal & Hobbs Company

4951 Lake Brook Dr., Ste. 500

Glen Allen, VA 23060

Phone: (804) 747-6500

Fax: (804) 747-6046

www.hrh.com

HSBC Finance Corporation

2700 Sanders Road

Prospect Heights, IL 60070

Phone: (847) 564-5000

Fax: (847) 205-7401

www.household.com

ING Americas

5780 Powers Ferry Rd. NW

Atlanta, GA 30327-4390

Phone: (770) 980-3300

Fax: (770) 980-3301

www.ing-usa.com

Jefferson-Pilot Corporation

100 N. Greene St.

Greensboro, NC 27401

Phone: (336) 691-3000

Fax: (336) 691-3938

www.jpfinancial.com

John Hancock Financial Services, Inc.

John Hancock Place

Boston, MA 02117

Phone: (617) 572-6000

Fax: (617) 572-9799

www.johnhancock.com

Liberty Mutual Insurance Companies

175 Berkeley Street

Boston, MA 02116

Phone: (617) 357-9500

Fax: (617) 350-7648

www.libertymutual.com

Marsh Inc.

1166 Avenue of the Americas

New York, NY 10036

Phone: (212) 345-6000

Fax: (212) 345-4808

www.marsh.com

Massachusetts Mutual Life Insurance Company

1295 State St.

Springfield, MA 01111

Phone: (413) 788-8411

Fax: (413) 744-6005

Toll Free: (800) 767-1000

www.massmutual.com

MasterCard International

2000 Purchase St.

Purchase, NY 10577

Phone: (914) 249-2000

Fax: (914) 249-4206

www.mastercard.com

MBNA

1100 North King Street

Wilmington, DE 19884-0131

Phone: (302) 453-9930

Fax: (302) 432-3614

www.mbna.com

Mellon Financial

1 Mellon Financial Center

Pittsburgh, PA 15258-0001

Phone: (412) 234-5000

Fax: (412) 234-9495

www.mellon.com

Merrill Lynch

4 World Financial Center

250 Vesey Street

New York, NY 10080

Phone: (212) 449-1000

www.ml.com

MetLife, Inc.

200 Park Ave.

New York, NY 10166

Phone: (212) 578-2211

Fax: (212) 578-3320

Toll Free: (800) 638-5433

www.metlife.com

Moody's

99 Church St.

New York, NY 10007

Phone: (212) 553-0300

Fax: (212) 553-7194

www.moody's.com

Morgan Keegan & Company

Morgan Keegan Tower

50 Front St., 17th Floor

Memphis, TN 38103

Phone: (901) 524-4100

www.morgankeegan.com

Mutual of Omaha Companies, The

Mutual of Omaha Plaza

Omaha, NE 68175

Phone: (402) 342-7600

Fax: (402) 351-2775

Toll Free: (800) 775-6000

www.mutualofomaha.com

Nationwide

1 Nationwide Plaza

Columbus, OH 43215-2220

Phone: (614) 249-7111

Fax: (614) 249-7705

Toll Free: (800) 882-2822

www.nationwide.com

Visit Vault at **www.vault.com** for insider company profiles, expert advice, career message boards, expert resume reviews, the Vault Job Board and more.

VAULT CAREER LIBRARY

117

New York Life Insurance Company
51 Madison Ave.
New York, NY 10010
Phone: (212) 576-7000
Fax: (212) 576-8145
www.newyorklife.com

Northwestern Mutual Financial Network
720 E. Wisconsin Avenue
Milwaukee, WI 53202-4797
Phone: (414) 271-1444
Fax: (414) 665-9702
www.northwesternmutual.com

Physicians Mutual Insurance Company
2600 Dodge St.
Omaha, NE 68131
Phone: (402) 633-1000
Fax: (402) 633-1096
www.physiciansmutual.com

Principal Financial Group, The
711 High Street
Des Moines, IA 50392
Phone: (515) 247-5111
Fax: (515) 246-5475
www.principal.com

Progressive Corporation, The
6300 Wilson Mills Rd.
Mayfield Village, OH 44143
Phone: (440) 461-5000
Fax: (440) 603-4420
www.progressive.com

Prudential Financial
751 Broad Street
Newark, NJ 07102-3777
Phone: (973) 802-6000
Fax: (973) 802-4479
www.prudential.com

Raymond James Financial
880 Carillon Parkway
St. Petersburg, FL 33716
Phone: (727) 567-1000
Fax: (727) 567-8915
www.rjf.com

Sallie Mae
12061 Bluemont Way
Reston, VA 20190
Phone: (703) 810-3000
www.salliemae.com

St. Paul Travelers Companies
385 Washington Street
St. Paul, MN 55102
Phone: (651) 310-7911
Fax: (651) 310-3386
www.stpaultravelers.com

Standard & Poor's
55 Water Street
New York, NY 10041
Phone: (212) 438-1000
Fax: (212) 438-2000
www.standardandpoors.com

State Farm Insurance Companies
One State Farm Plaza
Bloomington, IL 61710-0001
Phone: (309) 766-2311
Fax: (309) 766-3621
www.statefarm.com

Thrivent Financial for Lutherans
625 4th Ave. South
Minneapolis, MN 55415-1624
Phone: (800) 847-4836
www.thrivent.com

UBS Financial Services
1285 Avenue of the Americas
UBS Building, 20th Floor
New York, NY 10019
Phone: (212) 713-2000
Fax: (212) 713-9818
financialservicesinc.ubs.com

Unitrin
1 E. Wacker Dr.
Chicago, IL 60601
Phone: (312) 661-4600
Fax: (312) 494-6995
www.unitrin.com

UnumProvident
1 Fountain Square
Chattanooga, TN 37402
Phone: (423) 755-1011
Fax: (423) 755-3962
www.unumprovident.com

Visa USA
900 Metro Center Blvd.
Foster City, CA 94404
Phone: (650) 432-3200
Fax: (650) 432-7436
www.visa.com

Washington Mutual
1201 3rd Avenue
Seattle, WA 98101
Phone: (206) 461-2000
Fax: (206) 554-4807
www.wamu.com

Wells Fargo & Company
420 Montgomery Street
San Francisco, CA 94163
Phone: (800) 411-4932
www.wellsfargo.com

W. R. Berkley Corporation
475 Steamboat Rd.
Greenwich, CT 06830
Phone: (203) 629-3000
Fax: (203) 629-4359
www.wrbc.com

Government and Politics

Washington, DC has largely been an untapped source of career opportunities for business school students and MBAs. However, several recent trends indicate that MBAs may start looking to Washington for positions not available elsewhere. These trends include a heightened interest in employment with non-profits and a burgeoning effort by some Federal agencies to recruit MBAs. Additionally, there are MBA employers that exist only in Washington, such as the World Bank.

Despite increased interest in hiring MBAs by many of these employers, in general, these organizations have limited and spotty recruiting efforts on business school campuses. The onus remains on interested students to research appropriate opportunities and network with individuals with similar interests. The section below contains a guide to several of the employment options for MBAs in Washington along with advice on how to identify opportunities and successfully apply for positions.

Federal Government

Washington, DC is slowly, but increasingly, becoming more aware of the benefits of the MBA as well as the need to bring in qualified managers with more than just government experience. When George W. Bush was sworn in as the 43rd President of the United States, he was commonly referred to as the "MBA President," since, as a graduate of the Harvard Business School he is the first chief executive of the United States to hold the degree. Several of his appointments to fill key administration posts were also MBAs, including Elaine Chao, the Secretary of Labor, who received her MBA from the Harvard Business School and Don Evans, the Secretary of Commerce, who received an MBA from the University of Texas. Many other of his top appointments were culled from the world of business, including Paul O'Neil, his first Secretary of the Treasury and former CEO of Alcoa, as well as his replacement, John Snow, who was the head of CSX Corp.

The change at the top has not translated yet into widespread opportunities for MBAs, but the government has grown more receptive to MBAs as it begins to appreciate the skills and capabilities they bring to bear. For example, there have been recent efforts to recruit on MBA campuses. In the 2003 recruiting season, the U.S. Department of the Treasury has visited select campuses seeking to fill internships and full time positions. At times, the CIA has promoted opportunities with MBA programs and advertised for MBAs as part of its financial analysis teams on popular job posting sites, such as HotJobs.com and the Washington Post.

In 2002, Secretary Chao of the U.S. Department of Labor launched an initiative specifically to recruit MBAs to the department. With a large proportion of senior department personnel scheduled to retire in the coming years, Secretary Chao moved aggressively to create a new pipeline of talent and specifically identified hiring MBAs as the future of the department.

Finding a position with the Federal government

As would be expected with the Federal government, bureaucracy rules the hiring process. However, as with any organization, there are paths around the human resources quagmire. MBAs interested in finding an appropriate position with the Federal government should apply the tools emphasized by any career counseling office: identify your interests, find out the general requirements for position, network, and utilize internships.

Since the Federal government is required to post nearly all vacancies, one potential resource to use in identifying appropriate opportunities is its career listing website, www.usacareers.com. However, a word of warning: while the site provides a useful starting point and a valuable research tool, using it exclusively for a job search with the Federal government would sell your efforts short. Instead, for MBAs it can be best used as means to examine the types of positions available and the general salary ranges. Still, even the position descriptions can be overly bureaucratic, and therefore the site should only be considered a starting point in the research process.

Visit Vault at **www.vault.com** for insider company profiles, expert advice, career message boards, expert resume reviews, the Vault Job Board and more.

VAULT CAREER LIBRARY 119

According to several MBAs employed by the federal government in Washington, the best way to identify opportunities is by networking with those already working in the Federal government and with those in the nonprofits and other entities that regularly partner or interact with the Federal agencies. Two good ways to make such contacts are through MBA alumni networks and student or school sponsored conferences focusing on the public sector and non-profit management.

Applying for positions can also be highly bureaucratic, and again, interested applicants are well advised to use their networks to begin the application process. While all applicants must eventually go through the human resources department to determine whether they are qualified and if so, their pay level, it is far more fruitful to begin the application process with the office one wishes to join than with the human resources department. This is where networking can pay off, since ultimately hiring decisions are made within a specific office for high-level candidates. In fact, many government managers already have an applicant in mind before a position is posted.

One MBA graduate who returned to the Federal government after graduation says that while finding government position can take effort, the MBA is definitely seen as a benefit. "There are a lot of hiring managers who will be receptive to talking with MBAs simply because they hold the credential," he says. "MBAs with a specific interest should seek out managers in the Federal government, send them their resumes, and then try to follow up."

The insider also confirmed that there is a growing awareness of the value of an MBA, but that the government hasn't been fast enough to quickly establish the right recruiting policies to bring more business students into the Federal workforce. "The fact of the matter is that the government just doesn't pay what the private sector does," he says. "But, for those with a strong interest in government work, there are many ways in and many rewarding career paths."

Areas of Interest to MBAs

Since most MBAs aren't interested in becoming lifetime bureaucrats, they usually consider specific opportunities in order to gain the experience they need to advance in their chosen professions. The following are areas of the Federal government that provide career enhancing opportunities:

Community and economic development

Community and economic development is an area that has captured the interest of MBAs. Since community and economic development is often the result of cooperation among ublic sector, private sector and non-profit entities, a position with the Federal government can be an effective way to build experience, gain contacts within the development community and gain an understanding of the government's role in community and economic development and the resources it makes available.

There are several agencies within the Federal that have community and economic development functions. These include the U.S. Department of Treasury, the U.S. Department of Commerce, and the Small Business Administration. Since roles within each agency will vary with the specific mission of the department, interested candidates should try to learn about each department's operations and opportunities through networking with organizations such as Net Impact, alumni, and by contacting hiring managers directly to discuss opportunities.

Management

There are many opportunities within the Federal government for MBAs to gain management experience. However, these opportunities must be ferreted out, and will depend on what the MBA hopes to gain by joining the Federal government. For example, an MBA with an interest in the Federal budget process could attempt to locate an analyst position with the Office of Management and Budget. Another potential source of management positions will be the newly created Department of Homeland Security. Since the Homeland Security Department will be free of some of the Federal employment regulations imposed on virtually every other Federal entity, there may be more opportunities for MBAs to utilize their management abilities to a greater degree than elsewhere in the Federal bureaucracy. MBAs need to think creatively about how their skills relate to government management. Since the Department of Homeland Security is being created from programs and agencies run by a variety of Federal entities, it could be thought of in business terms as a "post-merger integration project." (As of this writing, the Department of Homeland is still being formed. Openings, as they are identified, are posted at the Federal government's employment site, www.usajobs.opm.gov.

One avenue for MBAs into the Federal government is through the Presidential Management Internship (PMI) program, which is open to all students pursuing masters or doctoral degrees. To be considered for the program, students must submit an application and be nominated by the dean, chairperson, or program director of their academic program. Once accepted, PMIs must find an appropriate position within the Federal government. The program lasts two years, with PMIs beginning at the GS-9 level (approximately $35,500 to $46,100. After one year, they are eligible for promotion to the GS-11 level ($42,900 to $55,800). At the end of the program, PMI program participants may be converted to a permanent position with the Federal government and are eligible for the GS-12 grade level ($51,500 to $66,900). For detailed information on the program, see its web site at www.pmi.opm.gov.

Additionally, the Department of Labor has begun to actively recruit MBAs for general management positions with strong results. For 2002, its first year in operation, Department's MBA recruitment program reported receiving more than 250 applications for thirty openings. While MBAs start at the GS-9 level, the Department is offering other incentives, including recruitment bonuses and loan forgiveness programs.

Upon acceptance into the program, MBAs will be allowed to rotate through several different assignments before being placed in a permanent position. The permanent assignments are based on the needs of the Department and the long-term interests of each participant.

A senior official working on the program glows about its initial results: "We didn't know what to expect when we fist put the program into place, but we have been very pleased with the results. In fact, several other offices within the Federal government have approached us about putting up similar recruitment programs for themselves."

Application information is available on the Department's website at www.dol.gov.

International development

The Federal government also provides options for MBA students interested in International development, a field that has traditionally and still remains dominated by economists.

Since there are no formal recruitment programs in place for MBAs for international development positions with the Federal government, interested students will have to network with both on-campus and outside organizations to uncover opportunities.

The U.S. Department of Treasury's Office of International Affairs often recruits MBAs for financial analysis positions covering such issues as debt policy or international trade. It particularly is interested in MBA with strong experience in the banking and financial service sector as well as international experience. The office's recruitment efforts include posting position openings with MBA career offices and general advertising.

Visit Vault at www.vault.com for insider company profiles, expert advice,
career message boards, expert resume reviews, the Vault Job Board and more.

VAULT CAREER LIBRARY   121

Employer Directory

Inter-American Development Bank

1300 New York Ave. NW
Washington, DC 20577
Phone: (202) 623-1000
Fax: (202) 623-3096
www.iadb.org

International Finance Corporation

2121 Pennsylvania Avenue, NW
Washington, DC 20433
IFC switchboard: (202) 473-1000
www.ifc.org

International Monetary Fund (IMF)

700 19th Street, N.W.
Washington, DC 20431
Phone: (202) 623-7000
Fax: (202) 623-4661
www.imf.org

Office of Management and Budget

725 17th Street, NW
Washington, DC 20503
Phone: (202) 395-3080
Fax: (202) 395-3888
www.whitehouse.gov/omb

Small Business Administration

409 Third Street, SW
Washington, DC 20416
Phone: 1-800-U-ASK-SBA
www.sba.gov

U.S. Department of Commerce

1401 Constitution Avenue NW
Washington, DC 20230
(202) 482-2000
www.commerce.gov

U.S. Department of Education

400 Maryland Avenue, SW
Washington, DC 20202
Phone: (800)- USA-LEARN
www.ed.gov

U.S. Department of Justice

950 Pennsylvania Avenue, NW
Washington, DC 20530-0001
Phone: (202) 353-1555
www.justice.gov

U.S. Department of Treasury

1500 Pennsylvania Avenue NW
Washington, DC 20220
(202) 622-1260
www.treasury.gov

U.S. Department of Labor

200 Constitution Ave. NW
Washington, DC 20210 U.S.A.
Phone: (202) 693-6000
Fax: (202) 219-5721
Toll free: (866) 487-2365
www.dol.gov

U.S. Department of State

2201 C Street NW
Washington, DC 20520
Phone: (202)-647-6575
www.careers.state.gov

The World Bank Group

1818 H Street, N.W.
Washington, DC 20433
Phone: (202) 473-1000
Fax: (202) 477-6391
www.worldbank.org

Health Care

Industry Overview

An industry in flux

You can't live with it, you can't live without it – this pretty much sums up the attitude many Americans have toward today's health care industry. The industry is made up of a variety of providers of patient care, including hospitals, nursing homes and physicians' offices, as well as those who help coordinate, manage and pay for that care, like HMOs and other health insurers. It's no secret that the sector is a volatile one. Despite making up nearly 15 percent of the nation's gross domestic product (GDP) – U.S. health care spending totaled $1.8 trillion in 2004 – the industry has had a tough time figuring out how to turn healthy profits in a way that benefits both providers and patients. The growth rate in the industry has consistently outpaced the growth rate of the overall economy in recent years. Economists predict health spending will make up 18.7 percent of the country's GDP in 2014, a percentage considered "unsustainable" by many analysts. In fact, it is estimated that the public sector will pay for nearly half of all health spending in the U.S. by 2014.

Having a senior moment

By the year 2050, seniors will outnumber children for the first time ever, according to the AARP. With approximately one million people turning age 60 each month worldwide, the phenomenon known as "global aging" promises to have a deep impact on the demand for and delivery of health care services. In the U.S., the Baby Boom generation – those born shortly after World War II up to the mid-1960s – makes up a sizable portion of the total population. In fact, people aged 50 and older are the fastest-growing demographic group in the nation. This shift is already sparking interest in all issues affecting senior health – from preventive health care to ward off problems later in life, to programs promoting home care and assisted living as alternatives to the dreaded nursing home option for seniors who can't take care of themselves.

Creaky Medicare

With an aging population comes growing pressure on the nation's reimbursement system for seniors and low-income patients. In the U.S., the federal government looms large in health care – though not as large as some patient advocates would prefer (we'll get to health care reform later). In fact, ranked by sales, the government's own Centers for Medicare & Medicaid Services (CMS, formerly known as the Health Care Financing Administration) ranks No. 1 in the industry, according to data from Hoovers.com. Around 40 million Americans are eligible for Medicare coverage, more than twice as many as when the program was first established in 1966 under President Lyndon Johnson. In 2002, Medicare spending made up about 17 percent of total health care expenditures, or $267 billion, roughly equal to the 16 percent coming from Medicaid (which is administered by the states and covers low-income patients as well as senior citizens). From 2003 to 2004, Medicare expenditures increased 15.2 percent, nearly twice as high as the largest growth percentage in recent years. The Centers for Medicare and Medicaid Services estimate premiums for enrollees will rise to $89.20 per month in 2006, roughly $1.50 more than Medicare trustees projected.

Medicare claims are submitted by health care providers through intermediaries or carriers, entities that have contracted through the government to serve as middlemen in the payment process. After navigating a tricky labyrinth of rules regarding coverage, these claims are either accepted or denied by the contractors. Top Medicare contractors include BlueCross BlueShield organizations in a number of states, plus other companies such as Palmetto GBA and Empire Medicare Services.

The Medicare program, perennially the subject of reform packages in Congress, is a political hot potato. Under the Bush administration, a heated battle was waged between patient advocates and lobbyists for insurers and pharmaceutical companies in an effort to get prescription drug costs under control. In 2003 the administration established a prescription drug dis-

Visit Vault at www.vault.com for insider company profiles, expert advice, career message boards, expert resume reviews, the Vault Job Board and more.

VAULT CAREER LIBRARY 123

count card for Medicare beneficiaries, but critics argued that it wasn't the solid overhaul the program truly requires. Bush's plans in his second term for Medicaid have also come under fire. Among his administration's proposed changes are reducing the federal matching rate for targeted case management (which often funds mental health services and assertive community treatment), reducing pharmacist reimbursement rates for prescription medications provided to Medicaid beneficiaries and capping the federal funding match for state administrative services costs, including outreach, enrollment and quality assurance. Also in the works is a proposal to fix faulty pricing techniques, which have caused Medicaid to overpay for some of the drugs it bought in the past, according to a March 2005 report by the Government Accountability Office.

Flying without a net

The rest of the population – those who aren't eligible for Medicare or Medicaid coverage – either have to buy private insurance on their own, get it at discounted rates through an employer, or just go without and hope for the best. An alarming number of Americans, including many children, are in the latter category. In early 2004, almost 44 million Americans (about 15 percent of the population) were uninsured. Additionally, an April 2005 report by the Health Affairs Policy Journal predicted that the number of non-elderly uninsured Americans will grow to 56 million by 2013. Not only do these people risk financial meltdown when faced with unexpected medical emergencies, they're also less likely to rely on routine visits to doctors, dentists, and the like to maintain good health and prevent the onset of more serious conditions down the line. In addition, reports indicate that health care is more expensive overall for the uninsured. For example, some hospitals bill uninsured clients a higher rate for the same procedures provided to those with health coverage, since big insurance companies are able to negotiate discounts with providers.

The situation isn't so rosy for consumers fortunate enough to have coverage, either. Private health insurance companies paid for 35 percent of the total health expenditures in the U.S. in 2002, nearly $550 billion. But as the cost of providing health care coverage continues to rise, many employers are finding they can no longer afford this benefit, and are passing more of the costs on to employees in the form of higher premiums and stingier reimbursement plans. The American Medical Association is currently at work to put together a plan that mixes private and public sector financing to benefit the uninsured and improve quality of care and patient choice, with features like tax credits for the purchase of insurance and a wide range of affordable insurance options.

Unmanageable care

Managed care, which came into prominence in the 1980s and 1990s as a response to rampant inflation in health care costs, has changed the face of the industry. Under these systems, insurers (also known as "payors") figured out that they could rein in costs by establishing networks of providers who participate in a network or health maintenance organization (HMO), which in turn covers a host of covered patients' needs. But in order for the reimbursement to be profitable, health care providers have to curb their own costs. This includes keeping strict limits on the amount of time they spend with patients to maximize the number of appointments they can squeeze in during a day – leading to the hour-in-the-waiting-room, five-minutes-in-the-exam-room doctor visits many Americans experience today. Top managed care corporations include Anthem, HealthNet and UnitedHealth Group.

As illustrated by Hollywood dramas, prime time news programs and even the Gore presidential campaign, the public largely sees HMOs as stingy and heartless, willing to deny society's neediest members basic procedures that are deemed too costly or unnecessary through an impenetrable system of rules and limits. For their part, managed care organizations argue that without these limits, the cost of health care would rise for everyone in the network (and society at large), nullifying the benefits of such a system. Meanwhile, the government has gotten into the managed care game, allowing patients to participate in the "Medicare+Choice" program, which also operates under the provider network philosophy. As with much government-speak, the program actually controls costs by limiting patient choice, not adding to it, skeptics contend.

The doctor will see you now

At the other end of the spectrum, consumers who can flash the cash increasingly are turning to "concierge" or "boutique" physician practices. These private practices offer the attentive, personal and thorough care associated with the pre-HMO days of house calls and Norman Rockwell paintings – for a price. Patients shell out an annual fee up front that can range from several hundred to tens of thousands of dollars to join an exclusive roster of clients seen by a participating internist. So rather than scrambling to see up to 30 patients a day as in a typical managed care practice, boutique physicians can limit their number of cases to a select handful. Some of these practices charge for appointments above and beyond the annual fee (which is just a sort of retainer for their services); some accommodate reimbursement by health plans for things like specialized tests. As health care costs skyrocket and patients grow frustrated with insurance plans and the quality of managed care, these practices are becoming more popular – and profitable – business options for those doctors who don't see exclusive care for the well-off as an ethical dilemma.

The quest for reform

Every time a campaign season rolls around, the health care coverage crisis gets a lot of buzz – but since Hilary Clinton's attempt to create a universal coverage plan was shot down early in her husband's tenure as president, few mainstream candidates have been willing to outline a specific, coherent strategy for reform. In fact, rejection of sweeping health care reform is somewhat of a tradition in the U.S., going back to the days when President Truman stumbled in the 1940s after introducing a universal coverage proposal. In addition, of those citizens who actually get out and vote each season, a large majority (92 percent in the 2000 election) have health insurance anyway, so officials aren't exactly running to fix the problem of the uninsured, according to an April 2004 BusinessWeek article. So while many reformers say a "single-payer plan" – one in which the government takes over the administration of all health care costs – is the only reasonable way to tame the coverage dragon, it may take a while before a viable plan takes shape.

Liability looms

Another type of reform that gets plenty of Congressional buzz is in the area of medical malpractice liability. In fact, the powerful American Medical Association has made the issue its top priority recently. The association has taken to identifying states that are in a "medical liability crisis" owing to exploding insurance premiums and their effect – providers limiting or halting certain services because of liability risks. In June 2004, there were 20 such states on the AMA's list. One such state, Massachusetts, is a case in point – according to Massachusetts Medical Society research, 50 percent of the state's neurosurgeons, 41 percent of orthopedic surgeons and 36 percent of general surgeons had been forced to limit their scopes of practice because of insurmountable medical liability costs.

The Bush administration cited an end to "junk lawsuits" as one of its primary goals for the president's second term, calling for "medical liability reform that will reduce health care costs and make sure patients have the doctors and care they need." In the early months following his January 2005 inauguration, Congress passed Bush-backed legislation to restrain class-action lawsuits and overhaul bankruptcy laws. However, Bush's influence has not fared as well for the "med-mal" bill, which is expected to be passed through the House, but stands to be blocked by Senate Democrats. Bush's proposal limits to $250,000 the amount a health provider could be required to pay a patient for "pain and suffering" beyond actual cost of medical services provided and provides for payout of judgments over time instead of in a lump sum. Lobbyists from the Association of Trial Lawyers of America are also aiming to block the medical malpractice proposal.

It's a seemingly unending loop: With multi-million-dollar judgments against providers making headlines regularly, a solid industry of trial lawyers is devoted to representing patients who complain of poor care (and in some cases, abuse or the deaths of loved ones). At the same time, such judgments cause liability insurers to panic, and many are refusing to cover health care

Visit Vault at **www.vault.com** for insider company profiles, expert advice, career message boards, expert resume reviews, the Vault Job Board and more.

VAULT CAREER LIBRARY 125

providers at all. The insurers who have stayed in the medical liability market can charge a premium that providers increasingly can't afford to pay.

For lawmakers, the issue is a tough one – how do you set a cap on the amount a plaintiff can receive for the preventable death of a loved one? Patient advocates frame the issue as a David-versus-Goliath scenario, charging that the monolithic medical community wants to limit consumers' rights to sue providers for poor care. Meanwhile, as the industry waits for the federal government to come up with a solution, states have begun to tackle the issue themselves, setting their own limits on the amount of money a malpractice judgment can reap for the plaintiff. Voters in the state of Texas, which was listed on the AMA's liability list, recently approved a constitutional amendment that caps awards for non-economic damages at $250,000. Similar tort reform measures are in place in West Virginia and Ohio. Though the actions of these states are a far cry from the kind of national reform physicians and insurers are gunning for, it is a start in a definitive direction.

Hot hospitals

In 2002, hospital spending increased by 9.5 percent from the year before, to $486.5 billion. Growing demand for hospital services, along with higher rates from private insurers, have led to the fourth straight year of growth in this sector. Among the approximately 6,100 hospitals in the U.S., a few tower over the rest. Each year, *U.S. News & World Report* publishes a ranking of the nation's top hospitals, surveying doctors around the country about hospitals' reputations in 17 medical specialties as well as other factors like staffing, morbidity rates and technology. In 2004, *U.S. News & World Report's* list named Baltimore's Johns Hopkins Hospital as No. 1 overall – a position the institution has held for 14 years running. The Mayo Clinic was ranked second, followed by Massachusetts General, The Cleveland Clinic and UCLA Medical Center.

In 2005, the government launched a new web site, www.hospitalcompare.hhs.gov, comparing nearly 4,200 hospitals that volunteered data in 17 different areas related to heart attack, heart failure and pneumonia in an effort to help physicians and patients see how hospitals nationwide compare in terms of quality of care. Federal officials plan to use the site as a model for future efforts to publicize hospital results and assess Medicare participants, which they hope will lead to quality improvements within practices.

The downfall of the health care business

Tenet Healthcare, the nation's second-largest hospital chain, provides a cautionary tale about the perils of doing business in this industry. The company, with 98 acute care hospitals and numerous other facilities nationwide, has been the subject of federal investigations into the way it handled Medicare payments over the last few years. Charles Grassley, chair of the Senate Finance Committee, has said that Tenet "appears to be a corporation that is ethically and morally bankrupt." In May 2003, beleaguered CEO Jeffrey Barbakow stepped down after 10 years of heading the firm. The company paid a record settlement amount of $375 million in 1994 for alleged kickbacks and bribes to doctors as inducements to refer patients to its psychiatric hospitals. Tenet made headlines again 10 years later as it began talking to the feds about a possible $1 billion settlement to end an investigation into charges it performed unnecessary heart surgeries on patients – and industry insiders speculated about a possible bankruptcy filing. Another headline-grabbing health care scandal recently involved HealthSouth, the nation's largest provider of physical rehab, outpatient surgery and diagnostic services. In 2003, the Securities and Exchange Commission hit HealthSouth with charges of cooking the books, accusing the company and its founder and CEO, Richard Scrushy, of overstating earnings by $1.4 billion since 1999.

The dreaded "home"

The term "nursing home" strikes fear in the hearts of many Americans, primarily due to media reports detailing abuse and unsanitary conditions at many facilities – and often because of consumers' first-hand experiences with these institutions. But the nation's nursing homes – also sometimes called "skilled nursing facilities" (SNFs) or "long-term care facilities" – have traveled a rocky road in recent years. Indeed, their crisis helps illustrate larger trends in the health care industry as a whole, particularly among providers that, like nursing homes, rely heavily on federal and state dollars to reimburse them for the cost of patient care. By 2001, nine of the top nursing home corporations in the country, including top names like Genesis Health Ventures, Vencor, Sun Healthcare Systems and Mariner Post-Acute Networks, had passed through the bankruptcy court system, saddled with hundreds of millions in debt.

What brought these billion-dollar companies to this low point, when they have such a steady stream of consumers desperate for their services? For one thing, many long-term care facilities overextended their debt burdens in the 1990s, investing in rehab facilities and other ancillary services that promised big (some would say "inflated") paybacks from Medicare. Then Medicare struck back, as Congress passed the Balanced Budget Act of 1997, which, among other things, sought to reduce federal health care spending by instituting entirely new payment systems for major health entities like nursing homes, home care agencies, hospitals and doctors. Under the old system, providers were basically paid a fixed amount, or fee, for each service they provided to Medicare patients. Fair enough, but patient advocates and Congress began to worry that nursing home clients were receiving a bit too much care – excessive and unnecessary therapy services, for instance – simply because facilities could make more money by providing and charging the feds for it. In the BBA, Congress mandated a new "prospective payment system" (PPS) that set up strict guidelines for how long-term care facilities were to be reimbursed for care provided to Medicare and Medicaid patients. Under PPS, facilities are basically paid a fixed per-diem for a patient's care depending on the severity of her needs (or "acuity level"), which is determined using a host of intricate rules. The system also set certain limits, or "caps," on services such as rehab, under which Medicare would only pay a fixed amount per patient annually.

The combination of leftover debt and poor financial management, plummeting federal dollars and skyrocketing liability insurance due to high-profile malpractice judgments – plus a host of other factors like low staffing due to undesirable working conditions and a higher acuity level among the patient population – sent at least 10 percent of the nursing home industry into Chapter 11 by 2001, by some estimates. Most of the nursing home giants have recovered and are learning to adjust to the new payment system, but the situation provided a valuable lesson to other health care providers, like rehab hospitals, whose new Medicare PPS systems took effect after the long-term care revamp had done its damage. Congress, acknowledging that it may have been a bit enthusiastic with the red ink, also kicked in some million-dollar concessions to boost reimbursements after intense industry lobbying.

Others weren't so lucky – many providers of those once high-paying ancillary services, like physical therapy, were forced to close their doors in the aftermath of PPS. Home health care providers, also highly dependent on Medicare and Medicaid payments, weathered a similar crisis to that of long-term care under their own new payment system – and, like their counterparts, managed to eke out some financial givebacks from Congress during the last few years.

Virtual care

Despite fancier defibrillators and sleeker MRIs, many observers have argued that the health care industry actually is a dinosaur when it comes to technology. In fact, less than 5 percent of the total amount of health care spending in the U.S. will go toward information technology in 2004, CMS estimates. But both providers and payors have begun to catch on to the benefits of doing business electronically. From the providers' side, patient advocates argue that care can be improved by standardizing practices using digital technology – for instance, using hand-held devices to transcribe, translate and store doctors' near-illegible notes from patient records. These types of solutions may help cut down on the estimated 44,000 to 98,000 patient deaths per year said to be caused by provider errors (as outlined in a widely publicized 1999 Institutes of Medicine report).

One Chicago-area hospital profiled in a July 2004 *BusinessWeek* article has taken the plunge and gone entirely "paperless" over the past three years. Evanston Northwestern Healthcare's $60 million project has made nearly every point along the

Visit Vault at **www.vault.com** for insider company profiles, expert advice, career message boards, expert resume reviews, the Vault Job Board and more.

VAULT CAREER LIBRARY   **127**

patient care continuum virtual, putting everything from surgical bay orders to medical records transcription online. The hospital predicts the overhaul will save $10 million per year. Patients benefit from such a system, too – at Evanston, doctors can access results of mammograms in just one day, as opposed to three weeks under the old system, and the hospital has slashed the late administration of meds to patients by 70 percent. Among the IT solutions health care systems will be investing in over the coming decade are information systems that can standardize the clinical treatment of diseases and bar-code systems for managing drugs and lab samples. Even the government has gotten onboard the IT bandwagon – the Bush administration has said it wants all U.S. patient care records in an electronic format by 2014.

Going with the flow

Payors also have gone digital, requiring electronic filing of claims by providers and switching to online systems to provide essential information like updates on Medicare rules. As more and more patient health information flows through virtual data streams, however, systems needed to be put in place to help the disparate entities in the health care chain communicate with one another in a standardized way, and, most importantly, to protect the privacy of that free-flowing patient data. Thus was born the Health Insurance Portability and Accountability Act (HIPAA), signed by President Clinton, which covers both the privacy of medical records and the transmission of claims among payors and providers.

HIPAA, which promises hefty fines if providers violate a host of complex stipulations, sent the health care world into a minor panic – and thus a multi-million-dollar software, education and consulting industry was born. As the HIPAA rules began to be enforced in 2003, patients in doctors' offices may have noticed subtle changes, such as the "Notice of Privacy Practices" form attached to their clipboards upon check-in, one requirement of the law. Such requirements often are seen as busywork by harried health care providers, but some of the law's provisions respond to very real concerns – such as the fear that prospective employers or other decision-makers could hijack a patient's medical records off the Information Superhighway. Other, less extreme examples include the regulation of how much information hospitals and other providers can reveal regarding patients under their care, and the setting of limits on the amount of time patient records can be left to molder in basement file drawers. On the claims-processing side, HIPAA mandates an electronic transaction standard for Medicare claims sent between providers and Medicare contractors. The reward for compliance with the standard, in theory anyway, is more efficient and timely payment of these claims.

CDHC – the new wave of care?

One plan for health care that has generated a buzz in the Bush administration is the idea of "consumer-driven health care," or CDHC. The idea is simple: If consumers can control their own health care spending, providers and insurers will be forced to compete for business, thus (hopefully) increasing quality of care while driving down costs. At the crux of CDHC are health savings accounts (HSAs), or tax-free accounts offered along with low-cost, high-deductible insurance plans. Either employee or employer (or both) stow away a certain amount of money in the HSA each year, which consumers can spend on virtually any health treatment or medication they want; whatever is unused is theirs to keep.

Early forms of CDHC have shown up in a number of employer health care plans, including Sara Lee and Aetna. Benefits consultancy Mercer expects 73 percent of firms to add HSAs to their benefits offerings by 2006. Advocates for CDHC plans use the example of cosmetic surgery: Since consumers must pay for procedures completely out of pocket, they almost always find the best care at the lowest price. Since 1998, the average price of a tummy tuck has risen 19 percent, only slightly higher than inflation – and far below the 49 percent rise in per capita spending on health care for the same period. Opponents of the plan suggest that employers will use CDHC as a cover to drive up health care costs, and create a further schism between the quality of care received by the rich and the poor.

Becoming the biggest

According to Philip Pfrang, the national director of Life Sciences and Health Care at Deloitte's Merger & Acquisition Services practice, M&A activity among managed-care companies is alive and well as regional firms try to expand their brands to reach more U.S. workers stateside and abroad. Pfrang likens the managed care sector of health care to the pharmaceutical business, which has seen a select few companies emerge as large organizations through acquisitions. The hospital sector has also seen its fair share of venture/mergers recently, as competitive pressures in the industry increase.

WellPoint, today's largest leading health plan, gained its No.-1 ranking through a 2004 merger with Anthem worth $16.4 billion. Humana, the third-largest HMO in the nation, nearly became the top provider back in 1998, but failed to complete a merger with UnitedHealth, which chose instead to grow through its own acquisitions, including the 2002 purchase of AmeriChoice and the 2003 buyout of Mid Atlantic Medical Services worth $2.95 billion. One merger that proved to be a huge success was the 1997 combination of Beckman Instruments and the Coulter Corporation. The resulting company, Beckman Coulter, is currently one of the world's largest providers of instrument systems and products for laboratory work. Additionally, Coventry Health Care, among the largest HMO providers nationwide, was formed in 1998 through Coventry Corporation's acquisition of the Principal Financial Group's health care unit.

Sometimes, in the health care industry, reinvention can be an equally powerful tool to gaining market share. A number of the top companies in health care today survived bankruptcy scandals during the 1990s and re-emerged as successful businesses. Kindred, one of the nation's largest health care providers, was formerly Vencor Inc.; Caremark Rx, one of the nation's largest pharmaceutical services providers, used to be a division of the now-defunct MedPartners; and DaVita, the country's largest independent provider of dialysis services, was once Total Renal Care Holdings.

Other top companies in health care today include Cardinal Health, one of the largest wholesalers of pharmaceutical products and surgical supplies; HCA, one of the largest hospital operators in the U.S.; Guidant, a top medical device makers; and Medtronic, one of the world's leading medical technology companies.

Where the jobs are

In spite of its daunting complexity, the health care industry has one big upside – it's a reliable producer of job opportunities. The health services industry, the largest of all industries categorized by the Bureau of Labor Statistics (BLS) as of 2002, provided nearly 13 million jobs that year. Of the 20 occupations the BLS projects to grow the fastest in coming years, half are in the health services sector. And of new wage and salary jobs that will be created by 2012, about 16 percent will be in health services – more than in any other industry. According to a February 2005 report by CNN/Money, many of the fastest growing employment opportunities are in health care. The Labor Department predicts more than 600,000 jobs in nursing will open up by 2012, while physician's assistant jobs will grow by 50 percent and occupational therapist jobs by 35 percent. Additionally, positions for home care workers will increase by 40 percent. Fitness trainers and dental hygienists are also expected to be popular professions.

While the suggestion of working in the health care industry may conjure visions of crushing med school debt and grueling internships, in fact the majority of jobs in the sector require less than four years of college education. Graduates of one- and two-year certification programs might work as medical records and health information technicians. Service occupations abound, including medical and dental assistants, nursing and home health aides and facility cleaning jobs. The BLS predicts particularly strong growth in jobs outside the inpatient hospital sector, such as medical assistants and home health aides. There is a constant clamor for more nurses, as facilities face growing regulatory pressure to meet mandatory staffing levels.

Visit Vault at **www.vault.com** for insider company profiles, expert advice, career message boards, expert resume reviews, the Vault Job Board and more.

VAULT CAREER LIBRARY 129

MBAs in Health Care

Got a hankering to use that MBA for health as well as wealth? Here's a quick look at some of the options available to MBAs in the health care industry.

MBA with no health care experience

New MBAs with no health care experience often find jobs in similar venues as undergraduate liberal arts majors: consulting or financial services firms. While they come in with more responsibility and a much higher salary than undergraduates, MBAs without previous experience in health care are unlikely to be assigned to work exclusively within the health care industry. MBAs with a strong interest in developing health care experience should seek out opportunities as internal analysts or administrators for managed care companies, hospital or corporate health benefits offices. Other routes include finding work in the marketing offices of large pharmaceutical companies and physician groups.

MBA with health care experience

MBAs with previous health care experience have a range of options working in the health care industry or in related service industries such as consulting and public relations. Consulting firms often hire these individuals exclusively to work and develop new business among health care clients. McKinsey & Company hires individuals with substantial health care experience (either in consulting or industry) as "practice experts," a track separate from the more the general business analyst and associate tracks.

Depending on the nature of their previous experience, MBAs with previous health care experience join hospitals or hospital systems as junior administrators with the option of staying and rising through the ranks of the institution's administrative hierarchy. MBAs with clinical experience as physicians have the most lucrative opportunities: Many of these individuals are called on to oversee and manage the intersection of financial and clinical processes as hospital quality administrators or managed care medical directors.

Health Care Consulting

Once you land a job in the health care consulting, what you can expect depends largely on the type of firm your choose. Graduate degree holders with health care-related degrees or those who have substantial experience in the health care industry prior to attending graduate school are usually pegged early in the recruiting process to the firm's health care industry practice.

New hires at larger firms are more likely to have a standardized, predictable experience compared to their counterparts at smaller firms without formal internal processes for allocating work. But a "can-do" attitude regardless of the nature or size of the task is rewarded at all firms.

Kinder and gentler

The organizational motivation of most consulting firms includes an unspoken irony – each project implies a strong commitment to a client's interests without any guarantees of a long-term relationship or of any follow-up beyond the project's contractual boundary. In this environment the motivations of consultants stem largely from the project's intellectual challenges. While consultants often "believe" in what they are trying to accomplish for a client on a project, their visceral rise results from the application of intellectual muscle to complex questions.

Government involvement in regulating and purchasing health care reflects public opinion that health care is a social good that government should work to preserve. Even private health care market participants (and their consultants) tend to have a more humanitarian orientation compared to other industries that are more exclusively concerned with "bottom-line" issues. On the other hand, bottom-line issues are still the focus as the government looks to control public spending on health care and publicly traded technology providers and managed care organizations seek profit-increasing efficiencies. All in all, health care consultants are expected to have the same skill set as all other consultants, but may be seen as "kinder and gentler" than their counterparts consulting in other industries.

Visit Vault at **www.vault.com** for insider company profiles, expert advice, career message boards, expert resume reviews, the Vault Job Board and more.

V∧ULT CAREER LIBRARY   131

Employer Directory

Roche Diagnostics

9115 Hague Road
Indianapolis, Indiana 462520
http://careers.ind.roche.com

Roche Diagnostics is the world's leading provider of diagnostic systems and decision-oriented health information. We are dedicated to the discovery, development, manufacturing, marketing and servicing of products and solutions for medical laboratories, physicians and patients, as well as for research and industry. Roche Diagnostics is a diverse, inclusive company that seeks, celebrates and leverages diversity to maximize the competitive advantage of people. We offer a variety of opportunities at our U.S. diagnostics marketing and sales headquarters in Indiana and at our global molecular business area headquarters in California.

Business schools Roche Diagnostics recruits from

University of Chicago; Northwestern (Kellogg); Indiana University (Kelley); Harvard Business School, Duke University (Fuqua); U.C.L.A.; University of Michigan; Purdue University; MIT (Sloan); University of Pennsylvania (Wharton); Yale University, Stanford University; UC Berkeley (Haas); Washington University (Olin)

Aetna Inc.

151 Farmington Ave.
Hartford, CT 06156
Phone: (860) 273-0123
Fax: (860) 273-3971
Toll Free: (800) 872-3862
www.aetna.com

Amerigroup Corporation

4425 Corporation Lane
Virginia Beach, VA 23462
Phone: (757) 490-6900
Fax: (757) 490-7152
www.amerigrp.com

Applera Corporation

301 Merritt 7
Norwalk, CT 06851-1070
Phone: (203) 840-2000
Fax: (203) 840-2312
www.applera.com

Beckman Coulter Inc.

4300 N. Harbor Blvd.
Fullerton, CA 92834-3100
Phone: (714) 871-4848
Fax: (714) 773-8283
www.beckman.com

Beverly Healthcare

1000 Beverly Way
Fort Smith, AR 72919
Phone: (479) 201-2000
Fax: (479) 201-1101
www.beverlyhealthcare.com

Boston Scientific Corporation

1 Boston Scientific Place
Natick, MA 01760-1537
Phone: (508) 650-8000
Fax: (508) 647-2393
www.bostonscientific.com

Caremark Rx, Inc.

211 Commerce Street, Suite 800
Nashville, TN 37201
Phone: (615) 743-6600
Fax: (205) 733-9780
www.caremark.com

CIGNA

1 Liberty Place
Philadelphia, PA 19192-1550
Phone: (215) 761-1000
Fax: (215) 761-5515
www.cigna.com

Community Health Systems, Inc.

155 Franklin Road, Ste. 400
Brentwood, TN 37027-4600
Phone: (615) 373-9600
Fax: (615) 371-1068
www.chs.net

Coventry Health Care, Inc.

6705 Rockledge Drive
Suite 900
Bethesda, MD 20817
Phone: (301) 581-0600
Fax: (301) 493-0731
www.cvty.com

DaVita, Inc.

601 Hawaii Street
El Segundo, CA 90245
Phone: (310) 536-2400
Fax: (310) 536-2675
www.davita.com

Express Scripts, Inc.

13900 Riverport Drive
Maryland Heights, MO 63043
Phone: (314) 770-1666
Fax: (314) 702-7037
www.express-scripts.com

Fresenius Medical Care AG

Else-Kröner-Straße 1
61346 Bad Homburg, Germany
Phone: +49-6172-608-0
Fax: +49-6172-608-2488
www.fmc-ag.com

Guidant Corporation

111 Monument Circle, 29th Floor
Indianapolis, IN 46204
Phone: (317) 971-2000
Fax: (317) 971-2040
www.guidant.com

HCA, Inc.

1 Park Plaza
Nashville, TN 37203
Phone: (615) 344-9551
Fax: (615) 344-2266
www.hcahealthcare.com

Health Management Associates, Inc.

5811 Pelican Bay Blvd., Suite 500
Naples, FL 34108-2710
Phone: (239) 598-3131
Fax: (239) 598-2705
www.hma-corp.com

Health Net, Inc.

21650 Oxnard Street
Woodland Hills, CA 91367
Phone: (818) 676-6000
Fax: (818) 676-8591
www.healthnet.com

HealthSouth Corporation

1 HealthSouth Pkwy.
Birmingham, AL 35243
Phone: (205) 967-7116
Fax: (205) 969-6889
www.healthsouth.com

Hillenbrand Industries, Inc.

700 State Route 46 East
Batesville, IN 47006-8835
Phone: (812) 934-7000
Fax: (812) 934-7371
www.hillenbrand.com

Humana Inc.

The Humana Building
500 W. Main Street
Louisville, KY 40202
Phone: (502) 580-1000
Fax: (502) 580-3677
www.humana.com

Kaiser Permanente

1 Kaiser Plaza, Suite 2600
Oakland, CA 94612-3673
Phone: (510) 271-5800
Fax: (510) 267-7524
www.kaiserpermanente.org

Kindred Health Care

680 S. 4th Street
Louisville, KY 40202-2412
Phone: (502) 596-7300
Fax: (502) 596-4170
www.kindredhealthcare.com

Laboratory Corp. of America

358 S. Main Street
Burlington, NC 27215
Phone: (336) 229-1127
Fax: (336) 436-1205
www.labcorp.com

Magellan Health Services, Inc.

16 Munson Road
Farmington, CT 06032
Phone: (860) 507-1900
Fax: (410) 953-5200
www.magellanhealth.com

Manor Care, Inc.

333 N. Summit Street
Toledo, OH 43604-2617
Phone: (419) 252-5500
Fax: (419) 252-5596
www.hcr-manorcare.com

Mariner Health Care, Inc.

1 Ravinia Dr., Ste. 1500
Atlanta, GA 30346
Phone: (678) 443-7000
Fax: (770) 393-8054
www.marinerhealth.com

Medco Health Solutions

100 Parsons Pond Drive
Franklin Lakes, NJ 07417-2604
Phone: (201) 269-3400
Fax: (201) 269-1109
www.medco.com

Medical Mutual of Ohio

2060 E. 9th Street
Cleveland, OH 44115-1300
Phone: (216) 687-7000
Fax: (216) 687-6044
www.mmoh.com

Medtronic, INC.

710 Medtronic Pkwy. NE
Minneapolis, MN 55432-5604
Phone: (763) 514-4000
Fax: (763) 514-4879
www.medtronic.com

NeighborCare, Inc.

601 East Pratt Street, 3rd Floor
Baltimore, MD 21202
Phone: (410) 528-7300
Fax: (410) 528-7473
www.neighborcare.com

PacifiCare Health Systems, Inc.

5995 Plaza Drive
Cypress, CA 90630
Phone: (714) 952-1121
Fax: (714) 226-3581
www.pacificare.com

Quest Diagnostics Incorporated

1 Malcolm Avenue
Teterboro, NJ 07608
Phone: (201) 393-5000
Fax: (201) 462-4715
www.questdiagnostics.com

Sierra Health Services, Inc.

2724 N. Tenaya Way
Las Vegas, NV 89128
Phone: (702) 242-7000
Fax: (702) 242-9711
www.sierrahealth.com

Visit Vault at **www.vault.com** for insider company profiles, expert advice,
career message boards, expert resume reviews, the Vault Job Board and more.

VAULT CAREER LIBRARY   133

St. Jude Medical, Inc.
1 Lillehei Plaza
St. Paul, MN 55117-9983
Phone: (651) 483-2000
Fax: (651) 482-8318
www.sjm.com

Stryker Corporation
2725 Fairfield Road
Kalamazoo, MI 49002
Phone: (269) 385-2600
Fax: (269) 385-1062
www.strykercorp.com

Sun Healthcare Group, Inc.
18831 Von Karman, Ste. 400
Irvine, CA 92612
Phone: (949) 255-7100
Fax: (949) 255-7054
www.sunh.com

Tenet Healthcare
13737 Noel Road
Dallas, TX 75240
Phone: (469) 893-2200
Fax: (469) 893-8600
www.tenethealth.com

UnitedHealth Group Inc.
UnitedHealth Group Center
9900 Bren Road East
Minnetonka, MN 55343
Phone: (952) 936-1300
Fax: (952) 936-7430
www.unitedhealthgroup.com

Universal Health Services
Universal Corporate Center
367 S. Gulph Road
King of Prussia, PA 19406-0958
Phone: (610) 768-3300
Fax: (610) 768-3336
www.uhsinc.com

WellChoice, Inc.
11 W. 42nd Street
New York, NY 10036
Phone: (212) 476-7800
Fax: (212) 476-1281
www.wellchoice.com

WellPoint, Inc.
120 Monument Circle
Indianapolis, IN 46204
Phone: (317) 488-6000
Fax: (317) 488-6028
www.wellpoint.com

Hedge Funds

What is a Hedge Fund?

In a recent article by *The Wall Street Journal*, Tremont Advisors reported that hedge funds took in approximately $72.2 billion in assets in 2003 and that worldwide hedge fund investment is now as high as $750 billion in assets.

Hedge funds are considered an "alternative investment" vehicle. The term "alternative investment" is the general term under which unregulated funds operate; this includes private equity and real estate funds. The total "alternative" category (would include private equity and real estate) is not covered within the scope of this section but it is useful to know that often people refer to hedge funds as alternative investments. Mainstream funds are investment funds that everyday investors can purchase, mutual funds are the prime example of a mainstream fund.

Over the past decade, hedge funds have grown tremendously in terms of assets under management and also garnered a lot of media attention. Although, despite their growth and popularity, hedge funds still remain a mystery to many people who do not understand exactly what they are and how they work. So what exactly is a hedge fund?

A Concise Definition of "Hedge Fund"

A 'private unregistered investment pool' encompassing all types of investment funds, companies and private partnerships that can use a variety of investment techniques such as borrowing money through leverage, selling short, derivatives for directional investing and options.

During the early years of the hedge fund industry (1950s to 1970s), the term 'hedge fund' was used to describe the 'hedging' strategy used by managers at the time. "Hedging" refers to the hedge fund manager making additional trades in an attempt to counterbalance any risk involved with the existing positions in the portfolio. Hedging can be accomplished in many different ways but the most basic technique is to purchase a long position and a secondary short position in a similar security. This is used to offset price fluctuations and is an effective way of neutralizing the effects of market conditions.

Today, the term 'hedge fund' tells an investor nothing about the underlying investment activities, similar to the term "mutual fund." So how do you figure out what the hedge fund manager does? You are able to figure out a little more about the underlying investment activities by understanding the trading/investment strategies that the hedge fund manager states he trades. The "investment strategy" is the investment approach or the techniques used by the hedge fund manager to have positive returns on the investments. If a manager says he trades long/short equity then you know he is buying undervalued equities and selling overvalued equities. Although this description is the long/short equity strategy at its most basic, it is important to understand the strategies that the manager says he employs. For more information on specific hedge fund investment strategies, see the *Vault Career Guide to Hedge Funds*.

Visit Vault at **www.vault.com** for insider company profiles, expert advice, career message boards, expert resume reviews, the Vault Job Board and more.

VAULT CAREER LIBRARY 135

Distinguishing Characteristics

So now that you have reviewed some of the basic terminology in the industry, we will explain the key points in depth. The main distinguishing characteristics of hedge funds are the following:

- Hedge funds can "hedge" their portfolio

- Hedge funds use derivatives

- Hedge funds can short sell

- Hedge funds have the ability to use leverage.

These characteristics make hedge funds different from most other investment funds, especially mutual funds. To get a good understanding of how a hedge fund manager operates, it is very important to understand these concepts. The four concepts are now defined in detail:

Hedging

Hedging refers to the execution of additional trades by the hedge fund manager in an attempt to counterbalance any risk involved with the existing positions in the portfolio. Hedging can be accomplished in many different ways, although the most basic technique is to purchase a long position and a secondary short position in a similar security (See Gap example). This is used to offset price fluctuations and is an effective way of neutralizing the effects of market conditions.

Hedging Example

Courtney is a hedge fund manager who invested in the Gap stores. Here we will see how he hedges his risk. Courtney is 'long' (he's bought) 100 shares of Gap Stores but he now believes the retail industry may be vulnerable to a down turn in the market. He wants to hedge this risk and does this by going "short" (selling) Abercrombie & Fitch, which is in the same retail industry.

Q. What would happen if the retail industry did poorly?
A. The share prices of both Gap and Abercrombie & Fitch might decline.

Q. How would this affect any money Courtney makes?
A. Since Courtney is long on Gap (he owns it) he would lose money on this trade. Since Courtney is also short (he has already sold it) Abercrombie & Fitch, he would make money on that trade. Therefore he can offset some of his losses from Gap with gains from Abercrombie & Fitch. He reduces his risk of Gap by hedging with Abercrombie & Fitch.

Q. When you say Courtney gains from the Abercrombie & Fitch trade, what does this mean?
A. When Courtney goes short A&F it means he has sold it before he owns it. So say he sold 100 A&F shares short for $50 each. He receives $5,000 cash for doing so. This transaction is conducted through his broker and he now owes 100 A&F shares to his broker, to be paid back at some time the future. As time goes by the retail industry does poorly and the share price of A&F falls to $40.

Q. If the stock price of A&F falls to $40, what does this mean for Courtney's profits?
A. Since Courtney owes 100 A&F shares to his broker he can now go out and buy the 100 shares for $40 each, costing him a total of $4,000. Therefore Courtney has made $1,000 profit. (He received $5,000 from the original short sale and then paid $4,000 to buy A&F, so his profit is $1,000)

Derivatives

Derivatives that are used by hedge funds can take on many forms, and the more complex derivatives (interest rate swaps, foreign currency swaps, contract for differences, total return swaps, etc.) are not covered in this book. Discussed now are the most basic forms of derivatives: 'put' and "call' options on stocks:

Option Definitions

Put option

A 'put' option gives the holder the right to sell the underlying stock at a specified price (strike price) on or before a given date (exercise date).

Call option

A 'call' option gives the holder the right to buy the underlying stock at specified price (strike price) on or before a given date (exercise date).

Option writer

The seller of these options is referred to as the "writer" – many hedge funds will often write options in accordance with their strategies. This is the person who originates an option contract by promising to perform a certain obligation in return for the price or premium of the option. Any investor can sell options (write options) provided they have answered an options questionnaire provided to them by their broker. This would determine the knowledge of the investor and whether they understand the risks associated with writing options.

How does a hedge fund manager use options to reduce risk?

Consider Kristin, a long/short hedge fund manager, who in January 2004 owns 1,000 Wal-Mart shares. The current share price is $73 per share. Kristin is concerned about developments in Wal-Mart's illegal immigrant lawsuit that may cause the share price to decline sharply in the next two months and wants to protect herself from this risk. The process that Kristin would go through to hedge the risk of Wal-Mart's share price falling would be:

- Kristin could buy 10 July 'put' options with a strike price of $65 on the Chicago Board Options Exchange (www.cboe.com).

- This 'put' option gives Kristin the right to sell 1,000 shares for $65 per share at any time before it expires in July. If the market price of Wal-Mart falls below $65, the options can be exercised so that Kristin received $65,000 for the entire holding. When the cost of the options is taken into account, the amount realized is $62,500.

- If the quoted option price is $2.50, each option contract would cost $250. Since each option contract is valued per 100 shares, the total cost of the hedging strategy would be 10* $250 = $2,500.

- Although this strategy costs $2,500, it guarantees that the shares can be sold for at least $65 per share for the life of the option (it expires in July).

- But if the market price stays above $65, the options are not exercised because Kristin can make more money by just selling the shares for market price.

Visit Vault at **www.vault.com** for insider company profiles, expert advice, career message boards, expert resume reviews, the Vault Job Board and more.

V\ULT CAREER LIBRARY   **137**

The Chicago Board Options Exchange (CBOE)

The CBOE created an orderly market with well-defined contracts on 16 stocks when it began trading call option contracts in 1973. The exchange began trading put options in 1977. The CBOE now trades options on over 1,200 stocks and many different stock indices. Many other exchanges throughout the world also trade option contracts. To learn more, visit the exchange's web site at www.cboe.com.

Short selling (going "short")

Short selling involves the selling of a security that the seller does not own. Short sellers believe that the stock price will fall and that they will be able to repurchase the stock at a lower price in the future. Thus, they will profit from selling the stock at a higher price, then buy it in the future at a lower price. (The opposite of going "short" is going "long," when investors buy stocks they believe will rise.)

Short Selling Example

Jimmy believes that McDonalds is overvalued and that he can profit by selling short "MCD." Jimmy sells short 100 shares at $50 which means he has sold stock that he does not yet own, this is a stock loan. In the future he has to buy the stock to repay the stock loan he entered into when shorting the stock. But, McDonald's price continues to rise to $75, this means that in order to buy the stock (this is called "covering" his stock loan), Jimmy pays $75 per share which results in him losing $2,500 (100 * $25)

Before Jimmy enters into the short sale, he must ensure that he is able to borrow the stock (get a stock loan), usually through its prime broker. Jimmy will call the stock loan department of the prime broker to see if the prime broker has the stock available to lend to him. If the stock loan department has the stock to lend, then Jimmy can short sell the stock (borrowing it from the prime broker). If the stock is not available for borrow, Jimmy cannot sell short the security.

Leverage

Leverage measures the amount of assets being borrowed for each investment dollar. Leverage (borrowing additional funds) is utilized by hedge fund managers when they believe that the cost of the borrowed funds will be minimal compared to the returns of a particular position. It can be a key component to hedge fund management since it gives the hedge fund managers the ability to have higher returns (and potentially lose more) with borrowed funds.

Typical hedge fund leverage depends on the type of financial instruments that the hedge fund trades. Fixed income has lower risk levels so it is not uncommon to have four or five times the value of the fund borrowed. Equities have a higher risk profile and therefore typical leverage is one and a half to two times the value of the fund. However hedge funds are usually comprised of long and short positions, so a large market rise or fall has little impact if their profitable positions were equally balanced by their losing positions.

The simplest examples in everyday life of leverage are house mortgages and car loans. The bank manager uses the house or the car as collateral for the loan from the bank. The bank manager can then sell the house or the car if you default on your loan. Similarly, the hedge fund manager uses the financial instruments in his account as collateral for the funds they have borrowed from their bank (prime broker). The primary sources of leverage are financial institutions and banks. If the hedge fund manager cannot pay the loan back, the financial institution can then sell the collateral (the financial instruments in the account) to pay back the loan.

Leverage Calculation Example

If the hedge fund has $1 million of invested money and is borrowing another $2 million, to bring the total dollars invested to $3 million, then the leverage used is 200 percent. The amount of leverage typically used by the fund is shown as a percentage of the fund.

Organizational Structure of a Typical Hedge Fund

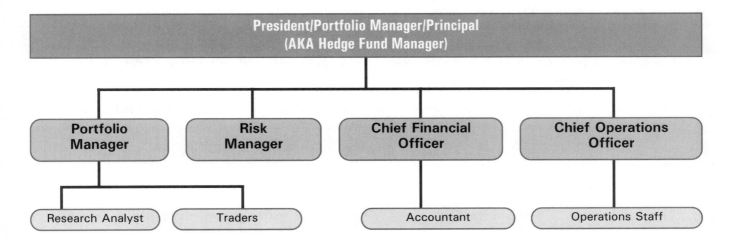

So what exactly are hedge fund managers and what do they do? A hedge fund manager is normally the founder and the key person in charge of overseeing the whole operation of the hedge fund. This means that he/she is responsible for overseeing the portfolio, often making trading decisions, hiring personnel, monitoring the risk of the portfolio and ensuring that the accounting and operations departments are in order. The hedge fund manager is often referred to as the principal or president and can often also be called the portfolio manager.

Hedge funds vary in size from assets under management from as little as $1 million to over $10 billion. Unlike a typical investment bank, the roles of the employees at hedge funds are not the same for each hedge fund. Someone entering an investment bank as a trader will likely have a similar role to someone else entering another investment bank as a trader. Traders at hedge funds are likely to have different responsibilities, which are usually determined by the size of the fund. At a smaller fund the trader is much more likely to be involved with the operations of the trade whereas a larger hedge fund would have a separate operations person to handle this element. A smaller hedge fund may have 3- 4 employees whereas a larger hedge fund may employ over 300 people.

A typical hedge fund will have various departments: operations, accounting, trading, and risk and investor relations. These departments support the trading decisions and operations of the hedge fund. Since the size of hedge funds vary dramatically, the number of people in each department can range from one to over 20. As a hedge fund grows in size (manages more money), more personnel are added to support the increased trading volume.

In the next few pages we will attempt to clearly outline the different departments at hedge funds and the distinct roles within each department. While you read through the different roles it is very important to note that specific job titles are not important at hedge funds. This is because one role (job) can have many different titles depending on the hedge fund. For example, an Operations Analyst can also be called Portfolio Analyst, Trading Assistant or Accountant depending on the size and environment of the fund.

Visit Vault at **www.vault.com** for insider company profiles, expert advice, career message boards, expert resume reviews, the Vault Job Board and more.

VAULT CAREER LIBRARY   **139**

In addition, due to the varying sizes of hedge funds, employees tend to have a more diverse range of responsibilities, which may overlap between several different departments. This unique nature of the hedge fund job requires superior teamwork skills and the ability to deal with a variety of people.

Director of Operations

Most individuals carrying this title either have several years of experience in the same capacity, a MBA or both. At this stage one generally has a staff of two to 10 people who are direct reports. The job functions are similar to the Operations Specialist although there is much more responsibility for the employees working under you as well as maintaining relationships between prime broker, banks, and off shore administrators.

Most individuals carrying this title either have several years of experience in the same capacity, a MBA or both. At this stage one generally has a staff of two to 10 people who are direct reports. The job functions are similar to the Operations Specialist although there is much more responsibility for the employees working under you as well as maintaining relationships between prime broker, banks, and off shore administrators.

This position will generally pay between $100,000 and $250,000 depending on experience, background and size of hedge fund.

A Day in the Life: Director of Operations

7:30 a.m. – Arrive at the office and log on to the computer, along will various back office and portfolio systems such as DTC. (See Glossary)

8:15 a.m. – Go over exception reports (available only to a manager) that show trades that have not settled and any Margin Calls for accounts and speak to the member of staff who works on it to get status on the item.

9:00 a.m. – Have weekly team meeting and go over team workload and coverage for the week.

10:00 a.m. – Get on a call with a manager in the prime broker because a large wire needs to be sent out for management fees and there needs to be extra attention give to it to make sure it goes through properly. The Prime Broker is described in detail in a few pages. In summary it is a department at an investment bank that offers products, technology and clearing services to a hedge fund.

11:00 a.m. – Have a meeting with the head trader on the convertible trading desk who does not agree with the final position on a particular security. Go over each transaction and see if anything was incorrectly booked. Have one of the staff members print all transaction reports internally and at the prime broker to find a solution to this problem as it may involve large losses for the desk.

1:00 p.m. – Have lunch at the desk while browsing through some stories on Bloomberg.

2:00 p.m. – Field calls and help the staff resolve any pending problems.

4:00 p.m. – Re-review all reports from the morning and make sure all highlighted discrepancies are resolved otherwise jot them down as "open items'.

5:00 p.m. – Create a list of agenda items for the next day and look at the calendar of any meetings.

6:00 p.m. – Leave work and meet the prime broker for dinner who is taking the operations team out.

7:00 p.m. – Discuss rates with the prime broker over dinner and get to know them better.

10:00 p.m. – Head home and try to get the motivation to go to the gym before crashing.

Risk Management

The risk department proactively monitors each hedge fund, identifying potential risks and then determining and understanding the importance of various types of risks. This department uses various propriety or vendor tools and methodologies for risk management and implements strategies to prevent any risk completely or to deal with them if they occur.

At a hedge fund, a risk management role can vary depending on the size of the fund. At a small fund generally the principals or the trading group may monitor the risk and there are no specific risk personnel versus at a larger fund there is a group who is solely responsible for monitoring risk. Many hedge funds are also known to outsource their risk controls through third party vendors specialized in providing this service to corporations, hedge funds, mutual funds etc. Many investment banks also provide such added value service through their prime broker departments (described later in the book).

Fund of funds are known to have a very large risk teams because of two reasons: Firstly, due to the way fund of funds operate they are dealing with a large variety of securities product base and secondly the risk group plays a large role in alleviating concerns of existing and potential investors.

Risk Associate

This associate level position will play a supporting role in the risk department. Many hedge funds don't have a separate risk department but this position would be available at an investment banks prime broker department.

At a prime broker the risk associate will perform the same duties except he will be monitoring risk for several hedge funds that are prime broker clients. This position generally requires a minimum of a bachelor's degree and a few years of relevant experience. A thorough understanding of a variety of trading products (i.e. options, fixed income, mortgage backed securities, swaptions), options risks (i.e. delta, gamma, Vega, rho, and theta)* and strong analytical skills are strongly recommended. The daily job duties include but are not limited to maintaining Value at Risk (VAR) data, back-testing and stress-testing securities within a portfolio and reporting the analyzed data to senior risk management.

For example, Heather works with the trading group to monitor risk. The hedge fund where she works subscribes/utilizes a risk monitoring system designed by a large investment bank. Every morning she will perform analysis to the short portfolio measuring how minor changes in the stock market such as the Dow Jones Industrial Average decreasing substantially in one day, could affect the value of the portfolio. Heather does not have to compute everything manually because the Risk system has built in mathematical models to attribute for different scenarios, although Heather needs to understand what the output of results mean and be able to verbally communicate those clearly to the traders and portfolio mangers along with having spreadsheets and graphs as back up of her analysis.

This position generally pays from $50K to $70K, depending on geographical location, previous experience, education skills and size of the corporation. The risk position could potentially have interaction with clients (investors) depending on the size of the fund. Some hedge funds have a designated investor relations employee whose sole responsibility is to field calls form investors. Although, in smaller funds investors may call the risk group directly to state and address any risk concerns. It is important that a hedge fund has a strong risk monitoring system because this reduces the likelihood of error and losses in the fund and will also help alleviates the investor's worries.

Risk jobs are found through job agencies or through connections. Generally traders also are well aware of job openings in the risk groups and can be a good source of contact/network.

Visit Vault at **www.vault.com** for insider company profiles, expert advice, career message boards, expert resume reviews, the Vault Job Board and more.

V/\ULT CAREER LIBRARY   **141**

Day in the Life: Risk Analyst at a Large Hedge Fund

7:30 a.m. – Get into the office and check e-mail. Chat with colleagues about interesting stories in the WSJ.

8:00 a.m.– Daily risk conference call with traders, portfolio manager and principals

9:30 a.m.– Monitoring the portfolios on one screen while looking at the markets affecting the various securities on another screen. Quantify illiquid positions and valuations risk and compare margin requirements of all positions with the custodian/prime broker making sure you are in agreement.

10:00 a.m.– Call the prime broker risk department and discuss risks involved in utilizing more leverage for a particular option arbitrage fund. Write up a report based on the call to present to the principals.

11:00 a.m.– Compile statistics for the ongoing exception report for non-investment risk issues such as trade settlement, particular trader leaving the organization, etc.

12:00 p.m. – Making sure that the portfolio is maintained within established risk parameters

1:00 p.m. – Eat lunch at the desk while preparing for the 1:30 meeting with potential investors of the hedge fund who want to discuss business and corporate structure of the hedge fund and its links to the investment manger.

1:30 – 2:30 p.m. – Meeting with investors in a conference room.   Emphasize the safety of assets to the investor because of proper risk monitoring.

2:30 p.m. – Re cap the meeting with principals, see how it went and make a list of items to follow up with the investor. It is very important that the risk manager gets rid of any potential investors concerns of sudden losses.

4:00 p.m. – Work with the CFO to have him clarify a problem you noticed on last month's audit.

5:00 p.m. – Field calls and answer e-mails on all risk and portfolio inquiries to internal and external people.

7:00 p.m. – Look over notes from today and jot down any items that needs to be addressed tomorrow.

7:15 p.m. – Review schedule for next day.

7:30 – 8 p.m. – Head home and get to bed early for a good night's sleep.

Employer Directory

Andor Capital Management
153 E. 53rd St., 58th Fl.
New York, NY 10022
Phone: (212) 224 5800
Fax: (212) 224 6010
www.andorcap.com

Angelo, Gordon & Co.
245 Park Ave.
New York, NY 10167
Phone: (212) 692 2042
Fax: (212) 867 9328
www.angelogordon.com

Caxton Associates
625 Madison Ave, 15th floor
New York, NY 10022
www.caxton.com

Citadel Investment Group
131 South Dearborn Street
Chicago, IL 60603
Phone: (312) 395-2100
Fax: (312) 368-1348
www.citadelgroup.com

Farallon Capital Management
1 Maritime Plaza Suite 1325
San Francisco, CA 94111

Maverick Capital
767 Fifth Avenue
11th floor
New York, NY 10153
Phone: (212) 418-6900
Fax: (212) 418-6901

Moore Capital Management
1251 Avenue of the Americas, 53rd Fl.
New York, NY 10020
www.moorecap.com

Pequot Capital Management
500 Nyala Farm Road
Westport, CT 06880
Phone: (203) 429-2200
Fax: (203) 429-2400
www.pequotcap.com

Soros Fund Management LLC
888 Seventh Ave., 33rd Fl.
New York, NY 10106
Phone: (212) 262-6300
Fax: (212) 245-5154

Visit Vault at **www.vault.com** for insider company profiles, expert advice, career message boards, expert resume reviews, the Vault Job Board and more.

V∧ULT CAREER LIBRARY **143**

We are Honeywell

We are building a world that's safer and more secure ...
More comfortable and energy efficient ...
More innovative and productive.
We are Honeywell.

To explore career opportunities with Honeywell, please logon to:
www.honeywell.com\careers

Honeywell

High Tech

Technology is Everywhere

Information Technology (IT) is a huge, ever-changing field. It encompasses the products and services necessary to store, convert, and deliver information electronically. This includes the entire computer infrastructure of an organization: computer hardware, packaged software, computer system architecture, documents outlining technical procedures, many other computer-related products, and lots and lots of people.

Computers and IT continue to have an explosive impact of on life and business. More than ever, companies must rapidly evolve, incorporating new technologies into their daily operations to remain competitive. From one-man sales companies to international medical labs, almost every type of business utilizes an IT infrastructure to run, to expand, and occasionally, to simply comply with the law.

IT is essential to business because it allows people to communicate faster, more efficiently, and with more capabilities than older technologies. A lone costume maker in Illinois can suddenly turn her enterprise into an international business by putting up a web site. A corporate executive can instantaneously deliver vital information to associates in Japan, South Africa, and England through the power of a secure network. A student whose laptop gets stolen can immediately retrieve all of his lost information from a backup database server. A doctor can use a computer program that makes all of his patients' correspondences and information secure from prying eyes. There is power in IT.

Since technology issues are so critical to a company's health, a significant portion of business is involved with IT. In fact, one in every 14 jobs in America is an IT or IT-related position. IT careers cover a broad range of businesses, skill paths, office sizes, and backgrounds.

The scope of IT

Today, IT is integral in most businesses, and its definition is still being redefined. Although most jobseekers know that IT involves widespread technologies, few trying to enter the field probably know just which technologies or which jobs it encompasses.

Authorities describing IT demonstrate how widespread yet "blurry" the field is. First of all, "There is not a government-wide definition of who is classified as an Information Technology worker," says Roger Moncarz, an economist for the U.S. Bureau of Labor Statistics. "There's a wide sampling of estimates out there, for exactly how to define an Information Technology worker."

Moncarz continues, "Based on our definition of information technology workers, and based on government occupational surveys, we come up with 3.3 million to 3.5 million IT workers in America. The Information Technology Association of America (ITAA), in their recently released study, says there are 10.4 million IT workers. So there's wide discrepancy."

Regardless of who may define it, one thing is certain: IT is everywhere. Offices large and small must maintain, utilize, and upgrade IT infrastructures to be effective in the marketplace. Because of the ubiquitous and demanding nature of the technology, IT jobs run the gamut from entry-level, low-tech positions to tech-savvy engineering managers.

The MBA in Tech

So you're in IT and you decided to get an MBA. Perhaps your degree even came with a technology specialty, which is an increasingly common option. Where will your degree get you?

Visit Vault at **www.vault.com** for insider company profiles, expert advice, career message boards, expert resume reviews, the Vault Job Board and more.

VAULT CAREER LIBRARY   145

Despite the lore of the 1970s-era computer "hackers" who revolutionized personal computing by working out of garages, many other people even then were studying for MBA degrees and were interested in technology. In the five-year period from 1976 to 1981, Harvard Business School produced Dan Bricklin (VisiCalc), Scott Cook (Intuit), Donna Dubinsky (Palm), Meg Whitman (eBay), and many others. Bricklin was an MIT-educated engineer, but has stated that he thought of many core ideas for the electronic spreadsheet while in business school.

Today, working in IT or working at a technology manufacturer offers many opportunities for MBAs to advance. Some of the popular fields are consulting, director-level positions, finance, law, marketing, project management, sales, training, and the ultimate, which is C-level leadership.

Project management

As a project (or product) manager, you have a very specific set of goals to meet. They typically include detailed technology specifications to follow, deadlines to make, and of course a budget to stick with. Maybe you'd be put in charge of an IT department's rollout of a new software product for internal users, or in charge of a certain operating system version of a certain piece of hardware. Either way, acquiring an MBA as a project/product manager can lead to doing the same job but with a bigger company, or to a position with a VP title. As in marketing, project/product managers need a very wide range of skills and knowledge, so having your MBA can only help. If you're a hardcore engineer or programmer, the MBA will help you break into project/product management.

Marketing

If the intensity of the IT lifestyle makes you feel burned out, and you have some creative DNA, then you may be a good fit for a position in technology marketing. The field involves dealing with advertising, partners, the press, and anything related to corporate outreach. In technology marketing, more so than in other fields, you will be expected to know quite a bit about the technology in question. By getting that MBA you can also understand the technology's business strategic situation, and have a good chance at moving up into upper management.

Tech consulting

Many tech consultants are former successful technologists who desire to share what they've learned with others. With just IT experience, you can get an entry-level consulting job, which means interfacing with your client's own IT staff about their special needs. With a few years of experience and the addition of an MBA degree, you can open your own consulting firm, be invited to participate in panels at trade shows, or perhaps move from out of consulting and into the exciting world of venture capital. (To be a VC, you need to excel at understanding business and technology hand-in-hand, just as good consultants do.) You can also become an in-house consultant for a very large company, which may involve more deadlines and politics to play, but leaves you not having to worry about finding new customers.

Director jobs

If you work for a company that makes technology products, instead of working in the IT department of a company that simply utilizes technology, then possessing an MBA degree will often lead you into a "director" level job. For example, you might become the director of printers for a company that makes business technology, or the director of R&D for a military software contractor. As a director, your role is a notch below the division vice president and a notch above the various product managers. Product managers work on just one thing, but as director you're also working on a technology group's sales, marketing, manufacturing, etc.

Finance and law

Finance and law positions in an IT department or at a technology vendor have some aspects that are unique compared to working in other fields. You may have to deal with patent issues, foreign employee visas, international licensing laws, making sure the IT staff follows legal compliance rules for backing up data, and working with multiple layers of distributors, partners, and resellers. By getting an MBA degree as well, you are in good position to become a company's operations director, or even to get a C-level position if you have extensive sales or technology experience as well.

Sales

In sales the job description is very clear: generate revenue for the company. By having an MBA you can manage entry-level staff, get the best and biggest clients, get into working with partners and resellers, or even enter the field of "competitive intelligence" which is a nice way of saying corporate espionage.

Training

As an IT trainer you have many career options. You can work in a classroom setting, manage advanced customer support, become involved with technical writing, educate the sales staff, or work with your company's technology partners. With an MBA degree you can become a manager and get a title such as call center director or VP of user experience.

Upper management

Last, and the hardest job to get, is technology upper management. To become a CIO, CTO, or even a CEO in the technology field, an MBA degree is almost a requirement, especially at large companies. There are a lucky few who become business leaders straight out of core technology jobs (and with a lot of natural talent) – the world's richest person, Bill Gates, never even finished his undergraduate degree. But for mere mortals, if you want to become an IT business leader, you can't go wrong with an MBA: it will help you close big sales, manage your company's logistics, strategize for growth, and prepare you for the executive suite.

Tech Experience and the MBA

Of course, getting an MBA is not enough for a successful career in tech. "My gut reaction is, get the real-world experience," says Paul Buonaiuto, director of recruiting for Computer Associates International Inc., the Islandia, N.Y. company specializing in business management software. The problem with classroom experience alone, he says, is that "Unless you're really out in the trenches, it's difficult to implement sometimes what you read in a book. Real-world experience I hold in more high regard." And even when a rookie MBA gets hired, there is usually the need for some amount of re-training, as "A lot of the [MBA] case studies are dot-com [or] an Enron or a latest-greatest merger," Buonaiuto explains.

To really stand out in the hiring process, the ideal job candidate should also have some kind of hands-on technology experience, Buonaiuto said. Candidates that well rounded come along "almost never," he says. When a pure MBA interviews in technology, "What's sorely lacked in those folks looking for a job is research skills. It becomes painfully evident in the interview" that they know about CA's stock performance but know nothing about its technology other than what's on the web site, he said.

Many future executive candidates start out as technical employees or lower-level managers. For them, many companies will pay for a portion of their MBA educations. There are a wide range of choices for where to get it – a traditional MBA program gives you the recognition that business is business and profits are profits, regardless of your industry, while a specialized technology MBA program (such as in e-commerce or systems management) will make you stand out but can be risky if

Visit Vault at **www.vault.com** for insider company profiles, expert advice,
career message boards, expert resume reviews, the Vault Job Board and more.

V/\ULT CAREER LIBRARY   **147**

your chosen specialty market has a downturn. Magazines like *Computerworld*, *BusinessWeek*, and *U.S. News & World Report* sometimes publish features dedicated to ranking the graduate programs. The relative newness of specialized degrees is another common point of debate: it's been noted many times before that the leading rankings often wildly disagree.

Employer Directory

Honeywell International

101 Columbia Road
Morristown, New Jersey 07962
Phone: (973) 455-2000
www.honeywell.com\careers

Honeywell International is a $23 billion diversified technology and manufacturing leader, serving customers worldwide with aerospace products and services; control technologies for buildings, homes and industry; automotive products; turbochargers; specialty chemicals; fibers; and electronic and advanced materials. Based in Morris Township, N.J., Honeywell's shares are traded on the New York, London, Chicago and Pacific Stock Exchanges. It is one of the 30 stocks that make up the Dow Jones Industrial Average and is also a component of the Standard & Poor's 500 Index.

Business schools Honeywell recruits from

University of Arizona; Arizona State University; Brigham Young University; Carnegie Mellon University; Columbia; Cornell; Emory; Georgia Tech; University of Illinois; University of Maryland; University of Michigan; Michigan State; University of Minnesota; Massachusetts Institute of Technology; Northwestern; Notre Dame; Ohio State; Penn State; Purdue University; University of Tennessee; Thunderbird; UCLA; USC; Vanderbilt; Vault of Virginia

3Com

350 Campus Drive
Marlborough, MA 01752-3064
Phone: (508) 323-5000
Fax: (508) 323-1111
www.3com.com

Advanced Micro Devices, Inc.

One AMD Place
P.O. Box 3453
Sunnyvale, CA 94088-3453
Phone: (408) 749-4000
Fax: (508) 323-1111
www.amd.com

Agilent Technologies

395 Page Mill Road
Palo Alto, CA 94306
Phone: (650) 752-5000
Fax: (650) 752-5300
www.agilent.com

Analog Devices, Inc.

1 Technology Way
Norwood, MA 02062-9106
Phone: (781) 329-4700
Fax: (781) 461-3638
www.analog.com

Apple Computer, Inc.

1 Infinite Loop
Cupertino, CA 95014
Phone: (408) 996-1010
Fax: (408) 974-2113
www.apple.com

Applied Materials, Inc.

3050 Bowers Avenue
Santa Clara, CA 95054-8039
Phone: (408) 727-5555
Fax: (408) 748-9943
www.appliedmaterials.com

Ariba Inc.

807 11th Avenue
Sunnyvale, CA 94089
Phone: (650) 390-1000
Fax: (650) 390-1100
www.ariba.com

Boeing Company, The

100 N. Riverside Plaza
Chicago, IL 60606-2609
Phone: (312) 544-2000
Fax: (312) 544-2082
www.boeing.com

Bose Corp.

The Mountain
Framingham, MA 01701
Phone: (508) 879-7330
Fax: (508) 766-7543
www.bose.com

Cisco Systems, Inc.

170 West Tasman Drive
San Jose, CA 95134
Phone: (408) 526-4000
www.cisco.com

Computer Associates International, Inc.

1 Computer Associates Plaza
Islandia, NY 11749
Phone: (631) 342-6000
Fax: (631) 342-5329
www.ca.com

Compuware Corporation

1 Campus Martius
Detroit, MI 48266-5099
Phone: (313) 227-7300
Fax: (248) 737-7108
www.compuware.com

Visit Vault at **www.vault.com** for insider company profiles, expert advice, career message boards, expert resume reviews, the Vault Job Board and more.

VAULT CAREER LIBRARY   149

Cypress Semiconductor Corporation
3901 N. 1st Street
San Jose, CA 95134-1599
Phone: (408) 943-2600
Fax: (408) 943-6841
www.cypress.com

Dell Inc.
One Dell Way
Round Rock, TX 78682
Phone: (512) 338-4400
Fax: (512) 728-3653
www.dell.com

EMC Corporation
176 South Street
Hopkinton, MA 01748
Phone: (508) 435-1000
Toll Free: (877) 362-6973
Fax: (508) 497-6912
www.emc.com

Gateway, Inc.
7565 Irvine Center Drive
Irvine, CA 92618
Phone: (949) 471-7000
Fax: (949) 471-7041
www.gateway.com

Hewlett-Packard Company
3000 Hanover Street
Palo Alto, CA 94304
Phone: (650) 857-1501
Fax: (650) 857-5518
www.hp.com

Intel Corporation
2200 Mission College Blvd
Santa Clara, CA 95052
Phone: (408) 765-8080
Fax: (408) 765-9904
www.intel.com

International Business Machines Corporation (IBM)
New Orchard Road
Armonk, NY 10504
Phone: (914) 499-1900
Fax: (914) 765-7382
www.ibm.com

Intuit Inc.
2632 Marine Way
Mountain View, CA 94043
Phone: (650) 944-6000
Fax: (650) 944-3699
www.intuit.com

LSI Logic Corporation
1621 Barber Lane
Milpitas, CA 95035
Phone: (408) 433-8000
Fax: (408) 954-3220
www.lsilogic.com

Microsoft Corporation
1 Microsoft Way
Redmond, WA 98052-6399
Phone: (425) 882-8080
Fax: (425) 936-7329
www.microsoft.com

Motorola, Inc.
1303 E. Algonquin Road
Schaumburg, IL 60196
Phone: (847) 576-5000
Fax: (847) 576-5372
www.motorola.com

NCR Corporation
1700 S. Patterson Blvd.
Dayton, OH 45479
Phone: (937) 445-5000
Toll Free: (800) 225-5627
Fax: (937) 445-1682
www.ncr.com

Oracle Corporation
500 Oracle Parkway
Redwood City, CA 94065
Phone: (650) 506-7000
Fax: (650) 506-7200
www.oracle.com

SAP Aktiengesellschaft
Dietmar Hopp Allee 16
69190 Walldorf
Germany
Phone: +49-6227-7-47474
Toll Free: (800) 225-5627
Fax: +49-6227-7-57575
www.sap.com

Science Applications International Corporation
10260 Campus Point Drive
San Diego, CA 92121
Phone: (858) 826-6000
Fax: (858) 826-6800
www.saic.com

Siebel Systems, Inc.
2207 Bridgepointe Pkwy.
San Mateo, CA 94404
Phone: (650) 295-5000
Fax: (650) 295-5111
www.siebel.com

Siemens AG, Inc.
Wittelsbacherplatz 2
D-80333 Munich, Germany
Phone: +49-89 636-00
Fax: +49-89 636-52 000
www.siemens.com

Sony Corporation
7-35, Kitashinagawa, 6-chome,
Shinagawa-ku
Tokyo, 141-0001
Japan
Phone: +81-3-5448-2111
Fax: +81-3-5448-2244
www.sony.net

Sun Microsystems, Inc.
4150 Network Circle
Santa Clara, CA 95054
Phone: (650) 960-1300
Fax: (408) 276-3804
www.sun.com

Sybase Inc.
1 Sybase Drive
Dublin, CA 94568
Phone: (925) 236-5000
Fax: (925) 236-4321
www.sybase.com

Symantec Corporation
20330 Stevens Creek Blvd.
Cupertino, CA 95014-2132
Phone: (408) 517-8000
Fax: (408) 253-3968
www.symantec.com

Texas Instruments Incorporated
12500 TI Blvd.
Dallas, TX 75266-4136
Phone: (972) 995-2011
Toll Free: (800) 336-5236
Fax: (972) 995-4360
www.ti.com

Unisys Corporation
Unisys Way
Blue Bell, PA 19424
Phone: (215) 986-4011
Fax: (215) 986-2312
www.unisys.com

Xerox Corporation
800 Long Ridge Road
Stamford, CT 06904
Phone: (203) 968-3000
Fax: (203) 968-3218
www.xerox.com

Visit Vault at **www.vault.com** for insider company profiles, expert advice, career message boards, expert resume reviews, the Vault Job Board and more.

VΛULT CAREER LIBRARY

151

"I found myself sharing thoughts from day one with the most respected professionals in the industry, who originated some of the deals on the FT covers that we read back in university. For me that was quite impressive."

ENRIQUE BECERRA, ASSOCIATE
INVESTMENT BANKING

Global Banking

Global Capital Markets

Global Transaction Services

Corporate Infrastructure

Investment Research

Private Bank

Working at Citigroup means being part of a team that is making history in the financial services world. If this appeals to you, come see us. We're looking forward to meeting you.

apply online at **www.oncampus.citigroup.com**

Investment Banking

What is investment banking? Is it investing? Is it banking? Really, it is neither. Investment banking, or I-banking, as it is often called, is the term used to describe the business of raising capital for companies and advising them on financing and merger alternatives. Capital essentially means money. Companies need cash in order to grow and expand their businesses; investment banks sell securities to public investors in order to raise this cash. These securities can come in the form of stocks or bonds, which we will discuss in depth later.

The Firms

The biggest investment banks include Goldman Sachs, Merrill Lynch, Morgan Stanley, Credit Suisse First Boston, Salomon Smith Barney, J.P. Morgan Chase and Lehman Brothers, among others. Of course, the complete list of I-banks is more extensive, but the firms listed above compete for the biggest deals both in the U.S. and worldwide.

You have probably heard of many of these firms, and perhaps have a brokerage account with one of them. While brokers from these firms cover every major city in the U.S., the headquarters of every one of these firms is in New York City, the epicenter of the I-banking universe. It is important to realize that investment banking and brokerage go hand-in-hand, but that brokers are one small cog in the investment banking wheel. As we will cover in detail later, brokers sell securities and manage the portfolios of "retail" (or individual) investors.

Many an I-banking interviewee asks, "Which firm is the best?" The answer, like many things in life, is unclear. There are many ways to measure the quality of investment banks. You might examine a bank's expertise in a certain segment of investment banking. Those who watch the industry pay attention to "league tables," which are rankings of investment banks in several categories (e.g., equity underwriting or M&A advisory). The most commonly referred to league tables are published quarterly by Thomson Financial Securities Data (TFSD), a research firm based in Newark, N.J. TFSD collects data on deals done in a given time period and determines which firm has done the most deals in a given sector over that time period. Essentially, the league tables are rankings of firm by quantity of deals in a given area.

Corporate Finance

Stuffy bankers?

The stereotype of the corporate finance department is stuffy, arrogant (white and male) MBAs who frequent golf courses and talk on cell-phones nonstop. While this is increasingly less true, corporate finance remains the most white-shoe department in the typical investment bank. The atmosphere in corporate finance is, unlike that in sales and trading, often quiet and reserved. Junior bankers sit separated by cubicles, quietly crunching numbers.

Depending on the firm, corporate finance can also be a tough place to work, with unforgiving bankers and expectations through the roof. Although decreasing, stories of analyst abuse abound, and some bankers come down hard on new analysts to scare and intimidate them. The lifestyle for corporate finance professionals can be a killer. In fact, many corporate finance workers find that they literally dedicate their lives to the job. Social life suffers, free time disappears, and stress multiplies. It is not uncommon to find analysts and associates wearing rumpled pants and wrinkled shirts, exhibiting the wear and tear of all-nighters. Fortunately, these long hours pay remarkable dividends in the form of six-figure salaries and huge year-end bonuses.

Personality-wise, bankers tend to be highly intelligent, motivated, and not lacking in confidence. Money is important to the bankers, and many anticipate working for just a few years to earn as much as possible, before finding less demanding work. Analysts and associates tend also to be ambitious, intelligent and pedigreed. If you happen to be going into an analyst or

Visit Vault at **www.vault.com** for insider company profiles, expert advice, career message boards, expert resume reviews, the Vault Job Board and more.

VAULT CAREER LIBRARY 153

associate position, make sure to check your ego at the door but don't be afraid to ask penetrating questions about deals and what is required of you.

The deal team

Investment bankers generally work in deal teams which, depending on the size of a deal, vary somewhat in makeup. In this chapter we will provide an overview of the roles and lifestyles of the positions in corporate finance, from analyst to managing director. (Often, a person in corporate finance is generally called an I-banker.) Because the titles and roles really do not differ significantly between underwriting to M&A, we have included both in this explanation. In fact, at most smaller firms, underwriting and transaction advisory are not separated, and bankers typically pitch whatever business they can scout out within their industry sector.

The Players

Analysts

Analysts are the grunts of the corporate finance world. They often toil endlessly with little thanks, little pay (when figured on an hourly basis), and barely enough free time to sleep four hours a night. Typically hired directly out of top undergraduate universities, this crop of bright, highly motivated kids does the financial modeling and basic entry-level duties associated with any corporate finance deal.

Modeling every night until 2 a.m. and not having much of a social life proves to be unbearable for many an analyst and after two years many analysts leave the industry. Unfortunately, many bankers recognize the transient nature of analysts, and work them hard to get the most out of them they can. The unfortunate analyst that screws up or talks back too much may never get quality work, spending his days bored until 11 p.m. waiting for work to come, stressing even more than the busy analyst. These are the analysts that do not get called to work on live transactions, and do menial work or just put together pitchbooks all the time.

When it comes to analyst pay, much depends on whether the analyst is in New York or not. In NYC, salary often begins for first-year analysts at $45,000 to $55,000 per year, with an annual bonus of approximately $30,000. While this seems to be a lot for a 22-year-old with just an undergrad degree, it's not a great deal if you consider per-hour compensation. At most firms, analysts also get dinner every night for free if they work late, and have little time to spend their income, often meaning fat checking and savings accounts and ample fodder to fund business school or law school down the road. At regional firms, pay typically is 20 percent less than that of their New York counterparts. Worth noting, though, is the fact that at regional firms 1) hours are often less, and 2) the cost of living is much lower. Be wary, however, of the small regional firm or branch office of a Wall Street firm that pays at the low end of the scale and still shackles analysts to their cubicles. While the salary generally does not improve much for second-year analysts, the bonus can double for those second-years who demonstrate high performance. At this level, bonuses depend mostly on an analyst's contribution, attitude, and work ethic, as opposed to the volume of business generated by the bankers with whom he or she works.

Associates

Much like analysts, associates hit the grindstone hard. Working 80- to 100-hour weeks, associates stress over pitchbooks and models all night, become experts with financial modeling on Excel, and sometimes shake their heads wondering what the point is. Unlike analysts, however, associates more quickly become involved with clients and, most importantly, are not at the bottom of the totem pole. Associates quickly learn to play quarterback and hand-off menial modeling work and research projects to analysts. However, treatment from vice presidents and managing directors doesn't necessarily improve for associates versus analysts, as bankers sometimes care more about the work getting done, and not about the guy or gal working away all night to complete it.

Usually hailing directly from top business schools (sometimes law schools or other grad schools), associates often possess only a summer's worth of experience in corporate finance, so they must start almost from the beginning. Associates who worked as analysts before grad school have a little more experience under their belts. The overall level of business awareness and knowledge a bright MBA has, however, makes a tremendous difference, and associates quickly earn the luxury of more complicated work, client contact, and bigger bonuses.

Associates are at least much better paid than analysts. An $80,000 starting salary is typical, and usually bonuses hit $25,000 and up in the first six months. (At most firms, associates start in August and get their first prorated bonus in January.) Newly minted MBAs cash in on signing bonuses and forgivable loans as well, especially on Wall Street. These can amount to another $25,000 to $30,000, depending on the firm, providing total first-year compensation of up to $150,000 for top firms. Associates beyond their first year begin to rake it in, earning $250,000 to $400,000 and up per year, depending on the firm's profitability and other factors.

Vice Presidents

Upon attaining the position of vice president (at most firms, after four or five years as associates), those in corporate finance enter the realm of real bankers. The lifestyle becomes more manageable once the associate moves up to VP. On the plus side, weekends sometimes free up, all-nighters drop off, and the general level of responsibility increases – VPs are the ones telling associates and analysts to stay late on Friday nights. In the office, VPs manage the financial modeling/pitchbook production process in the office. On the negative side, the wear and tear of traveling that accompanies VP-level banker responsibilities can be difficult. As a VP, one begins to handle client relationships, and thus spends much more time on the road than analysts or associates. You can look forward to being on the road at least two to four days per week, usually visiting clients and potential clients. Don't forget about closing dinners (to celebrate completed deals), industry conferences (to drum up potential business and build a solid network within their industry), and, of course, roadshows. VPs are perfect candidates to babysit company management on roadshows.

Directors/Managing Directors

Directors and managing directors (MDs) are the major players in corporate finance. Typically, MDs set their own hours, deal with clients at the highest level, and disappear whenever a drafting session takes place, leaving this grueling work to others. (We will examine these drafting sessions in depth later.) MDs mostly develop and cultivate relationships with various companies in order to generate corporate finance business for the firm. MDs typically focus on one industry, develop relationships among management teams of companies in the industry and visit these companies on a regular basis. These visits are aptly called sales calls.

Pay scales for vice presidents and managing directors

The formula for paying bankers varies dramatically from firm to firm. Some adhere to rigid formulas based on how much business a banker brought in, while others pay based on a subjective allocation of corporate finance profits. No matter how compensation is structured, however, when business is slow, bonuses taper off rapidly. For most bankers, typical salaries may range from $100,000 to $200,000 per year, but bonuses can be significantly greater. Total packages for VPs on Wall Street often hit over $500,000 level in the first year – and pay can skyrocket from there.

Top bankers at the MD level might be pulling in bonuses of up to $1 million or more a year, but slow markets (and hence slow business) can cut that number dramatically. It is important to realize that for the most part, MDs act as relationship managers, and are essentially paid on commission. For top performers, compensation can be almost inconceivable.

Visit Vault at **www.vault.com** for insider company profiles, expert advice,
career message boards, expert resume reviews, the Vault Job Board and more.

V\ULT CAREER LIBRARY **155**

SATISFACTION IS GOOD.

PRIDE IS BETTER.

Join Merrill Lynch and you'll share in a sense of pride that runs throughout our organization. Pride in the world's premier financial services brand. Pride in our continued leadership in products and services. And pride in our intellectual capital that continues to foster groundbreaking innovation.

Know the exhilaration of working alongside some of the finest minds in financial services. Stretch yourself to reach for – and achieve – the success you dream of. And take pride in contributing your talent to a team that defines exceptional in every sense of the word.

If you seek a truly outstanding employment experience, there's never been a better time to join Merrill Lynch.

Opportunities for undergraduates:

- Global Markets
- Investment Banking
- Private Client

- Credit
- Investment Management
- Operations

- Technology
- Accounting & Finance
- Human Resources

EXCEPTIONAL *WITHOUT EXCEPTION*

Merrill Lynch is an equal opportunity employer.

ml.com/careers/americas

Day in the Life: Associate, Corporate Finance

We've asked insiders at leading investment banks to offer us insight into a day in the life of their position. Here's a look at a day of an associate I-banker at Goldman Sachs.

8:15 a.m. Arrive at 85 Broad Street. (Show Goldman ID card to get past the surly elevator guards).

8:25 a.m. Arrive on 17th Floor. Use "blue card" to get past floor lobby. ("Don't ever forget your blue card. Goldman has tight security and you won't be able to get around the building all day.")

8:45 a.m. Pick up work from Word Processing, review it, make changes.

9:00 a.m. Check voice mail, return phone calls.

9:30 a.m. Eat breakfast; read The Wall Street Journal. ("But don't let a supervisor see you with your paper sprawled across your desk.")

10:00 a.m. Prepare pitchbooks, discuss analysis with members of deal team.

12:00 p.m. Conference call with members of IPO team, including lawyers and client.

1:00 p.m. Eat lunch at desk. ("The Wall Street McDonald's delivers, but it's the most expensive McDonald's in New York City; Goldman's cafeteria is cheaper, but you have to endure the shop talk.")

2:00 p.m. Work on restructuring case studies; make several document requests from Goldman library.

3:00 p.m. Start to prepare analysis; order additional data from DRG (Data Resources Group).

5:00 p.m. Check in with vice presidents and heads of deal teams on status of work.

6:00 p.m. Go to gym for an abbreviated workout.

6:45 p.m. Dinner. ("Dinner is free in the IBD cafeteria, but avoid it. Wall Street has pretty limited food options, so for a quick meal it's the Indian place across the street that's open 24 hours.")

8:00 p.m. Meet with VP again. ("You'll probably get more work thrown at you before he leaves.")

9:45 p.m. Try to make FedEx cutoff. Drop off pitchbook to Document Processing on 20th Floor. ("You have to call ahead and warn them if you have a last-minute job or you're screwed.")

10:00 p.m. Order in food again. ("It's unlikely that there will be any room left in your meal allowance – but we usually order in a group and add extra names to bypass the limit.")

11:00 p.m. Leave for home. ("Call for a car service. Enjoy your nightly 'meal on wheels' on the way home.")

Visit Vault at **www.vault.com** for insider company profiles, expert advice, career message boards, expert resume reviews, the Vault Job Board and more.

VAULT CAREER LIBRARY   **157**

Employer Directory

Citigroup

388 Greenwich Street

New York, NY 10013

www.oncampus.citigroup.com

citigroup♪

global corporate &
investment banking group

Citigroup Corporate and Investment Banking is a full service investment banking and securities brokerage firm, providing a complete range of financial advisory, research and capital raising services to corporations, governments and individuals. Citigroup (NYSE: C) and its affiliates, have a reach that spans over 100 countries and territories. This enables us to offer a unique combination of local market insight, as well as the expertise necessary for today's global economy.

What we give you is the chance to gain invaluable experience, leverage the insights of multicultural backgrounds and broaden your experience through global working relationships and a wide variety of work opportunities.

Business schools Citigroup recruits from

Berkeley; Carnegie Mellon; Columbia University Graduate School of Business; Cooper Union; Cornell (Johnson); Dartmouth (Tuck); Duke (Fuqua); Georgetown; Harvard Business School; Illinois; MIT (Sloan); Northwestern (Kellogg); NYU Stern; Princeton; Stanford Graduate School of Business; UCLA (Anderson); University of Chicago Graduate School of Business; University of Michigan (Ross); University of Pennsylvania (Wharton); University of Texas (McCombs); University of Virginia (Darden); Yale School of Management

Credit Suisse First Boston

11 Madison Avenue
New York, New York 10010
www.csfb.com

Diversity Contact: Tanji Dewberry - Head of Diversity Recruiting, Phone: 212-538-2594
E-mail: Diversity.recruiting@csfb.com

CSFB MBA EXPLORER PROGRAM - FIRST YEAR MBA STUDENTS

The MBA Explorer Program is a two-day educational outreach program that brings together women and students of color who are entering business school in the fall. This unique program offers students who may not have an investment banking background a chance to learn first-hand about Wall Street and specifically CSFB. Participants learn about the firm's core businesses and culture and get to meet with school teams and recruiters months in advance of the Summer Associate recruiting season.

THE CSFB MBA FELLOWSHIP PROGRAM - FIRST YEAR MBA STUDENTS

The MBA Fellowship Program is designed to increase the level of interest in, and awareness of careers in the investment banking industry among students of color attending business school.

Credit Suisse First Boston (CSFB) will offer a one-year, full-tuition fellowship to top MBA students of Black and/or Hispanic heritage at the following business schools:

Chicago Graduate School of Business • Columbia Business School • Cornell Johnson School of Management • Harvard Business School • MIT Sloan School of Management • Stern School of Business • Stanford Graduate School of Business • The Wharton School

Eligible candidates must be admitted as entering first-year MBA students and be interested in pursuing a career in the investment banking industry including sales, trading, research, investment banking, and alternative capital.

Once selected the fellowship recipients will be assigned junior and senior mentors at the beginning of the academic year. Finally, the CSFB Fellowship requires that recipients participate in and complete the CSFB summer internship interview process.

Business schools CSFB recruits from

Columbia Business Schools; Cornell Johnson School of Management; Harvard Business School; Stanford Graduate School of Business; Wharton School of Business; Sloan School of Management; Stern School of Business; University of Chicago Graduate School of Business

Visit Vault at **www.vault.com** for insider company profiles, expert advice,
career message boards, expert resume reviews, the Vault Job Board and more.

VAULT CAREER LIBRARY   **159**

Goldman, Sachs and Co.

85 Broad Street

New York, NY 10004

www.gs.com/careers

Goldman Sachs is a global investment banking, securities and investment management firm. We provide a wide range of services to a substantial and diversified client base that includes corporations, institutional investors, governments, non-profit organizations and individuals. Our headquarters is in New York and we maintain significant offices in London, Frankfurt, Tokyo, Hong Kong and other financial centers around the world.

Founded in 1869, Goldman Sachs has long sustained a commitment to hiring and training outstanding leaders. Our business principles are rooted in integrity, a commitment to excellence, innovation and teamwork. These values enable us to execute successfully a business strategy that is focused on extraordinary client service and superior long-term financial performance for our shareholders.

We conduct our business in increasingly complex markets. Our people must continually find new ways to provide access to capital, manage risk and provide investment opportunities for our clients to enable them to realize their goals. We judge ourselves on our ability to help clients anticipate and respond to changing market conditions and to create opportunities that merit the trust they place in us.

Schools Goldman recruits from

We actively recruit at schools across the United States and welcome applications for both full-time positions and summer internships. Please contact your school's career center to find out when we may be on your campus.

Merrill Lynch

250 Vesey Street

New York, New York 10080

www.ml.com/careers

Merrill Lynch is a leading global financial management and advisory company with a presence in 36 countries across six continents. It serves the needs of both individual and institutional clients with a diverse range of financial services, including:

> Personal financial planning • Securities underwriting • Trading and brokering • Investment banking and advisory services • Trading of foreign exchange • Commodities and derivatives • Banking and lending • Insurance • Research

With private client assets of approximately $1.5 trillion, Merrill Lynch is the undisputed leader in planning-based financial advice and management for individuals and small businesses. As an investment bank, it is a top global underwriter of debt and equity securities and a leading strategic advisor to corporations, governments, institutions and individuals worldwide. Through Merrill Lynch Investment Managers, the company operates one of the world's largest mutual fund groups.

Business schools Merrill recruits from

Merrill recruiters from a variety of top tier graduate business schools.

SG Cowen & Co.

1221 Avenue of the Americas

New York, New York 10020

Phone: 646-562-1818

Recruiting E-mail: associate.us-ib@sgcowen.com

www.sgcowen.com

SG Cowen is a mid-size investment banking firm with a focus on emerging growth companies. We specialize in value added, high margin investment banking services and products. The product groups include equity capital markets, private equity, and mergers and acquisitions. The corporate finance groups include technology, media, and telecom; health care; and consumer products. We have opportunities for about a dozen associates and summer associates in our New York, San Francisco, and Boston Investment Banking offices annually.

Business schools SG Cowen recruits from

Tuck; Columbia; Cornell; Darden; Emory; UCLA; USC

A.G. Edwards & Sons

One North Jefferson Ave.

St. Louis, MO 63103

Phone: (314) 955-3000

Fax: (314) 955-5402

www.agedwards.com

ABN AMRO Holdings

Gustav Mahlerlaan 10

1082 PP Amsterdam, The Netherlands

Phone: +31-10-282-0724

www.abnamro.com

Allen & Company

711 Fifth Avenue

9th Floor

New York, NY 10022

Phone: (212) 832-8000

Banc of America Securities

9 West 57th Street

New York, NY 10019

Phone: (888) 583-8900

www.bofasecurities.com

Bank of America Corporation

100 North Tryon Street

Charlotte, NC 28255

Phone: (800) 432-5000

Fax: (704) 386-6699

www.bankofamerica.com

Barclays Capital

World Headquarters

5 The North Colonnade

Canary Wharf

London, E14 4BB

Phone: +44 (0) 20 7623 2323

Americas Headquarters

200 Park Avenue

New York, NY 10166

Phone: (212) 412-4000

www.barcap.com

Bear Stearns

383 Madison Avenue

New York, NY 10179

Phone: (212) 272-2000

Fax: (212) 272-4785

www.bearstearns.com

BNP Paribas

World Headquarters

16, Blvd. Des Italiens

Paris Cedex 09, 75009

Phone: +33-1-4014-4546

U.S. Headquarters

787 Seventh Avenue

New York NY 10019

Phone: (212) 841-2000

www.bnpparibas.com

Brown Brothers Harriman

140 Broadway

New York, NY 10005-1101

Phone: (212) 483-1818

www.bbh.com

CIBC World Markets

300 Madison Avenue

New York, NY 10017

Phone: (212) 856-4000

www.cibcwm.com

Citigroup Corporate & Investment Banking

388 Greenwich Street

38th Floor

New York, NY 10013

Phone: (212) 816-6000

www.citigroupgcib.com

Citigroup Inc.

399 Park Avenue

New York, NY 10043

Phone: (212) 559-1000

Fax: (212) 793-3946

www.citigroup.com

Credit Suisse Corporate & Investment Banking

11 Madison Avenue

New York, NY 10010-3629

Phone: (212) 325-2000

Fax: (212) 325-6665

www.csfb.com

Visit Vault at **www.vault.com** for insider company profiles, expert advice, career message boards, expert resume reviews, the Vault Job Board and more.

VAULT CAREER LIBRARY   161

Deutsche Bank

60 Wall Street
New York, NY 10003
Phone: (212) 250-2500
www.db.com

Dresdner Kleinwort Wasserstein

1301 Avenue of the Americas
New York, NY 10019
Phone: (212) 969-2700
Fax: (212) 429-2127
www.drkw.com

Evercore Partners

55 East 52nd Street
43rd Floor
New York, NY 10055
Phone: (212) 857-3100
Fax: (212) 857-3101
www.evercore.com

Friedman Billings Ramsey Group

1001 19th St. North
Arlington, VA 22209
Phone: (703) 312-9500
www.fbr.com
Gleacher Partners
660 Madison Avenue
19th Floor
New York, NY 10021
Phone: (212) 418-4200
www.gleacher.com

Goldman Sachs

85 Broad Street
New York, NY 10004
Phone: (212) 902-1000
Fax: (212) 902-3000
www.gs.com

Greenhill & Co.

300 Park Avenue
New York, NY 10022
Phone: (212) 389-1500
www.greenhill-co.com

Houlihan Lokey Howard & Zukin

1930 Century Park West
Los Angeles, CA 90067
Phone: (310) 553-8871
www.hlhz.com

HSBC Holdings plc

World headquarters:
8 Canada Square
London E145HQ
United Kingdom
Phone: 44-020-7991-8888
Fax: +44-020-7992-4880
www.hsbc.com

HSBC Bank USA

452 5th Ave.
New York, NY 10018
Phone: (212) 525-5000
www.us.hsbc.com

Jefferies & Company, Inc.

520 Madison Ave.
12th Floor
New York, NY 10022
Phone: (212) 284-2550
www.jefferies.com

JPMorgan Chase

270 Park Avenue
New York, NY 10017
Phone: (212) 270-6000
Fax: (212) 270-2613
www.jpmorganchase.com

Keefe, Bruyette & Woods

The Equitable Building
787 Seventh Avenue, 4th Floor
New York, NY 10019
Phone: (212) 887-7777
www.kbw.com

Lazard

30 Rockefeller Plaza
New York, NY, 10020
Phone: (212) 632-6000
www.lazard.com

Legg Mason

100 Light Street
Baltimore, MD 21202-1099
Phone: (410) 539-0000
Fax: (410) 454-4923
www.leggmason.com

Lehman Brothers

745 Seventh Ave
New York, NY 10019
Phone:(212) 526-7000
www.lehman.com

MBNA Corp.

1100 N. King St.
Wilmington, DE 19884-0115
Phone: (302) 453-9930
Fax: (302) 432-3614
www.mbna.com

Merrill Lynch

4 World Financial Center
250 Vesey Street
New York, NY 10080
Phone: (212) 449-1000
www.ml.com

Morgan Keegan & Company

Morgan Keegan Tower
50 Front St., 17th Floor
Memphis, TN 38103
Phone: (901) 524-4100
www.morgankeegan.com

Morgan Stanley

1585 Broadway
New York, NY 10036
Phone: (212) 761-4000
www.morganstanley.com

Nomura Holdings

1-9-1, Nihonbashi, Chuo-ku
Tokyo, 103-8645, Japan
Phone: +81-3-5255-1000

2 World Financial Center
Building B
New York, NY 10281
Phone: (212) 667-9300
www.nomura.com

Peter J. Solomon Company

520 Madison Avenue
New York, NY 10022
Telephone: (212) 508-1600
www.pjsc.com

Piper Jaffray & Co.

800 Nicollet Mall
Suite 800
Minneapolis, MN 55402-7020
Phone: (612) 303-6000
www.piperjaffray.com

Raymond James Financial

880 Carillon Parkway
St. Petersburg, FL 33716
Phone: (727) 567-1000
www.raymondjames.com

RBC Capital Markets

165 Broadway
One Liberty Plaza, 4th Floor
New York, NY 10006
Phone: (212) 428-6600

Royal Bank Plaza

200 Bay Street
Toronto, Ontario, M5J 2W7
Phone: (416) 842-2000
www.rbccm.com

Robert W. Baird & Co. (Baird)

777 East Wisconsin Avenue
Milwaukee, WI 53201-0672
Phone: (414) 765-3500; (800) RW
BAIRD
www.rwbaird.com

Rothschild

New Court, St. Swithin's Lane
London
EC4P 4DU, United Kingdom
Phone: +44-20-7280-5000
Fax: +44-20-7929-1643
www.nmrothschild.com

Rothschild North America

1251 Avenue of the Americas
51st Floor
New York, NY 10020
Phone: (212) 403-3500
Fax: (212) 403-3501
www.rothschild.com

Royal Bank of Scotland

RBS Gogarburn
P.O. Box 1000
Edinburgh
EH112 1HQ
United Kingdom
Phone: +44-131-556-8555
Fax: +44-131-557-6140
www.rbs.com

SG Cowen & Co., LLC

1221 Avenue of the Americas
New York, NY 10020
Phone: (646) 562-1000
www.sgcowen.com

The Bank of New York

One Wall Street
New York, NY 10286
Phone: (212) 495-1784
www.bankofny.com

The Blackstone Group

345 Park Avenue
New York, NY 10154
Phone: (212) 583-5000
www.blackstone.com

Thomas Weisel Partners

Montgomery Tower
One Montgomery Street
San Francisco, CA 94104
Phone: (415) 364-2500
Fax: (415) 364-2695
www.tweisel.com

U.S. Bancorp

800 Nicolett Mall
Minneapolis, MN 55402
Phone: (800) 872-2657
www.usbancorp.com

UBS Investment Bank

299 Park Avenue
New York, NY 10171
Phone: (212) 821-3000

677 Washington Boulevard
Stamford, CT 06901
Phone: (203) 719-3000
www.ibb.ubs.com

Wachovia Corporation

301 S. College Street
Suite 400
Charlotte, NC 28288
Phone: (704) 374-6161
www.wachovia.com

Wachovia Securities

Riverfront Plaza
901 East Byrd Street
Richmond, Virginia 23219
www.wachoviasec.com

Wells Fargo & Company

420 Montgomery Street
San Francisco, CA 94163
Phone: (800) 411-4932
www.wellsfargo.com

William Blair & Company

222 West Adams St.
Chicago, IL 60606
Phone: (312) 236-1600
www.williamblair.com

WR Hambrecht + Co.

539 Bryant Street
Suite 100
San Francisco, CA 94107
Phone: (415) 551-8600
www.wrhambrecht.com

Visit Vault at **www.vault.com** for insider company profiles, expert advice,
career message boards, expert resume reviews, the Vault Job Board and more.

V/ULT CAREER LIBRARY   **163**

Investment Management

How many industries can you think of that impact households all over the world? Very few. That is one of the many exciting aspects of the asset management industry – more people than ever before are planning for their future financial needs, and as a result, the industry is more visible and important than ever.

Investment management vs. asset management

A quick note about the terms investment management and asset management: these terms are often used interchangeably. They refer to the same practice – the professional management of assets through investment. Investment management is used a bit more often when referring to the activity or career (i.e., "I'm an investment manager" or "That firm is gaining a lot of business in investment management"), whereas "asset management" is used more with reference to the industry itself (i.e., "The asset management industry").

More stability

Because of the stability of cash flows generated by the industry, investment management provides a relatively stable career when compared to some other financial services positions (most notably investment banking). Investment management firms are generally paid a set fee as a percentage of assets under management. (The fee structure varies, and sometimes is both an asset-centered fee plus a performance fee, especially for institutional investors.) Still, even when investment management fees involve a performance incentive, the business is much less cyclical than cousins like investment banking. Banking fees depend on transactions. When banking activities such as IPOs and M&A transactions dry up, so do fees for investment banks, which translates into layoffs of bankers. In contrast, assets are quite simply always being invested.

History

To better understand why asset management has become such a critical component of the broader financial services industry, we must first become acquainted with its formation and history.

The beginnings of a separate industry

While the informal process of managing money has been around since the beginning of the 20th century, the industry did not begin to mature until the early 1970's. Prior to that time, investment management was completely relationship-based. Assignments to manage assets grew out of relationships that banks and insurance companies already had with institutions – primarily companies or municipal organizations with employee pension funds – that had funds to invest. (A pension fund is set up as an employee benefit. Employers commit to a certain level of payment to retired employees each year and must manage their funds to meet these obligations. Organizations with large pools of assets to invest are called institutional investors.)

These asset managers were chosen in an unstructured way – assignments grew organically out of pre-existing relationships, rather than through a formal request for proposal and bidding process. The actual practice of investment management was also unstructured. At the time, asset managers might simply pick 50 stocks they thought were good investments – there was not nearly as much analysis on managing risk or organizing a fund around a specific category or style. (Examples of different investment categories include small cap stocks and large cap stocks. We will explore the different investment categories and styles in a later chapter.) Finally, the assets that were managed at the time were primarily pension funds. Mutual funds had yet to become broadly popular.

Visit Vault at **www.vault.com** for insider company profiles, expert advice, career message boards, expert resume reviews, the Vault Job Board and more.

V/\ULT CAREER LIBRARY 165

ERISA, 401(k) plans and specialist firms

The two catalysts for change in the industry were: 1) the broad realization that demographic trends would cause the U.S. government's retirement system (Social Security) to be underfunded, which made individuals more concerned with their retirement savings, and 2) the creation of ERISA (the Employment Retirement Income Secruity Act) in 1974, which gave employees incentives to save for retirement privately through 401(k) plans. (401(k) plans allow employees to save pre-tax earnings for their retirement.) These elements prompted an increased focus on long-term savings by individual investors and the formation of what can be described as a private pension fund market.

These fundamental changes created the opportunity for professional groups of money managers to form "specialist" firms to manage individual and institutional assets. Throughout the 1970s and early 1980s, these small firms specialized in one or two investment styles (for example, core equities or fixed income investing).

During this period, the investment industry became fragmented and competitive. This competition added extra dimensions to the asset management industry. Investment skills, of course, remained critical. However, relationship building and the professional presentation of money management teams also began to become significant.

The rise of the mutual fund

In the early to mid 1980s, driven by the ERISA laws, the mutual fund came into vogue. While mutual funds had been around for decades, they were only used by financially sophisticated investors who paid a lot of attention to their investments. However, investor sophistication increased with the advent of modern portfolio theory (the set of tools developed to quantitatively analyze the management of a portfolio; see sidebar on next page). Asset management firms began heavily marketing mutual funds as a safe and smart investment tool, pitching to individual investors the virtues of diversification and other benefits of investing in mutual funds. With more and more employers shifting retirement savings responsibilities from pension funds to the employees themselves, the 401(k) market grew rapidly. Consequently, consumer demand for new mutual fund products exploded (mutual funds are the preferred choice in most 401(k) portfolios). Many specialists responded by expanding their product offerings and focusing more on the marketing of their new services and capabilities.

Modern Portfolio Theory

Modern Portfolio Theory (MPT) was born in 1952 when University of Chicago economics student Harry Markowitz published his doctoral thesis, "Portfolio Selection," in the Journal of Finance. Markowitz, who won the Nobel Prize in economics in 1990 for his research and its far-reaching effects, provided the framework for what is now known as Modern Portfolio Theory. MPT quantifies the benefits of diversification, looking at how investors create portfolios in order to optimize market risk against expected returns. Markowitz, assuming all investors are risk averse, proposed that investors, when choosing a security to add to their portfolio, should not base their decision on the amount of risk that an individual security has, but rather on how that security contributes to the overall risk of the portfolio. To do this, Markowitz considered how securities move in relation to one another under similar circumstances. This is called "correlation," which measures how much two securities fluctuate in price relative to each other. Taking all this into account, investors can create "efficient portfolios," ones with the highest expected returns for a given level of risk

Consolidation and globalization

The dominant themes of the industry in the 1990s were consolidation and globalization. As many former specialists rapidly expanded, brand recognition and advanced distribution channels (through brokers or other sales vehicles) became key success factors for asset management companies. Massive global commercial and investment banks entered the industry, taking business away from many specialist firms. Also, mutual fund rating agencies such as Lipper (founded in 1973, now a part of

Reuters) and Morningstar (founded in Chicago in 1984) increased investor awareness of portfolio performance. These rating agencies publish reports on fund performance and rate funds on scales such as Morningstar's 4-star rating system.

These factors led to a shakeout period of consolidation. From 1995 to 2001, approximately 150 mergers took place, creating well-established and formidable players such as Capital Group and Citigroup. As opposed to specialist firms, these large financial services firms provide asset management products that run the gamut: mutual funds, pension funds, management for high-net-worth individuals, etc. While many excellent specialist firms continue to operate today, they are not the driving force that they once were.

The Industry Today

Wealth creation in the 1990s has led to even greater demand for money management services today. In the U.S. alone, 2.8 million families have reached millionaire status. Mutual fund demand has continued to increase; as of 2002, there were 8,000 different funds in the market, up from just 3,000 in 1990. In fact, nearly 50 million households invest in mutual funds, with a total worth of $8.5 trillion, up from only $340 billion in 1984 and $1 trillion as recently as 1990.

As the industry has matured, total assets under management (AUMs) in the United States have grown to $20 trillion. Consolidation and globalization have created a diverse list of leading industry players that range from well-capitalized divisions of investment banks, global insurance companies and multinational commercial banks to independent behemoths, such as Fidelity and Capital Group.

Below is a list of the 20 largest worldwide asset management companies as of 2001. Pay attention to one critical component that may not be immediately obvious: the leading players in the industry are located all over the U.S. Working in the industry, unlike other areas of financial services like investment banking, does not require that you live in a particular region of the country.

Portfolio Management

The portfolio management segment of the firm makes the ultimate investment decision; it's the department that "pulls the trigger." There are three jobs that typically fall under this component of the firm: portfolio managers, associate portfolio managers and portfolio manager assistants. Recent college graduates often fill portfolio assistant positions, while individuals with many years of investment experience hold associate and senior portfolio manager assignments. MBAs are not hired as portfolio managers right out of business school unless they have a ton of experience. Typically, MBAs who wish to pursue a career in portfolio management join investment management firms in their investment research divisions. After two years in research, MBAs will then have a choice: either stay in research or leverage their research experience to move into an associate portfolio manager position.

Senior portfolio manager

Portfolio managers are responsible for establishing an investment strategy, selecting appropriate investments and allocating each investment properly. All day long, portfolio managers are presented with investment ideas from internal buy-side analysts and sell-side analysts from investment banks. It is their job to sift through the relevant information and use their judgment to buy and sell securities. Throughout each day, they read reports, talk to company managers and monitor industry and economic trends looking for the right company and time to invest the portfolio's capital.

The selection of investments must adhere to the style of the portfolio. For instance, a large-capitalization growth manager might be screening for only companies that have a market-capitalization in excess of $3 billion and earnings growth charac-

Visit Vault at **www.vault.com** for insider company profiles, expert advice, career message boards, expert resume reviews, the Vault Job Board and more.

V/\ULT CAREER LIBRARY   **167**

teristics that exceed its industry. Therefore, the portfolio manager would not even consider a $500 million utility stock with a 6 percent dividend yield.

Associate portfolio manager

The associate portfolio manager position requires an MBA, CFA or considerable investment experience. Typically, the job is filled by successful research analysts who have at least 3 to 5 years of post-MBA experience. The job itself is very similar to that of the senior portfolio manager with one main exception: associates interact less with clients than senior managers do. Associate portfolio managers are usually assigned smaller, less sophisticated portfolios to manage or serve as lieutenants on large, complicated portfolios.

The role of the associate portfolio manager differs depending on which segment of the market is being served – mutual fund, institutional or high-net-worth. For instance, associate portfolio managers at many mutual fund firms will either act as the lead investor on a sector fund or as second-in-command on a large diversified fund. Depending on the firm, an associate could also act as a lead on a sector fund and a second-in-command on a diversified fund at the same time. Alternatively, on the institutional side, associate portfolio managers typically apprentice with seasoned portfolio managers on the largest and most complicated portfolios. After they have succeeded in that role, the firm will assign them smaller institutional accounts to manage on their own.

Successful associate portfolio managers will usually be promoted to senior portfolio managers within 2 to 5 years.

Investment Research

The investment research segment is responsible for generating recommendations to portfolio managers on companies and industries that they follow. Similar to the portfolio management segment, there are three potential positions: senior research analyst, investment research associate and investment research assistant. Senior research analysts typically have 2 to 4 years of post-MBA research experience. Research associates are usually recent MBA graduates, while assistants are recent college graduates.

Senior research analyst

Senior research analysts are investment experts in their given industry focus. An equity analyst covers stocks; a fixed income analyst covers bonds.

Their role is to predict the investment potential of the companies in their sector. For instance, take an equity analyst covering computer hardware companies, including Apple Computer. The analyst would be responsible for predicting Apple's future earnings and cash flow, and comparing the fair value of Apple to the expectations of the stock market. To do this, the analyst would build a financial model that included all of the potential variables to derive Apple's earnings and appropriate value (e.g., sales growth and business costs, as well as research and development).

A fixed income analyst focusing on telecom, for example, might be looking at a new high-yield corporate bond issued by Qwest. The main thing the analyst will be looking for is Qwest's ability to pay off that loan – the amount of the bond. The analyst will look at historical cash flows, project future cash flows and look at other debt obligations that might be more senior to the new bond. This will tell the analyst the likelihood that Qwest will be able to pay off the bond.

Analysts spend a considerable amount of time attending industry conferences, meeting with company management and analyzing industry supply and demand trends to derive business forecasts. Many analysts follow 20 to 30 companies and must be an expert on each.

An important part of a senior research analyst's job is to convey their recommendations to the portfolio management teams. Therefore, senior analysts spend considerable time presenting to portfolio managers and issuing investment reports. Because of this, senior research analysts must be articulate and persuasive in their convictions in order to earn respect within the firm.

Senior research analysts typically have served as investment research associates for two to four years, post MBA or CFA, before assuming their position. If successful in their role, many senior analysts move into portfolio management roles later in their careers.

Investment research associate

This is the role for most MBAs or those with equivalent experience. Essentially, investment research associates have the same responsibilities as senior research analysts with one exception: associates are given smaller industries to follow. Typically, the industry assigned to an associate is a component of a broader sector that is already being analyzed by a senior analyst. For instance, a research associate might be assigned HMOs and work closely with the senior analyst in charge of insurance companies.

The associate analyst creates investment recommendations in the same manner as a senior analyst. In general, new associates spend several weeks familiarizing themselves with their industry by reading industry papers, journals and textbooks, and attending industry conferences. A large percentage of a research analyst's time is spent monitoring industry and company trends to predict financial results for the company. Therefore, research associates are constantly speaking with management, customers and suppliers to gauge the current status of the company they are analyzing. Armed with financial models and fundamental company analysis, they develop investment recommendations that they distribute to the firm's portfolio managers.

One of the greatest challenges for a new associate is the steepness of the learning curve. Portfolio managers don't have the patience or the luxury to allow an analyst to be uninformed or consistently incorrect. New associates work extremely hard building trust with portfolio managers.

Obviously, financial acumen and quantitative skills are a must for a research associate, but communication skills are also critical. Research associates need to be able to clearly and persuasively communicate their investment recommendations. These associates must also be able to respond to detailed inquiries from portfolio managers that challenge their ideas – which requires a strong tact and a great deal of patience. Furthermore, associates need to be energetic, diligent and intellectually curious.

Research associates are usually promoted to larger industries within two to four years of joining the firm.

Visit Vault at **www.vault.com** for insider company profiles, expert advice, career message boards, expert resume reviews, the Vault Job Board and more.

VAULT CAREER LIBRARY   **169**

Employer Directory

Advest
90 State House Sq.
Hartford, CT 06103
Phone: (860) 509-1000; (800)
243-8115
Fax: (860) 509-3849
www.advest.com

AIG Global Investment Group
175 Water Street
New York, NY 10038
Phone: (212) 458-2000
Fax: (212) 458-2200
www.aiggig.com

Alliance Capital Management
1345 Avenue of the Americas
New York, NY 10105
Phone: (212) 969-1000
Fax: (212) 969-2229
www.alliancecapital.com

American Century Investments
4500 Main Street
Suite 1500
Kansas City, MO 64111
Phone: (816) 531-5575
Fax: (816) 340-7962
www.americancentury.com

AMVESCAP
30 Finsbury Square
London
EC2A 1AG, United Kingdom
Phone: 44-20-7638-0731
Fax: 44-20-7065-3962
www.amvescap.com

AIM Investments
11 Greenway Plaza, Suite 100
Houston, TX 77046
Phone: (713) 626-1919; (800)
959-4246
Fax: (713) 993-9890
www.aiminvestments.com

AIM Trimark
120 Bloor Street East
Suite 700
Toronto Ontario
M4W 1B7
Canada
Phone: (800) 588-4880
Fax: (416) 590-7742

INVESCO North America
One Midtown Plaza
1360 Peachtree Street, N.E.
Atlanta, Georgia 30309
Phone: (404) 892-0896
Fax : (404) 436-4911
www.invesco.com

INVESCO Perpetual
Henley-on-Thames
Oxfordshire RG9 1HH
United Kingdom
Phone: 44 0 1491 417 000
Fax: 44 0 1491 416 000
www.perpetual.co.uk

Barclays Global Investors
45 Fremont St.
San Francisco, CA 94105
Phone: (415) 597-2000
Fax: (415) 597-2010
www.barclaysglobal.com

BlackRock
40 East 52nd Street
New York, NY 10022
Phone: (212) 754-5560
Fax: (212) 935-1370
www.blackrock.com

CalPERS
Lincoln Plaza
400 P Street
Sacramento, CA 95814
Phone: (916) 326-3000
Fax: (916) 558-4001
www.calpers.ca.gov

Credit Suisse Asset Management
(CSAM)
466 Lexington Avenue
New York, NY 10017
Phone: (212) 875-3500
Fax: (646) 658-0728
www.csam.com

D.E. Shaw & Co. L.P.
120 West 45th Street
39th Floor, Tower 45
New York, NY 10036
Phone: (212) 478-0000
Fax: (212) 478-0100
www.deshaw.com

Deutsche Asset Management
345 Park Avenue
New York, NY 10154
Phone: 212 454 6260
www.deam-us.db.com

Dreyfus Corporation
200 Park Ave.
New York, NY 10166
Phone: (212) 922-6000
Fax: (212) 922-7533
www.dreyfus.com

Evergreen Investments
200 Berkeley Street
Boston, MA 02116
Phone: (617) 210-3200
www.evergreeninvestments.com

Federated Investors Inc.
Federated Investors Tower,
1001 Liberty Avenue
Pittsburgh, PA 15222-3779
www.FederatedInvestors.com

Fidelity Investments
82 Devonshire St.
Boston, MA 02109
Phone: (617) 563-7000
Fax: (617) 476-6150
www.fidelity.com

Franklin Resources
One Franklin Parkway
San Mateo CA, 94403
Phone: (650) 312-2000
www.franklintempleton.com

Gabelli Asset Management Inc.
One Corporate Center
Rye, NY 10580-1422
Phone: (914) 921-5100
Fax: (914)921-5392
www.gabelli.com

Janus Capital Group
Janus Capital Group Inc.
151 Detroit Street
Denver, CO 80206
Phone: (303) 333-3863
Fax: (303) 336-7497
www.janus.com

Legg Mason
100 Light Street
Baltimore, MD 21202-1099
Phone: (410) 539-0000
Fax: (410) 454-4923
www.leggmason.com

MFS Investment Management
500 Boylston Street
Boston, MA 02116
Phone: (617) 954-5000
Fax: (617) 954-5000
www.mfs.com

Nuveen Investments
333 West Wacker Drive
Chicago, IL 60606
Phone: (312) 917-7700
Fax: (312) 917-8049
www.nuveen.com

Pequot Capital Management
500 Nyala Farm Road
Westport, CT 06880
Phone: (203) 429-4400
Fax: (203) 429-2400
www.pequotcap.com

PIMCO
840 Newport Center Dr.
Newport Beach, CA 92660
Phone: (949) 720-6000
Fax: (949) 720-1376
www.pimco.com

Putnam Investments
1 Post Office Square
Boston, MA 02109
Phone: (617) 292-1000
Fax: (617) 482-3610
www.putnaminvestments.com

State Street Corporation
State Street Financial Center
One Lincoln Street
Boston, MA 02111
Phone: (617) 786-3000
www.statestreet.com

TIAA-CREF
730 Third Avenue
New York, NY 10017
Phone: (212) 490-9000
Fax: (212) 916-4840
www.tiaa-cref.org

T. Rowe Price
100 E. Pratt St.
Baltimore, MD 21202
Phone: (410) 345-2000
Fax: (410) 345-2394
www.troweprice.com

UBS Global Asset Management
UBS Tower
One North Wacker Drive,
38th Floor
Chicago, IL 60606
Phone: (312) 525-7100
Fax: (312) 525-7199
globalam-us.ubs.com

The Vanguard Group
100 Vanguard Blvd.
Malvern, PA 19355
Phone: (610) 648-6000
Fax: (610) 669-6605
www.vanguard.com

Wellington Management
75 State Street
Boston, MA 02109
Phone: (617) 951-5000
www.wellington.com

Visit Vault at **www.vault.com** for insider company profiles, expert advice,
career message boards, expert resume reviews, the Vault Job Board and more.

V/\ULT CAREER LIBRARY   171

Managment Consulting

What is Consulting?

A giant industry, a moving target

Consulting, in the business context, means the giving of advice for pay. Consultants offer their advice and skill in solving problems, and are hired by companies who need the expertise and outside perspective that consultants possess. Some consulting firms specialize in giving advice on management and strategy, while others are known as technology specialists. Some concentrate on a specific industry area, like financial services or retail, and still others are more like gigantic one-stop shops with divisions that dispense advice on everything from top-level strategy, to choosing training software, to saving money on paper clips.

But consulting firms have one thing in common: they run on the power of their people. The only product consulting firms ultimately have to offer is their ability to make problems go away. As a consultant, you are that problem-solver.

Not the kind of consulting we mean

As a standalone term, "consulting" lacks real meaning. In a sense, everyone's a consultant. Have you ever been asked by a friend, "Do I look good in orange?" Then you've been consulted about your color sense. There are thousands upon thousands of independent consultants who peddle their expertise and advice on everything from retrieving data from computers to cat astrology. There are also fashion consultants, image consultants, and wedding consultants. For the purposes of this section, we are going to use the term "consulting" to refer specifically to management consulting.

Management consulting firms sell business advisory services to the leaders of corporations, governments, and non-profit organizations. Typical concentrations in consulting include strategy, IT, HR, finance, and operations. Types of problems in consulting include pricing, marketing, new product strategy, IT implementation, or government policy. Finally, consulting firms sell services in virtually any industry, such as pharmaceuticals, consumer packaged goods, or energy.

Firms can be organized or broken up according to topic, type of problem, or industry. For example, a firm might focus on strategy problems only, but in virtually any industry. Bain & Company is an example of one such firm. Another firm might focus on a specific industry, but advise on nearly any type of issue. Oliver, Wyman and Company, which focuses on the financial services industry, is an example of this type of firm. Many of the larger firms have a "matrix" organization, with industry practice groups but also functional practice groups. And some firms are extremely specialized. For example, a firm might have only two employees, both focusing solely on competitive analysis in the telecommunications industry. All of these are examples of management consulting.

Caveats about consulting

All this might sound great, but before we go on, we should address some common misconceptions about consulting.

- **Implementation** – You might be thinking, "All consultants do is figure out problems at companies and explain them. Awesome. I'm going to be making great money for doing something really easy." Unfortunately, that's not true. Spotting a client's problems is a mere fraction of the battle. (Most people with a fair amount of common sense and an outsider's perspective can identify a client's problems. And in many cases, clients also understand where the problems lie.)

  The job of the consultant, therefore, isn't just about knowing what's wrong. It's about figuring out how to make it right. Even finding the solution isn't the end of the story. Consultants must make sure the solution isn't too expensive or impractical to implement. (Many consulting firms have what's called an 80 percent rule: It's better to put in

Visit Vault at **www.vault.com** for insider company profiles, expert advice, career message boards, expert resume reviews, the Vault Job Board and more.

VAULT CAREER LIBRARY 173

place a solution that takes care of 80 percent of the problem than to strive for a perfect solution that can't be put into place.) A corollary to this is the 80/20 rule: 80 percent of a problem can be solved in 20 percent of the time. Consultants must also get buy-in from the clients. Not only does bureaucracy often make implementation tough, but consultants must also convince individual client employees to help them make solutions work.   It's tough to solve problems – and that's why clients hire consultants.

- **Glamour** – Consulting can indeed be exciting and high profile, but this is the exception, not the rule. Chances are, you won't be sitting across from the CEO at your next project kick-off, and you probably won't be staying in four-star hotels in the coolest cities in the world (though both are possible). Depending on the industry and location of your client's business, your environment might be a mid-range hotel in a small city, and you might be working with the senior vice president of one of the company's many business units.

- **Prestige** – Consulting is widely thought of as a prestigious career among business circles, particularly MBAs. But you should realize that in contrast to work in investment banking, your work in consulting will probably never get mentioned in The Wall Street Journal. Very few consulting firms are publicly recognized for the help they give.

  As a result, few people outside of the industry really understand what consulting is. In fact, a running joke about consulting is that no one can explain it, no matter how hard or many times one tries. If you want a job you can explain to your grandmother, consulting isn't for you. Most "civilians" won't have heard of your firm – unless it has been involved in a scandal, that is.

- **Income** – The salary looks attractive on paper, but remember, it's not easy money.   Divide your salary over the (large) number of hours, and the pay per hour isn't much better than other business careers.

So what does a consultant actually do, anyway?

Most "non-consultants" are mystified by the actual job and its day-to-day responsibilities. There are good reasons why this is so. While you're used to giving advice and solving problems, you may not understand how this translates into a career path. The problem is compounded because consultants tend to use a very distinctive vocabulary. You may not know what your skill set is, or how not to boil the ocean, or what the heck consultants mean when they talk about helicoptering. In addition, many consulting firms have their own specific philosophies and problem-attacking frameworks, which only raise the level of jargon.

The short answer is that you will be working on projects of varying lengths at varying sites for different clients. What you do will depend on your seniority, experience, phase of the project and your company. If you are a partner, you are selling work most of the time, whereas if you have a recent MBA degree, you are probably overseeing a couple of entry-level consultants doing research. For the most part, we'll describe the job that entry-level and mid-level (MBA or the equivalent) consultants do. Generally, projects follow the pitching/research/analysis/report writing cycle.

Depending where you are in the project lifecycle, here are some of the things you could be doing:

Pitching

- Helping to sell and market the firm (preparing documents and researching prospective clients in preparation for sales calls)
- Helping to write the proposal
- Presenting a sales pitch to a prospective client (usually with PowerPoint, Microsoft's presentation software)

Research

- Performing secondary research on the client and its industry using investment banking reports and other research sources (these include Bloomberg, OneSource, Hoover's Online, Yahoo! News and SEC filings)
- Interviewing the client's customers to gather viewpoints on the company

- Checking your firm's data banks for previous studies that it has done in the industry or with the client, and speaking to the project leads about their insights on the firm

- Facilitating a weekly client team discussion about the client company's business issues

Analysis

- Building Excel discounted cash flow (DCF) and/or other quantitative financial models

- Analyzing the gathered data and the model for insights

- Helping to generate recommendations

Reporting

- Preparing the final presentation (typically a "deck" of PowerPoint slides, though some firms write up longer reports in Microsoft Word format)

- Helping to present the findings and recommendations to the client

Implementation

- Acting as a project manager for the implementation of your strategy, if your firm is typically active during the implementation phase of a project

- Executing the coding, systems integration, and testing of the recommended system, if you work for an IT consulting practice

- Documenting the team's work after the project is over

Administration

- Working on internal company research when your firm has no projects for you. (Being unstaffed is referred to as being "on the beach," a pleasant name for what is often a tedious time.)

- Filling out weekly time tracking and expense reports

Keep in mind that the analysis phase – usually the most interesting part – is probably the shortest part of any assignment. Consultants staffed on projects typically do a lot of research, financial analysis, Excel model building and presentation. You will attend lots of meetings in your quest to find the data, create the process and meet the people who will help you resolve the issues you've been hired to address. And, when you're not staffed, you will spend time "on the beach" doing research on prospective clients and helping with marketing efforts. (It's called "on the beach" because the time when you're not staffed on a paid engagement is usually less frenetic – though not always so!) Consulting firms spend a lot of time acquiring the work, and depending on how the firm is structured or how the economy is doing, you could spend significant amounts of time working on proposals. For you, this usually means lots of research, which is then elucidated on the omnipresent PowerPoint slides.

To some extent, though, the boundaries of the job are virtually limitless. Each project carries with it a new task, a new spreadsheet configuration, a new type of sales conference, or an entirely new way of thinking about business. To top it all off, you often must travel to your work assignment and work long hours in a pressurized environment. It's not easy.

Consulting Skill Sets

Consultants focus their energies in a wide variety of practice areas and industries. Their individual jobs, from a macro level, are as different as one could imagine. While a supply chain consultant advises a client about lead times in their production facility, another consultant is creating a training protocol for a new software package. What could be more different?

Visit Vault at **www.vault.com** for insider company profiles, expert advice, career message boards, expert resume reviews, the Vault Job Board and more.

VAULT CAREER LIBRARY 175

Despite the big picture differences, however, consultants' day-to-day skill sets are, by necessity, very similar. (Before we go any further: by skill set, we mean "your desirable attributes and skills that contribute value as a consultant." Skill set is a handy, abbreviated way to refer to same.)

Before we talk about the skill sets, keep in mind that there is a big difference between the job now and the job six to eight years from now, if and when you are a partner. We are going to talk about whether you would like the job now, but you should think about whether this might be a good long-term career for you. Is your goal to see it through to partner? If you would rather have an interesting job for six years, you just have to know you have the qualities to be a good consultant and manager. To be a partner, you have to be a persuasive salesperson. You will spend nearly 100 percent of your time selling expensive services to companies who don't think they need help. Your pay and job security will depend on your ability to make those sales.

Do you have the following characteristics in your skill set?

- **Do you work well in teams?** Consultants don't work alone. Not only do they frequently brainstorm with other consultants, but they also often work with employees at the client company, or even with consultants from other companies hired by the client. Consultants also frequently attend meetings and interview potential information sources. If you're the sort of person who prefers to work alone in quiet environments, you will not enjoy being a consultant.

- **Do you multi-task well?** Not only can consulting assignments be frenetic, but consultants are often staffed on more than one assignment. Superior organizational skills and a good sense of prioritization are your friends. Would your friends describe you as a really busy person who's involved in a ton of activities, and still able to keep your personal life on track?

- **Speaking of friends, do you like talking to people?** Do you find yourself getting into interesting conversations over lunch and dinner? If you consider yourself a true introvert and find that speaking to people all day saps your energy, you will likely find consulting quite enervating. On the other hand, if you truly relish meetings, talking to experts, explaining your viewpoints, cajoling others to cooperate with you and making impromptu presentations, you've got some valuable talents in your consulting skill set.

- **Did you love school?** Did you really like going to class and doing your homework? There's a high correlation between academic curiosity and enjoyment of consulting.

- **Are you comfortable with math?** Consulting firms don't expect you to be a math professor, but you should be comfortable with figures, as well as commonly used programs like Excel, Access and PowerPoint. If you hate math, you will hate consulting. On a related note, you should also relish and be good at analysis and thinking creatively. Consultants have a term, now infiltrating popular culture, called "out of the box thinking." This means the ability to find solutions that are "outside of the box" – not constrained by commonly accepted facts.

- **Are you willing to work 70, even 80 hours a week?** Consultants must fulfill client expectations. If you must work 80 hours a week to meet client expectations, then that will be your fate. If you have commitments outside work, for example, you may find consulting hours difficult. Even if you have no major commitments outside work, understand what such a schedule means to you. Try working from 8 a.m. to 10 p.m. one day. Now imagine doing so five days a week for months on end.

- **Last, but certainly not least, are you willing to travel frequently?** Be truthful. If you can't answer most of these points with a resounding "yes," consulting is most likely not for you. The point is not just to get the job, but also to know what you're getting into – and to truly want to be a consultant. (See the next section for a discussion of travel in consulting.)

The Traveling Salesman Problem

A lot of people go into the consulting field with the notion that travel is fun. "Traveling four days a week? No problem! My last vacation to Italy was a blast!" However, many soon find the traveling consultant's life to be a nightmare. Many consultants leave the field solely because of travel requirements.

Here's what we mean by consulting travel. Different consulting firms have different travel models, but there are two basic ones:

- A number of consulting firms (the larger ones) spend four days on the client site. This means traveling to the destination city Monday morning, spending three nights in a hotel near the client site, and flying home late Thursday night. (This will, of course, vary, depending on client preference and flight times.) The same firms often try to staff "regionally" to reduce flying time for consultants.

- The other popular travel model is to go to the client site "as needed." This generally means traveling at the beginning of the project for a few days, at the end of the project for the presentation, and a couple of times during the project. There is less regularity and predictability with this travel model, but there is also less overall time on the road.

Here are some variations of these travel modes that pop up frequently:

- International projects involve a longer-term stay on the client site. (Flying consultants to and from the home country every week can get expensive.) For example, the consultant might stay two or three weeks on or near the client site (the client might put you up in a corporate apartment instead of a hotel to save costs) and then go home for a week, repeating the process until the end of the project.

- Then, there is the "local" project that is really a long commute into a suburb, sometimes involving up to two hours in a car. Examples of this include consulting to Motorola (based in not-so-convenient Schaumburg, IL) while living in Chicago, or consulting to a Silicon Valley client while living in San Francisco. In these cases, you might opt to stay at a local hotel after working late, instead of taking the long drive home. This is not very different from non-local travel, and it can be more grueling, due to the car commute.

You need to ask yourself a number of questions to see if you are travel-phobic. For example, when you pack to go on vacation, do you stress about it? Do you always underpack or overpack? Do you hate flying? Do you hate to drive? Do you mind sleeping in hotel rooms for long periods of time? Are you comfortable with the idea of traveling to remote cities and staying there for three or four nights every week for ten weeks? If you're married, do you mind being away from your spouse (and children if you have them) for up to three nights a week? Does your family mind? Will your spouse understand and not hold it against you if you have to cancel your anniversary dinner because the client wants you to stay a day later? If you and your spouse both travel for work, who will take care of the pets? Does the idea of managing your weekly finances and to-do lists from the road bother you?

If these questions make your stomach churn, look for consulting companies that promise a more stable work environment. For example, if you work in financial consulting and live in New York City, most of your clients may be local. But because consulting firms don't always have the luxury of choosing their clients, they can't guarantee that you won't travel. Moreover, many large companies build their corporate campus where they can find cost-effective space, often in the suburbs or large corporate parks. (If you absolutely can not travel, some of the largest consulting firms, such as Accenture, have certain business units that can guarantee a non-traveling schedule. Ask.)

Note that travel is common in the consulting field, but not all consultants travel. And not all clients expect you to be on site all the time. It absolutely depends on the firm's travel model, industry, your location, and most importantly, your project.

Visit Vault at **www.vault.com** for insider company profiles, expert advice, career message boards, expert resume reviews, the Vault Job Board and more.

VAULT CAREER LIBRARY   **177**

Day in the Life: Associate Strategy Consultant

Greg Schneider is an associate at the Boston office of a top strategy consulting firm office. He kindly agreed to share a "typical" workday with Vault, noting that no day at any consulting firm can be called typical.

6:15 a.m.: Alarm goes off. I wake up asking myself why I put "run three times per week" into the team charter. I meet another member of the team, and we hobble out for a jog. At least it's warm out – another advantage of having a project in Miami.

7:15 a.m.: Check voice mail. Someone in London wants a copy of my knowledge building document on managing hyper-growth. A co-worker is looking for information about what the partner from my last team is like to work with.

7:30 a.m.: Breakfast with the team. We discuss sports, Letterman, and a morning meeting we have with the client team (not necessarily in that order). We then head out to the client.

9:00 a.m.: Meet with the client team. We've got an important progress review with the CEO next week, so there's a lot going on. We're helping the client to assess the market potential of an emerging technology. Today's meeting concerns what kind of presentation would be most effective, although we have trouble staying off tangents about the various analyses that we've all been working on. The discussion is complicated by the fact that some key data is not yet available. We elect to go with a computer-based slide show and begin the debate on the content.

10:53 a.m.: Check voice mail. The office is looking for an interviewer for the Harvard Business School hell weekend. The partner will be arriving in time for dinner and wants to meet to discuss the progress review. A headhunter looking for a divisional VP. My wife reminding me to mail off the insurance forms.

11:00 a.m.: I depart with my teammate for an interview. We meet with an industry expert (a professor from a local university) to discuss industry trends and in particular what the prospects are for the type of technology we're looking at. As this is the last interview we plan to do, we are able to check many of our hypotheses. The woman is amazing – we luck out and get some data we need. The bad news is, now we have to figure out what it means.

12:28 p.m.: As I walk back in to the client, a division head I've been working with grabs me and we head to lunch. He wanted to discuss an analysis he'd given me some information for, and in the process I get some interesting perspectives about the difficulties in moving the technology into full production and how much it could cost.

1:30 p.m.: I jump on a quick conference call about an internal knowledge building project I'm working on for the marketing practice. I successfully avoid taking on any additional responsibility.

2:04 p.m.: Begin to work through new data. After discussing the plan of attack with the engagement manager, I dive in. It's a very busy afternoon, but the data is great. I get a couple "a-ha"s – always a good feeling.

3:00 p.m.: Short call with someone from Legal to get an update on the patent search.

6:00 p.m.: Team meeting. The engagement manager pulls the team together to check progress on various fronts and debate some issues prior to heading to dinner with the partner. A quick poll determines that Italian food wins – we leave a voice mail with the details.

6:35 p.m.: Call home and check in with the family. Confirm plans for weekend trip to Vermont. Apologize for forgetting to mail the insurance forms.

7:15 p.m.: The team packs up and heads out to dinner. We meet the partner at the restaurant and have a productive (and calorific) meal working through our plans for the progress review, the new data, what's going on with the client team, and other areas of interest. She suggests some additional uses for the new data, adds her take on our debates, and agrees to raise a couple issues with the CFO, whom she's known for years. She takes a copy of our draft presentation to read after dinner.

9:15 p.m.: Return to hotel. Plug in computer and check e-mail, since I hadn't had a chance all day. While I'm logged in, I download two documents I need from the company database, check the Red Sox score, and see how the client's stock did.

10:10 p.m.: Pre-sleep voice mail check. A client from a previous study is looking for one of the appendices, since he lost his copy. The server will be down for an hour tomorrow night.

10:30 p.m.: Watch SportsCenter instead of going right to sleep, as I know I probably should.

Note: Had this been an in-town study, the following things would have been different: I wouldn't have run with another member of my team, and we'd have substituted a conference call for the dinner meeting, so we could go home instead. Also, I probably wouldn't have watched SportsCenter.

Visit Vault at **www.vault.com** for insider company profiles, expert advice, career message boards, expert resume reviews, the Vault Job Board and more.

V/\ULT CAREER LIBRARY **179**

Employer Directory

Booz Allen Hamilton

101 Park Avenue
New York City, New York 10178
To Apply: www.boozallen.com/mba

Booz Allen Hamilton is a global strategy consulting firm. We work hand-in-hand with our clients-senior executives of Fortune 500 companies and public sector agencies-to transform their organizations and their industries with our combination of strategy, technology, operations, and change management capabilities.

Business schools Booz Allen Hamilton recruits from

Carnegie Mellon; Columbia; Darden; Fuqua; Harvard; IESE; INSEAD; Kellogg; London Business School; MIT; NYU; Stanford; Tuck; U of Chicago; U of Michigan; University of Texas; and Wharton

Deloitte

1633 Broadway
New York, NY 10013-6754
www.deloitte.com/careers

Deloitte, one of the nation's leading professional services firms, provides audit, tax, consulting, and financial advisory services through nearly 30,000 people in more than 80 U.S. cities. Known as an employer of choice for innovative human resources programs, the firm is dedicated to helping its clients and its people excel. "Deloitte" refers to the associated partnerships of Deloitte & Touche USA LLP (Deloitte & Touche LLP and Deloitte Consulting LLP) and subsidiaries. Deloitte is the U.S. member firm of Deloitte Touche Tohmatsu.

Business schools Deloitte recruits from

There are too many to list. All candidate are to submit to opportunities via our career website located at www.deloitte.com

A.T. Kearney
222 West Adams Street
Chicago, IL 60606
Phone: (312) 648-0111
www.atkearney.com

Accenture
1345 Avenue of the Americas
New York, NY 10105
Phone: (917) 452-4400
Fax: (917) 527-5387
www.accenture.com

The Advisory Board Company
2445 M Street, N.W.
Washington, D.C. 20037
Phone: (202) 266-5600
Fax: (202) 266-5700
www.advisoryboardcompany.com

Analysis Group
111 Huntington Avenue
10th Floor
Boston, MA 02199
Phone: (617) 425-8000
Fax: (617) 425-8001
www.ag-inc.com

Arthur D. Little
68 Fargo Street
Boston, MA 02210
Phone: (617) 443-0309
Fax: (617) 443-0166
www.adlittle-us.com

Bain & Company
131 Dartmouth Street
Boston, MA 02116
Tel: (617) 572-2000
Fax: (617) 572-2427
www.bain.com

BearingPoint
1676 International Drive
McLean, VA 22102
Phone: (703) 747-3000
Fax: (703) 747-8500
www.bearingpoint.com

Booz Allen Hamilton
8283 Greensboro Drive
McLean, VA 22102
(703) 902-5000
Fax: (703) 902-3333
www.boozallen.com
www.bah.com

Boston Consulting Group
Exchange Place
31st Floor
Boston, MA 02109
Phone: (617) 973-1200
Fax: (617) 973-1339
www.bcg.com

Cambridge Associates
100 Summer Street
Boston, MA 02110-2112
Phone: (617) 457-7500
Fax: (617) 457-7501
www.cambridgeassociates.com

Capgemini
Five Times Square
New York, NY 10036
Phone: (917) 934-8000
Fax: (917) 934-8001
www.capgemini.com

Charles River Associates
John Hancock Tower
200 Clarendon Street, T-33
Boston, MA 02116-5092
Phone: (617) 425-3000
Fax: (617) 425-3132
www.crai.com

Cornerstone Research
599 Lexington Avenue, 43rd Floor
New York, NY 10022-7642
Phone: (212) 605-5000
Fax: (212) 759-3045

1000 El Camino Real, Suite 250
Menlo Park, CA 94025
Phone: (650) 853-1660
www.cornerstone.com

Corporate Executive Board
2000 Pennsylvania Avenue, NW
Suite 6000
Washington, D.C. 20006
Phone: (202) 777-5000
Fax: (202) 777-5100
www.executiveboard.com

Dean & Company
8065 Leesburg Pike, Suite 500
Vienna, VA 22182
Phone: (703) 506 3900
Fax: (703) 506 3905
www.dean.com

Deloitte
1633 Broadway, 35th Floor
New York, NY 10019
Phone: (212) 492-4500
Fax: (212) 492-4743
www.deloitte.com

DiamondCluster International
Suite 3000
John Hancock Center
875 N. Michigan Avenue
Chicago, IL 60611
Phone: (312) 255-5000
Fax: (312) 255-6000
www.diamondcluster.com
info@diamondcluster.com

First Manhattan Consulting Group
90 Park Avenue
19th Floor
New York, NY 10016
Phone: (212) 557-0500
Fax: (212) 338-9296
www.fmcg.com

Gallup Consulting
901 F Street, NW
Washington, D.C. 20004
Phone: (877) 242-5587
or (202) 715-3030
Fax: (202) 715-3041
www.gallup.com

Gartner, Inc.
56 Top Gallant Road
Stamford, CT 06904
Phone: (203) 964-0096
www.gartner.com

Giuliani Partners
5 Times Square
New York NY 10036
Phone: (212) 931-7300
Fax: (212) 931-7310
www.giulianipartners.com

Hay Group
The Wanamaker Building
100 Penn Square East
Philadelphia, PA 19107
Phone: (215) 861-2000
Fax: (215) 861-2111
www.haygroup.com

Hewitt Associates
100 Half Day Road
Lincolnshire, IL 60069
Phone: (847) 295-5000
Fax: (847) 295-7634
www.hewitt.com

IBM Business Consulting Services
1133 Westchester Avenue
White Plains, NY 10604
Phone: (800) IBM-7080, ext. BCS
www-
1.ibm.com/services/us/bcs/html/bcs_ind
ex.html

Katzenbach Partners LLC
381 Park Avenue South
5th Floor
New York, NY 10016
Phone: 212-213-5505
Fax: 212-213-5014
www.katzenbach.com

Visit Vault at **www.vault.com** for insider company profiles, expert advice,
career message boards, expert resume reviews, the Vault Job Board and more.

V∆ULT CAREER LIBRARY   **181**

Kurt Salmon Associates

1355 Peachtree Street, NE
Suite 900
Atlanta, GA 30309
Phone: (404) 892-0321
Fax: (404) 898-9590
www.kurtsalmon.com

L.E.K. Consulting

28 State Street
16th Floor
Boston, MA 02109
Phone: (617) 951-9500
Fax: (617) 951-9392
info@lek.com
www.lek.com

LECG

2000 Powell Street, Suite 600
Emeryville, CA 94608
Phone: (510) 985-6700
Fax: (510) 653-9898
www.lecg.com

Marakon Associates

245 Park Avenue
44th Floor
New York, NY 10167
Phone: (212) 377-5000
Fax: (212) 377-6000
www.marakon.com

Mars & Company

124 Mason Street
Greenwich, CT 06830
Phone: (203) 629-9292
Fax: (203) 629-9432
www.marsandco.com

Mercer Human Resource Consulting

1166 Avenue of the Americas
New York, NY 10036
Phone: (212) 345-7000
Fax: (212) 345-7414
www.mercerhr.com

Mercer Management Consulting

1166 Avenue of the Americas
32nd Floor
New York, NY 10036
Phone: (212) 345-8000
Fax: (212) 345-8075
www.mercermc.com

Mercer Oliver Wyman

99 Park Avenue, 5th Floor
New York, NY 10016
Phone: (212) 541-8100
Fax: (212) 541-8957/8958
www.merceroliverwyman.com

Mitchell Madison Group

575 Madison Ave.
8th Floor
New York, NY 10022
(212) 605-0141
www.mitchellmadison.com

Monitor Group

Two Canal Park
Cambridge, MA 02141
Phone: (617) 252-2000
Fax: (617) 252-2100
www.monitor.com

Navigant Consulting

615 North Wabash Avenue
Chicago, IL 60611
Phone: (312) 573-5600
Fax: (312) 573-5678
www.navigantconsulting.com

NERA Economic Consulting

50 Main Street, 14th Floor
White Plains, NY 10606
Phone: (914) 448-4000
Fax: (914) 448-4040
www.nera.com

OC&C Strategy Consultants

U.S. Headquarters:
244 Madison Avenue #420
New York, NY10016
(646) 479-7127
www.occstrategy.com

PA Consulting Group

123 Buckingham Palace Road
London
SW1W 9SR
United Kingdom
Phone: +44 20 7730 9000
Fax: +44 20 7333 5050
www.paconsulting.com

Parthenon Group, The

200 State Street
Boston, MA 02109
Phone: (617) 478-2550
Fax: (617) 478-2555
www.parthenon.com

PRTM

1050 Winter Street
Waltham, MA 02451
Phone: (781) 647-2800
Fax: (781) 647-2804

650 Town Center Drive, Suite 820
Costa Mesa, CA 92626
Phone: (714) 545-9400
Fax: (714) 545-8600
www.prtm.com

Putnam Associates

25 Burlington Mall Road
Burlington, MA 01803
Phone: (781) 273-5480
Fax: (781) 273-5484
www.putassoc.com

Roland Berger Strategy Consultants

Arabellastrasse 33
81925 Munich
Germany
Phone: +49 89 9230-0
Fax: +49 89 9230-8202
www.rolandberger.com

Stern Stewart & Company

780 Third Avenue, 6th Floor
New York, NY 10017
Phone: (212) 261-0600
Fax: (212) 581-6420
www.sternstewart.com

Strategic Decisions Group (SDG)
735 Emerson Street
Palo Alto, CA 94301-2411
Phone: (650) 475-4400
Fax: (650) 475-4401
www.sdg.com

Towers Perrin
335 Madison Avenue
New York, NY 10017-4605
Phone: (212) 309-3400
www.towersperrin.com

Value Partners
Via Leopardi, 32
20123 Milano
Tel. +39 02 4854-81
Fax +39 02 480090-10
www.valuepartners.com

Watson Wyatt Worldwide
1717 H Street, NW
Washington, DC 20006
Phone: (202) 715-7000
Fax: (202) 715-7700
www.watsonwyatt.com

ZS Associates
1800 Sherman Avenue
Suite 700
Evanston, IL 60201
Phone: (888) 972-4173
Fax: (888) 972-7329
www.zsassociates.com

Visit Vault at **www.vault.com** for insider company profiles, expert advice, career message boards, expert resume reviews, the Vault Job Board and more.

V\ULT CAREER LIBRARY   **183**

Manufacturing

The Engine Driving the Economy

The manufacturing industry

America's manufacturing industry is a powerful engine driving the nation's economy, making up roughly one-fifth of all U.S. economic activity. Between 1992 and 2000, the industry contributed 22 percent of the country's economic growth, or 28 percent with the addition of software production. It's a major force in employment, as well, comprising 12 percent of all jobs. Through its "multiplier effect," manufacturing actually creates economic output in other industries by using intermediate goods and services in its production process – so that every $1 of a manufacturing product sold to a final user creates an additional $1.43 in intermediate economic output, according to the Department of Commerce. The U.S. continues to lead the world in many manufacturing sectors, including automobiles, aerospace, steel, telecommunications and consumer goods, and it also maintains the lead in exports of manufactured products. It's no wonder economists pay such close attention to U.S. manufacturing stats and figures – and no wonder that the pronounced slump in the sector since 2000 has been cause for concern.

The big slump

Beginning in 2000, following a boom that spanned most of the 20th century, manufacturing was hit by a recession that eventually led to the loss of more than 2.7 million jobs, or about 17 percent of the sector's workforce. A number of circumstances led to the slump, including high interest rates, increased natural gas prices, and a strong U.S. dollar that weakened the export trade, according to the National Association of Manufacturers (NAM). Recovery began in 2003, though at the slowest pace recorded since the Federal Reserve started keeping track of such things in 1919. And though overall hiring came back, the industry, which had seen job losses each month for more than three years in a row, was still on shaky ground.

More efficiency, fewer jobs

Like many industries, manufacturing has seen a steady push toward technologies that promise greater efficiency and productivity – while reducing the need for manpower. So even as employment figures edged up in early 2004, manufacturing giants like 3M continued to make cuts. The Bureau of Labor Statistics (BLS) predicts total manufacturing employment will decrease by 1 percent through 2012. It's likely that many of the factory jobs lost since the beginning of the century will never return, signaling a fundamental shift in the industry as a whole.

A shift also has taken place in the makeup of the industry. According to the NAM, chemicals, industrial machinery and equipment, and electronics are the three largest manufacturing sectors today, making up a third of the industry's gross domestic product. Fifty years ago, the three largest sectors in manufacturing were food, primary metals and motor vehicles.

The auto sector

Still, manufacturing is closely tied to the production of automobiles – indeed, an assembly line in Michigan may be what many people think of when they hear the term "manufacturing." In 2002, the latest year for which BLS data is available, the auto sector accounted for about 1.2 million jobs. For the most part, the U.S. was able to ward off the competitive threat from Japanese companies that surfaced in the early 1990s by improving their quality and product lines domestically (a bullish environment on Wall Street and economic weakness in Asia also helped). The so-called "Big Three" automakers – General Motors, DaimlerChrysler and Ford – had about 57 percent of the domestic passenger car market in 2000. But since big-ticket purchases like cars are closely tied to consumer confidence, the terrorist attacks of September 11 and the resulting econom-

Visit Vault at **www.vault.com** for insider company profiles, expert advice, career message boards, expert resume reviews, the Vault Job Board and more.

VAULT CAREER LIBRARY   185

ic turmoil forced car makers to offer customers heavy discounts (such as the zero-percent financing campaign initiated by GM) and cash-back incentives to keep inventory moving. Capacity also needed to be slashed to bring inventories in line with reduced demand, leading to an unhealthy combination of diminished productivity and weak prices. All of this has led to major job cuts, as well as negative ripple effects for related sectors like steel companies.

Though the auto industry has attempted to rebound by revamping cars to meet consumer demand for items like SUVs and, in contrast, fuel-efficient hybrid vehicles, analysts warn that U.S. companies need to look to the east again as the Asian markets improve and manufacturers like Toyota (currently number four in terms of sales) pick up the pace.

Steely resolve

Steel is another traditional mainstay in U.S. manufacturing. Like its manufacturing counterparts, the steel sector recently experienced its worst days since the Depression, with more than 30 U.S. steel companies, including giants like Bethlehem Steel and National Steel, filing for bankruptcy since 2000. But more recently, steel has rebounded, largely due to the lifting of tariffs on steel imports to avoid reprisals from Europe. With efficiency in line, steel producers raised prices by 20 percent in late 2003, and have continued to post strong orders. The sector isn't slowing down – in fact, the U.S. is actually producing 50 percent more steel today than it did in the early 1980s.

Flying the friendly skies

Aerospace also contributes significantly to U.S. manufacturing. In the commercial sphere, aerospace manufacturing is dominated by Boeing and European rival Airbus. These companies and others, like Lockheed Martin, Northrop Grumman, and Raytheon, also are involved in the production of military aircraft, missiles, and equipment for space. But following 2001's domestic terrorist attacks, civilian air travel plummeted, and major airlines like United were driven into bankruptcy. Fewer planes were being ordered, leading to massive layoffs in the sector. Though the industry has been bolstered a bit by innovations such as Boeing's new 7E7 Dreamliner, a fuel-efficient passenger jet that should take to the skies by 2008, total sales for civilian and military planes in 2004 were expected to grow by less than one percent, to $148 billion – down $7 billion from 2002, according to the Aerospace Industries Association.

All about chemicals

In the chemical manufacturing sector, high-profile names like BASF, DuPont, and Dow Chemical lead the market. The chemical giants have struggled in recent years, since they're dependent on materials like natural gas and petroleum, which have seen sharp increases in prices. And when prices for energy increase, the chemical manufacturers' customers – such as automakers – cut back on production, weakening demand for chemicals. This all has added up to decreased revenues during the first years of the century, along with an increased drive toward mergers and acquisitions. Notable deals recently have included Dow Chemical's purchase of Union Carbide and Valspar's purchase of Lilly Industries.

Other manufacturing sectors include the forest products industry, estimated at around 7 percent of U.S. manufacturing output. Here again, employment figures have plummeted in recent years due to a convergence of unfavorable economic conditions and changes in demand due to the new "paperless" business environment. Additional heavy manufacturing sectors include plastics, textiles, apparel, rubber and minerals.

What is the Supply Chain?

Suppliers and vendors

A simple definition of supply chain is the network of vendors that provides materials for a company's products, but in reality, the supply chain is more complicated. There is a stream of flows from supplier to supplier until a product reaches an end user. For example, oil is rigged from the ground, sent to a refinery, plastic is made, an injection molding shop buys plastic pellets, makes plastics components, ships the components to a customer, the customer assembles the plastic parts into their machine, and then sells the machine to their customer. The further away from the customer, the farther "upstream" a supplier is considered to be.

The network of vendors in a supply chain often includes tiered suppliers (meaning a company does not receive materials directly from the supplier, but is involved in getting materials or parts from an upstream supplier to a downstream supplier). The more complex a product, the more significant the upstream supplier's roles are. From a supply chain manager's perspective, his suppliers are primarily responsible for managing their own supply chain but he should have some involvement.

Oftentimes, a manufacturing facility acts as a supplier to a downstream manufacturing facility. For example, a company could have their manufacturing plant in the U.S. and their assembly plant in Mexico. The U.S. plant would be considered an internal supplier, since it's part of the same company. The transportation of materials throughout the supply chain is often called logistics. This includes air, land, and sea shipping as well as customs processing to allow materials to cross borders. The supply chain does not end until the product reaches the consumer. For this reason, distribution centers, distributors, and wholesalers are all part of the supply chain. It is not rare for a supply chain to involve a dozen parties.

The relationship between a supplier and a manufacturing company is not as simple as a supply chain manager ordering parts and the supplier shipping them. There are continuous flows between the supplier and the customer. Figure X below shows these flows in chronological order from top to bottom. (Note that this figure is for an already established supplier and material.) In the case of a new supplier, a supplier audit (a verification that a supplier has the potential to meet the manufacturer's needs) should be conducted first to determine if the supplier is appropriate for the work.

In the case of new material, the customer must first supply the anticipated number of units required, along with all of the drawings and specifications, to the supplier to get a quotation of unit price and lead time. After the quotes are received and a supplier is chosen, a purchase order should be done for the setup costs and samples. Setup costs can be a few hundred to hundreds of thousands of dollars (mostly tooling costs). A supply chain manager should always present the setup costs along with the piece price quote when working with engineers (so manufacturing methods are not specified solely on unit cost). For example, making a simple part by thermoforming would cost about $50 each, whereas making it by injection molding would cost $5 each. However, injection molding requires a $10,000 mold. If you only need 20 pieces annually, you are better off using thermoforming.

Depending on whether prototypes or the component have already been made or not, the samples ordered may be just to verify the ability of the supplier to make the parts, or to verify the design of the finished product. In other words, the supplier may fabricate a part correctly, but a manufacturer's engineering department may determine that the part needs to be redesigned. This would start the process over. Once samples have been approved, the flow of Figure X can be followed.

A manufacturing company has to furnish a forecast (usually annually) so the supplier can then go through his supply chain and make sure that all the materials needed (i.e. material, lubricant, machine capacity, labor resources) for the component the supplier provides will be available. A manufacturer then issues a purchase order, which serves as a commitment to purchase a defined number of units. A purchase order must have terms and conditions accompanying it to protect your company. Usually, a customer will not want to receive the entire forecast amount at once. Instead, a manufacturer could issue multi-

Visit Vault at **www.vault.com** for insider company profiles, expert advice, career message boards, expert resume reviews, the Vault Job Board and more.

V/\ULT CAREER LIBRARY   **187**

ple purchase orders throughout the year, or do what is called a blanket purchase order for a large amount and then make releases against that purchase order for small amounts when they actually want it.

For example, a company uses 1,000 rods of aluminum in a year. They may lock into a price for the entire year (the price of aluminum changes daily), but not take delivery of all 1,000 rods at once. Instead, the supply chain manager would request economic order quantity (EOQ) releases. An EOQ is the optimal balance between taking delivery for the entire 1,000 rods at once and paying for material that will not be used for months, and paying transportation, inspection, and transaction costs for receiving frequent smaller shipments. The formula for EOQ is

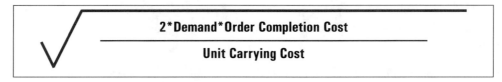

$$\sqrt{\frac{2*Demand*Order\ Completion\ Cost}{Unit\ Carrying\ Cost}}$$

where the Order Completion Cost is the total cost of placing the purchase order, paying for a setup at the vendor (if applicable), and paying the transportation and in-house handling to get the components to the production floor. The unit carrying cost is the cost of holding inventory (insurance, warehouse lease, shrinkage costs, security, cost of capital, etc.)

Customers can do releases to the supplier at specific time intervals or specific inventory intervals. With inventory intervals, when a customer gets to a certain number of rods left, they would issue a release for the next shipment of rods.

A supplier should send a confirmation to the customer acknowledging they have received the purchase order and agreed to the terms and conditions described therein. The supplier sends the material per the purchase order and then sends an invoice for the amount shipped. Once the goods have been accepted by the customer, a payment is sent to the supplier equal to the amount of the invoice.

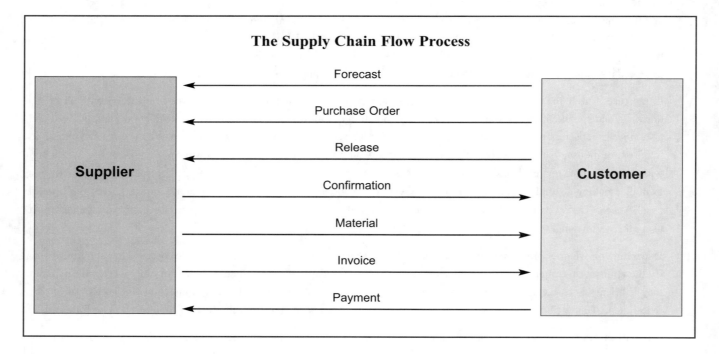

The Supply Chain Flow Process

OEM suppliers

There are basically three types of suppliers. In the first, or most conventional scenario, a company provides a design for what they want the supplier to furnish and the supplier makes it to the company's specifications. The second is the Original Equipment Manufacturer (OEM) supplier. In this case, the company does not specify the design for a custom product, but in fact buys a product that the supplier sells to many customers. These products are called off-the-shelf (a screw is an example of a component that is usually purchased as an off-the-shelf product rather than being custom designed).

Contract manufacturers

Contract manufacturers are the third type of suppliers, in which formal contracts between the supplier (the contract manufacturer) and your manufacturing company are relied upon. The contract manufacturer purchases or makes all of the components, assembles the product, tests it, and ships the finished product either directly to the customer or to a warehouse. Companies that want to get out of the manufacturing aspect of their products turn to contract manufacturers. The supply chain manager finds suitable contract manufacturers and manages the relationship after a contract has been signed. A company has to put a huge amount of trust into the contract manufacturer, since the customer does not have the same level of visibility or control over the manufacturing of the product as they do when they are making the product themselves. Contract manufacturing is an option in almost every industry from food processing to semiconductors.

Freight forwarders and transportation providers

Transportation providers and freight forwarders are also controlled by a supply chain management practitioner. Transportation providers pick up product from one location and deliver them to another. Obviously, it is very costly to pick up some cargo in Los Angeles and drive it all the way to New York for delivery. For this reason, these companies consolidate shipments from different places in a departing hub (whether it be a port, a warehouse, or an airport), send them to an arriving hub, and then deliver them to their final destination. It is quite common for a transportation provider to hand off a shipment to another company to carry out some or all of the transportation. This is called subcontracting or third party carriers. Specialty transportation providers also exist (i.e. for transporting explosive materials, refrigerated cargo, etc.). Some manufacturing companies have traffic, transportation, or logistics departments that take care of most of this work so a supply chain manager can concentrate on suppliers only.

Freight forwarders specialize in transportation across borders. They coordinate the paperwork, book the space with a transportation provider, and track the goods from pickup to delivery. Because of the complexity of customs requirements, tariff codes, and language barriers for different countries, it is better to have freight forwarders involved if a company is dealing with more than a few countries or commodities.

Job Responsibilities

Supply chain management occupations

Below are brief summaries of the duties for supply chain management occupations. Not every organization will have all of these positions and the duties of the positions will not be limited to those described here.

Buyer: Buyers do purchasing just like supply chain managers. The difference is that supply chain managers buy parts and materials for the company's products, whereas buyers purchase everything else. Some examples of items that buyers procure are desktop computers, office supplies, and hand tools.

Visit Vault at **www.vault.com** for insider company profiles, expert advice, career message boards, expert resume reviews, the Vault Job Board and more.

VAULT CAREER LIBRARY   **189**

Planner: A planner takes the forecast from marketing/sales and breaks that into a build schedule of what products should be built and when they should be built to meet inventory goals. Planners also work with supply chain managers to control inventory of parts and materials.

Purchasing Administrative Assistant: A purchasing administrative assistant takes care of the filing of paperwork for the purchasing department. S/he will also coordinate travel arrangements.

Logistics Manager: A logistics manager is responsible for the traffic of goods coming to and going from the factory. This encompasses air, land, and ocean traffic, both domestic and international.

Supply Chain Engineer: A supply chain engineer works on technical issues with the supplier. This involves working with suppliers to improve their quality, helping them to analyze failures, and developing new products.

Commodity Manager: A commodity manager is similar to a supply chain manager. Some companies separate the ownership of parts and materials for the supply chain managers by product line. For example, if a company makes binoculars, telescopes, cameras, and microscopes, and they have four supply chain managers, they might assign one supply chain manager for each product family. Another approach is to distribute the work by commodity. One supply chain manager would be responsible for the optics on all of the product families and one supply chain manager would be responsible for the plastic parts on all of the product families. When this is the case, the supply chain managers can be called commodity managers.

Receiving Inspector: A receiving inspector is responsible for checking the quality of the parts and materials that come from the vendor before they get moved to the production floor for consumption and before the supplier gets paid. There are statistics charts that define the number of samples from a shipment that need to be checked to meet the desired confidence level that the entire lot received is acceptable, so a receiving inspector does not check 100% of the incoming items.

Procurement Manager: A procurement manager is in charge of the buyers and supply chain managers. The procurement manager sets the goals for the department and provides a level of escalation when a supply chain manager is having trouble managing a supplier.

Receiving Coordinator: The receiving coordinator processes the parts and materials delivered. This includes doing a receiving transaction in ERP, moving the parts to their location, and making sure the paperwork the supplier sends matches what was received.

Receiving Supervisor: The receiving supervisor is responsible for the receiving department. Besides supervising receiving department workers, the receiving supervisor is in charge of creating and improving department processes.

Accounts Payable Coordinator: The accounts payable coordinator works in the accounting department and processes the invoices from the suppliers. After verifying the invoices match what was actually received, the accounts payable coordinator sends a payment to the supplier.

The MBA in Supply Chain Management

MBA graduates seeking opportunities in supply chain management usually pursue either a Project Manager or Director of Materials position. Both of these vocations require previous experience in supply chain management, so the likelihood of a new graduate landing one of these positions is low.

A Project Manager is responsible for large transitions related to supply chain management. One example of these transitions is a plant shutdown. A company may decide that it is more cost-effective to stop manufacturing their products themselves, and instead have a vendor do it for them. The management of a plant shutdown project requires cross-functional teamwork between accounting (working out the costs), engineering (helping the vendors get up and running), human resources (laying off the production workers), and manufacturing (managing the inventory to make a seamless transition). Another example of a transition is a large scale vendor change. A company may have a contract manufacturer in Mexico making its products. In an effort to reduce costs, the company may want to partner with a contract manufacturer in Vietnam instead. Making this transition can be even harder than a plant shutdown, because the existing supplier may become bitter and refuse to cooperate. Most often, these transitions are done without notifying the existing supplier until the new supplier is running at the required capacity.

A Director of Materials is responsible for the strategy of the purchasing group. He does not get involved in the details of the day-to-day operations of the supply chain management department, but will assume the reins when issues get out of control or need upper-management attention. A Director of Materials also sets the practices of his departments and approves large dollar item purchases. Similarly, the Director of Materials participates in vendor relationship management for the suppliers with whom the company spends the most money. In addition to providing strategic direction to the purchasing group, the Director of Materials spends significant time meeting with the other executives in the company, sharing expertise, championing causes, and staying abreast of issues facing the company. A Director of Materials also spends a lot of time networking with people outside of the company (i.e. industry experts, competitors, and prospective vendors).

Visit Vault at **www.vault.com** for insider company profiles, expert advice, career message boards, expert resume reviews, the Vault Job Board and more.

V/\ULT CAREER LIBRARY 191

Employer Directory

Pitney Bowes Inc.

1 Elmcroft Road
Stamford, CT 06926-0700
Phone: (203) 356-5000
www.pb.com/careers

Pitney Bowes is the world's leading provider of integrated mail and document management systems, services and solutions. The $5.0 billion company helps organizations of all sizes efficiently and effectively manage their mission-critical mail and document flow in physical, digital and hybrid formats. Its solutions range from addressing software and metering systems to print stream management, electronic bill presentment and presort mail services.

Pitney Bowes values, actively pursues, and leverages diversity in our employees, and through our relationships with customers, business partners and communities, because it is essential to innovation and growth. Pitney Bowes' commitment to diversity is also consistent with and further supports the company's values and practices.

Business schools Pitney Bowes recruits from
Open to all competitive undergraduate programs

3M Company

3M Center
St. Paul, MN 55144
Phone: (651) 733-1110
Fax: (651) 736-2133
www.mmm.com

ABB Ltd.

Affolternstrasse 44
8050 Zurich, Switzerland
Phone: +41-43-317-7111
Fax: +41-43-317-4420
www.abb.com

Alcoa, Inc.

201 Isabella Street
Pittsburgh, PA 15212-5858
Phone: (412) 553-4545
Fax: (412) 553-4498
www.alcoa.com

Applied Materials, Inc.

3050 Bowers Avenue
Santa Clara, CA 95054-8039
Phone: (408) 727-5555
Fax: (408) 748-9943
www.appliedmaterials.com

BASF

Carl-Bosch Street 38
67056 Ludwigshafen, Germany
Phone: +49-621-60-0
Fax: +49-621-60-42525
www.basf.com

Regional Subsidiary
BASF Corporation
100 Campus Drive
Florham Park, NJ 07932

Bayerische Motoren Werke (BMW)

Petuelring 130
D-80788 Munich, Germany
Phone: +49-89-382-0
Fax: +49-89-382-2-44-18
www.bmwgroup.com

Boeing Company, The

100 N. Riverside Plaza
Chicago, IL 60606-2609
Phone: (312) 544-2000
Fax: (312) 544-2082
www.boeing.com

Boise Cascade, LLC

1111 W. Jefferson Street
P.O. Box 50
Boise, ID 83728-0001
Phone: (208) 384-6161
Fax: (208) 384-7189
www.bc.com

Caterpillar, Inc.

100 NE Adams Street
Peoria, IL 61629
Phone: (309) 675-1000
Fax: (309) 675-1182
www.cat.com

DaimlerChrysler

Epplestrasse 225
70546 Stuttgart, Germany
Phone: +49-711-17-0
Fax: +49-711-17-94022

1000 Chrysler Drive
Auburn Hills, Michigan 48326-2766
Phone: (248) 512-5420
Fax: (248) 512-4885
www.daimlerchrysler.com

Dana Corporation
4500 Dorr Street
Toledo, OH 43615
Phone: (419) 535-4500
Fax: (419) 535-4643
www.dana.com

Deere & Company
One John Deere Place
Moline, IL 61265
Phone: (309) 765-8000
Fax: (309) 765-5671
www.johndeere.com

The Dow Chemical Company
2030 Dow Center
Midland, MI 48674
Phone: (989) 636-1000
Fax: (989) 636-3518
www.dow.com

E.I. Du Pont De Nemours and Company
1007 Market Street
Wilmington, DE 19898
Phone: (302) 774-1000
Fax: (302) 999-4399
www.dupont.com

Eaton Corporation
Eaton Center
1111 Superior Avenue
Cleveland, OH 44114-2584
Phone: (216) 523-5000
Fax: (216) 523-4787
www.eaton.com

Federal-Mogul Corporation
26555 Northwestern Highway
Southfield, MI 48034
Phone: (248) 354-7700
Fax: (248) 354-8950
www.federal-mogul.com

Ford Motor Company
1 American Road
Dearborn, MI 48126-2798
Phone: (313) 322-3000
Fax: (313) 845-6073
www.ford.com

GE Advanced Materials
1 Plastics Avenue
Pittsfield, MA 01201
Phone: (413) 448-7110
Fax: (413) 448-7465
www.geadvancedmaterials.com

General Dynamics Corp.
3190 Fairview Park Drive
Falls Church, VA 22042-4523
Phone: (703) 876-3000
Fax: (703) 876-3125
www.gendyn.com

General Motors
300 Renaissance Center
Detroit, MI 48265-3000
Phone: (313) 556-5000
Fax: (248) 696-7300
www.gm.com

Georgia-Pacific Corporation
133 Peachtree Street, NE
Atlanta, GA 30303
Phone: (404) 652-4000
Fax: (404) 230-1674
www.gp.com

Honeywell International Inc.
101 Columbia Road
Morristown, NJ 07962-1219
Phone: (973) 455-2000
Fax: (973) 455-4807
www.honeywell.com

Ingersoll-Rand Company Limited
Clarendon House, 2 Church Street
Hamilton, HM 11, Bermuda
Phone: (441) 295-2838
www.irco.com

International Paper Company
400 Atlantic St.
Stamford, CT 06921
Phone: (800) 223-1268
Fax: (203) 541-8200
www.ipaper.com

ITT Industries, Inc.
4 W. Red Oak Lane
White Plains, NY 10604
Phone: (914) 641-2000
Fax: (914) 696-2950
www.ittind.com

Johnson Controls
5757 N. Green Bay Avenue
Milwaukee, WI 53201
Phone: (414) 524-1200
Fax: (414) 524-2077
www.johnsoncontrols.com

Lockheed Martin Corporation
6801 Rockledge Drive
Bethesda, MD 20817-1877
Phone: (301) 897-6000
Fax: (301) 897-6704
www.lockheedmartin.com

Newell Rubbermaid Inc.
10 B Glenlake Pkwy., Suite 600
Atlanta, GA 30328
Phone: (770) 407-3800
Fax: (770) 407-3970
www.newellrubbermaid.com

Northrop Grumman Corporation
1840 Century Park East
Los Angeles, CA 90067-2199
Phone: (310) 553-6262
Fax: (310) 553-2076
www.northgrum.com

PPG Industries, Inc.
1 PPG Place
Pittsburgh, PA 15272
Phone: (412) 434-3131
Fax: (412) 434-2448
www.ppg.com

Raytheon Company
870 Winter Street
Waltham, MA 02451-1449
Phone: (781) 522-3000
Fax: (781) 522-3001
www.raytheon.com

Visit Vault at **www.vault.com** for insider company profiles, expert advice, career message boards, expert resume reviews, the Vault Job Board and more.

VAULT CAREER LIBRARY 193

Solectron Corporation
777 Gibraltar Drive
Milpitas, CA 95035
Phone: (408) 957-8500
Fax: (408) 957-6056
www.solectron.com

Thermo Electron Corporation
81 Wyman Street
Waltham, MA 02454-9046
Phone: (781) 622-1000
Fax: (781) 622-1207
www.thermo.com

Toyota Motor Company
1, Toyota-cho
Toyota City, Aichi Prefecture 471-8571, Japan
Phone: +81-565-28-2121
Fax: +81-565-23-5800
www.toyota.co.jp (Worldwide)
www.toyota.com (North America)

United States Steel Corporation
600 Grant Street
Pittsburgh, PA 15219-2800
Phone: (412) 433-1121
Fax: (412) 433-5733
www.ussteel.com

United Technologies
One Financial Plaza
Hartford, CT 06103
Phone: (860) 728-7000
Fax: (860) 728-7979
www.utc.com

Weyerhaeuser Company
33663 Weyerhaeuser Way South
Federal Way, WA 98063-9777
Phone: (253) 924-2345
Fax: (253) 924-2685
www.weyerhaeuser.com

Media and Entertainment

Media and Entertainment MBAs

Not long ago, the creative types in media kept a wary eye on the suits or the bean counters, as the business side of media is known. For years, Wall Street paid little attention to the media biz, an industry it didn't take that seriously. Now, with the rise of the global conglomerates and the aftermath of dot-com meltdown, many media professionals, both on the creative and business sides, are finding it necessary to pursue an MBA.

A new order

"When we started, I had two courses and we had about 40 people in each. Today, in any given semester we have about 400 to 500 students taking one or more classes," says Al Lieberman, Executive Director of NYU Stern's Entertainment, Media and Technology Initiative. Started in 1996, Stern's EMT program awards a certificate to those students who complete at least nine credits in courses like Entertainment Finance and The Business of Sports Marketing. Over at Fordham Business School, Dr. Everette Dennis, Chair of the Communications and Media Management program has also seen an increased interest over the last couple of years, "We have a relatively small program, but we've had probably a 20 to 25 percent increase in applications." Fordham's program, believed to be one of the first in the country, began in the mid-1980s when Arthur Taylor, a former president of CBS, arrived as the business school's new dean and brought in William Small, another CBS executive, to head up the program.

So why are more and more media professionals interested in an MBA? Of course, many can argue that a wave of dot-com dropouts have decided to hide out in business school in the wake of the collapse of the dot-coms and the weak ad market. Lieberman argues that this is no trend. "It's a fundamental change because the competitive factors that are driving this are not going away. They are intensifying." He is talking about the shakeup of the media landscape. Deregulation and mergers have given rise to media behemoths.

Technology, without a doubt, has wrought havoc in the industry, forcing firms to rethink their business strategies. That's one reason why Jason Oberlander, a first-year student at Columbia Business School, has finds the business side of media so attractive. "The technology that comes out, it's coming out so quickly that it requires people who are able to adapt and think on their feet and are able to pursue new opportunities in order to be successful and compete effectively."

Consumers today have a rainbow of media products to choose from. Dennis says the media industry has become an important economic engine and Wall Street has taken notice. "All of the sudden this was an industry to be reckoned with." Lieberman points to a shift towards cooperation and the building of alliances as well, in an industry that has been notoriously competitive. The current negotiations between CNN and ABC News would have been unheard of just ten years ago. Not only has media seen enormous domestic growth, but abroad as well; says Lieberman, "For every dollar that is generated in the United States, 15 years ago the most they could look for was maybe 25 cents outside, as an export. Now it is dollar for dollar."

What does an MBA really offer?

"A few years ago, I would have said, 'An MBA that would be nice, but it really isn't necessary.' Now, I think an MBA, or at least some exposure to business practices, is probably essential," says Dennis. He cites a growing need for better understanding of market research, audiences, how to manage change and the cash position of a company. In the mid-80s, Lieberman started a marketing firm focused on entertainment and media. At the time, he couldn't find enough qualified candidates to keep pace with the growth of the firm. He ended up recruiting people right out of one of the courses he was teaching at NYU. "I taught this course that I created, called The Marketing of Entertainment Industries at the NYU School of

Visit Vault at **www.vault.com** for insider company profiles, expert advice, career message boards, expert resume reviews, the Vault Job Board and more.

VAULT CAREER LIBRARY 195

Continuing Education. Out of the 40 or 45 adults that would come in from all kinds of industries to learn about this, I'd pick one or two that were the best and offer them jobs."

Oberland left Showtime as a Communications Manager in Sports and Event Programming, but felt an MBA was the only way to increase his chances for advancement. "I felt that doing the transition within the company would have been difficult. I certainly would have had to take a significant step down in title and in compensation." Dennis concurs that an MBA is increasingly becoming a requirement for management in media companies. "I think people on the creative side are not going to move into major management and executive roles unless they either get this kind of background and experience on their own in some way, or they go to a business school and get it where it is taught systematically."

Bridging the gap

"One of the biggest problems was the business people who stepped into this world of creativity, didn't understand the creative product, didn't understand how it made money, didn't understand how to apply the basic strategic thinking, therefore there was a huge disconnect," says Lieberman. It takes two to tango, and the creative side has also contributed to the disconnect. Fordham, recognizing the interest by some creative folks to bridge this gap, will be launching a new MS program soon, "It's really tailored to the people from the creative side who do need to know and understand more about business." Stern is also helping the business types better understand the creative process by encouraging Stern students to take courses in filmmaking at the Tisch School of the Arts. "They're not going to make films, but at least they understand the skills, so they don't come on a set and make complete idiots of themselves." At the end of the day, Oberland argues that you need the overall package to get ahead. "I think someone who balances the creative skills with business skills is the most suitable person to run a business from a general management standpoint."

Media Business Positions

Strategic planning

Strategic planning groups are small groups of about five to 40 professionals that serve as in-house consulting and investment banking arms. Not coincidentally, most employees are ex-consultants and bankers. Strategists are involved in valuation and negotiation decisions for acquisitions, business plans for new ventures, the expansion of the current business lines (and sometimes creating new ones), forward-looking financial plans to provide budgeting and overall prognosis for the health of all divisions of the company, and any other high-level issues that the company as a whole may be facing.

Because these projects affect the overall health of the company, meetings are often power sessions in the corporate dining room or top-floor board rooms with the company's senior executives, including the CEO, COO and CFO. While exposure to these individuals is one of the perks of this position, the jobs also tend to be incredibly challenging and taxing, as inordinate amounts of background data, research and information are synthesized and spun into a story prior to the presentation of findings. This group's job is all the more challenging, given that the recommendations that strategic planning groups deliver must necessarily be at odds with decisions that have already been made. Strategic planners, after all, are constantly trying to maximize the returns on the company's capital, which means analyzing and dismissing many current projects.

This function is also sometimes called corporate development, business development or in-house consulting. Because of the frequent exposure to high-level executives, the overall clout of the group and its impact in the major decisions of media conglomerates, these tend to be highly sought-after jobs, mostly filled by top-notch MBAs.

Corporate finance

Corporate finance is a sister group to strategic planning. Corporate financiers are the people who work in concert with investment bankers (or in lieu of them) to price deals, investigate options and plot the course of the company's growth through acquisitions of other companies.

Nearly all the major entertainment companies have grown through major acquisitions in the past two decades, increasing the importance of their corporate financiers. Corporate finance professionals investigate acquisition opportunities, gather competitive intelligence on other companies, determine synergies and negotiate deals. Likewise, they also divest businesses that may be undesirable in exchange for cash.

Most individuals in the corporate finance function are former investment bankers, accounting wizards and CFOs-to-be who bring their expertise in finance and public company performance to the entertainment industry.

Corporate marketing

Corporate marketing assesses consumer reaction to new projects, initiatives and endeavors. Often these groups are direct reports of business units (where each division has its own marketing group), but there are also many cases in which these groups are centralized under corporate and provide their services on an as-needed basis. The benefit of centralized marketing is that it enables the sharing of data across the company since the information is compiled by one group that can then spread the information. It also provides leverage with outside vendors (advertising agencies, media placement agencies, market research firms) when negotiating fees: the more money a company plans on spending with one deal, the better its negotiating position when choosing among competing agencies.

Corporate marketing encompasses many objectives:

- Market research and the execution of both quantitative and qualitative research
- The management of outside vendors who oversee new software, focus groups or large research studies
- Determining revenue projections for new products
- Soliciting consumer feedback on new and existing products
- Creating pricing models
- Estimating market penetration and rollout strategies
- Authoring marketing plans
- Supervising advertising and direct mail
- Overseeing overall brand equity and elements of brand differentiation like logo and identity
- Overseeing product-specific public relations efforts that drive coverage in the media

Corporate marketers often have an extensive background with advertising agencies or marketing consultancy firms.

Corporate public relations

For years, corporate PR was considered to be exclusively for damage control during events like the Exxon Valdez or the Tylenol cyanide scare. Whenever a CEO had problems with the press,, the white knights of corporate PR came to the rescue to help avert a worse catastrophe. Corporate PR groups still perform this function. However, the work of corporate PR groups is much broader than just handling crisis management. Corporate PR groups now manage corporate spokespersons, serve as experts on media training and public appearances and coach CEOs as they prepare for media appearances and event marketing.

Visit Vault at **www.vault.com** for insider company profiles, expert advice, career message boards, expert resume reviews, the Vault Job Board and more.

VAULT CAREER LIBRARY   197

The corporate PR group is also known for initiating major press coverage in industry and business trade publications, as well as corporate-focused articles in general interest magazines like Time, Newsweek or Vanity Fair. PR professionals also develop relationships with government officials and lobbying groups that may have influence over legislation affecting the company's growth and development. Often, this group works with outside public relations agencies like Edelman Worldwide, Bozell or Hill & Knowlton.

Internet strategy

As content becomes increasingly commoditized due to the fact that so much on the Internet is free, there are challenges in protecting the hallowed material that entertainment companies create. While studios would love to use the Internet to hoard their content and prevent anyone else from distributing and profiting from it (sort of a preemptive strike against companies like Napster), the Internet is also an incredibly seductive resource for marketing, mainly because information can be communicated broadly and cheaply – much more inexpensively than TV commercials, billboards and bus shelters. The popularity of The Blair Witch Project, a surprise hit, was partially attributed to a very effective web site.

This tension (to promote our properties or protect them?) feeds the very complex and critical role that Internet strategy plays in the growth of media and entertainment companies. Because of the constantly evolving and still uncertain nature of the business, there are hundreds of individuals at nearly all major entertainment companies, tracking evolving technologies, coding pages, maintaining fresh web site content and otherwise marketing via the Web. Media companies with Internet strategy groups include Walt Disney/ABC and AOL Time Warner.

Real estate development

Real estate development within an entertainment company involves not only theme parks, but also extensions of an entertainment empire's brands, including themed restaurants (Hard Rock Café), sports stadiums, entertainment complexes (Sony Metreon) and other destinations that involve large tracts of land that can both provide steady revenue streams and impress an entertainment-seeking audience. The major entertainment companies often have proprietary lots of their own land that were either part of the company's origin (as Disney does with its land in Florida and Southern California, now managed under the aegis of the Disney Development Corporation), were results of acquisitions or were acquired over time.

As real estate development is its own unique business with special financing rules and its own intrinsic rewards, the field generally attracts individuals from outside the entertainment industry. The most successful individuals in these divisions are those with substantial experience managing vendors, contractors and landscape architects, working with community development offices, leveraging tax benefits and executing visionary blueprints. Real estate development is a particularly exciting division for individuals wishing to combine interests in the hospitality industry, finance and real estate.

Our Survey Says: Lifestyle and Pay

Hours

Like so many industries, there is a work-life tradeoff that comes in the entertainment industry. "There are tons of tradeoffs," says one longtime employee in the strategic planning group of a studio. "The entertainment industry definitely doesn't come to mind when I think about a balanced lifestyle. It's a rare day I don't put in 12 hours."

But that's not always the case. There are many individuals that report (mostly outside of strategic planning and other corporate groups) consistently being home by 6. While the career trajectory is slower and the compensation is lower in the "business units" (versus the "corporate side"), the hours and the requirements are less demanding. There are always exceptions.

Says one theme park executive: "Hours are usually 9 to 6, but every year for a few weeks in the spring during our five-year planning process, it's not uncommon for us to put in 12 hours a day, seven days a week."

One rule of thumb: Corporate jobs that report to the CEO typically face "fire drills" (i.e. urgent deadlines imposed at the last minute) on a regular basis. Jobs that are more predictable (i.e., positions with business units rather than corporate-level positions) generally have more predictable hours.

Pay

"The pay in corporate jobs is usually up there with investment banking and management consulting," reports one former consultant-turned-analyst at a publishing house. The business units, however, are typically known for paying less, both because they are responsible for profit and loss (high salaries come straight out of the topline) and because of the less grueling hours. (For the difference between corporate and business units, see Organizational Chart of Media Companies.)

At the corporate level, beginning-level analysts out of college typically start at around $40,000, with several thousand dollars in bonus and a 15 percent raise after a year. Managers make at least $80,000 and directors usually crack six figures. VPs earn in the low $100k range.

In business units, the pay can be anywhere from 10 to 30 percent lower.

Other perks

Entertainment is attractive partly because of its perks. "Let's face it, I got into the industry hoping to hang out with rock stars," confesses one record industry insider. Employees get discounts on products, invitations to advance screenings of movies and tickets to movie premieres and gala parties. That said, the perks are not nearly as lavish as the expense accounts and freebies that come on the creative side of the business. There are the stories of the business folks who occasionally get free lunches, tickets to movie premieres and celebrity wedding invitations, but these are mostly the result of a person's personal connections.

Another practice, widely considered a perk, is that many within the industry itemize taxes and deduct all their entertainment expenses in the name of the job. "I itemized everything from my stereo to my movie tickets," boasts one corporate finance manager.

Promotions and competition

There is indeed jockeying for certain roles and positions, as there is in any industry, but the business side is not as ugly as the creative side when it comes to competition. Promotion decisions are not based on whether people like you, or on how your last film did, but rather on the body of your professional work. Even though there is an oversupply of people vying for the available jobs, it is a largely meritocratic industry.

Visit Vault at **www.vault.com** for insider company profiles, expert advice, career message boards, expert resume reviews, the Vault Job Board and more.

VAULT CAREER LIBRARY 199

Day in the Life: Strat Planning Executive

While there's no "typical" day in strat planning at a media company, below are some of the most common day-to-day tasks:

- Interfacing with other business units, domestically and abroad, either in calls or in meetings (25%)

- Presentations to the senior executive team on key decisions (25%)

- Presentations from the business units on growth initiatives within other groups (10%)

- Responding to requests from senior management (25%)

- Managing junior team members (15%)

If this sounds murky or unclear, read on for an illustration of the specifics. Overall, the hours are long. There are often stories of many executives who do not have families or children, or often forsake them for their careers.

7:00 a.m.: Arrive at work, make conference calls to Europe to discuss progress on a major new initiative to expand in Europe.

8:00 a.m.: Breakfast meeting with a manager in another business unit, to update one another on work and "keep both ears close to the ground."

9:00 a.m.: Review a subordinate's presentation, assigned last night. The presentation is due early tomorrow for the CEO – revisions must be made with haste.

10:00 a.m.: Return some morning phone calls. Glance at e-mail for anything urgent.

10:30 a.m.: Leave for an off-site meeting to discuss what to do with a waning division in which the top chief just left.

10:45 a.m.: Call my assistant. Have her type up e-mail responses to some new e-mails and send them off on my behalf.

10:55 a.m.: Arrive at off-site meeting. Listen to presentations from key leaders on what to do next.

12:00 p.m.: Depart for lunch meeting with a senior VP at another small entertainment company to propose an acquisition.

1:30 p.m.: Return to office to debrief with CFO on the numbers needed for a 5-year plan.

3:00 p.m.: Answer e-mails, review daily trade publications, The Hollywood Reporter and Daily Variety.

3:45 p.m.: For fun and to build team morale, respond to office pool on what the weekend's box office will be.

3:47 p.m.: Spontaneous meeting with CEO in the hallway – turns out the presentation originally due tomorrow is not that urgent.

4:00 p.m.: Tell junior manager to call off work and go home since she's been pulling all-nighters for a couple of days.

4:10 p.m.: Start reviewing budget requests and expense reports of department employees.

5:00 p.m.: Peruse the proposals from three top management consulting firms, all vying for a piece of a major project.

6:30 p.m.: Make a conference call to Asia executives to discuss progress on their latest initiative.

7:30 p.m.: Answer all outstanding e-mails.

8:30 p.m.: Leave the office.

Employer Directory

ABC, Inc.
77 W. 66th Street
New York, NY 10023-6298
Phone: (212) 456-7777
Fax: (212) 456-1424
www.abc.go.com

Bertelsmann AG
Carl-Bertelsmann-Strasse 270
D-33311 Gütersloh, Germany
Phone: +49-5241-80-0
Fax: +49-5241-80-9662
www.bertelsmann.com

Black Entertainment Television
One BET Plaza
1235 W. Street, NE
Washington, DC 20018
Phone: (202) 608-2000
Fax: (202) 608-2589
www.bet.com

Bloomberg L.P.
499 Park Avenue
New York, NY 10022
Phone: (212) 318-2000
Fax: (917) 369-5000
www.bloomberg.com

Creative Artists Agency
9830 Wilshire Blvd.
Beverly Hills, CA 90212-1825
Phone: (310) 288-4545
Fax: (310) 288-4800
www.caa.com

CBS, Inc.
51 W. 52nd Street
New York, NY 10019
Phone: (212) 975-4321
Fax: (212) 975-4516
www.cbs.com

Clear Channel Communications
200 E. Basse Road
San Antonio, TX 78209
Phone: (210) 822-2828
Fax: (210) 822-2299
www.clearchannel.com

CNN News Group
1 CNN Center
Atlanta, GA 30303
Phone: (404) 827-1500
Fax: (404) 827-2437
www.cnn.com

Comcast Corporation
1500 Market Street
Philadelphia, PA 19102-2148
Phone: (215) 665-1700
Fax: (215) 981-7790
www.comcast.com

Cox Communications, Inc.
1400 Lake Hearn Drive
Atlanta, GA 30319
Phone: (404) 843-5000
Fax: (404) 843-5975
www.cox.com

Discovery Communications, Inc.
1 Discovery Place
Silver Spring, MD 20910
Phone: (240) 662-2000
Fax: (240) 662-1868
www.discovery.com

Dow Jones & Company, Inc.
1 World Financial Center
200 Liberty Street
New York, NY 10281
Phone: (212) 416-2000
Fax: (212) 416-4348
www.dj.com

DreamWorks SKG L.L.C.
1000 Flower Street
Glendale, CA 91201
Phone: (818) 733-7000
Fax: (818) 695-7574
www.dreamworks.com

Fox Entertainment Group
1211 Avenue of the Americas
New York, NY 10036
Phone: (212) 852-7111
Fax: (212) 852-7145
www.fox.com

Gannett Company, Inc.
7950 Jones Branch Drive
McLean, VA 22107-0910
Phone: (703) 854-6000
Fax: (703) 854-2046
www.gannett.com

HarperCollins Publishers, Inc.
10 E. 53rd Street
New York, NY 10022
Phone: (212) 207-7000
Fax: (212) 207-7145
www.harpercollins.com

Home Box Office (HBO)
1100 Avenue of the Americas
New York, NY 10036
Phone: (212) 512-1000
Fax: (212) 512-1182
www.hbo.com

Houghton Mifflin Company
222 Berkeley St.
Boston, MA 02116-3764
Phone: (617) 351-5000
Fax: (617) 351-1105
www.hmco.com

International Data Group
1 Exeter Plaza, 15th Floor
Boston, MA 02116-2851
Phone: (617) 534-1200
Fax: (617) 423-0240
www.idg.com

Visit Vault at **www.vault.com** for insider company profiles, expert advice,
career message boards, expert resume reviews, the Vault Job Board and more.

V∧ULT CAREER LIBRARY   **201**

John Wiley & Sons, Inc.

111 River St.

Hoboken, NJ 07030

Phone: (201) 748-6000

Fax: (201) 748-6008

www.wiley.com

Liberty Media

12300 Liberty Blvd.

Englewood, CO 80112

Phone: (720) 875-5400

Fax: (720) 875-7469

www.libertymedia.com

Martha Stewart Living Omnimedia, Inc.

11 W. 42nd Street

New York, NY 10036

Phone: (212) 827-8000

Fax: (212) 827-8204

www.marthastewart.com

The McGraw-Hill Companies, Inc.

1221 Avenue of the Americas

New York, NY 10020

Phone: (212) 512-2000

Fax: (212) 512-3840

www.mcgraw-hill.com

Metro-Goldwyn-Mayer Inc.

10250 Constellation Blvd.

Los Angeles, CA 90067

Phone: (310) 449-3000

Fax: (310) 449-8857

www.mgm.com

National Public Radio, Inc.

635 Massachusetts Avenue NW

Washington, DC 20001-3753

Phone: (202) 513-2000

Fax: (202) 513-3329

www.npr.org

News Corporation

1211 Avenue of the Americas

8th Floor

New York, NY 10036

Phone: (212) 852-7017

Fax: (212) 852-7145

www.newscorp.com

Paramount Pictures

5555 Melrose Avenue

Hollywood, CA 90038

Phone: (323) 956-5000

Fax: (323) 862-1204

www.paramount.com

Pearson PLC

80 Strand

London

WC2R ORL

United Kingdom

Phone: +44-20-7010-2000

Fax: +44-20-7010-6060

www.pearson.com

Penguin group

80 Strand

London

WC2R ORL

United Kingdom

Phone: +44-2070103396

Fax: +44-2070106642

www.penguin.com

Pixar Animation Studios

1200 Park Avenue

Emeryville, CA 94608

Phone: (510) 752-3000

Fax: (510) 752-3151

www.pixar.com

Primedia

745 Fifth Avenue

New York, NY 10151

Phone: (212) 745-0100

Fax: (212) 745-0121

www.primedia.com

Reed Elsevier PLC

1-3 Strand

London

WC2N 5JR, United Kingdom

Phone: +44-20-7930-7077

Fax: +44-20-7166 5799

www.reedelsevier.com

Reed Elsevier NV

Raderweg 29

1043 NX Amsterdam

The Netherlands

Phone: +31 20 485 2222

Fax: +31 20 618 0325

Reuters Group PLC

85 Fleet Street

London

EC4P 4AJ, United Kingdom

Phone: +44-20-7250-1122

Fax: +44-20-7542-4064

www.reuters.com

Scholastic Corporation

557 Broadway

New York, NY 10012

Phone: (212) 343-6100

Fax: (212) 343-6934

www.scholasticinc.com

Simon & Schuster, Inc.

1230 Avenue of the Americas

New York, NY 10020

Phone: (212) 698-7000

Fax: (212) 698-7099

www.simonsays.com

SourceMedia

One State Street Plaza

27th Floor

New York, NY 10004

Phone: (212) 803.8200

www.sourcemedia.com

Time Warner

1 Time Warner Center

New York, NY 10019

Phone: (212) 484-8000

Fax: (212) 489-6183

www.timewarner.com

USA Network, Inc.

152 West 57th Street

New York, New York 10019

Phone: (212) 314-7300

Fax: (212) 314-7309

www.usanetwork.com

Viacom Inc.
1515 Broadway
New York, NY 10036
Phone: (212) 258-6000
Fax: (212) 258-6464
www.viacom.com

Vivendi Universal
42 avenue de Friedland
75380 Paris Cedex 08
France
Phone: +33-1-71-71-10-00
Fax: +33-1-71-71-10-01
www.vivendiuniversal.com

W.W. Norton & Company
500 5th Avenue
New York, NY 10110
Phone: (212) 354-5500
Fax: (212) 869-0856
www.wwnorton.com

Visit Vault at **www.vault.com** for insider company profiles, expert advice, career message boards, expert resume reviews, the Vault Job Board and more.

V∧ULT CAREER LIBRARY   **203**

Use the Internet's
MOST TARGETED
job search tools.

Vault Job Board

Target your search by industry, function, and experience level, and find the job openings that you want.

VaultMatch Resume Database

Vault takes match-making to the next level: post your resume and customize your search by industry, function, experience and more. We'll match job listings with your interests and criteria and e-mail them directly to your in-box.

Real Estate

History of the Real Estate Industry in the United States

Real estate is tangible. It's a piece of land and any building or structures on it, as well as the air above and the ground below. Everyone comes into direct contact with real estate. The places we live, work, go to school, vacation, shop and exercise, are all assets to be bought, sold and rented. And it's always been an important element of the economy. .

Real estate has always been big business in the United States. Shortly after the signing of the Constitution, the federal government began transferring one billion acres of land to private owners through land sales and land grants. In the 1830s, for example, the government sold 20 million acres at roughly $1.25 per acre. This sounds like a bargain to us today, but at the time the vast majority of citizens couldn't afford that price. Consequently, a grassroots group called the Free Soil Movement formed and lobbied the government for an alternate method of distributing land.

The Homestead Act of 1862 was Congress' answer to the appeal. Settlers who did not already own what was considered a "judicious" amount of land were given title to 160 acres for each adult in the family. There was no cash exchange. Instead, the understanding was that the settlers would live on and improve the land for a period of at least five years. This program was very successful and similar federal land distribution programs followed until the later part of the nineteenth century. In total, the U.S. government distributed more than 300 million acres of public property to private landowners through the Homestead Act, creating the basis for the real estate market.

For the first time in the history of the young country, there was a system in place by which one landowner could transfer property rights to another through sale, lease or trade. This led to a tremendous amount of speculation. Some investors accumulated a tremendous amount of wealth, while others lost everything.

At the end of the 19th century, America was transitioning from an agricultural society to a manufacturing economy. Citizens flocked to urban areas to work at the burgeoning factories. For example, as the Midwest's industrial center, Chicago reached a population of one million people more rapidly than any other city in history. Settled in the 1830s, the city grew from less than 1,000 inhabitants to become the fifth largest city in the world by 1900.

The values of urban properties skyrocketed. By 1920, 50 percent of America's population lived in cities. This urban density created opportunities for real estate development as housing, office buildings, industrial facilities, hotels and retail centers were constructed to meet the demands of city dwellers.

Skyrocketing property values and associated costs began pushing people and businesses outside the city, just as advances in transportation made living outside the city easier. Suburbs, communities just outside urban centers, began to spread. Developers made these planned communities attractive by building along the transportation routes so people could easily commute to their jobs in the cities.

Technological advances influenced the building boom of the 1920s. Communities were wired for electricity, new machines such as elevators helped meet additional demand for space and allowed the construction of ever-taller buildings. Planned communities began taking shape in the suburbs, while skyscrapers changed the way the cities looked. One hundred buildings higher than 25 stories were constructed in this decade, most of them in New York City, with Chicago a distant second.

The Great Depression crippled most industries – including real estate. Values dipped below debt levels, causing a collapse. The federal government put the domestic financial markets through a major overhaul and was shrewd enough to include real estate financing as part of the New Deal programs. The Federal Housing Administration (FHA) was created in 1930 to provide mortgage insurance, lowering the risk on real estate loans and making lending more palatable for savings and loans and banks. The government also created the Federal Home Loan Bank System (FHLB) to supervise and regulate local banks. In 1938, the Federal National Mortgage Association (FNMA or Fannie Mae) was created to provide a secondary mortgage market as well as to lure investment capital in the mortgage market, and continues to play a very important role in supplying cap-

Visit Vault at **www.vault.com** for insider company profiles, expert advice, career message boards, expert resume reviews, the Vault Job Board and more.

VAULT CAREER LIBRARY 205

ital to the mortgage market today. These New Deal programs ultimately made the real estate finance market more sophisticated and secure.

America and the real estate industry slowly climbed out of the Depression only to fall headlong into the Second World War. Development was put on hold during the war, but once the GIs returned from overseas, another era of prosperity began. A tremendous amount of demand for housing emerged virtually overnight. By 1946, new housing construction quadrupled to over 500,000 homes. In the postwar period, a white picket fence and peaceful green lawn proved very appealing. Two-thirds of the 15 million homes built in the 1950s were in the suburbs.

The decade was also a period of expansion for the highways, which provided access to more areas by car and truck. This enabled all types of real estate (e.g., hotels, industrial and retail centers) to be located further outside the city. Hotel chains like Holiday Inn started popping up along roadways across the country. The suburban shopping mall also became popular in this era.

As the suburbs grew, the cities slumped. By 1960, many urban centers hadn't seen new office building development in 30 years. The decay of America's urban areas didn't go unnoticed. Community activism and political pressure led to the creation of a cabinet position in 1965 focused on improving urban housing – what today is known as the Department of Housing and Urban Development (HUD). The central business districts of America's urban centers saw a number of new buildings (both commercial and retail) constructed during the last three decades of the twentieth century, spurred by growth in the service industry, increased access to financing and municipal incentives.

Today, the real estate industry is considered one of the most dynamic and healthy sectors in the American economy – people may divest their stocks, but they always need a place to live, work and shop. (To read more about the history of real estate, read Real Estate Development by Miles, Berns and Weiss.)

Industry Trends

As of 2003, the real estate business employed close to five million people. Opportunities abound for candidates to earn staggering income levels. Those who work in this sector often enjoy greater flexibility in job responsibilities than in other industries.

There can be drawbacks, though, in the form of low paying entry-level positions, competitive co-workers and long hours when starting out. Furthermore, once you're established relocation can be detrimental to your career, as this industry is often geography-specific.

The real estate sector is largely dependent on the economy; small shifts can impact trends significantly. For example, the technology industry boom certainly helped the real estate industry in the 1990s. There was more demand for space-both commercial and residential-and asset values skyrocketed. The subsequent technology bust had a dramatic effect on some parts of the sector. Commercial firms that focused on office and retail development projects now find the market glutted with available space.

The residential real estate market is also affectecd by economic swings. Unemployment and interest rates impact both consumer confidence and buying power. Although the U.S. economy was mired in recession for the first several years of the 21st century, the residential real estate market was one of the few bright spots. In 2002, home sales shot up 8 percent and housing starts grew by 7 percent.

There are many reasons for the current residential housing boom. The aging United States population and the influx of immigrants has increased the demand for households. The rockiness of the stock market makes investing in real estate look very appealing. The Federal Reserve is playing a big part as well. Lower mortgage rates and minimal inflations meant that in 2003, a 30-year home mortgage could be had at a 5 percent rate. The drop in mortgage rates meant that homeowners could refinance, freeing up more cash for them − and in the process making real estate look like an even more attractive investment.

The wealth isn't spread equally. Residential real estate values continue to soar on the coasts. During the real estate boom that began after the end of the 1991 recession, homes and apartments in the Boston-to-Washington corridor and California have doubled, tripled or quadrupled in value. Even in fast-growing areas in other parts of the country, such as Las Vegas, gains have been more modest because there is more land on which to build houses and apartments.

The remarkable gains in the residential real estate market have provoked fears among some economists and homeowners that the real estate market is a bubble about to burst. The prices of homes, especially on the West and East Coast, have outpaced the ability of many prospective first-time buyers to purchase a place to live. A jump in mortgage rates would stop the current trend of refinancing in its tracks and make it more difficult for many homeowners to make mortgage payments. A revival in the economy could cause investors to stop investing in real estate and start investing in stocks. (Such a revival would, on the other hand, help the commercial and industrial real estate markets.) In the meantime, however, the residential real estate market continues to be an engine of the economy − and of the real estate job market.

Valuing Real Estate

There are three generally accepted approaches to valuing real estate: the sales approach, the cost approach and the income approach. Professional appraisers will reach a valuation after carefully considering each approach. You should make sure to review all three approaches before any real estate interview.

The sales approach

The sales approach arrives at a value for a property based on recent sales of similar properties. This approach can be used for both residential and commercial properties. There are proprietary databases that track home and commercial building sales, which make it easier for real estate professionals to access market information used in valuing properties. One of the most popular databases is the Multi-listing Service (MLS), which is used to track residential properties. The MLS contains useful information about homes, such as the sales history, tax records and property amenities that can be accessed for an annual fee. In the sales approach, appraisers will use databases, such as the MLS, to look for homes with similar characteristics (e.g. location and house specifics), as the subject property. For example, when valuing a four-bedroom, two-bathroom house in the Pacific Heights section of San Francisco, it is logical to value that property based on the most recent sales information for properties in the same area with similar characteristics. Bear in mind that no two properties are alike, so when valuing a property using the sales approach you must adjust for differences between the properties.

The cost approach

In markets where it is difficult to find similar properties, an appraiser can value a property based on the cost approach. This approach focuses on a few steps. First, you must determine the cost of replacing or reconstructing the improvements or building. Next, the age of the improvements must be considered and an appropriate amount of depreciation is subtracted from the value of improvements. Finally, the value of the land must be taken into consideration. The land value is added to the improvements minus the estimated property depreciation. The cost approach is used for truly unique properties like churches, which cannot use either the sales or income approach to arrive at a valuation.

The income approach

The income approach is the most quantitative of the three approaches. The income approach involves the use of net operating income (NOI) in calculating the value of the property. (See the Appendix for a detailed explanation of Net Operating Income.) Think of NOI as the reason most investors buy a building. The investment community talks about NOI incessantly, so make sure to understand this concept if you plan on being involved with real estate investing.

Visit Vault at **www.vault.com** for insider company profiles, expert advice, career message boards, expert resume reviews, the Vault Job Board and more.

V∧ULT CAREER LIBRARY   **207**

There are two forms of the income approach. One form involves isolating NOI for one year, while the other form involves a longer time horizon. Both forms use a capitalization (cap) rate to calculate a value. The cap rate is a market mechanism, so don't worry about what goes in the calculation. Just be concerned with how it is used. In practice the cap rate is generally used in a formula with the NOI to arrive at a property value. For example, suppose you were buying an industrial facility whose net operating income in the following year was projected to be $500,000. If you knew the market cap rate for similar properties, you could arrive an estimated value of the property. Assume the market cap rate for industrial facilities was 10 percent. To arrive at the value of the building, divide NOI by the cap rate. In our example, the value of the building would be:

$$\text{Value} = \frac{\text{NOI}}{\text{Cap Rate}} = \frac{\$500,000}{.10} = \$5,000,000$$

The yield capitalization form uses a longer time horizon. It involves calculating a discounted cash flow to arrive a property value.

$$\text{Value} = \frac{\text{NOI year n}}{(1+\text{discount rate})^n} + \frac{\text{NOI year n}+1}{(1+\text{discount rate})^{n+1}} + \frac{\text{residual value}}{(1+\text{discount rate})^{n+1}}$$

In the example above, the numerator represents the cash flows that the building generates today and in the coming years, which theoretically provides a value for the asset. Note, that there is also a future residual value listed in the formula. The discount rate reflects the cost of capital. Your client may provide this cost, or you may have to estimate the discount rate based on similar transactions and knowledge of the market. The discount rate is necessary because it allows you to bring all the future cash flows back to today's dollars or present value (PV). The discount rate factors in the opportunity cost of money or the return that you could expect elsewhere with the cash flows. The exponent "n" in the denominator represents the period or number of years in the future that you would receive that cash flow. The DCF is calculated based on a stated number of years and adds up the PVs. At some point in the future cash flows you have a residual value because it is assumed the property is eventually sold. The residual value is calculated by taking the NOI of the year after the assumed time horizon and then dividing that year's NOI by an assumed cap rate. Some investors use different time periods when calculating the DCF but 10 years is the generally accepted period to value an asset. The DCF is normally used for income-producing property, while a single-family house is typically valued by the sales comparison approach.

Although there are different ways to value real estate, there are a few common variables such as location, the property's condition and market demand that make real estate valuable regardless of the asset type. There is a popular industry saying, "The three most important things in real estate are location, location, location." You simply cannot underestimate the importance of location. While you can restore and upgrade a property as much as you want, there is no substitute for being located close to: transportation, good schools, attractive retail and an aesthetically pleasing area. While location is important, keeping the property in good working order also creates value because it lessens the need to make improvements or contribute capital to the property. In addition, fundamental macroeconomics plays a major role in real estate values. For example, when interest rates offered by lenders are low, people will rush to buy a house to take advantage of the low financing costs. If this new market demand is greater than the market supply, property prices will increase.

The Real Estate MBA

One possible educational route into real estate is to get an MBA at an institution with a specific real estate program. Some of the best programs, based on U.S. News & World Report rankings, are Wharton, University of California-Berkeley's Haas Business School, MIT's Sloan School of Management, University of Wisconsin-Madison and Ohio State University's Fisher School of Business. These schools also have strong real estate clubs that produce annual conferences and other activities.

Job Seeking Advice for Real Estate MBAs

Joseph Pagliari, a clinical assistant professor and director of the Real Estate Center at the Kellogg School of Management, says, "There are host of opportunities in real estate for MBAs. The issue is identifying the best fit for the candidate. Positions that are good fits for MBAs are with firms that supply capital to the industry. Typically these are large, sophisticated, financially-oriented firms. MBAs should identify these institutions and aggressively pursue them for employment. In today's marketplace, this means looking at REITs, mezzanine funds (funds built around mezzanine financing, which combines equity and fixed income investments) and private equity firms.

"In general the high profile real estate positions and financially rewarding jobs are on the capital side," adds Pagliari, who is also a principal of a real estate investment firm. "These jobs are almost self-selecting because they are tough to get and you have to be smart and aggressive to succeed. Given that positions in the capital side of the business are reserved for the elite, MBAs should pursue these positions because many of them possess the necessary qualities for these roles."

Employers look for a variety of skill sets. "It is difficult to narrow it to just a few things," he says. "Some positions are very quantitative while others emphasize strong interpersonal skills. Having a combination of both is a competitive advantage. In general, I tell all my students to look for roles that speak to their skill sets. It is going to be hard enough to get the interview, so don't blow it by going after a job that probably doesn't fit your background. MBAs should do their homework on the types of roles out there and match your background and interest with the best fit. However, you still want to shoot for the sky and leverage your MBA."

Job seekers shouldn't be shy about using their contacts "This industry is very tough for outsiders or newcomers to break into and students should be ready to accept that," he advises. "Get in the hunt as soon as possible and network, network, network. Using alums or anyone else you know in the industry is something I always recommend." When you have the interview, be prepared to talk about the local market – or any other in which the company operates. If it's a public firm, check The Wall Street Journal for the scuttlebutt. Also, be certain they'll welcome your MBA.

"In the interview you will most likely be asked about why you are interested in real estate and a few technical questions," Pagliari warns. "Be ready to describe a cap rate and market specifics like rental rates and general economic conditions."

To MBA students just starting a real estate program who know they want to enter the industry, he stresses, "Don't rely on simply taking real estate classes, especially if you have no prior real estate experience." You need to demonstrate passion by joining a real estate club or getting active in real estate-related activities at school. "Do whatever it takes to be able to demonstrate your enthusiasm for the industry," he adds. "If it takes starting a real estate club or being the driving force behind an event, then so be it."

The professor also advises individuals who are evaluating MBA programs that offer real estate curriculums to: make sure the professors have some practical experience and the curriculum will give you a skill set that will meet your end goal. Don't sacrifice the overall MBA experience for a school that simply offers a strong real estate curriculum and is lacking in other areas.

For MBA students who are interested in real estate but whose programs do not offer real estate classes, Pagliari offers a solution. "Classes related to finance and economic principles that help you price risks are very useful," he says, noting that the ability to price risk is a strong differentiating factor. Pagliari also recommends taking business law classes because there are many legal issues involved in the industry. "Which is why you should not be surprised to find so many attorneys in the business," he says.

"I was a career switcher and was repeatedly asked in interviews about why I was interested in real estate," says Rich Monopoli, a recent graduate from business school. "Many of the interviewers wanted an explanation of how my background

Visit Vault at **www.vault.com** for insider company profiles, expert advice, career message boards, expert resume reviews, the Vault Job Board and more.

V/\ULT CAREER LIBRARY   **209**

tied to my interest in real estate. I can't emphasize enough how important it is to be prepared to answer the question of why you are interested in real estate."

Employer Directory

AMB Property Corporation
Pier 1 Bay 1
San Francisco, CA 94111
Phone: (415) 394-9000
Fax: (415) 394-9001
www.amb.com

Boston Properties, Inc.
111 Huntington Avenue
Boston, MA 02199-7602
Phone: (617) 236-3300
Fax: (617) 536-5087
www.bostonproperties.com

CB Richard Ellis Group, Inc.
865 South Figueroa Street
34th Floor
Los Angeles, CA 90017
Phone: 213.438.4880
Fax: 213.438.4820
www.cbre.com

Century 21 Real Estate Corporation
1 Campus Drive
Parsippany, NJ 07054
Phone: (877) 221-2765
Fax: (973) 496-7564
www.century21.com

Cushman & Wakefield, Inc.
51 West 52nd Street
New York, NY 10019-6178
Phone: (212) 841-7500
Fax: (212) 841-7767
www.cushwake.com

Duke Realty Corporation
600 East 96th Street
Suite 100
Indianapolis, IN 46240
Phone: (317) 808-6000
Fax (317) 808.6794
www.dukerealty.com

Equity Office Properties Trust
Two North Riverside Plaza
Chicago, IL 60606
Phone: (312) 466-3300
Fax: (312) 454-0332
www.equityoffice.com

General Growth Properties, Inc.
110 North Wacker Drive
Chicago, IL 60606
Phone: (312) 960-5000
Fax: (312) 960-5475
www.generalgrowth.com

Hines Interests L.P.
Williams Tower
2800 Post Oak Boulevard
Houston, TX 77056
Phone: (713) 621-8000
Fax: (713) 966-2053
www.hines.com

HomeServices of America
6800 France Ave. South, Ste. 710
Edina, MN 55435
Phone: (952) 928-5900
Fax: (952) 928-5590
www.homeservices.com

Jones Lang LaSalle Incorporated
200 E. Randolph Drive
Chicago, IL 60601
Phone: (312) 782-5800
Fax: (312) 782-4339
www.joneslanglasalle.com

Julien J. Studley, Inc.
300 Park Ave.
New York, N.Y. 10022
Phone: (212) 326-1000
Fax: (212) 326-1034
www.studley.com

Lend Lease Corporation Limited
Level 46, Tower Building
Australia Square
Sydney, 2000 Australia
Phone: +61-2-9236-6111
www.lendlease.com.au

RE/Max International, Inc.
8390 E. Crescent Parkway, Suite 500/600
Greenwood Village, CO 80111-2800
Phone: (303) 770-5531
Fax: (303) 796-3599
www.remax.com

RREEF Funds L.L.C.
101 California Street
26th Floor
San Francisco, CA 94111
Phone: (415) 781-3300
Fax: (415) 391-9015
www.rreef.com

Trammell Crow Company
2001 Ross Avenue
Suite 3400
Dallas, TX 75201
Phone: (214) 863-3000
Fax: (214) 863-3138
www.trammellcrow.com

Visit Vault at **www.vault.com** for insider company profiles, expert advice,
career message boards, expert resume reviews, the Vault Job Board and more.

V\LT CAREER LIBRARY   211

VAULT
THE MOST TRUSTED NAME IN CAREER INFORMATION

Sales and Trading

The War Zone

If you've ever been to an investment banking trading floor, you've witnessed the chaos. It's usually a lot of swearing, yelling and flashing computer screens: a pressure cooker of stress. Sometimes the floor is a quiet rumble of activity, but when the market takes a nosedive, panic ensues and the volume kicks up a notch. Traders must rely on their market instincts, and salespeople yell for bids when the market tumbles. Deciding what to buy or sell, and at what price to buy and sell, is difficult when millions of dollars at stake.

However, salespeople and traders work much more reasonable hours than research analysts or corporate finance bankers. Rarely does a salesperson or trader venture into the office on a Saturday or Sunday; the trading floor is completely devoid of life on weekends. Any corporate finance analyst who has crossed a trading floor on a Saturday will tell you that the only noise to be heard on the floor is the clocks ticking every minute and the whir of the air conditioner.

Shop Talk

Here's a quick example of how a salesperson and a trader interact on an emerging market bond trade.

SALESPERSON: Receives a call from a buy-side firm (say, a large mutual fund). The buy-side firm wishes to sell $10 million of a particular Mexican Par government-issued bond (denominated in U.S. dollars). The emerging markets bond salesperson, seated next to the emerging markets traders, stands up in his chair and yells to the relevant trader, "Give me a bid on $10 million Mex Par, six and a quarter, nineteens."

TRADER: "I got 'em at 73 and an eighth."

Translation: I am willing to buy them at a price of $73.125 per $100 of face value. As mentioned, the $10 million represents amount of par value the client wanted to sell, meaning the trader will buy the bonds, paying 73.125 percent of $10 million plus accrued interest (to factor in interest earned between interest payments).

SALESPERSON: "Can't you do any better than that?"

Translation: Please buy at a higher price, as I will get a higher commission.

TRADER: "That's the best I can do. The market is falling right now. You want to sell?"

SALESPERSON: "Done. $10 million."

S&T: A Symbiotic Relationship?

Institutional sales and trading are highly dependent on one another. The propaganda that you read in glossy firm brochures portrays those in sales and trading as a shiny, happy integrated team environment of professionals working for the client's interests. While often that is true, salespeople and traders frequently clash, disagree, and bicker.

Simply put, salespeople provide the clients for traders, and traders provide the products for sales. Traders would have nobody to trade for without sales, but sales would have nothing to sell without traders. Understanding how a trader makes money and how a salesperson makes money should explain how conflicts can arise.

Traders make money by selling high and buying low (this difference is called the spread). They are buying stocks or bonds for clients, and these clients filter in through sales. A trader faced with a buy order for a buy-side firm could care less about

Visit Vault at **www.vault.com** for insider company profiles, expert advice, career message boards, expert resume reviews, the Vault Job Board and more.

VAULT CAREER LIBRARY   213

the performance of the securities once they are sold. He or she just cares about making the spread. In a sell trade, this means selling at the highest price possible. In a buy trade, this means buying at the lowest price possible.

The salesperson, however, has a different incentive. The total return on the trade often determines the money a salesperson makes, so he wants the trader to sell at a low price. The salesperson also wants to be able to offer the client a better price than competing firms in order to get the trade and earn a commission. This of course leads to many interesting situations, and at the extreme, salespeople and traders who eye one another suspiciously.

The personalities

Salespeople possess remarkable communication skills, including outgoing personalities and a smoothness not often seen in traders. Traders sometimes call them bullshit artists while salespeople counter by calling traders quant guys with no personality. Traders are tough, quick, and often consider themselves smarter than salespeople. The salespeople probably know better how to have fun, but the traders win the prize for mental sharpness and the ability to handle stress.

The MBA in S&T

Do I need an MBA to be promoted on a sales and trading desk?

Generally, sales and trading is a much less hierarchical work environment than investment banking. For this reason, it is widely believed that you don't need an MBA to get promoted on sales and trading desks. This view is often perpetuated be people who work on trading desks, but just because you hear this once or twice, don't accept it as truth. Whether you need an MBA or not is really a function of the firm you work for and the desk you're on. If the firm you're considering hires both associates and analysts, but you notice that associates are offered twice as much pay as analysts, then this is certainly an indication that MBAs are better paid. This doesn't mean that you can't be promoted without an MBA; you'll just have to work much harder to get recognized. When it's time for a promotion, you may also be somewhat behind in the pecking order. Some firms, on the other hand, don't want MBAs. This may result from budgetary constraints, or explicit firm policy. Some firms also hold the view thatit's hard to teach an old dog new tricks, so they will hire exclusively out of undergraduate programs.

A more subtle point to discern are the desk dynamics. A lot about being on a trading desk is about fitting in, and if everyone else, including the boss, doesn't have an MBA, then chances are that having an MBA won't add too much value in this environment. In fact, an MBA degree may even hurt your career prospects if there's a downright disdain for MBA-types. Alternatively, if the desk you're on is populated with MBAs, then not having an MBA could potentially limit your career advancement. Alternatively, you can be in a situation where you're the only MBA and everyone thinks that you're the brain, which can work to your advantage even if the boss has no personal biases about the value of the degree.

The bottom line is that there are no hard and fast rules. Depending on the particular firm and desk, an MBA may not advance your career. Be aware of the aforementioned issues, and ask some good questions to get a better feel for whether an extra degree is a benefit.

What are some of the tangible benefits of an MBA?

The pay is better and you will generally have a faster track for promotion to salesperson or trader. The MBA associate will typically have to do the same demeaning things that an undergraduate analyst does, but mercifully for a shorter period of time. In some cases, MBAs are also more likely to be assigned the desk that they'd like to work for. Undergraduate sales and trading recruiting programs, on the other hand, may hire you as part of a generalist pool and place you on a desk that isn't your top choice.

Another tangible benefit for the MBA candidate is the availability of more exit options.

Day in the Life: Sales-Trader

Here's a look at a day in the life of a sales-trader, given to us by an associate in the Equities division at Lehman Brothers.

6:30 a.m. Get into work. Check voice mail and e-mail. Chat with some people at your desk about the headlines in the Journal.

7:15 a.m. Equities morning call. You find out what's up to sell. ("I'm sort of a liaison between the accounts [clients] and the block traders. What I do is help traders execute their trading strategies, give them market color. If they want something I try to find the other side of the trade. Or if I have stuff available, I get info out, without exposing what we have.")

9:30 a.m. Markets open. You hit the phones. ("You want to make outgoing calls, you don't really want people to call you. I'm calling my clients, telling them what research is relevant to them, and what merchandise I have, if there's any news on any of their positions.")

10:00 a.m. More calls. ("I usually have about 35 different clients. It's always listed equities, but it's a huge range of equities. The client can be a buyer or seller – there's one sales-trader representing a buyer, another representing the seller.")

10:30 a.m. On the phone with another Lehman trader, trying to satisfy a client. ("If they have questions in another product, I'll try to help them out.")

11:00 a.m. Calling another client. ("It's a trader at the other end, receiving discussions from portfolio manager; their discretion varies from client to client.")

12:00 p.m. You hear a call for the sale for a stock that several of your clients are keen on acquiring. ("It's usually a block trader, although sometimes it's another sales-trader. The announcement comes 'over the top,' – over the speaker. It also comes on my computer.")

12:30 p.m. Food from the deli comes in. (You can't go to the bathroom sometimes, say you're working 10 orders, you want to see every stock. We don't leave to get our lunch, we order lunch in.")

1:00 p.m. Watching your terminal ("There's a lot of action. If there's 200,000 shares trade in your name [a stock that a client has a position in or wants] and it's not you, you want to go back to your client and say who it was.)

2:00 p.m. Taking a call from a client. ("You can't miss a beat, you are literally in your seat all day.")

2:05 p.m. You tell the client that you have some stock he had indicated interest in previously, but you don't let him know how much you can unload. ("It's a lot of how to get a trade done without disclosing anything that's going to hurt the account. If you have to one stock is up you don't want the whole Street to know, or it'll drive down the price.")

4:30 p.m. Head home to rest a bit before going out. ("I leave at 4:30 or sometimes 5:00. It depends.")

7:00 p.m. Meet a buy-side trader, one of your clients, at a bar. ("We entertain a lot of buy-side traders – dinner, we go to baseball games, we go to bars. Maybe this happens once or twice a week.")

MBA Career Path

First-year MBA students and recent MBA graduates are eligible for summer associate and full-time associate positions respectively. Associates start with similar responsibilities as analysts, but add more responsibility quickly and are typically on a faster track for promotion.

Visit Vault at **www.vault.com** for insider company profiles, expert advice, career message boards, expert resume reviews, the Vault Job Board and more.

V/\ULT CAREER LIBRARY   **215**

MBAs are also more likely to have the opportunity to get staffed abroad. For example, Goldman Sachs, Morgan Stanley and Lehman Brothers have recently hired MBAs from American business schools directly into their European trading desks. MBAs interested in pursuing sales and trading opportunities abroad must be able to demonstrate local language proficiency, and a strong desire to make a long-term commitment to the region. Each of these firms has recently also offered summer internship opportunities, but these programs are less established than the New York-based opportunities, and therefore shouldn't be counted on as a stable source of MBA hiring demand.

Associate pay: To infinity and beyond

Sales and trading associates will start at about the same base pay as their investment banking counterparts. The going rate has held up around $80,000 to $85,000 per year plus an end of year bonus of $20,000 to $30,000. While signing bonuses were the norm during the bull market of the late 1990s, they are now rare. Salaries increase primarily through performance bonuses, especially if you've become a position trader for the firm. Bonuses are normally computed as a percentage of the trading revenues you generate (or commission dollars that you generate if you're a salesperson), so depending on how cheap or generous your firm is, this number can be normally expected to fluctuate between 0 percent and 10 percent in any given year.

If you make $10 million for the firm, however, don't expect to receive a cool million for your efforts. Wall Street firms are highly conscious of expense control, and the largest expense item is compensation. To keep compensation expense at or below 50 percent of revenues, investment banks hand out compensation packages that include among other things, cash, stock options and restricted stock. Generous stock option grants are a non-cash form of compensation that doesn't hit the income statement, but aren't quite as motivating as cash. Another game in the compensation is the granting of restricted stock. This is a major component of pay as you move up the ladder, and you can only convert this compensation into cash according to a vesting schedule that stretches out for years.

Finally, keep in mind that investment banks are operating across all markets and products sectors. In a simplified world, the investment bank operates a bond desk and an equity desk. The bond traders make more money and the salespeople sell more bonds when the economy is in recession. On the other hand, the stock traders make more money and the sales traders sell more stock when the economy is robust. What happens at the end of the year when the compensation committee is determining how big the bond bonus pool and the equity bonus pool should be? Most firms tend to cross-subsidize the equity desk with the bond desk's revenues when the stock market falls on hard times, and to return the favor to the bond desk when the bond market falls on hard times. This makes sense at the corporate level (preventing mass defections, for example), but the immediate consequence to the stock trader that generated $10 million in revenues and is expecting a $1 million check is that he'll see a lot less than $1 million. The small consolation to the expectant stock trader is that when he makes substantially less than his budget, maybe the bond desk will stuff his stocking.

The winding promotion road in S&T

The path to promotion on a sales and trading desk is less standard than it is in investment banking. Investment banking analysts really don't have much too look forward to except perhaps a third year and then back to business school or some other career. By contrast, undergraduate analysts who have a demonstrated ability to add value to a desk have the potential to move up without an MBA.

One common scenario that unfolds is that after several years, the restless undergraduate analyst decides to apply to business school and gets accepted. If this analyst is a prized employee, then the boss might offer the analyst a promotion to associate in order to keep the analyst on the desk.

Promotions on trading desks are generally not much to celebrate, except that it leads to potentially higher pay. Investment banking associates can look forward to moving out of the bullpen and into a real office with a secretary. Salespeople and traders settle for better accounts and more trading responsibility. The focus of promotions shouldn't be to achieve a particular title (vice president, director, managing director etc.), but rather, to earn real sales and trading responsibility. Of course if you do your job well, you'll be duly compensated and promoted, but after reaching a level of significant responsibility, you shouldn't be expecting to get promoted every couple of years.

Visit Vault at **www.vault.com** for insider company profiles, expert advice, career message boards, expert resume reviews, the Vault Job Board and more.

V∧ULT CAREER LIBRARY   **217**

Employer Directory

Banc of America Securities LLC
9 West 57th Street
New York, New York 10019
Phone: (888) 583-8900
www.bofasecurities.com

Barclays Capital
200 Park Avenue
New York, NY 10166
Phone: (212) 412-4000
www.barcap.com

Bear, Stearns & Co., Inc.
383 Madison Avenue
New York, NY 10179
Phone: (212) 272-2000
Fax: (212) 272-4785
www.bearstearns.com

Cantor Fitzgerald
135 East 57th Street
New York, NY 10022
Phone: (212) 938-5000
Fax: (212) 829-5280
www.cantor.com

CIBC World Markets
425 Lexington Ave.
New York, NY 10017
Phone: (212) 856-4000
www.cibcwm.com

Credit Suisse First Boston
11 Madison Avenue
New York, NY 10010-3629
Phone: (212) 325-2000
Fax: (212) 325-6665
www.csfb.com

Deutsche Bank
60 Wall Street
New York, NY 10003
Phone: (212) 250-2500
www.db.com

Dresdner Kleinwort Wasswerstein
1301 Avenue of the Americas
New York, NY 10019
Phone: (212) 969-2700
www.drkw.com

Jefferies & Co.
520 Madison Avenue
12th Floor
New York, NY 10022
Phone: (212) 284-2550
www.jefco.com

J.P. Morgan Chase
270 Park Avenue
New York, NY 10017
Phone: (212) 270-6000
Fax: (212) 270-2613
www.jpmorganchase.com

Keefe, Bruyette & Woods
The Equitable Building
787 Seventh Avenue, 4th Floor
New York, NY 10019
Phone: (212) 887-7777
www.kbw.com

Legg Mason
100 Light Street
Baltimore, MD 21202
Phone: (877) 534-4627
www.leggmason.com

Lehman Brothers
745 Seventh Avenue
New York, NY 10019-6801
Phone: (212) 526-7000
www.lehman.com

Morgan Stanley
1585 Broadway
New York, NY 10036
Phone: (212) 761-4000
www.morganstanley.com

RBC Capital Markets
Royal Bank Plaza
200 Bay Street
Toronto, Ontario M5J 2W7
Phone: (416) 842-2000
Fax: (416) 842-8033
www.rbccm.com

Thomas Weisel Partners
1 Montgomery St.
San Francisco, CA 94104
Phone: (415) 364-2500
Fax: (415) 364-2695
www.tweisel.com

UBS Investment Bank
299 Park Avenue
New York, NY 10171
Phone: (212) 821-3000
www.ibb.ubs.com

Piper Jaffray & Co.
800 Nicollet Mall, Suite 800
Minneapolis, MN 55402-7020
Phone: (800) 333-6000
www.piperjaffray.com

Wachovia
301 S. College Street
Suite 4000
Charlotte, NC 28288
Phone: (704) 374-6161
Fax: (704) 383-0996
www.wachovia.com

WR Hambrecht + Co.
539 Bryant Street
Suite 100
San Francisco, CA 94107
Phone: (415) 551-8600
www.wrhambrecht.com

Technology Consulting

The State of Technology Consulting

Origins

Technology consulting traces its roots back to several parents. As information technology (IT) grew in complexity in the early 1990s, management consultants found that their strategic recommendations often involved complex and costly internal IT changes. Consulting clients demanded information system implementation assistance along with high-level business advice, so management consulting firms like McKinsey and Booz Allen Hamilton built up practice areas to provide it. As the consulting business model proliferated in the 1980s and 1990s, all of the major U.S. accounting firms created consulting practices that could leverage their massive existing client bases, offering both business strategy consulting and IT consulting expertise to private sector and government clients. Moreover, software firms like Oracle have moved into the consulting field to capture some of the enormous new demand for design, implementation and management of all sorts of technology-based business information processes. Finally, newer "pure play" IT consulting firms such as Infosys and DiamondCluster have formed their entire business models around providing clients with technology strategy advice, systems implementation support and/or outsourcing services.

Businesses across all industries now realize that effective technology and technological processes are essential to maintaining competitive footing in the marketplace. As a result, decision-makers turn to outside IT consulting firms for world class expertise on technical questions, third-party perspective on optimizing their business processes, and sheer headcount to execute large IT initiatives.

Blue skies?

Like many businesses, technology consulting firms suffered in recent years as the U.S. economy fell into a recession. IT improvements are sometimes considered luxuries as opposed to necessities, so corporations cut back on technology spending during the slump; this meant falling revenues at technology consulting firms. After demand for IT consulting services dropped in 2001 – 2003, 2004 saw mild growth and 2005 is expected to yield more of the same. As of yet, few industry experts have predicted a sustained, substantive revival in corporate IT spending.

That said, half of all IT spending in this country occurs in small and medium-sized enterprises (SMEs), and much of the spending growth that is predicted will originate from this business segment. Included in the SME category are many government agencies, health care companies and professional services firms. In fact, government contracting is one source of IT consulting work that has withstood the economic downturn rather well. Computer Sciences Corporation, for example, is one of the notable beneficiaries of some large U.S. government contracts in 2005.

IT consulting salaries have stagnated for the past few years, as firms aim to let generous, boom-era pay rates back in line with the rest of the job market. The buyer's market of the past few years has also been manifested in the ability of many corporations to expand their internal IT consulting groups, picking top talent out of an oversupplied market. Joining such an internal consulting group is certainly one attractive alternative for someone looking to enter the technology consulting field.

The internationalization of technology consulting

One of the most noteworthy trends in technology consulting has been the offshore outsourcing ("offshoring") of technical work. Plain old business process outsourcing (BPO) involves a corporation contracting out some of its more technical and/or repetitive work to another firm (often to an IT consulting firm). Companies might outsource activities like application development, back office reporting functions, HR-related processing, data warehousing and user or customer technical support.

Visit Vault at **www.vault.com** for insider company profiles, expert advice, career message boards, expert resume reviews, the Vault Job Board and more.

V/\ULT CAREER LIBRARY 219

BPO is one of the major types of IT consulting firms' work. Increasingly, however, companies are now offshoring jobs as well, meaning they outsource work to their overseas branches or to overseas IT consulting firms. At first, skeptics suggested that low wages paid to IT workers in emerging markets would be offset by a higher cost of management, lesser work ethic, decreased accuracy, etc. However, there is now a broad consensus that the cost savings are real. U.S.-based IT consulting firms have also begun offshoring jobs themselves. Opening up branches in low-wage countries allows these firms to complete some of the work on their client engagements at a lower cost, which they can reflect in competitive pricing.

While outsourcing from corporations to IT consulting firms is a huge revenue source for the consulting firms, the offshoring trend is a threat. Offshore outsourcing diverts revenue from U.S. consultancies and their employees to overseas firms and workers. According to US Banker, a Forrester Research report projects that 3.3 million service- and knowledge-based jobs will migrate to other countries by 2015. Market research firm Gartner predicts that up to 40 percent of U.S. companies will have developed or tested software, provided tech support or provided storage functions overseas by 2004. Accordingly, this trend has become a hot-button political issue swirling around within trade policy debates.

As far as the U.S. IT consulting job market goes, offshoring has the effect of somewhat tempering the growth that would otherwise be expected. India-based IT consulting firms (Infosys Technologies, Tata Consulting Services) are growing at a faster rate than their U.S. competitors. Given their ability to pay employees only about 20 percent of prevailing tech wages in the U.S. and price their service offering accordingly, these firms are experiencing strong volume growth. Offshoring started in India, where the government provided economic incentives to grow the domestic IT services industry. But as the competition for top Indian talent has intensified, offshoring is now spreading to places like China, the Philippines, eastern Europe and Pakistan.

However, there is a limit to what type of work can effectively be offshored – to date it has typically been the pure technical work such as programming or pure IT support, and not the higher-value consulting work like business process reengineering and system integration. Ultimately, most types of IT consulting work are delivered more effectively by highly-educated, domestically-based consultants who bring broad business skills to the table.

Who's who

Over the past several years, we have seen each of the large U.S. accounting firms split off and rename its business/IT consulting division. This phenomenon started with Andersen Consulting's difference-of-vision distancing from Arthur Andersen in 1989 (formalized as a complete divorce through arbitration in 2000) and renaming itself Accenture in 2001. With the SEC discussing the potential for conflict of interest between accounting/audit and consulting services under one roof (e.g. audit team fudges numbers to curry favor with the client, who then buys more consulting services), the other four major accounting firms followed suit. The 2001 Enron scandal at Arthur Andersen then provided further impetus for most of these consultancies to shed vestiges of their accounting firm pasts from their names:

• KPMG Consulting split from KPMG in 2000, and rebranded itself as BearingPoint in 2003;

• Ernst & Young sold its consulting division to Cap Gemini in 2000, and the resulting Cap Gemini Ernst & Young consulting group was rebranded as Capgemini in 2004;

• Deloitte Consulting split off from accounting firm Deloitte Touche Tohmatsu in 2002;

• PWC Consulting was bought up by IBM in 2002 after parting ways with PricewaterhouseCoopers that year.

All of these ex-accounting firm consulting groups have a focus on technology consulting. Their IT practices grew out of the need to advise clients on storing and processing the mountains of accounting- and audit-related financial data. Today, their consulting work retains a distinctly IT- and finance-oriented flavor.

While the ex-accounting firms remain many of the biggest names in technology consulting, any list of technology consulting firms is overwhelmingly dominated by "pure play" firms that exclusively deliver IT services. There are literally hundreds of such firms in the U.S., and many of them are highly specialized around one technology solution that they developed. Most of the big players that made our list, however, are the full-service technology consulting firms who offer a broad range of services to clients in a wide array of business sectors.

In addition to the ex-accounting IT behemoths and the plethora of technology consulting firms, there are two other types of firms that play a more minor role in this space. First, many of the large management consultancies have technology strategy groups. However, they do focus primarily on technology strategy (as opposed to the implementation work that overwhelmingly dominates pure technology consulting firms), and are not for the most part involved in outsourced services or technical development work. Secondly, for years large software providers like SAP and Oracle have been working on their implementation service offerings to compete with the big consulting firms. Ultimately, a firm like Accenture, with deeply entrenched client relationships, has proven to be on balance more successful selling an Oracle integration project than Oracle itself. Still, job seekers should consider that most of the major software companies offer technology consulting job opportunities very similar to those at professional services firms.

Engagements

System integration

This is one of the traditional jobs of the IT consultant, and a growth area today as companies add more IT systems to their business processes. When two companies merge, or a single company wants to implement new hardware or software, they turn to consultants to make all the technology compatible. Sometimes, this is a simple matter of installing upgrades or changing settings. More often, it's a long and arduous process of writing new code to force all the machines and existing software to play nicely together.

Outsourcing

Another long-time area of tech consulting expertise, business process outsourcing (BPO) is the bread and butter of many firms. Some companies find it easier and more cost-effective to pay somebody else to manage their technology for them. The consultants, in effect, become the client's IT department. They handle everything from help desk and call center operations to server maintenance to passkey and ID tag issuance. Even governments and their armies outsource nowadays; CIBER has a number of contracts with the U.S. Army Reserve's Regional Support Commands and the U. S. Army Civil Affairs and Psychological Operations Command, while Computer Sciences Corporation has outsourcing deals with the U.K., Germany's armed forces and Australia.

Enterprise solutions

Besides motivating some of the ex-accounting IT consulting firms to change their names, another impact of the Enron (2001) and Worldcom (2002) accounting scandals was the summer 2002 passage of the Sarbanes-Oxley Act. "SOX" mandates that companies publicly listed in the U.S. market conduct internal audits, provide more detailed financial information to investors, and store financial data for a certain period of time. Many companies initially thought they could manage the IT implications of SOX on their own, and it has taken a couple of years for huge SOX-compliance IT contracts to become common. Companies have found that they need vastly improved data storage and records management systems, security systems to maintain confidentiality of their newly prodigious amounts of financial information, and process management software systems to facilitate audit, tracking and reporting requirements.

Sarbanes-Oxley compliance is just one of the major types of consulting that is generally bundled into the "enterprise solutions" category. Supply chain consulting, for example, is an even larger piece of the enterprise solutions pie. Supply chain consultants help client companies streamline parts and materials ordering processes and reduce manufacturing input costs. Supply chain projects can focus on inventory reduction, throughput enhancement and manufacturing cost containment.

Visit Vault at **www.vault.com** for insider company profiles, expert advice, career message boards, expert resume reviews, the Vault Job Board and more.

VAULT CAREER LIBRARY   221

Enterprise resource planning (ERP) is an extension of supply chain management that further integrates product planning, customer service, order tracking, finance and HR processes.

Customer relationship management (CRM) systems garnered a lot of hype in the late 1990s, only to be hit hard by an economic downturn that meant even the most technologically sophisticated customer management wasn't going to grow sales. CRM consulting engagements involve developing organized and efficient ways for clients to manage relationships, usually through a complex software solution for storing and mining large amounts of customer data.

IT strategy

IT consulting engagements that involve a broad view of the client's business or high-level technology decisions are usually called simply "consulting" or "strategy" projects and often involve aligning a client's IT infrastructure with its overall business strategy. Most of the large, brand-name management consulting firms have technology strategy practices: Booz Allen's technology strategy group, Accenture's Strategic IT Effectiveness (SITE) group within its business consulting (i.e. distinct from IT consulting) division. These technology strategy consulting groups are often managed by industry specialists (e.g. utilities, financial services) who are deeply familiar with the specific information challenges faced by potential clients.

Many technology strategy engagements fall into the business process reengineering (BPR) category. When a company decides to purchase a new software package, or to simply improve its business processes, the result is not just a new IT system of some sort, but usually a dramatic shift in the way people interact. BPR assignments involve rewriting work rules and shaping communication paths, calling upon the consultant's general business know-how more than technical computer knowledge.

Web services

Long the domain of design and hosting companies based in Silicon Alley (New York's tech center), web services include e-commerce implementation and other secure-transaction work, though consultancies do some page design and site hosting as part of their overall deliverables as well. This specialty is receiving a lot of attention from major technology players like IBM, Hewlett-Packard and Accenture. Gartner predicts Web services spending will reach $14.3 billion by 2006. (Note that many major hardware companies like Cisco are involved in "managed services," providing underlying hosting, monitoring and technical support to their e-commerce customers. These activities are more akin to a product offering than a consulting-style problem-solving service, and thus such firms are not featured in our technology consulting review.)

Security

Four years after the September 11 terrorist attacks and the resulting heightened awareness of security threats to U.S. residents and U.S.-based businesses, information security consulting work is still a hot area. IT businesses have realized there's money to be made in designing and implementing better security and identification methods. Strides have been made in biometrics (the science of identifying a person via retina patterns, voice, fingerprints and other unique biological characteristics), contraband detection and secure communications.

Research and development

Some consultants spend their time in the lab creating new hardware and software. Often, this work is geared toward creating new products (servers, analysis software and the like) that will help the consultancy sell work or complete the engagements it undertakes. In other cases, the consultants must create something entirely new for a client's use; for example, military contractors like Raytheon.

Day in the Life: IT Consultant

Kristine is a consultant at a major consulting firm with many IT consulting engagements. Her role is Team Lead of the design and developer for eight Web-based training modules. She has five analysts on her team.

4:30 a.m.: It's Monday morning. Time to wake up. There's time for a shower this Monday morning – such luxury!

5:30 a.m.: I am in a cab on the way to the airport, making a mental list of anything that could have been forgotten. I ask the cabbie to tune the radio to NPR.

6:10 a.m.: At the airport I go up to the self check-in kiosk. I take the boarding pass and head down to the security line, laptop and small carry-on in hand.

6:25 a.m.: At security, I remove my laptop from my bag and place it on the tray. I move through security quickly. No alarms beep.

6:35 a.m.: After a quick stop at Starbucks, I arrive at the gate. I say hello to three other members of my project and check out the other passengers I see every week on this Monday morning flight. I board early along with the other premier fliers – one of the perks of being a frequent traveler.

7:00 a.m.: The flight departs on time. Yay! I relish my window seat close to the front of the airplane.

8:00 a.m.: The beverage cart wakes me up. I ask for coffee and scan *The Wall Street Journal* as I drink.

9:30 a.m.: I arrive at my destination and share a ride with my fellow consultants to the project site.

10:30 a.m.: At the project site. As I crawl underneath my desk to hook my laptop to the client LAN connection, one of my team members informs me that he still hasn't received feedback from his client reviewer. That's not good news.

11:00 a.m.: After checking and responding to e-mail, I call my team member's client reviewer. The reviewer agrees to send me the team member feedback on the training material by noon tomorrow.

11:15 a.m.: I remind the team of the 1 p.m. status meeting. I've got to start it on time – I have a meeting downtown at 3:15 p.m. I start to review the content outlines for the training modules.

12:00 p.m.: I scurry, along with two teammates, to get sandwiches at a nearby eatery. Mine is turkey and cheddar.

12:20 p.m.: Back at my desk, I get a call from the project manager, who is working at a client site in another state. He tells me that clients in the training department are nervous about their job security and asks that the entire team be sensitive to how the training changes may affect the training positions in the organization.

1:00 p.m.: The team holds a status meeting. I pass on the message from the project manager. Each member discusses what has been completed and what he or she expects to complete that week. Two other team members are having difficulty obtaining feedback from their client reviewers. We all brainstorm ideas on how to obtain the feedback.

2:00 p.m.: I finish up the meeting and get directions to my meeting downtown.

2:40 p.m.: Off to the 3:15 p.m. meeting.

3:15 p.m.: I meet the head of the training department to discuss the training courses. He calls in a close associate who has opinions on how the courses should be organized. The associate wants to add several more Web-based training modules. I politely suggest that part of the additional subject matter could be covered in the modules that have been agreed to in the scope of the project. We all sketch out the course structure on a white board.

4:45 p.m.: Back at the project site. I check in with my team members via e-mail.

Visit Vault at **www.vault.com** for insider company profiles, expert advice, career message boards, expert resume reviews, the Vault Job Board and more.

V/\ULT CAREER LIBRARY 223

5:45 p.m.: I complete a draft of the course flow in PowerPoint and send it to the client and my manager for review.

7:00 p.m.: I have reviewed 50 percent of the course outlines. It's time to head back to the hotel. I stop by a local diner for a quick dinner.

8:30 p.m.: Time for a workout in the hotel gym.

9:15 p.m.: I'm ready for bed. Clothes for the next day are hanging in the closet. The alarm clock is set to 6:30 a.m.

10:30 p.m.: I go to sleep.

Employer Directory

Deloitte

1633 Broadway
New York, NY 10013-6754
www.deloitte.com/careers

Deloitte, one of the nation's leading professional services firms, provides audit, tax, consulting, and financial advisory services through nearly 30,000 people in more than 80 U.S. cities. Known as an employer of choice for innovative human resources programs, the firm is dedicated to helping its clients and its people excel. "Deloitte" refers to the associated partnerships of Deloitte & Touche USA LLP (Deloitte & Touche LLP and Deloitte Consulting LLP) and subsidiaries. Deloitte is the U.S. member firm of Deloitte Touche Tohmatsu.

Business schools Deloitte recruits from

There are too many to list. All candidate are to submit to opportunities via our career website located at www.deloitte.com

Roche Diagnostics

9115 Hague Road
Indianapolism, Indiana 462520
http://careers.ind.roche.com
www.roche.com

Roche Diagnostics is the world's leading provider of diagnostic systems and decision-oriented health information. We are dedicated to the discovery, development, manufacturing, marketing and servicing of products and solutions for medical laboratories, physicians and patients, as well as for research and industry. Roche Diagnostics is a diverse, inclusive company that seeks, celebrates and leverages diversity to maximize the competitive advantage of people. We offer a variety of opportunities at our U.S. diagnostics marketing and sales headquarters in Indiana and at our global molecular business area headquarters in California.

Business schools Roche recruits from

University of Chicago; Northwestern (Kellogg); Indiana University (Kelley); Harvard Business School, Duke University (Fuqua); U.C.L.A.; University of Michigan; Purdue University; MIT (Sloan); University of Pennsylvania (Wharton); Yale University, Stanford University; UC Berkeley (Haas); Washington University (Olin)

Accenture

1345 Avenue of the Americas
New York, NY 10105
Phone: (917) 452-4400
Fax: (917) 527-5387
www.accenture.com

Atos Origin

North America Headquarters
Atos Origin, IT Services Inc.
5599 San Felipe, Ste. 300
Houston, TX 77056
Phone: (713) 513-3000

Corporate Headquarters
Da Vincilaan 5
1930
Zaventem
Belgium
Phone: +31 (0)23 566 70 00

Corporate Financial Headquarters
Immeuble Ile de France
3, place de la Pyramide
92067 Paris La Defence Cedex
France
Phone: +33 1 4900 9000

BearingPoint

1676 International Drive
McLean, VA 22102
Phone: (703) 747-3000
Fax: (703) 747-8500
www.bearingpoint.com

Booz Allen Hamilton

8283 Greensboro Drive
McLean, VA 22102
Phone: (703) 902-5000
Fax: (703) 902-3333
www.boozallen.com

Visit Vault at **www.vault.com** for insider company profiles, expert advice, career message boards, expert resume reviews, the Vault Job Board and more.

VAULT CAREER LIBRARY **225**

Capgemini

Five Times Square
New York, NY 10036
Phone: (917) 934-8000
Fax: (917) 934-8001
www.us.capgemini.com

CGI Group

1130 Sherbrooke St. West
5th Floor
Montreal Quebec H3A 2M8
Canada
Phone: (514) 841-3200
Fax: (514) 841-3299
www.cgi.com

Computer Sciences Corporation

2100 East Grand Avenue
El Segundo, CA 90245
Phone: (310) 615-0311
Fax: (310) 322-9768
www.csc.com

Deloitte Consulting LLP

1633 Broadway, 35th Floor
New York, NY 10019
Phone: (212) 492-4500
Fax: (212) 492-4743
www.deloitte.com

DiamondCluster International Inc.

John Hancock Center
Suite 3000
875 N. Michigan Avenue
Chicago, IL 60611
Phone: (312) 255-5000
Fax: (312) 255-6000
E-mail: www.diamondcluster.com
info@diamondcluster.com

EDS

5400 Legacy Drive
Plano, TX 75024
Phone: (972) 604-6000
www.eds.com

Fujitsu Consulting

333 Thornall Street
Edison, NJ 08837
Phone: (732) 549-4100
Fax: (732) 632-1826
www.fujitsu.com/us/services/consulting

Getronics

290 Concord Road
Billerica, MA 01821-4130
Phone: (978) 625-5000

Rembrandttoren
Amstelplein 1
1096 HA Amsterdam
The Netherlands
Phone: +31 (20) 586-1412
Fax: +31 (20) 586-1568

HP Technology Solutions

3000 Hanover Street
Palo Alto, CA 94304-1185
Phone: (650) 857-1501
Fax: (650) 857-5518
www.hp.com/hps

IBM Global Services

New Orchard Road
Armonk, New York 10504
Phone: (914) 499-1900
Fax: (914) 765-7382
www.1.ibm.com/services/us/index.wss

Infosys Technologies Ltd.

Plot No. 44 & 97A, Electronics City
Hosur Road, Bangalore
560 100
India
Phone: (080) 28520261
Fax: (080) 28520362
www.infosys.com

Keane

100 City Square
Boston, MA 02129
Phone: (617) 241-9200 or (800) 73-KEANE
Fax: (617) 241-9507
www.keane.com

LogicaCMG

Stephenson House
75 Hampstead Road
London, NW1 2PL, UK
Phone: +44 20 7637 9111
Fax: +44 20 7468 7006

U.S. HQ:
32 Hartwell Avenue
Lexington, MA 02421
Phone: (617) 476-8000
Fax: (617) 476-8010
www.logicacmg.com

PA Consulting Group

123 Buckingham Palace Road
London
SW1W 9SR
United Kingdom
Phone: +44 20 7730 9000
Fax: +44 20 7333 5050
www.paconsulting.com

Perot Systems

2300 W. Plano Pkwy.
Plano, TX 75075
Phone: (972) 577-0000
Fax: 972 340-6100
www.perotsystems.com

Sapient

25 First Street
Cambridge, MA 02141
Phone: (617) 621-0200
Fax: (617) 621-1300
www.sapient.com

Tata Consultancy Services (TCS)

Corporate HQ
Air India Bldg., 11th Fl.,Nariman Point
Mumbai, 400 021, India
Phone: +91-22-56689999
Fax: +91-22-56689333

www.tcs.com
U.S. HQ:
101 Park Avenue, 26th Floor
New York, NY 10178
Phone: (212) 557-8038
Fax: (212) 867-8652

Telcordia Technologies
One Telcordia Drive
Piscataway, NJ 08854-4157
Phone: (732) 699-2000
www.telcordia.com

Titan Corporation, The
3033 Science Park Rd.
San Diego, CA 92121-1199
Phone: (858) 552-9500
Fax: (858) 552-9645
www.titan.com

UNISYS
Corporate Headquarters
Unisys Way
Blue Bell, PA 19424
Phone: (215) 986-4011
www.unisys.com

Wipro Ltd.
Doddakannelli, Sarjapur Road
Bangalore, Karnataka 560035
Phone: +91(80) 844 0011
Fax: +91(80) 844 0056
www.wipro.com

Visit Vault at **www.vault.com** for insider company profiles, expert advice, career message boards, expert resume reviews, the Vault Job Board and more.

V∧ULT CAREER LIBRARY   **227**

Telecommunications

Telecom Calling

In simpler times, the word "telecommunications" might conjure an image of a telephone – and not much else. These days, telecom is an industry encompassing everything from local and long-distance phone services to wireless communication, Internet access, and cable and digital television. In the U.S., total spending for telecom services reached more than $720 billion in 2004, and is expected to hit the $1 trillion mark in 2007, according to the Telecommunications Industry Association (TIA). Internationally, the TIA predicts telecom spending, estimated at $1.5 trillion in 2004, to top $2 trillion by 2007.

For whom the bell tolls

Established in 1877 as American Bell, AT&T enjoyed the largest share of the industry pie for nearly a century, thanks to the government's belief that the utility constituted a "natural" monopoly. That monopoly crumbled in 1969, when the Federal Communications Commission (FCC) allowed other companies to play in Ma Bell's sandbox. Companies like MCI were quick to get in the game. But monopolies don't disappear overnight – to encourage competition in the long-distance market, the Department of Justice followed up with an antitrust suit against AT&T in 1974, resulting in the division of AT&T into a long-distance retailer and seven regional Bell operating companies (RBOCs), which would compete in the local call market as independent local exchange carriers (LECs). The final breakup took place in 1984.

The industry thrived under the breakup, exploding into hundreds of smaller competitors, lowering the cost of long-distance calling dramatically. While AT&T held about 70 percent of the market in 1984, it holds about a third today, according to Hoover's. Still, it's these so-called "Tier 1" carriers – AT&T, Sprint, and WorldCom – that make up the bulk of the long-distance market.

Untangling the wires

As the long distance market diversified, the local exchange market remained relatively homogenous. The Telecommunications Act of 1996 aimed to change that, deregulating entry into local markets and requiring that the so-called Baby Bells, or incumbent local phone companies (ILECs), retail their network elements to smaller competitors. The incumbents were required to unbundle their networks for reasonable prices, with the goal of decentralization of the system into a "network of networks." The act also temporarily blocked an RBOC from entering the long-distance market until it could prove that there was sufficient competition in its local territory.

Another provision of the Telecom Act, allowing RBOCs the right to sell cable television services and phone equipment, proved to be a boon for the strongest RBOCs. Thanks to those services and the entry of the Babies into long distance, the Telecom Act actually had the opposite of its intended effect, allowing a few RBOCs to solidify their positions and dominate the market through mergers and acquisitions. Today, there are just four RBOCs – Verizon Communications, BellSouth, SBC Communications, and Qwest Communications International – dominating both local phone service access and the burgeoning DSL (digital subscriber line) markets.

Still, sniping among the RBOCs and long distance giants like MCI and AT&T over network-access rights continues. As late as May 2004, the FCC was engaged in a dispute between the Baby Bells and the long distance carriers, as the LD companies argued for increased access to local calling networks.

Merger mania

The Telecom Act ushered in an era of merger fever among telecom companies. In 1997, Bell Atlantic purchased little sib NYNEX for $25.6 billion, and SBC bought Pacific Telesis. The following year, SBC acquired local and long-distance

Visit Vault at **www.vault.com** for insider company profiles, expert advice, career message boards, expert resume reviews, the Vault Job Board and more.

VAULT CAREER LIBRARY 229

provider Southern New England Telecommunications, entering the LD market through this Telecom Act loophole. SBC also acquired Baby Bell Ameritech for $68.8 billion, and Bell Atlantic merged with GTE to form Verizon. Also in 1998, Qwest Communications International bought long-distance company LCI International, entering the struggle between the big three of long distance, AT&T, Sprint, and MCI. The next year, Qwest's bid to acquire US West (the smallest of the Baby Bells) defeated that of fiber optics leader Global Crossing of Bermuda. Also in 1999, AT&T acquired cable operator Tele-Communications, Inc. and merged with MediaOne Group in a $44-billion deal. Meanwhile, MCI was folded into WorldCom for $47 billion, (more on this later) becoming the world's leading Internet carrier and a full-fledged global telecom company, boasting a 25 percent share of the U.S. long-distance market after the deal.

The activity wasn't limited to America's shores. Telecom became truly global in 1997, when 70 members of the World Trade Organization agreed to open up their telecom markets to each other at the start of the following year. Those 70 countries control 90 percent of worldwide telecom sales. Nearly all telecom companies around the world had privatized in anticipation of this expanded level of competition. The accord led to a rush of international deals, especially in the world's second-largest telecom market, Japan. In 1999, British Telecommunications and AT&T partnered to acquire a 30 percent stake in LD operator Japan Telecom, combining their Japanese ventures under JT. Britain's Cable & Wireless bought Japan's No. 6 carrier, IDC, a few months later. Also in 1999, Global Crossing teamed up with Marubeni to build an entirely new network, called Global Access, to service Japan.

Wall Street highs and lows

As M&A activity heated up, Wall Street took notice – investors poured $1.3 trillion into telecom industry companies in the five years following the Telecom Act's passage, according to Forbes magazine. But with this activity came increased scrutiny and risk. Ultimately, the industry was subject to the same meltdown that hit the rest of the tech sector beginning in late 2000. According to Forbes, the industry's market value plummeted by $1 trillion after the Dow Jones took its dive. Mergers also fell by the wayside. In July 2000, a proposed deal between Sprint and WorldCom fell through when the Justice Department filed a lawsuit that attempted to block the deal. The prospect of a lengthy DOJ suit effectively killed the merger, and it may similarly discourage future unions.

Compounding the gloom in the industry, some major telecoms had high-profile problems in their accounting departments. The two biggest offenders were WorldCom and Global Crossing, both of which ran afoul of the feds in 2002. WorldCom filed for the largest bankruptcy in U.S. history in July 2002, racking up $41 billion in debts and an estimated $11 billion in fraudulent expenses – leading to a $100 billion loss to shareholders. Even as the company attempted a rebound, emerging from bankruptcy in April 2004 with a lighter debt load, a moderately healthy outlook, and a less tarnished name (the company reverted to the MCI brand), it had to contend with scores of class action lawsuits; former chief executive Bernard J. Ebbers also faced a growing list of federal fraud and conspiracy charges as late as Spring 2004. Accounting firm Citigroup announced in May 2004 that it would pay $2.65 billion to investors for its role in the scandal. The turmoil has led some industry analysts to speculate about a possible sale of MCI to one of its Baby Bell competitors.

A debt burden of $12.4 billion, along with an oversupply of high-speed network capacity, led to Global Crossing's Chapter 11 filing in January 2002. The outcome was predictable in this era of accounting scandals, including a Justice Department probe into the company's accounting practices, and lawyers rounding up plaintiffs. In April 2004, investors again had reason to worry as Global Crossing announced it would need to review and restate its financial statements for all of 2002 and 2003 thanks to a $50 million to $80 million understatement of liability costs.

In addition to WorldCom and Global Crossing, about a half-dozen other providers of telecom services began Chapter 11 bankruptcy proceedings in 2002, dumping customers and employees as they went. In September 2003, Sprint reported a reorganization into business and consumer lines in an effort to save $1 billion.

Wireless wins the day

Thanks to the booming wireless market, however, Sprint, which offers wireless service under the Sprint PCS name, faces less market risk, analysts say. The same holds true for other major telecoms that have devoted resources to wireless services. In fact, the wireless market, with $89 billion in spending in 2003, outpaced long distance for the first time that year, according to TIA research (LD posted $78 billion in spending). The number of wireless users was estimated at above 1 billion in 2003.

The boom in wireless may herald renewed business activity in telecom. One notable example is Cingular's $41 billion purchase of rival AT&T Wireless, announced in February 2004, following a fierce bidding battle with rival Vodafone. As an example of how complicated the industry's family ties are, consider this: Cingular happens to be owned by rival Baby Bells BellSouth and SBC; competitor Verizon Wireless is a joint venture of Verizon and the Vodafone Group. Competition began to sizzle in late 2003, as the first phase of a federal law allowing "portability" – the ability of consumers to retain their phone numbers when switching carriers – took effect. While the media emphasized a sudden boom in carrier-hopping among consumers, industry watchers like the Gartner Group pointed out

An end-run around the phone

Cell phones aren't the only way consumers are making calls these days – Voice over Internet Protocol (VoIP), offered by companies like Vonage, allows users to turn their personal computers into telephones by sending voice "data" over a broadband connection in the same way other data is sent online. Bypassing questions of local and long distance networks entirely, VOIP services allow complete number portability – users in Iowa can maintain Manhattan area codes. The technology also has an advantage in terms of cost – thanks to the FCC, VoIP is exempt from taxes and regulations regular phone carriers are saddled with. Of course, the major telecoms are busy on Capitol Hill, trying to level the playing field – meanwhile, most experts say the technology has a way to go in terms of reliability and simplicity for the average consumer.

But it isn't a simple question of phone companies competing with the Internet – indeed, telecom providers, seeing the Internet revolution early on, began expanding their data communication networks, constructing more than 90 million miles of fiber-optic cables alone. Cable lines, which are hooked up to 90 percent of American residences, have considerably greater bandwidth than current phone lines and appear to be the least painful replacement for the outdated phone lines connecting homes today. With AT&T currently gobbling up miles of cable wire, there's little mystery as to what its medium in the next few years will be.

A job market roller coaster

By some estimates, the telecom industry slashed 300,000 jobs during the troubled period beginning in late 2000. As recently as May 2004, MCI announced plans to lay off 7,500 workers – on top of 4,500 in cuts it had announced a few months prior to that. But outplacement firm Challenger Gray & Christmas sees the layoffs fading a bit – while more than 12,000 telecom workers lost their jobs in December 2002, that number was just over 8,700 in December of the following year. While employment prospects are expected to be limited in telecom for the time being, the U.S. Department of Labor's Bureau of Labor Statistics (BLS) says that rising demand for services will eventually boost hiring.

According to the BLS, telecom provided 1.2 million wage and salary jobs in 2002, the latest year for which statistics are available. Of these employees, just over half work in office and administrative support or in installation, maintenance and repair. Other positions in the industry include sales and IT-related functions like computer support, engineering and administration. Keeping job skills up-to-date is crucial in this rapidly changing industry, the BLS insists – many major employers offer training through web sites and other resources.

Visit Vault at **www.vault.com** for insider company profiles, expert advice, career message boards, expert resume reviews, the Vault Job Board and more.

VAULT CAREER LIBRARY   **231**

Employer Directory

Cox Communications, Inc.

1400 Lake Hearn Drive
Atlanta, Georgia 30319
Phone: (404) 843-5000
www.cox.com

Cox Communications is a multi-service broadband communications company serving approximately 6.3 million customers nationwide. Cox is the nation's third-largest cable television provider and offers both traditional analog video programming under the Cox Cable brand as well as advanced digital video programming under the Cox Digital Cable brand. Cox Communications, Inc. and its subsidiaries are Equal Opportunity Employers. We have a tradition of encouraging a wide diversity of talents through a broad range of hiring practices.

ALLTEL Corporation
1 Allied Dr.
Little Rock, AR 72202
Phone: (501) 905-8000
Fax: (501) 905-5444
www.alltel.com

AT&T
One AT&T Way
Bedminster, NJ 07921
Phone: (908) 221-2000
Fax: (908) 532-1675
www.att.com

BellSouth Corp.
1155 Peachtree Street, NE
Atlanta, GA 30309-3610
Phone: (404) 249-2000
Fax: (404) 249-2071
www.bellsouth.com

Charter Communications
12405 Powerscourt Dr.
Suite 100
St. Louis, MO 63131-3660
Phone: (314) 965-0555
Fax: (314) 965-9745
www.charter.com

Cingular Wireless
Glenridge Highlands Two
5565 Glenridge Connector
Atlanta, GA 30342
Phone: (404) 236-6000
Fax: (404) 236-6005
www.cingular.com

Cisco Systems, Inc.
170 W. Tasman Drive
San Jose, CA 95134-1706
Phone: (408) 526-4000
Fax: (408) 526-4100
www.cisco.com

Comcast Corporation
1500 Market St.
Philadelphia, PA 19102-2148
Phone: (215) 665-1700
Fax: (215) 981-7790
www.comcast.com

Corning Incorporated
1 Riverfront Plaza
Corning, NY 14831-0001
Phone: (607) 974-9000
Fax: (607) 974-5927
www.corning.com

Cox Communications, Inc.
1400 Lake Hearn Dr. NE
Atlanta, GA 30319
Phone: (404) 843-5000
Fax: (404) 843-5975
www.cox.com

The DIRECTV Group, Inc.
2230 East Imperial Highway
El Segundo, CA 90245
Phone: (310) 964-0700
Fax: (310) 535-5225
www.directv.com

EchoStar Communications Corp.
9601 South Meridian Blvd.
Englewood, CO 80112
Phone: (303) 723-1000
Fax: (303) 723-1399
www.dishnetwork.com

Lucent Technologies Inc.
600 Mountain Avenue
Murray Hill, NJ 07974
Phone: (908) 582-8500
Fax: (908) 508-2576
www.lucent.com

MCI, Inc.
22001 Loudoun County Pkwy.
Ashburn, VA 20147
Phone: (877) 624-1000
Fax: (212) 885-0570
www.mci.com

Motorola, Inc.
1303 E. Algonquin Rd.
Schaumburg, IL 60196
Phone: (847) 576-5000
Fax: (847) 576-5372
www.motorola.com

Nextel Communications
2001 Edmund Halley Drive
Reston, VA 20191
Phone: (703) 433-4000
Fax: (703) 433-4343
www.nextel.com

Nokia Corporation
Keilalahoentie 4
PO Box 226
Espoo, 02150
Finland
Phone: +358-7180-08000
Fax: +358-7180-38226
www.nokia.com

Nortel Networks Limited
8200 Dixie Road Suite 100
Brampton, Ontario, L6T 5P6
Canada
Phone: (905) 863-0000
Fax: (905) 863-8408
www.nortelnetworks.com

QUALCOMM Incorporated
5775 Morehouse Drive
San Diego, CA 92121-1714
Phone: (858) 587-1121
Fax: (858) 658-2100
www.qualcomm.com

Qwest Communications International, Inc.
1801 California Street
Denver, CO 80202
Phone: (800) 899-7780
Fax: (303) 992-1724
www.qwest.com

SBC Communications Inc.
175 E. Houston
San Antonio, TX 78205-2233
Phone: (210) 821-4105
Fax: (210) 351-2071
www.sbc.com

Sprint Corporation
6200 Sprint Parkway
Overland Park, KS 66251
Phone: (800) 829-0965
www.sprint.com

Verizon Communications
1095 Avenue of the Americas
New York, NY 10036
Phone: (212) 395-2121
Fax: (212) 869-3265
www.verizon.com

Visit Vault at **www.vault.com** for insider company profiles, expert advice,
career message boards, expert resume reviews, the Vault Job Board and more.

V/\ULT CAREER LIBRARY   **233**

Use the Internet's
MOST TARGETED
job search tools.

Vault Job Board

Target your search by industry, function, and experience level, and find the job openings that you want.

VaultMatch Resume Database

Vault takes match-making to the next level: post your resume and customize your search by industry, function, experience and more. We'll match job listings with your interests and criteria and e-mail them directly to your in-box.

VAULT
> the most trusted name in career information™

Transportation and Airlines

Turbulent Skies for Airlines

It's an understatement to say that airlines are struggling these days. The nearly $25 billion lost by the airline industry from 2001 through the first quarter of 2004 is greater than the total of the profits it earned during the six years between 1995 and 2000. The aftermath of the September 11 terrorist attacks in the U.S. is an obvious factor in this downturn, but the industry has been weakened by other factors, as well, including unprecedented competition both within the sector and from other forms of transportation; skyrocketing fuel prices; online technologies empowering travel consumers; the SARS epidemic; increased liability insurance premiums; and unsustainable labor and operating costs. Still, the mammoth industry managed to post revenues of approximately $80 billion in 2004.

For the airline sector, turbulence is nothing new – since the early days of flight at the start of the last century, it's always been tough for air carriers to turn a profit. Major airline swan-dives took place long before the travel and economic crisis spurred by the increased attention to global terrorism – do the names Pan Am, Braniff, and Eastern ring a bell? They're among the approximately 100 airlines estimated by the Air Transport Association to have gone bankrupt since deregulation of the industry in 1978. In fact, industry analysts say that the number of airlines that have gone out of business since the dawn of the air travel industry outweighs those that have managed to survive.

Big trouble for the Big Six

Since the September 11 tragedies, Congress has given well over $20 billion to the industry, in the form of reimbursements for losses incurred while planes were grounded following the attacks, help with new passenger and plane security requirements, and pension funding relief. But many of the industry's major players were forced to shoulder massive debt loads to continue operating, on top of debt they had begun accumulating even before the terrorist attacks. The "Big Six" in the airline industry – United, US Airways, American, Northwest, Continental, and Delta - all spent the past few years falling into or trying to stave off bankruptcy protection, while enduring massive restructuring efforts and leadership changes. In addition, Great Plains, Hawaiian, Midway, National, Sun Country, TWA, and Vanguard have shown up in bankruptcy court.

United fell into the red in 2002 with the largest bankrupt filing in aviation history, and, as of May 2005, was still struggling with a restructuring plan. The company hopes to emerge from Chapter 11 in the fall of 2005 thanks to a settlement in which the government would take over UAL's under-funded pension plans; United workers are currently appealing the decision, claiming the plan cuts them out of promised reimbursement money. After US Airways, which emerged from bankruptcy in March 2003, slipped into a loss again later that year, pressure from unions forced CEO David Siegal and CFO Neal Cohen out of their top spots at the start of 2004. Workers refused a second round of concessions totaling $800 million during the summer of 2004, and US Airways collapsed into bankruptcy protection again that September.

AMR Corp., operator of American Airlines and American Eagle, increased leisure fares and flights, but reported overall profit loss for the first half of 2005, coming off a fourth-quarter loss in 2004 triple that of the same period the year prior. Over at Continental, the airline hopes a $500 million savings plan (including cuts in wage and benefits to workers, and reductions in fees and stock-option grants to directors) will save it from Chapter 11, though a March 2005 filing with the Securities and Exchange Commission revealed Continental expected a significant loss for the upcoming fiscal year, despite a strong sales showing via the Continental Web site. Northwest has staved off bankruptcy filings thus far by closing a number of ticket offices, increased round-trip fares to certain cities, slashing pilots' pay over a two-year period by 15 percent, cutting jobs, and expanding code-sharing agreements with fellow airlines. These changes haven't been able to lift Northwest's bottom line, though - the company recorded a $450 million loss in April 2005. Delta's CEO Gerald Grinstein helped slice $700 million from his company's overhead in 2004 through a series of cost-cutting efforts, and more cuts are in place (including more than 7,000 jobs) to reduce debt by $2.7 billion by 2006, which Grinstein says is necessary to prevent a bankruptcy filing.

Visit Vault at **www.vault.com** for insider company profiles, expert advice, career message boards, expert resume reviews, the Vault Job Board and more.

V∧ULT CAREER LIBRARY 235

Airline aid

Though passenger confidence continued to grow in the years following the attacks, and an improved economy bodes well for the travel industry as a whole, the industry's red ink continues to flow – according to a June 2004 Senate report, the industry carried combined debts of more than $100 billion as of that year, with much of it due by 2006. So major carriers continue to lobby the feds for financial support, in the form of subsidies and loans. Delta and Northwest are currently pleading with members of Congress to pass legislation allowing the airlines to stretch their multi-billion dollar pension payments over a 25-year period. As it stands now, Northwest would contribute $900 million in pensions in 2006, while Delta would give up $500 million - amounts neither airline can afford. If the pension bill is rejected, Delta and Northwest will most likely file for bankruptcy.

A global network

Around the world, many airlines still are heavily subsidized – or owned outright – by their home nations. While this has been a successful set-up for many, others haven't been so lucky – Swissair and Belgium's airline, Sabena, both crumbled when their respective governments couldn't keep up with demands for subsidies. Global alliances have been formed between subsidized international and U.S. carriers to avoid some regulatory issues and to maximize profits by sharing resources, including routes and marketing strategies. Well-known alliances include Oneworld, an alliance between American Airlines and British Airways, and SkyTeam, a partnership made up of Delta Air Lines, Air France, and AeroMexico. Such partnerships aren't always successful – an alliance between Dutch carrier KLM and AlItalia fell apart, for instance, after AlItalia had trouble securing funding from its government patrons.

But partnerships aside, the airline industry remains remarkably competitive, and in today's tough climate, it's everyone for themselves. The only major merger between top airlines in the past few years was the early 2004 acquisition of KLM by Air France (a deal expected to create one of the world's largest airlines). Tight regulatory controls in the U.S. make it tough for major domestic carriers to even consider merging; a plan to join United Airlines and U.S. Airways was the last such proposal to be floated, and it has since fallen to earth. The U.S. Airways name showed up again in merger talks in June 2005, with the announcement of a deal to join America West for $1.5 billion. Nothing is set in stone yet, though – the merger is pending approval from a federal bankruptcy court and the Air Transportation Stabilization Board, since U.S. Airways is still operating under bankruptcy protection.

Going regional

Regional airlines, which benefit from smaller, newer jets and lower operating costs than the domestic giants, have gained ground in recent years, becoming the fastest-growing segment of the airline market. Approximately 25 to 30 regional, or commuter, carriers operate in the industry today, according to the Bureau of Labor Statistics. Recent statistics from the Regional Airline Association reveal that one in five domestic airline passengers travel on a regional airline, and that the regional fleet makes up one-third of the US commercial airline fleet on the whole. The big carriers have taken notice, and many now have controlling interests in newer regional airlines – Delta controls Delta Express, Atlantic Southeast, and Comair, for instance, while American has American Eagle. The trend is reflected in Europe, too. Both globally and domestically, regional airlines benefit from such partnerships as alliances with major carriers allow the upstart regionals access to major airport hubs. In some cases, however, regional and low-budget airlines have skirted the hub question altogether by choosing to operate out of slightly out-of-the-way airports – Southwest's use of Islip airport, in the New York area, and JetBlue's adoption of Long Beach, near Los Angeles, are two examples.

And in other cases, regional airlines have decided to spread their wings and join the burgeoning low-cost boom. Independence Air is a prime example – once a regional carrier called Atlantic Coast Airlines, it relied on United for 85 percent of its revenue. Going independent, the carrier re-branded, changed its looks, and began marketing itself with rock-bottom rates, using Washington's Dulles airport as a hub, in the summer of 2004.

The budget boom

The budget airline sector – consisting of top performers like Southwest Airlines and JetBlue, plus a growing number of upstarts, has gotten a good deal of attention lately. But budget flight isn't a new phenomenon in the industry – in fact, Southwest has been around since 1971. The difference is in the branding, and public acceptance, of these carriers, fueled in part by Southwest's customer-centric approach, and partly by customers' reduced service expectations post-September 11. Expanded routes have helped, too – where once low-budget carriers limited their flights to relatively short hauls in regional markets, today's top discount airlines regularly offer cross-country, and even international, flights. The budget carrier phenomenon has rocked Europe, too, where more than 50 low-cost carriers were in operation in 2004, compared to just four in 1999. European customers have warmed up to the budget boom as well. British-based easyJet increased its passenger flow more than eight-fold between 1999 and 2004, while low-cost carrier Ryanair, operating out of Ireland, ranked as one of the top performers in the industry worldwide, second in market capitalization only to Southwest as of mid-2004, according to Yahoo! Finance.

Around the world, carriers have come to realize that there just aren't as many passengers willing to pay for five-star air travel these days – at least, not enough to make these services profitable for most carriers. The demise of the Concorde in 2003 was seen by many analysts as yet another indication of this trend.

Cutting costs

But above all, cost-savings are seen as key to the success of low-budget carriers. One way air carriers measure their fiscal health is through cost per available seat mile (or CASM), a complex formula involving airplane capacity, operating costs, route lengths, and other factors. Whereas American Airlines spends about 9.4 cents for each seat on each mile flown, budget competitors like Southwest and JetBlue lighten their loads with CASMs of 7.6 cents and 6.4 cents, respectively, according to an MSNBC article from December 2003. Those pennies add up over time, and so-called "legacy" carriers are under pressure to pinch them ever harder. But with more liberal work rules and a less-senior workforce overall, low-cost carriers beat their established rivals in terms of labor costs. Making matters worse for the legacy airlines, they're now under pressure to match the rock-bottom ticket prices issued by upstarts like JetBlue (founded in 2000) and seasoned discounters like Southwest. Combine that pressure with the growing presence of those once-fringe carriers at major domestic airport hubs, and the stage is set for all-out price wars. One way in which legacy carriers have begun to compete is by spinning off their own low-cost subsidiaries – Delta's Song took to the skies in April 2003, followed by United's Ted in early 2004. Where legacy carriers once competed with low-cost rivals, now the low-cost carriers are waging wars amongst themselves – Southwest, feeling the burn of higher labor and fuel costs, posted a 54 percent lower profit in the second quarter of 2004.

If budget airlines represent the great hope of major passenger carriers, corporate jets are the bright light on the business travel horizon. Fractional jet firms like NetJet, which allow the sharing of jets between multiple partners for charter use, are flying high, and even industry skeptics like Warren Buffett are backing the idea, MSNBC has noted.

Investing in a dream(liner)

Major carriers hope to save money in the future by investing in new planes that offer a lower cost of ownership and operation. In early 2004, Boeing got the go-ahead from Japan's Al Nippon Airlines to begin work on a new 7E7 Dreamliner passenger jet, which promises fuel savings of up to 20 percent – other carriers' orders are expected to follow. Meanwhile, Airbus, the French aircraft maker, unveiled a brand new high-scale jumbo-jet, the A380, at the start of 2005 at a gala event during the Le Bourget air show in Toulouse, France. Designed to comfortably seat 555, the A380 rocked the airline industry and repre-

Visit Vault at **www.vault.com** for insider company profiles, expert advice, career message boards, expert resume reviews, the Vault Job Board and more.

VAULT CAREER LIBRARY   **237**

sented the joint efforts of France, Britain, Germany, and Spain, who all contributed to the 10-year, $13 billion program that designed the plane. The double-decker monstrosity, the largest plane ever built, boasts a 262-foot wingspan and extra space companies can use to install bedrooms, gyms, bars, and lounges. On the conservative end, though, is where the A380 packs its biggest punch: its carbon fiber components and fuel-efficient technology are estimated to match or exceed Boeing's 20 percent fuel savings, and slice cost per passenger.

Other cost-cutting measures in the airline industry overall include the streamlining of fleets and the retirement of older planes; the cancellation of unprofitable routes; greater efficiency in procurement processes involving suppliers; and the slashing of commissions once paid regularly to middlemen such as travel agencies. Many see technological advancements as their great hope – according to a January 2004 BusinessWeek article, Continental hopes to save $500 million annually in coming years partly by investing in Web-based check-in systems and wireless bag tracking.

Through these and other measures, legacy carriers have slashed annual operating expenses by $13.4 billion and annual capital expenditures by $8.1 billion since 2001, according to the Air Transport Association. The belt-tightening was beginning to pay off as of mid-2004: While industry capacity (a measure of per-seat miles flown) contracted by 8 percent in the three years following mid-2001, capacity was expected to expand by nearly 7 percent.

Labor pains

According to the Bureau of Labor Statistics, labor costs make up roughly 38 percent of many airlines' operating costs – that's around 40 cents for every dollar spent by an air carrier. Passenger safety regulations, a workforce made up of highly specialized – and rarely cross-trained – professionals, and a strong union presence in the industry make it tough for airlines to trim costs from their labor budgets. One way they've done this is by cutting workforces to the bare bones. Following September 11, Continental Airlines and US Airways were the first to make dramatic cuts, laying off about 20 percent of their respective workforces and paring flight schedules. Most other carriers followed suit. Unions have fought tooth and nail for fair compensation, pension, and benefits packages while enduring large-scale pay cuts at many major airlines. Overall, the cost for unfounded pensions in the airline industry topped $32 billion in June 2005. And, with well over 110,000 jobs lost since mid-2001, the U.S. airline industry's workforce is at its lowest level since 1996. These trends were reflected in Europe, too, where carriers like British Airways and Lufthansa also made cuts in staff and services.

Carrying the Load

The vast transportation sector is charged with carrying people and products (safely and on-time, of course) to destinations around the globe – no small feat. The industry can be broken into a handful of sectors: airlines; air cargo and express delivery carriers; trucks; railroads; and buses.

Carrying the load

Amidst all this choppy air, the air cargo business remains comparatively stable, with major cargo carriers posting profits even in the dark days of 2001 and 2002. Worldwide revenues for the air freight and express delivery market were $75 billion in 2003, and the market has doubled every ten years, according to the Air Line Pilots Association (ALPA). Still, a few air cargo carriers, including Arrow Air and Atlas Air, were forced into bankruptcy court alongside their passenger-carrier counterparts. Arrow emerged from Chapter 11 in June 2004, and Atlas Express (one of the world's largest cargo carriers) was expected to re-emerge shortly thereafter.

United Parcel Service, FedEx Kinko's, and DHL dominate the express-delivery sector, both operating their own modes of transportation and leasing space and services on other cargo haulers' vehicles. The Internet boom has had both a positive and negative effect on industry: while the rise in e-mail has curtailed the shipping of smaller-scale documents, more and more

Internet shoppers, e-tailers, and online small businesses are using express delivery companies for direct packaging and shipping services supply chain management.

Many of the challenges the sector faces, including tighter security requirements, high fuel costs, and the need to replace an aging fleet of planes, mirror those on the passenger side. Others are specific to the air cargo industry – for instance, the ALPA worries that international shippers may begin routing cargo through Canada and Mexico in response to the new security restrictions, meaning reduced activity in the domestic market. In addition, the ALPA notes that the need for hard copies of documents and other items has diminishes with the rise of e-signatures and other digital technologies, leading to load reductions. And air cargo services also have to contend with other forms of transport, like ships and trucks.

The Germans are coming

Run by German postal entity Deutsche Post, express delivery company DHL made aggressive steps to solidify its position in the U.S. market in 2003. In August of that year, DHL acquired Airborne Inc. for $1.1 billion, securing its American rival's number-three place domestically and further strengthening its dominance in the world market for express delivery services overall. As of September 2003, according to BusinessWeek, FedEx held 44 percent of the market, with UPS coming in at 34 percent and Airborne trailing at 13 percent. Meanwhile, FedEx Kinko's and UPS have attempted to beat back the upstart by challenging DHL on regulatory grounds, particularly citing a restriction barring foreign companies from controlling U.S. airlines (DHL's airline was spun off from the company in 2003). But DHL has forged ahead, pulling out all the marketing stops in a $150 million PR campaign beginning in the summer of 2004.

In the fiercely competitive delivery market, where the leaders vie for massive corporate contracts as well as business from average consumers, marketing has become a hardball game. In 2003, the employee-controlled UPS, with a fleet of about 88,000 ground vehicles and 575 planes, branded itself as the "brown" company. FedEx strengthened its market position by diversifying, namely through its $2.4 billion buyout in January 2004 of Kinko's document services provider and copy shop chain. The company, with approximately 42,000 ground vehicles and an air fleet of 643 planes, operates different Express, Ground, and Freight units. The companies have also grown internationally: FedEx Kinko's picked up the Global Express Guaranteed operations of DHL Worldwide Express in July 2004. Rival UPS, meanwhile, bought direct control of a jointly run Chinese Delivery company, Sinotrans Group, for $100 million in December 2004, and swallowed the remain stake of a UPS Yamato Express Company, a joint venture with Yamato Transport Company, in January 2004 to increase services to Japan.

Greening Brown

As for their ground services, both UPS and FedEx have taken steps recently to "green" their fleets, replacing diesel vehicles with environmentally friendlier options like compressed natural gas and electricity-powered vans. In March 2002, FedEx announced plans to eventually replace its entire 30,000-van fleet with hybrid electric vehicles over a number of years. While the companies get PR points for their efforts, what's really driving the green movement is, well, the green – cash, that is. An August 2003 BusinessWeek article notes that hybrid electric vehicles can cut operators' fuel costs in half. And as big companies like FedEx continue to place orders for the lower-emissions, fuel-friendly vehicles, prices of these vehicles will go down too, benefiting the entire sector over time.

Keep on truckin'

Express-delivery services also share ties – and in some cases overlap – with the trucking sector. Dominated by bulk truckers like Quality Distribution Inc., JB Hunt Transport Services, and Yellow Roadway Corporation (which recently beefed up its business with the May 2005 purchase of supply-chain management firm USF Corp. for $1.5 billion), the industry is seeing increased demand for its hauling services, with sales of $254 billion expected for 2004, according to Global Insight, Inc.

Visit Vault at **www.vault.com** for insider company profiles, expert advice,
career message boards, expert resume reviews, the Vault Job Board and more.

VAULT CAREER LIBRARY   **239**

The trucking sector also overlaps with the railroad world, with giants like JB Hunt and Schneider International teaming up with old hands on the rails such as Union Pacific, Norfolk Southern, and Burlington Northern Santa Fe. With new technologies allowing real-time cargo tracking and time-specific delivery, this sector of the transportation industry is expected to grow increasingly integrated. Both road and train shippers started adding jobs in 2004, keeping truck fleets and rail lines running at maximum capacity.

Railroad blues

While the shipping portion of the rail sector has continued to chug along, the passenger-train sector has contracted dramatically in previous decades. In fact, the rail sector has been in decline since the dawn of the automobile; in the 1960s, it was dealt a heavy blow when the U.S. Postal Service turned to trucks and airplanes for its first-class shipping needs. Amtrak took over the majority of U.S. passenger trains under its National Railroad Passenger Corporation umbrella following legislation in the 1970s intended to prop up the flagging sector, but the operator has had trouble turning any sort of profit. As of 2002, rail transportation workers held 101,000 jobs in the U.S., the BLS reports; this figure is expected to decline over the next decade. Occupations in the sector include conductors and yardmasters, engineers, brake, signal, and switch operators, and subway and streetcar operators.

Though still a top draw for commuter travel, particularly in the Northeast, Amtrak's fares usually can't compete with the speed offered by airlines. Following September 11, 2001 and the deadly Madrid train bombing in March 2004, security has become a primary focus. With these requirements, dwindling passenger rolls, and increased operating costs, Amtrak has become increasingly subsidized – the organization requested $1.8 billion from Congress in 2004 to help it stay on track.

Amtrak felt the squeeze even more when a House appropriations subcommittee voted to give the organization $550 million in June 2005 – less than half of its budget the year prior – and also forbid the company to run trains that lost more than $30 per passenger (which, at the time, was the case for many long-distance routes). Amtrak said such drastic budgetary restraints would further hinder its ability to meet debt service, fulfill obligations to the railroad retirement fund, and make required payments to workers it would have to lay off in the process, thus forcing Amtrak to shut down all operations. A House-Senate conference committee is set to decide the fate of the train service in the fall of 2005. To add salt to an open wound, Amtrak's Acela Express, a high-speed train running the Eastern corridor from Washington, D.C., New York City, and Boston, was shut down "indefinitely" in April 2005 because of cracks discovered in 300 of the Acela fleet's 1,440 disc brake rotors. Acela trains accounted for roughly 20 percent of Amtrak's Boston-New York-Washington weekday service.

On the bus

For long-haul passenger travel, about the only thing cheaper than a bus is sticking out your thumb. Intercity buses, also known as motor coaches, provide regular service to more than 42,000 U.S. communities. According to the American Bus Association (ABA), more passengers travel by motorcoach in the U.S. than on any other commercial mode of transportation. The bus sector is unique in its composition – unlike the heavily subsidized rail and airline sectors, motorcoach companies are more likely to go it alone (though the industry received about $25 million in grant funding for security following September 11).

There are more than 4,000 bus companies on the roads in the U.S., many of which are small, entrepreneurial operators – 90 percent operate fewer than 25 buses, the ABA reports. Major operators include Trailways, which has been around for nearly 70 years and operates a group of 65 member companies, and Greyhound, founded in 1914 and acquired in 1999 by Laidlaw Inc. As insurance rates have increased ten-fold in recent years, access to affordable coverage is a key challenge faced by the industry. Unaffordable rates have priced some operators out of the market.

The not-so friendly skies

Even the most phobic of flyers can find a career working in the airline industry. In fact, the majority of the approximately 559,000 workers (as of 2002) in the U.S. airline industry are employed in ground occupations, as mechanics, reservation agents, and customer service representatives and the like. Flight crew members make up another large portion (around 31 percent) of the workforce – they include pilots and flight attendants. The size of the airline workforce depends in large part on the fluctuations of the market, but other factors are more predictable – for instance, the BLS notes, the ranks of reservation and ticket agents will continue to thin as these positions are phased out by paperless tickets, Internet travel purchases, and online check-ins.

However, the events of September 11th coupled with the subsequent economic recession, skyrocketing cost of fuel, and rise in competition from low-cost low-fare carriers like JetBlue and Southwest have devastated the "Big Six" in the airline industry (United, Delta, US Airways, American, Continental, and Northwest) early on in the 21st century, forcing job cuts, union wars over wages, executive turnarounds, and, in most cases, Chapter 11 filing. Overall during the summer of 2005, most airlines hiked round-trip fares by at least $10 dollars to combat a 50 percent increase in oil prices. Meanwhile, larger airlines are arguing that smaller operations, such as charter planes and corporate jets, should pay the same landing and users fees imposed on them to help lift the burden on the commercial airline industry (smaller charter plane operators worry such measures would crush their industry).

Trucking along

In the truck sector, drivers hold about 44 percent of approximately 1.9 million jobs, with the remainder consisting of warehouse workers, dispatchers, and clerks. The number of wage and salary jobs in the sector is expected to grow 23 percent by 2012, according to the BLS, with opportunities opening up at all levels, particularly for service technicians and mechanics. Drivers will also be in high demand as the amount of freight moving across the country continues to grow. Statistics from Global Insight, an economics consulting firm, suggest the number of drivers needed will rise by over half a million in the next decade. According to a June 2005 report by the American Trucking Association, the long-haul, heavy-duty truck transportation industry is currently experiencing a national shortage of 20,000 drivers - a number that could swell to 110,000 by 2014 – in what many in the industry consider the tightest driver market in over 20 years. Long-haul truckers deliver roughly 62 percent of all freight in the U.S. Predicted economic and freight growth suggests a 2.2% increase in shipping need over the next decade, compared with a 1.6% estimated increase in the number of heavy-duty truckers on the road.

Road and Track

While the shipping portion of the rail sector has continued to chug along, the passenger-train sector has contracted dramatically in previous decades. In fact, the rail sector has been in decline since the dawn of the automobile; in the 1960s, it was dealt a heavy blow when the U.S. Postal Service turned to trucks and airplanes for its first-class shipping needs. Amtrak took over the majority of U.S. passenger trains under its National Railroad Passenger Corporation umbrella following legislation in the 1970s intended to prop up the flagging sector, but the operator has had trouble turning any sort of profit. Though still a top draw for commuter travel, particularly in the Northeast, Amtrak's fares usually can't compete with the rock-bottom rates and speed offered by airlines. Following September 11, 2001 and the deadly Madrid train bombing in March 2004, security has become a primary focus. With these requirements, dwindling passenger rolls, and increased operating costs, Amtrak has become increasingly subsidized – the organization requested $1.8 billion from Congress in 2004 to help it stay on track.

Visit Vault at **www.vault.com** for insider company profiles, expert advice, career message boards, expert resume reviews, the Vault Job Board and more.

V/\ULT CAREER LIBRARY   **241**

On the bus

For long-haul passenger travel, about the only thing cheaper than a bus is sticking out your thumb. Intercity buses, also known as motorcoaches, provide regular service to more than 42,000 U.S. communities. According to the American Bus Association (ABA), more passengers travel by motorcoach in the U.S. than on any other commercial mode of transportation. The bus sector is unique in its composition – unlike the heavily subsidized rail and airline sectors, motorcoach companies are more likely to go it alone (though the industry received about $25 million in grant funding for security following September 11).

There are more than 4,000 bus companies on the roads in the U.S., many of which are small, entrepreneurial operators – 90 percent operate fewer than 25 buses, the ABA reports. Major operators include Trailways, which has been around for nearly 70 years and operates a group of 65 member companies, and Greyhound, founded in 1914 and acquired in 1999 by Laidlaw Inc. As insurance rates have increased ten-fold in recent years, access to affordable coverage is a key challenge faced by the industry. Unaffordable rates have priced some operators out of the market.

A Life in Transportation

As a whole, the transportation industry offers a range of employment options for highly skilled professionals and newcomers alike.

The friendly skies

Even the most phobic of flyers can find a career working in the airline industry. In fact, the majority of the approximately 559,000 workers (as of 2002) in the U.S. airline industry are employed in ground occupations, as mechanics, reservation agents, and customer service representatives and the like. Flight crew members make up another large portion (around 31 percent) of the workforce – they include pilots and flight attendants. The size of the airline workforce depends in large part on the fluctuations of the market, but other factors are more predictable – for instance, the BLS notes, the ranks of reservation and ticket agents will continue to thin as these positions are phased out by paperless tickets, Internet travel purchases, and online check-ins.

Trucking along

In the truck sector, drivers hold about 44 percent of approximately 1.9 million jobs, with the remainder consisting of warehouse workers, dispatchers, and clerks. The number of wage and salary jobs in the sector is expected to grow 23 percent by 2012, according to the BLS, with opportunities opening up at all levels, particularly for drivers, service technicians and mechanics.

As of 2002, rail transportation workers held 101,000 jobs in the U.S., the BLS reports; this figure is expected to decline over the next decade. Occupations in the sector include conductors and yardmasters, engineers, brake, signal, and switch operators, and subway and streetcar operators.

Employer Directory

AMR Corporation (American Airlines)
4333 Amon Carter Blvd.
Fort Worth, TX 76155
Phone: 817-963-1234
www.amrcorp.com

Canadian National Railway Company (CN)
935 de la Gauchetière St. West
Montreal, Quebec H3B 2M9, Canada
Phone: 514-399-5430
Fax: 204-987-9310
www.cn.ca

Continental Airlines, Inc.
1600 Smith St., Dept. HQSEO
Houston, TX 77002
Phone: (713) 324-2950
Fax: (713) 324-2637

CSX Corporation
500 Water St., 15th Fl.
Jacksonville, FL 32202
Phone: (904) 359-3200
www.csx.com

Delta Air Lines, Inc.
Hartsfield Atlanta International Airport
1030 Delta Blvd.
Atlanta, GA 30320-6001
Phone: (404) 715-2600
Fax: (404) 715-5042
www.delta.com

DHL Worldwide Network
De Kleetlaan 1
B-1831 Diegem, Belgium
Phone: +32-2-713-4000
www.dhl.com

FedEx Corporation
942 S. Shady Grove Rd.
Memphis, TN 38120
Phone: (901) 369-3600
Fax: (901) 395-2000
www.fedex.com

Greyhound Lines, Inc.
15110 N. Dallas Pkwy., Ste. 600
Dallas, TX 75248
Phone: (972) 789-7000
Phone: (972) 387-1874
www.greyhound.com

JetBlue Airways Corporation
118-29 Queens Blvd.
Forest Hills, NY 11415
Phone: (718) 286-7900
Phone: (718) 709-3621
www.jetblue.com

Norfolk Southern Corporation
3 Commercial Place
Norfolk, VA 23510-2191
Phone: (757) 629-2600
Phone: (757) 664-5069
www.nscorp.com

Northwest Airlines Corporation
2700 Lone Oak Pkwy.
Eagan, MN 55121
Phone: (612) 726-2111
Phone: (612) 726-7123
www.nwa.com

Southwest Airlines Co.
2702 Love Field Dr.
Dallas, TX 75235
Phone: (214) 792-4000
Phone: (214) 792-5015
www.southwest.com

Trailways Transportation System, Inc.
3554 Chain Bridge Rd., Ste. 301
Fairfax, VA 22030-2709
Phone: (703) 691-3052
Phone: (703) 691-9047
www.trailways.com

UAL Corporation (United Airlines)
1200 E. Algonquin Rd.
Elk Grove Township, IL 60007
Phone: (847) 700-4000
Phone: (847) 700-4081
www.united.com

Union Pacific Corporation
1416 Dodge St.
Omaha, NE 68179
Phone: (402) 271-5777
Phone: (402) 271-6408
www.up.com

United Parcel Service, Inc. (UPS)
55 Glenlake Pkwy., NE
Atlanta, GA 30328
Phone: (404) 828-6000
Fax: (404) 928-6562
www.ups.com

Visit Vault at **www.vault.com** for insider company profiles, expert advice, career message boards, expert resume reviews, the Vault Job Board and more.

VAULT CAREER LIBRARY   **243**

This section was excerpted from the *Vault Guide to the Top Transportation Industry Employers.* Get the inside scoop on on transportation careers with:

- **Vault Guides:** *Vault Guide to the Top Transportation Industry Employers*
- **Employee Surveys:** Vault's exclusive employee surveys for UPS, FedEx, American Airlines, CSX and other top transportation employers
- **Employer Research:**Company snapshots providing business descriptions and the latest news on top transportation employers
- **Career Services:** Vault Resume and Cover Letter Reviews, rated the "Top Choice" by *The Wall Street Journal* for resume makeovers

Go to www.vault.com

or ask your bookstore or librarian for other Vault titles.

Venture Capital

The Financial Industry and Venture Capital

Where does VC fit into the world of finance? The financial industry can be divided into two general segments: the buy-side and the sell-side. Sell-side refers to those financial firms that have services to sell, such as investment banks, brokerages, and commercial banks.

For instance, when a large company wants to sell stock on the public stock exchanges, an investment bank's corporate finance department handles the legal, tax, and accounting affairs of the transaction as well as the sale of those securities to institutional or individual investors. For providing these services, the investment bank receives a fee (between 2 percent and 10 percent of the money raised by selling stock). An investment banking firm's primary motivation is to sell such services, characterizing them as sell-siders.

Brokerages are paid a fee for the service they provide of buying and selling stocks. Commercial banks are paid for managing deposit accounts, making and then managing loans, etc. Again, they sell these services, so they are sell-side firms.

Venture capital firms, on the other hand, are on the buy-side because they control a fund or pool of money to spend on buying an equity interest in, or assets of, operating companies.

For the sake of this discussion, most buy-side venture capital firms have only one way to realize a return on their investment: selling their ownership stake to another private investor, a corporation (trade sale) or to the public markets for more money than they paid (often termed to be "in the money"). While some later-stage private equity shops invest in or acquire companies for their cash flow potential, venture capital is about building young companies and finding an exit (liquidity event) on the back side for "x" times their original investment. Descriptions of each segment of the buy-side are included below. Keep in mind that these definitions are intended to be very general in nature and that many buy-side organizations cross organizational boundaries.

Friends and family

Sometimes referred to as "friends, family and fools," this is usually the first source of funding for startups at the idea stage of development. The amounts invested per individual are quite small, averaging $5,000 to $10,000. These people may not have an in-depth understanding of the business, product, technology or market, and are simply making an investment in someone they know. While this is probably the easiest money for an entrepreneur to find, it can also be bittersweet. If a startup fails, telling Aunt Edna that she's lost her nest egg could be the low point of one's career.

Angels

These are high net-worth individuals who normally invest between $15,000 and $1 million in exchange for equity in a young company throughout the seed and early stage rounds, averaging $50,000 to $500,000. Angels prefer to invest within their immediate geographic area, and on average within one day of travel. According to businessfinance.com, angels fund an estimated one-seventh of the 300,000 start-up/early growth firms in the U.S. They are often the first investor segment who have the opportunity to sit on the board of directors and contribute experience and contacts, guiding young companies through the difficult initial stages of growth. That said, most of the value added by angel investors occurs in the pre-institutional (or Series A) rounds of funding. As the professional investors come into play, venture capitalists take over board seats previously held by angels.

Angels can be doctors, lawyers, former investors, though increasingly they are former entrepreneurs who have had a lucrative exit in their chosen professional field. Microsoft co-founder and multi-billionaire Paul Allen has made headlines for his angel investing as well as his investments through his VC firm, Vulcan Ventures. Intel co-founder Andy Grove has made

Visit Vault at **www.vault.com** for insider company profiles, expert advice, career message boards, expert resume reviews, the Vault Job Board and more.

V∧ULT CAREER LIBRARY   245

angel investments in numerous companies, including Oncology.com. Given the large number of new companies seeking funding as well as the rise in the number of wealthy individuals, in recent years the industry has seen the emergence of angel groups. These investor alliances create more structure for angel investors, and a more efficient conduit for moving startups along from seed funding to professional venture investors. Perhaps the best-known group of angels is Silicon Valley's "Band of Angels," a formal group of about 150 former and current high tech entrepreneurs and executives who meet monthly to consider pleas from three start-ups for venture financing. This group has injected nearly $100 million across some 150 startups. Angels are often involved with hiring, strategy, the raising of additional capital, and fundamental operating decisions. These alliances also allow for better coordination of due diligence in "vetting" new deals. Angels are not without their own issues, however. Collectively, angel investors have been accused of being fair weather friends; one of the first sources of private equity to dry up when public markets fall or macroeconomic conditions deteriorate. With less money to invest across fewer deals than their vc brethren, many of these individuals have a lower tolerance for losses. This risk aversion is compounded by their generally lower position in the capital structure. While angel groups may be able to negotiate preferred stock instead of common, their equity rarely has the same level of preferences or security demanded by later stage investors. Though angels, of course, expect a significant return on their investment, they are also thrill-seekers of a sort – motivated by getting close to the excitement of a new venture.

High net worth private placements

Sell-side companies, such as investment banks, may organize a group of very wealthy individuals, corporations, asset management firms, and/or pension funds to make a direct investment into a private company. The amount raised from these sources is typically between $5 million and $50 million. In essence, the sell-side company enables investors to invest in the venture capital asset class.

While these transactions may include a traditional venture fund as part of the round, in many cases they do not. As a whole, investment banks have historically been seen as having less perceived value in the early stages of the venture process. Since early-stage investing is not Wall Street's core competency, the downside is that 1) the startup company may not benefit from the domain expertise, operational savvy and rolodex of the venture capital firm, and 2) the sell-side company takes a fee for its services, typically between 2 and 10 percent of capital raised. While there is a credible value proposition to using private placements and participation by investment banks in funding some types of deals, this is expensive money on several fronts.

Asset management firms and pension funds

These groups include a diverse collection of limited partnerships and corporations that manage between $5 million to $100 billion plus. Most focus on diversified investment strategies, typically with public instruments including stocks, bonds, commodities, currencies, etc. They rarely invest in private companies, due to the large amount of time required to find and execute a private transaction, as well as the ongoing commitment of time to monitor such an investment. Instead of directly participating in individual startup fundings, many will allocate 5% to 7% of total funds to higher-risk alternative investments like vc partnerships, hedge funds, and distressed turnaround situations. The California Public Employees' Retirement System (CalPERS) is one of the largest players in this space.

Leveraged buyout firms

These are limited partnerships or corporations that take over private or public firms using their own capital as equity, combined with debt (leverage) financing from third-party banks. After acquiring a company, the LBO firm normally changes management and strategic direction, or may divide and sell its assets. The size of LBOs ranges from a few million to many billions of dollars. These firms look and behave very much like venture capital firms, but their investments differ in size and purpose. Both LBOs and VCs fall under the umbrella descriptor "Private Equity."

Hedge funds

These are limited partnerships or corporations that buy and sell public market instruments including stocks, bonds, commodities, currencies, etc. These firms take bets on market fluctuations and are often considered high risk/high return investors. The size of these funds ranges from a few million to several billion dollars.

Trading

Sell-side companies such as merchant banks, commercial banks and investment banks have trading departments that control and invest huge sums of money into public markets. These groups also take relatively risky bets on market fluctuations.

Venture funds

Limited partnerships.

Day in the Life: Venture Capitalist

7:00 a.m.: Arrive at the office.

7:01 a.m.: Read *The Wall Street Journal*, paying careful attention to the Marketplace section covering your industry focus.

7:20 a.m.: Read trade press and notice four companies you haven't seen before. Check your firm's internal database to see if someone else on your team has contacted the companies. Search the Internet to find out more. Of the four companies you find, only one holds your interest. Send yourself an e-mail as a reminder to call them during business hours.

7:45 a.m.: Clip out some interesting articles and put them in the in-boxes of other associates or partners with a note explaining why you found the information interesting. The other members of your firm have more expertise in the areas covered by the articles. You stay and talk for a few minutes with each of the people in their offices, exchanging the latest word about the people and technology you follow.

8:00 a.m.: Respond to e-mails or voice mails from the day before. People you are communicating with are primarily entrepreneurs, other VCs, and personal acquaintances.

9:00 a.m.: You attend a meeting with a group of entrepreneurs who want to make their pitch. You read the business plan for five minutes. One general partner (GP) sits in with you. The other GP, who planned to be there, cannot make it because he has a conference call with a portfolio company facing some challenges. The computer projecting the entrepreneur's presentation crashes, so you have to take their paper version of their presentation and work with your assistant to make four photocopies before the meeting can proceed.

During the 10-minute delay, the partner talks with the team informally, and learns more about the opportunity than he or she would in any one-hour presentation. You sit politely through the presentation, and identify the three critical issues facing the company. During the question and answer phase, you think of how to politely extract more information about those three issues, all the while evaluating whether you would want to work with this team or not.

In the end, you decide to make some calls to gather more information about the market, but you feel that there's a very low probability you would ever invest. You wish you could just kill the deal, but the management team is reasonable (though not great), the customer need they have identified may actually exist (you don't know first-hand, so you will need to call around), and you may learn something by taking it to the next step. Plus, in the back of your mind, you know the market for good deals is very competitive, and you don't want to reject a deal too quickly.

Visit Vault at **www.vault.com** for insider company profiles, expert advice, career message boards, expert resume reviews, the Vault Job Board and more.

VAULT CAREER LIBRARY   **247**

11:00 a.m.: Phone the people who called during your meeting. These people include entrepreneurs, analysts, other VC's, and your lunch appointment. You find out from another VC that the company you almost invested in two months ago was just funded by a competing firm. You wonder if you made a mistake. You find out from an entrepreneur you were hoping to back that he wants his son to be a co-founder and owner of the firm. You abandon all hope. You learn from an analyst that AT&T has decided to stop its trial of a new technology because it doesn't work, which creates an opportunity for companies with an alternative solution. You happen to know about two small companies, one in Boston, one in Denver, that have alternative solutions. You make a note to yourself to call them back to get a status report.

12:30 p.m.: Lunch with an executive recruiter. This person is very experienced in finding management talent in your area of expertise. You have kept in touch with her over the years, and try to see her every quarter to hear the latest buzz and to make sure she will be available when you need her services quickly. It's a fun lunch, freely mixing personal and professional information.

2:00 p.m.: Call new companies you have heard about over the last few days. Ideally, you could do this task a little bit every day, but you find you need to be in a friendly and upbeat mood to make these calls, so you batch them. Also, if you actually get in touch with the CEO, you may be on the phone for 90 minutes, so you need to have an open block of time. You leave the standard pitch about your firm on the voice mail of the CEO's of four other companies. You get through to one CEO, and although you can tell in the first five minutes that you won't be interested in investing, you talk for 30 minutes. You spend most of the 30 minutes probing about competitors who might be better than the company you're talking to and finding out more about his market space.

3:00 p.m.: You and a partner meet with a portfolio company on a conference call. The company is facing some challenges and you offer to screen executive recruiters to help find a new CFO for it. The GP offers to talk to two M&A firms to get a first opinion about what might be done to sell the company over the next six months. At the end of the call, the GP gives you three names and numbers of recruiters, which you add to your own two contacts.

3:30 p.m.: You call the recruiters, explaining the situation and asking about their recent experiences in similar searches. The critical element is whether the recruiters actually have time and interest in doing the search. You talk to two recruiters and leave voice mails for the other three.

4:30 p.m.: You make due diligence calls for a potential investment you have been following for two months. Last week you called the company's customers, and they seemed happy for the most part. Today, you are calling the personal references of the management team. The idea is to get as much negative information as possible. You need to discover any potential character or personality flaws any member of the team may have. VC firms are "due diligence machines," doing the hard work of making sure a company is what it says it is.

5:30 p.m.: You make calls to the West Coast. You also check your stocks and confirm dinner plans. You do some miscellaneous surfing on the Web to gather some articles about the technology areas you cover.

6:30 p.m.: You stand around the halls talking with other members of your firm, brainstorming and filling each other in about what's happening in your area.

7:00 p.m.: Dinner with two other young VCs downtown. You talk mostly about life, sports, travel and relationships, but also about the latest deals, cool business ideas, and recent successes. You find out that a competing firm just made 30 times their money on a deal you never saw. You also find out that a company you turned down which was invested in by someone else is about to go bankrupt. A train missed; a bullet dodged.

VC Uppers and Downers

Uppers

- There is a reason that very few people ever willingly leave their VC careers. Where else can you have so much fun investing other people's money (plus some of your own), while being "in the middle of it all"?

- You often get to be the one making decisions because you have money.

- Over the long term, financial security will cease to be an issue, because the job is well paying and you should eventually get "carry" or equity in the firm.

- You have access to the best minds – the people you work with are typically some of the smartest and most interesting. Successful venture capitalists have interests and hobbies as diverse as mountain climbing to playing jazz in nightclubs.

- Your job is to absorb and enjoy the positive creative energy of entrepreneurs and direct it toward successful execution.

- You could suddenly become rich if one of your companies does extremely well and you were able to co-invest or you have carry.

- You have access to the best information systems.

Downers

Because so many think of the venture capital industry as "the hot job to have," people often forget to question whether it is the right job for them. Here is a list of some of the negatives we hear from those who have worked in the industry for a while.

- Unless you work with a hands-on early-stage VC firm known for taking an active role in building successful companies, you don't have pride of ownership in anything. You're just an investor, not a builder.

- VC is a slow path to wealth compared with the immediate cash income you get in investment banking, hedge funds or even management consulting.

- It can be argued that venture capital is fundamentally a negative process. Because you reject 99 of every 100 plans, year after year, over time you focus on figuring out what is wrong with a company. You can then reject it and get on to the next deal. What is wrong with the management? The technology? The deal terms? The strategy? If you tend to have a contrarian disposition, after just a few years, that mentality may bleed into your life. What is wrong with my partners? What is wrong with my spouse? What is wrong with me? Oh, the angst! If this reaction hits too close to home, venture capital might not be for you. What fun is it to search through hundreds and thousands of business plans and ideas for that one rare gem, if you aren't an eternal optimist?

- Because you reject 99 of every 100 entrepreneurs, you can make some enemies, no matter how nice and helpful you try to be. No one likes rejection, and passionate entrepreneurs have long memories.

Visit Vault at **www.vault.com** for insider company profiles, expert advice, career message boards, expert resume reviews, the Vault Job Board and more.

VAULT CAREER LIBRARY   **249**

Employer Directory

Accel Partners
428 University Avenue
Palo Alto, CA 94301
Phone: (650) 614-4800
Fax: (650) 614-488
www.accel.com

Apax Partners
495 Park Avenue, 11th Floor
New York, NY 10022
Phone: (212) 753-6300
Fax: (212) 319-6155
www.apax.com

ARCH Venture Partners
8725 W. Higgins Road
Suite 290
Chicago, IL 60631
Phone: (773) 380-6600
Fax: (773) 380-6606
www.archventure.com

Austin Ventures
300 West 6th Street
Suite 2300
Austin, TX 78701
Phone: (512) 485-1900
Fax: (512) 476-3952
www.austinventures.com

Benchmark Capital
2480 Sand Hill Road
Suite 200
Menlo Park, CA 94025
Phone: (650) 854-8180
Fax: (650) 854-8183
www.benchmark.com

Charles River Ventures
1000 Winter Street #3300
Waltham, MA 02451
Phone: (781) 487-7060
Fax: (781) 487-7065

Draper Fisher Jurvetson
2882 Sand Hill Road, Suite 150
Menlo Park, CA 94025
Phone: (650) 233-9000
Fax: (650) 233-9233
www.drapervc.com

Hummer Winblad Venture Partners
2 South Park, 2nd Floor
San Francisco, CA 94107
Phone: (415) 979-9600
Fax: (415) 979-9601
www.humwin.com

JAFCO America Ventures
505 Hamilton Avenue
Suite 310
Palo Alto, CA 94301
Phone: (650) 463-8800
Fax: (650) 463-8801
www.jafco.com

Kleiner Perkins Caufield & Byers
2750 Sand Hill Road
Menlo Park, CA 94025
Phone: (650) 233-2750
Fax: (650) 233-0300
www.kpcb.com

Mayfield Fund
2800 Sand Hill Road
Suite 250
Menlo Park, CA 94025
Phone: (650) 854-5560
Fax: (650) 854-5712
www.mayfield.com

Menlo Ventures
3000 Sand Hill Road, Building 4
Suite 100
Menlo Park, CA 94025
Phone: (650) 854-8540
Fax: (650) 854-7059
www.menloventures.com

New Enterprise Associates
1119 St. Paul St.
Baltimore, MD 21202
Phone: (410) 244-0115
Fax: (410) 752-7721
www.nea.com

Norwest Venture Capital
525 University Ave., Suite 800
Palo Alto, CA 94301
Phone: (650) 321-8000
Fax: (650) 321-8010
www.norwestvc.com

Sequoia Capital
3000 Sand Hill Road
Building 4, Suite 180
Menlo Park, CA 94025
Phone: (650) 854-3927
Fax: (650) 854-2977
www.sequoiacap.com

St. Paul Venture Capital
10400 Viking Drive Ste 550
Eden Prairie, MN 55344
Phone: (952) 995-7474
Fax: (952) 995-7475
www.stpaulvc.com

TL Ventures
435 Devon Park Drive
700 Building
Wayne, PA 19087
Phone: (610) 971-1515
Fax: (610) 975-9330
www.tlventures.com

U.S. Venture Partners
2735 Sand Hill Road
Menlo Park, CA 94025
Phone: (650) 854-9080
Fax: (650) 854-3018
www.usvp.com

Venrock Associates
30 Rockefeller Plaza
Room 5508
New York, NY 10112
Phone: (212) 649-5600
Fax: (212) 649-5788
www.venrock.com

APPENDIX

About the Author

Vault Editors

Vault is the leading media company for career information. Our team of industry-focused editors takes a journalistic approach in covering news, employment trends and specific employers in their industries. We annually survey 10,000s of employees to bring readers the inside scoop on industries and specific employers.

Much of the material in *The MBA Career Bible* is excerpted from Vault titles to specific industries or career titles. Vault publishes more than 80 titles for job seekers and professionals. To see a complete list of Vault titles, go to www.vault.com.

Visit Vault at **www.vault.com** for insider company profiles, expert advice, career message boards, expert resume reviews, the Vault Job Board and more.

VAULT CAREER LIBRARY 253